Luminos is the Open Access monograph publishing program from UC Press. Luminos provides a framework for preserving and reinvigorating monograph publishing for the future and increases the reach and visibility of important scholarly work. Titles published in the UC Press Luminos model are published with the same high standards for selection, peer review, production, and marketing as those in our traditional program. www.luminosoa.org

The Well-Tempered Reader

THE BERKELEY SERIES IN POSTCLASSICAL ISLAMIC SCHOLARSHIP

Series Editors

Asad Q. Ahmed, University of California, Berkeley
Margaret Larkin, University of California, Berkeley

1. *The Light of the World: Astronomy in al-Andalus*, by Joseph Ibn Naḥmias and edited, translated, and with a commentary by Robert G. Morrison
2. *Language between God and the Poets: Maʿnā in the Eleventh Century*, by Alexander Key
3. *Reason and Revelation in Byzantine Antioch: The Christian Translation Program of Abdallah ibn al-Fadl*, by Alexandre M. Roberts
4. *Avicenna's Theory of Science: Logic, Metaphysics, Epistemology*, by Riccardo Strobino
5. *Palimpsests of Themselves: Logic and Commentary in Postclassical Muslim South Asia*, by Asad Q. Ahmed
6. *Being Another Way: The Copula and Arabic Philosophy of Language, 900–1500*, by Dustin D. Klinger
7. *The Well-Tempered Reader: The Legitimization of* Adab *in the Arabic Literary Tradition*, by Sarah R. Bin Tyeer

The Well-Tempered Reader

The Legitimization of Adab *in the Arabic Literary Tradition*

Sarah R. Bin Tyeer

UNIVERSITY OF CALIFORNIA PRESS

University of California Press
Oakland, California

Suggested citation: Bin Tyeer, S. R. *The Well-Tempered Reader: The Legitimization of* Adab *in the Arabic Literary Tradition*. Oakland: University of California Press, 2026. DOI: https://doi.org/10.1525/luminos.254

Library of Congress Cataloging-in-Publication Data

Names: Bin Tyeer, Sarah R. author
Title: The well-tempered reader : the legitimization of adab in the Arabic literary tradition / Sarah R. Bin Tyeer.
Other titles: Berkeley series in postclassical Islamic scholarship 7.
Description: Oakland, California : University of California Press, [2026] | Series: The Berkeley series in postclassical Islamic Scholarship ; 7 | Includes bibliographical references and index.
Identifiers: LCCN 2025017310 (print) | LCCN 2025017311 (ebook) | ISBN 9780520424968 cloth | ISBN 9780520424975 paperback | ISBN 9780520424982 ebook
Subjects: LCSH: Arabic literature—History and criticism
Classification: LCC PJ7517 .B497 2026 (print) | LCC PJ7517 (ebook) | DDC 892.709—dc23/eng/20250827

LC record available at https://lccn.loc.gov/2025017310
LC ebook record available at https://lccn.loc.gov/2025017311

GPSR Authorized Representative: Easy Access System Europe, Mustamäe tee 50, 10621 Tallinn, Estonia, gpsr.requests@easproject.com

34 33 32 31 30 29 28 27 26 25
10 9 8 7 6 5 4 3 2 1

For my mother,
who taught me the meaning of murūʾa *and* adab

CONTENTS

Preface ix
Acknowledgments xi

Introduction: The Subject of *Adab* 1

1. *Adab* and/as *Murū'a*: The Ways of Being Human 18
2. *Adab* as Hospitality: The *Adab* Sphere: Reading *Mathal* and Discourse 37
3. *Adab* as Discourse: Text(s) as Interlocutor(s) 64
4. *Adab* as Critique: Reading as Critical Justice (*Inṣāf*): al-Maʿarrī's *Zajr al-nābiḥ* and a Typology of Negative Readers 85
5. *Adab* as Method: Philological Retaliation and the Seventy Names for a Dog: al-Maʿarrī's Insult and al-Suyūṭī's Exoneration 103
6. *Adab* as Resolve and Will: The Philological Gadfly and the Lexical Ark 122

Coda: The Sustainability of *Adab* 151

Appendix 171
Notes 175
Bibliography 201
Index 219

PREFACE

This book has been in the making long before its actual organic research and writing, and I may not know exactly when it started to form, but it has lived with me in mutual forbearance, growing and unexpectedly metamorphizing, and now it is time for it to *adab*fully make its way into the world. *The Well-Tempered Reader* prompts a discussion about adab as a hermeneutical praxis possessing a critical grammar constitutive of the Arabic-Islamic knowledge system. This argument expands the understanding and significance of accepted genres as linear, or serving one purpose only. It offers, I hope, new ways of considering adab but also novel readings of foundational literary works that can be extended and theoretically applied to the Arabic literary tradition. *The Well-Tempered Reader*'s approach reveals the socioethical dimensions of the term-institution adab, showing that its cultural influence exceeds the domain of the textual sphere. Instead of a focus on only the formal and aesthetic features of the textual corpus as a way of writing and thus as markers of adab, this book argues that it is an ethico-aesthetic way of sensing, knowing, and being, which results from the incessant critical posture of the individual, qua the adabized subject, and their environment, which therefore offers us a critical grammar. That critical posture of the adabized subject allowed them a nuanced understanding of reality but also a modulated reception of reality, in its complexity, as multilayered.

The Well-Tempered Reader is concerned with being in the world through adab as an intellectual tuning system that offers complex, diverse, and rich ways of perceiving and reading the world, and texts as part of this world, that are different than some modern-day tuning systems due to different methods, critical language, terminology, and institutional structures that emerged in the early modern period with the onset of colonial modernity to handle the perceived overabundance of new knowledge. *The Well-Tempered Reader* is therefore attentive to the study of this cultural grammar of the formation of the subject, to which adab as praxis and application is an attestation. It advances an analysis of the virtue-ethic *murū'a*, or the ideal human, demonstrating its immanent structure in premodern Arabic culture and the formation of the subject as a legitimization of the existence of adab and its transformative power. The book argues for adab's acceptation and function as praxis through its own legitimization by way of an examination of reading and literary practices to unearth adab's critical grammar. Through advancing a critical grammar of adab, *The Well-Tempered Reader* posits adab as a generative literary, analytical, and cultural framework and a discursive force for analyzing literary acts owing to adab's participatory role in knowledge systems.

سارة بن طيير

Sarah R. Bin Tyeer

New York City, February 14, 2025 / Shaʿbān 15, 1446

ACKNOWLEDGMENTS

The completion of this book would not have been possible without the support and presence of many individuals and institutions, and coffee houses and restaurants.

First and foremost, I would like to express my deep gratitude to Alison M. Vacca, who read this book in its entirety in all its various forms: from a rough draft to the published form, and she still read every page afresh. I thank her not only for reading, but for her sincere, cordial, and purposeful presence that made a significant difference. Hamid Dabashi and Joseph Massad have been supportive of my work since day one, and I thank them for their advice, conversations, and moral support. Elaine van Dalen and I tried to enforce disciplined writing times but ended up mostly discussing either our premodern colleagues' works or everything besides than writing. I cherish these almost-writing sessions for what they were rather than for what they wanted to achieve. I thank my colleague Najam Haider for his overall advice. I thank Haifa S. Alfaisal for reading parts of this book and offering comments, words of support, and encouragement. I thank Annette Damayanti Lienau for a beautiful and heartfelt conversation over dinner in New Orleans at the MLA about both our works—thank you for your words of encouragement.

Throughout the journey of this book, I had long, short, and very short conversations, and words of general encouragement, with colleagues, as well as questions and comments on past work or ongoing work, mine and theirs, which made this journey more enjoyable as I engaged in this adab sphere. I extend my appreciation to Stefan Sperl, Geert Jan van Gelder, Abdelfattah Kilito, Nizar F. Hermes, Bilal Orfali, Nuha al-Shaar, Claire Gallien, Huda J. Fakhreddine, Suzanne Stetkeyvych, Matthew L. Keegan, Lara Harb, Jamal J. Elias, Ali Karjo-Ravary, Pier Mattia Tommasino, Seth Kimmel, Rebecca C. Johnson, Michael Cooperson, Jeffrey Sacks, Nouri Gana, and Karim Matar.

I also thank my students in courses I taught that featured some of the works and ideas discussed in this book where I explained and developed my ideas on adab and reading.

A heartfelt thanks to the two anonymous readers/*adībs* of the book for their feedback and enthusiasm—your words meant a lot to me.

A warm thanks to the Library of Arabic Literature (LAL), NYU Abu Dhabi, for their generosity and for providing the wonderful English translations for some of the works used in this book.

I am grateful to Columbia University Provost's Grant for Junior Faculty, Lenfest Junior Development Grant, and the Hettleman Junior Faculty Summer Research Grant for the financial support that allowed me to write this book comfortably. The resources provided were crucial for research-related activities and for the completion of this book.

I presented material relevant to chapter 2 at Harvard University, Institute of World Literature, in 2019. I also presented materials from chapter 4 at Trans/Formations of Arabic Literary Theory at Columbia University in 2021 and at the University of Pennsylvania in 2022. Parts of chapter 4 appear in a slightly different form in *Beyond the Rose and Nightingale*, edited by Jamal Elias (University of Pennsylvania Press, forthcoming).

I appreciate the patience and meticulous work of Eric Schmidt, who commissioned this book, and his enthusiasm and conversation. I also want to extend heartfelt thanks to current editor Margo Irvin, Jyoti Arvey, Jeff Anderson, Chloe Wong, and their team at the University of California Press for bringing this manuscript to fruition. I express sincere thanks to Muhammad Ridwaan and Leah Caldwell for their patience and impressive copyediting.

Lastly, any errors or oversights in this book are unintentional and my own. As our premodern colleagues said, *in aṣabt fa-min Allāh wa-in akhṭaʾt fa-min nafsī.*

Introduction

The Subject of *Adab*

The past few years have witnessed an effort to expand the conceptual vocabulary of the fields of languages and literatures of the Islamicate, as well as comparative literature, with regard to adab. While MESA (Middle East Studies Association) panels may be the usual place to look for and organize discussions on adab in some of the languages of the Islamicate, those of others, including the ACLA (American Comparative Literature Association) and the MLA (Modern Language Association), have also featured the topic. Slowly but surely adab is requiring little glossing similar to *polis, oikos, technē, humanitas, civitas, Bildung,* and the like. These new developments in the field gloss the importance of adab not only qua adab but as a conceptual reservoir of many critical categories and theoretical potentialities yet to be unearthed. Adab has thus far been regarded within moral, ethical, pedagogical borders but rarely as a contender of more hermeneutical tools and critical categories of thought that have contributed to the cultivation of the adabized subject qua human.

This book advances the argument that the institution of adab legitimizes its own existence through the formation of adabized subjects. The term "legitimization" used in this study evokes a *nomocentric* framework, whereas adab as a way of life is informed by the moral code of murūʾa/humanism. In this respect, it is already accepted that adab is not only narrowly restricted in a textual corpus or a theoretical abstraction but also its ethical fountain is not an abstraction of ethics. Rather, adab's framework is one that reverts to the definition and ways of being human within the framework of murūʾa. Adab therefore has a bearing on what is now defined as the formation of the subject through self-cultivation and self-regulation where adab exercises a power over the subject, through the values of murū'a, because the subject elects to behave according to adab and not another framework.[1] The adabized subject therefore recognizes this about themself but also others acknowledge this adabful quality in the subject. Murū'a as the ideal way of being human becomes a law of truth for the subject propelling them to act in murū'a, whereas adab becomes the practical expression of this law for the subject. As Michel Foucault maintains, "Power applies itself to immediate everyday life which categorizes the individual, marks him by his own individuality, attaches him to his own identity, imposes a law of truth on him which he must recognize and which others have to recognize in him. It is a form of power which makes individuals subjects."[2] If the subject is formed "through self-cultivation and self-regulation within contexts of linguistic conventions, power dynamics, and discursive formation," it can be observed that premodern scholars regarded adab's normativity as an ideal to be cultivated and perpetually refined. This normativity of adab, then, can be best regarded as its own grounds for legitimacy. By legitimacy, I also mean that adab was not taken for a superfluous activity that celebrated its own excesses and aesthetics or a corpus representative of certain moments in history in abstraction. Rather, as this book argues, the institution of adab was conscious of its own role in the formation of the subject through its active involvement in linguistic expressions and the crafting of meaning, its norms, mitigation of conflict and power relationships and critique, and the construction of discourse. In this respect, adab as an observed discursive tradition was actively legitimizing itself.

While *The Legitimization of* Adab *in the Arabic Literary Tradition* seems like a forbidding subtitle due to the sheer claim on words like "legitimization," "adab," and "Arabic literary tradition"—admittedly the latter alone presupposes a responsibility that is difficult to exhaust in one book—the tasks of this book are derived, or rather orbit and inter-derive, from one word: adab. Raymond Williams proposes that one keyword has the power to teach us about not only its etymological indication but also its processes of social and cultural innovation and legitimation, since such processes impart to us the ways these keywords are used to construct and appraise the world socially and intellectually.[3] Adab therefore becomes an agent of disclosure due to its revelatory power because of the wide range of conceptual, intellectual, and social attitudes in which it is used in the Arabic literary tradition and in all languages of the Islamicate where adab became a social and intellectual agential force.[4] Indeed, very few concept-institutions of the South-South have gained as much growth and popularity, but also, recently, a critical consideration, like adab. A specific definition of adab may prove challenging not because it is a nebulous concept but because of its extensive development history. These developments can be thought of as positively cumulative, which is one factor that lends adab its complexity. Since the "word has acquired new senses over the course of time, it has never entirely shed the older ones. Its semantic evolution mirrors the changes which Arab society and culture have undergone."[5]

Indeed, poets in the pre-Islamic period did not speak of adab or mention it in the capacity it had later. One of the earliest uses and forms that existed was *ādib*, which means the host or one who invites to a meal. As poet Ṭarafa b. al-ʿAbd (d. 569 CE) maintains:

نحن في المشتاة ندعو الجفلى . . . لا ترى الآدب فينا ينتقر

> In winter, we invite everyone to food / You do not see us selecting one over the other.[6]

The original acceptation and use of this word meant a banquet (*maʾduba*) where people are invited to food, especially in harsh environmental conditions in the desert and during winter months. The one who extended the invitation or initiated it is called the *ādub*, with the verb forms *aduba-yaʾdubu* referring to the act of inviting people to such banquets. Some studies maintain that it is unlikely pre-Islamic poetry mentioned or used adab beyond the capacity of the verb as referred to in Ṭarafa's poem nor did its semantic range expand beyond this use.[7] This would suggest that adab carried a materialistic connotation, one that referred strictly to the generous act of hospitality and inviting others to one's table. It is uncertain if this supposition can be fully accepted. Perhaps the connotation and use eventually expanded to the nonmaterial. One of the earliest semantic expansions, and hence epistemic transformations, of adab's usage came during the Prophet's time when in a *ḥadīth* he says, "My Lord has taught me excellent manners and perfected my manners" (*addabanī rabbī fa-aḥsana taʾdībī*). This very ḥadīth is also explained and regarded as an invitation, whereby the Qur'an is regarded as a banquet of knowledge and virtuousness sent by the divine.[8] This constitutes a double aim of the word here: adab as banquet retains the original conceptions of hospitality, but the form of sustenance is one that edifies and also refines. It is an intellectual and moral nourishment. Although the ḥadīth is deemed "weak" in its chain of transmission, it is not weak in its meaning. Adab here is explained by scholars of ḥadīth like al-Fayyūmī (d. 870 AH/1465–66 CE) as "the unification of the refinement of both the outer self and inner self" (*ijtimāʿ tahdhīb al-ẓāhir wa-l-bāṭin*).[9] Sahm b. Ḥanẓala al-Ghanwī, a *mukhaḍram* poet (someone who lived during both the pre-Islamic period and also after Islam), used adab in its ethical capacity, evoking the same use that occurred in the aforementioned ḥadīth:

لا يمنعُ النّاسُ منّي ما أردتُ ولا أُعطيهمِ ما أرادوا حسنَ ذا أدَبا

> People do not delay giving me what I want;
> Do I not then give them what they want?
> What beautiful adab this is![10]

The poet here is describing social relations between people in general, and so did not use the word "friends." This highlights that he does not refer to a transactional relationship where emotional investments and expectations frame these encounters. The poet uses "people" (*al-nās*) in general and says that they are helpful and never delay assisting him or giving him what he wants; why, then, should he not reciprocate—is not this beautiful adab? This example points to a less common category of emotions and social relations. The people referred to in the couplet are not specified as friends or relations but they could be acquaintances and/or mere strangers. What is emphasized in this assertion is the upkeeping of social relations via adab as social *poiēsis*: the making of this social harmony through adab. In this respect, the poet's rhetorical self-reflexivity is an acknowledgment of this normative adab as an ideal and as an aspiration. Where social *poiēsis* and harmony would often be called upon in terms of framing the existing or defined social relationships or even conflicts, adab's role as an instrument of fostering trust among strangers, hence a potential agent for furthering social cohesion, must also be recognized.

Although adab may have been used in a nonmaterial capacity before Islam, it is with the advent of Islam that the word-concept gradually transformed from its material signification to a metaphorical-conceptual one.[11] The ethical meaning of adab infused with Islamic teachings persisted into the Umayyad (41–132 AH/661–750 CE) and Abbasid (132–656 AH/750–1258 CE) periods and another meaning was added to the ever-evolving concept: the pedagogical and gradually the totality of knowledge seen as a result not only of the encounter with foreign cultures (Persian and Greek) but also the "transformation from the oral/aural literary to the increasingly book-based and writerly."[12] As the nascent empire found itself creating and adopting bureaus, departments, and professions to acclimate to its rapid growth and increasingly diverse and professional populations, translating and encountering foreign knowledge, a new class was being created: the secretaries (*kuttāb*) and the teachers for young princes (*muʾaddibīn*, sing. *muʾaddib*), whose role would be to teach these young princes what their future positions would require of them in studying Arab culture (poetry, oration, battles/days of Arabs, biography of pre-Islamic times and Islam). Similarly, the *kuttāb* had to possess comparable knowledge of the aforementioned genres.[13] Arab literary historian and critic Shawqī Ḍaif argues that this transformation in the usage and praxis allowed adab to become taxonomized as a discipline or science (*ʿilm*), which was restricted to Islamic sciences only until the Umayyads.[14] With the rise of professional specialization, especially within the chancery culture, scholars framed their definitions of adab as a discipline in addition to an ethical and moral quality to be aspired to; adab became a developing discipline that grew and affected and became affected by the rest of the developing Arab-Islamic disciplines.[15]

In his commentary on Ibn Qutayba's *Adab al-kātib*, grammarian and lexicographer al-Jawālīqī (d. 539 AH/1144 CE) considers adab linguistically and ethically as "good morals" (*ḥusn al-akhlāq*) and "doing virtue" (*fiʿl al-makārim*), and that its designation after the named Arabic sciences was something that occurred in Islam (*iṭlāqahu ʿalā ʿulūm al-ʿarabiyya al-madhkūra muwalladun ḥadatha fī al-islām*).[16] Wolfhart Heinrichs addresses the question of whether adab "embodied a separate and distinctive ideal of education and intellectual pursuit" during the apogee of Abbasid culture and the separate designation of adab qua *ʿulūm adabiyya* and by extension the *adīb*.[17] Heinrichs maintains that "knowledge of literary texts (poetic, ornate prosaic, proverbial, historical-anecdotal, including Koranic and Hadith)" is expected and not elective; the "*adīb* is trained to know by heart, on any conceivable topic, all the relevant quotable materials from all the genres just mentioned."[18] Heinrichs's discussion of the *ʿulūm adabiyya* in the fourth century AH/tenth century CE and George Makdisi's *studia adabiyya*, with reference to the disciplines of adab in his discussion of the Niẓāmiyya school in the fifth century AH/eleventh century CE, point to the establishment of adab as an independent discipline and to its official institutionalization.[19]

Although Ḍaif's lifetime work, the monumental ten-volume history of adab, *Tārīkh al-ādāb al-ʿarabiyya*, which took thirty years to complete, attests to the evolutionary process of adab until reaching the modern definition as "eloquent expression that is meant to affect readers and listeners on an emotional level, whether it be poetry or prose" (*al-kalām al-inshāʾī al-balīgh al-ladhī yuqṣad bihi ilā al-taʾthīr fī ʿawāṭif al-qurrāʾ wa-l-sāmiʿīn sawāʾ kāna shiʿran am nathran*),[20] it still views adab within the framework of modern literary practice and as a textual corpus. Viewing adab anatomically through texts alone can still be useful in highlighting the field contours of adab. To further explain, Brockelmann's *Geschichte der Arabischen Litteratur* was (and still is) considered an indispensable reference, despite the later corrections, which organized or rather divided Arabic studies into the historical periods that have become customary in the field of Arabic studies: from the pre-Islamic through the Umayyads, Abbasids, Mongols, Mamluks, Ottomans, among others. In Brockelmann's *Geschichte*, despite using *Litteratur* as a translation for adab, Brockelmann includes more than literature proper; he lists philosophy, *kalam*, logic, and jurisprudence, to mention a few nonliterary disciplines. The reason for this, he argues, is that

> Bei den modernen Kulturvölkern drängen sich diese Erscheinungen in solcher Masse, dass der Literarhistoriker sich auf die Dichtung zu beschränken genötigt ist. Die arabische Poesie bedeutet aber für die Entwicklung der menschlichen Kultur nicht so viel wie die Wirksamkeit arabisch schreibender Gelehrter für den Aufbau der Wissenschaft. Denn das Arabische blieb nicht an die Schranken einer Nation gebunden, sondern ward in dem weiten Umkreis, den der Islām als Religion durchdrang, von den Ufern des Pontus bis nach Zanzibar, von Fez und Timbuktu bis nach Kašġar und den Sundainseln, die Trägerin aller Kultur und Bildung und trat diese Rolle erst spät und nur zum Teil an die Nationalsprachen ab.[21]
>
> Among the "civilised" nations these manifestations have accumulated to such a degree that the literary historian is compelled to limit himself purely to poetry. However, Arabic poetry did not have the same significance for the development of human culture and knowledge as a whole compared to the achievements of scholars writing in Arabic for the development of the sciences. This is because the Arabic language was not limited to a single nation, but was the bearer of all culture and education in the vast area where Islam penetrated as a religion, from the banks of the Pontus to Zanzibar, from Fez and Timbuktu to Kashgar and the Sunda islands, ceding this role only belatedly to various national languages, and then only in part.[22]

Brockelmann intimates that for the study of the premodern period the totality of knowledge production in Arabic must be considered absolutely necessary for reading and understanding culture. This is because, in his words, Arabic poetry is inadequate to be of any "significance for the development of human culture and knowledge." He relegates this to the difference in what he calls "modernen Kulturvölkern," or "'civilised' nations," where the study of poetry alone can be sufficient as a study of culture. This distinction in scope of study, between the premodern and modern literary output, according to Brockelmann, is necessary as far as the former is concerned, whereas literary "outputs of the modern era, in which the world of Islam has become more and more aligned with European culture, [for those] one can limit oneself to poetry alone."[23] Indeed, Brockelmann's organization and selections convey this concept as tied to literature but also the entirety of culture, for he does not believe that a full picture of culture can be actualized without all relevant sciences in the premodern era. It was therefore necessary that other disciplines and genres be considered. It is only in the modern period that Brockelmann accepts a study of literature to mean only "literature" as poetry or the literary proper during and after the *nahḍa*, as Brockelmann's work was published between 1889 and 1902 in Leiden. His differentiation between the comprehensiveness of the premodern and the specialization of the modern pertaining to both Arabic and European literatures is explained through what he describes as the "alignment with European culture." Perhaps cultural capital expatriation is a better term that explains how, under the external pressures of colonialism and other foreign influences, the shift in cultural priorities and resources was noticeable in favor of European alignment. The standardization of the specialized academic disciplines around the mid-nineteenth century is often explained through the thorough secularization of the university, on the one hand, and the establishment of widespread social mechanisms of control and their needs for classification, categorization, and ranking, on the other.[24] Adab's comprehensiveness and interdisciplinarity with other sciences and its moral law of truth can no longer be aligned with this cultural capital expatriation and its imported laws of truth.

Jurjī Zaydān's *Tārīkh ādāb al-lugha al-ʿarabiyya*—printed in 1899, after first appearing partially in periodicals and magazines—comes ten years after Brockelmann's intervention. Zaydān's posture is certainly that of the literary historian who references Brockelmann among an impressive list of Arabic, English, French, and German sources. Zaydān's seminal and important history follows the same format and periodization that was witnessed in Brockelmann's work and other Orientalist works, though he criticizes the latter as insufficient and falling short of a "history" of Arabic literature. Instead, Zaydān argues that Arabs pioneered this art since the *Fihrist* of Ibn al-Nadīm (d. 380 AH/990 CE), and he commends Ibn al-Nadīm for including, alongside what he calls the original Arabs' adab (*ādāb al-ʿarab al-aṣliyya*), the knowledge produced in Islamic sciences and linguistics (*al-ʿulūm al-islāmiyya wa-l-lisāniyya*).[25] In a similar vein, Zaydān acknowledges

Miftāḥ al-sa ʿāda wa-miṣbāḥ al-siyāda, also known as *Mawḍū ʿāt al- ʿulūm*, by Ottoman historian-chronicler Taşköprüzade (Ṭāsh Kubrā Zādeh) (d. 968 AH/1561 CE), which is organized by fields and includes more than 150 genres (*mi ʾa wa-khamsūn fannan*) as part of this literary history.[26] Similarly, he praises Ottoman historian, geographer, and biographer Kâtip Çelebi's (d. 1067 AH/1657 CE) *Kashf al-ẓunūn*, a bibliographical encyclopedia providing information on around fifteen thousand titles published in Arabic, Persian, and Ottoman Turkish—a method that follows the previous prototypes on the history of adab Zaydān mentions. Finally, Zaydān relates a contemporaneous example as part of this literature review, the three-volume *Abjad al- ʿulūm* by Indian scholar Ṣiddīq al-Qunūjī (d. 1307 AH/1890 CE), published in India in the nineteenth century. Zaydān's comprehensiveness and understanding of the interdisciplinarity of adab as seen in the titles he included is obvious, as is his inclusion of titles published by Ottoman and Indian authors where knowledge produced about Arabic is indeed considered part of the Arabic corpus, naturally before the Sykes-Picot agreement in 1916, where less of Zaydān's sentiment and posture was observed after the creation of the modern Middle East.

Zaydān concurs that these tomes are foundational for the study of Arabic language and literature but cannot be really called a "history" of literatures as a "literary history" was then understood. By extension, he does not consider Brockelmann's or Orientalists' works exhaustive of "literary history" either; they are, according to him, all bibliographic and encyclopedic references. Zaydān then credits himself as the first to have likely named this science in the Arabic language and academe as "*tārīkh ādāb al-lugha al- ʿarabiyya*," or rather he credits himself as the founder of "Arabic literary history" in Arabic scholarship when he, as editor in chief, used it for the first time in *al-Hilāl* magazine in 1894.[27] In his article, he maintains that *ādāb* constitutes all science and knowledge (*taqa ʿ ʿalā al- ʿulūm wa-l-ma ʿārif muṭlaqan*) and avers that no judgment on the status of knowledge and literature (*al- ʿilm wa-l-adab*) in any time of Arab history is possible except after studying the cultural and civilizational context (*al-ḥaḍāra wa-l- ʿumrān*).[28] Like Brockelmann's definition, Zaydān's definition, as well as the bibliographic lists encompassing the disciplines of science, philosophy, and history, attests that adab is interdisciplinary, or rather postdisciplinary, in its embracing of several fields in the one work but also the evident learnedness of *adībs* in more than one field at any point in history.

Although the previous discussion showed the gradual process of the institutionalization of adab and its establishment as a discipline in its own right; an exacting, committing, nonchanging definition of adab in the Arabic tradition is not possible owing to its history, evolution, development, and functions. Attesting to this intellectually stimulating difficulty, despite Ḍaif's gargantuan efforts, like those before him who attempted to historicize Arabic adab, such as Brockelmann and Zaydān, Ḍaif acknowledges the limitations of such a task, that it is by no means exhaustive but still exhilarating due to its research and intellectual challenges. Ḍaif writes that these endeavors are what his efforts allowed him to complete to a level of acceptable accuracy in a lifetime, given, as he intimates, that much of this adab is still in manuscript format, a fact that continues to change since the completion of his work but that will also improve future anthologizing and historicizing efforts.

My intention is not to trace adab's expansion, constriction, and/or transformation of its own meaning in the place it occupies in the Arabic literary tradition but rather to investigate the grammar of adab itself. It is accepted that adab may have had different and evolving and shifting acceptations that changed with time. But rather than look for the definition of a term, a purely theoretical enterprise that more often than not is considered in posterity after the phenomenon is observed, this book's purpose is to look for practical acceptations as the practitioners of adab used and practiced.

If we accept that adab is expansively defined as a system that has an aesthetic and ethical language, and this language may vary or shift across the ages as the aforementioned discussions maintain, then by definition every language has a grammar that makes it intelligible even if the language varies in its aesthetics or has evolved. If adab, as Ḍaif and others attest, seems to have changed or had different characteristics and articulations across the ages, it can be argued that adab as a structure would still have a recognizable grammar. The grammar of adab therefore is what would allow this aesthetic of adab to be constructed. It is adab's structural foundation that would allow it its source of legitimization. How, might we ask, is a grammar of adab constructed? One of the components of the grammar of adab is its prescriptive nature, which can be observed in manuals such as the "adab of scribes" (*Adab al-kātib*) or the "adab of a certain praxis." This prescriptive adab attests to the aforementioned normativity of adab in general, and it also involves setting rules for how a practice should be best performed, often based on notions of correctness or decorum as agreed upon by practitioners, hence an accepted mode of professionalism. If adab's personal ethics and morals are accepted as part of the personal sphere, the prescriptive regulations as adab can be considered professional ethics. On the other hand, adab possesses a critical grammar that acts as its framework of legitimization. As mentioned, the normativity of adab derives its legitimacy from the reciprocated trust shown by the subject in this institution and the institution's responsibility for enhancing the subject's life. For this to happen, adab's own grammar cannot be other than a deeper understanding of the qualities of the ideal human: murū'a.

What relationship do adab and reading have to the Arab-Islamic conception of murū'a or humanism and the "ideal human" and the ways of being human? What does it mean to be an adabized subject and a literate reader in the premodern Arab-Islamic world? This book argues for adab's acceptation and function as praxis through its own legitimization via an examination of reading and literary practices that unearth adab's critical grammar. Through a critical grammar of adab, the book posits adab as a generative literary, analytical, and cultural framework and a discursive force for analyzing literary acts. In so doing, it takes adab as a framework for investigation. This book identifies adab as a literary, analytical, and cultural force, a new locus for the grammar of critical thinking in and of itself and about adab. The following chapters, taking six case studies, span key historical periods: eighth-century Baghdad (Ibn al-Muqaffaʿ's *Kalīla wa-Dimna*), tenth-century Syria (al-Maʿarrī's *Zajr al-nābiḥ*), twelfth-century Andalusia (Ibn Ṭufayl's *Ḥayy b. Yaqẓān*), fifteenth-century Egypt (al-Suyūṭī's *al-Tabarrī min maʿarrat al-Maʿarrī*), and the nineteenth-century Lebanese *nahḍa* (al-Shidyāq's *Leg over Leg*). These authors and works are not case studies in the strictest sense. Rather, they are entryways to much broader questions and claims that each chapter explores. In light of this structure and organization, the book's assertion about "adab's legitimization of itself" should not be understood as a discussion about an activity exclusive to these authors or texts alone. Indeed, each chapter is an investigation of the critical grammar of adab that speaks to broader discourses. These discourses, raised by the texts and their authors, are in "filiative" conversations with other texts within what they create as an adab sphere.[29] This sphere can be best defined and understood as the interrelated adab environment, textual and otherwise, with its authors, readers, critics, and all participants who engage this sphere, thereby giving it its form through both affirmation and opposition. These affirmations and oppositions naturally reflect critical positions that can have a social purchase. The adab sphere therefore should not be understood as an abstract concept. Rather, it is one where adab's complex nature is reflected through these interrelated dynamics and where contestations about legitimacy occur. That said, every text chosen for discussion that constitutes a chapter in this book can be considered its own sphere where these connections and dynamics will come into full light.

This book takes adab as a discursive practice. In this respect, the purpose of this temporal span of the selected works is to show several things. (a) The discursive and interdisciplinary nature of adab, in a precolonial context, was transformed in the nineteenth century owing to what Brockelmann described as the "alignment with European culture." (b) This in turn will account for the meaning of "tradition" in the subtitle. As the book sets out to show the discursive nature of adab, it by default contours both the act of adab's own legitimization and the adabized reader in the premodern Arab-Islamic world at various temporal slices as presented in each chapter. (c) The selection and method in turn allow for a stronger argument on the ways adab was legitimized (i.e., justified its existence) through its streaming of intellectual virtues and virtue-ethics that are considered definitive of the ideal human (murūʾa) in more than one genre, period, and geography.

The criterion for selection is not arbitrary; rather, it ties this selection back to the conception of human through the notion of "reading" as a cross section of human praxis. How does one express the means of being human through reading and understanding? Is all reading stable and void of crises of comprehension and understanding? What creates an unstable reading praxis? What is the difference between literal versus figurative language? How does one read humiliation; how does one read and respond to an insult? How did epistemic transformations and cultural pressures affect ways of reading in the nineteenth-century *nahḍa*? It is possible that there are answers to these questions outside the frame of adab. The book endeavors to answer these questions within the frame of adab and the conception of the adabized subject. These questions comprise the skeletal logic holding these chapters together. They are the very questions that shaped and guided the book's development, writing process, and creative impetus. The skeletal logic therefore is the consideration of intellectual virtues as delineated by the definition of murūʾa that guides and defines the act of reading and understanding within the parameters of the human. In adab's privileging of the human, it allows the adabized subject to live with the discursive tradition of language and history and develop textual empathy. Adab creates the conditions of the well-tempered reader, the adabized subject, beyond the confines of the literal and restricted language as a result of relegating this lived tradition to an archive of textual corpus, thereby creating a restricted reader.

Like Johann Sebastian Bach's (1685–1750 CE) *The Well-Tempered Clavier*, BWV 846–893, which consists of two sets of preludes and fugues in all twenty-four major and minor keys for keyboard, and which moves effortlessly between all keys through the employment of a tuning system, the well-tempered reader was/is able to move effortlessly, "connectedly" through layers of language and history across time and tradition. Bach's work explored every aspect of the keyboard in the seventeenth century, and it continues to offer challenges, perhaps also innovations, to each new generation. Bach's aim was to present an innovative approach to tuning that allowed for performance in all twenty-four major and minor keys without excessively altering the qualities of harmony. That said, "'well-tempered' does not in itself imply a specific tuning, any more than 'clavier' implies a specific instrument. It means no more than a tuning in which it is possible to play tolerably in all keys."[30] This means that players performed within a wide range of both skill and emotional register. The opposite of the well-tempered would be a tuning that produces what is known as the "wolf intervals" or unpleasant and harsh "dissonance."

Like the typology of Bach's players, Ibn al-Muqaffaʿ also envisioned a typology of readers whom he, through the virtue of adab as a tuning system, saw as the well-tempered readers who would be able to read his *Kalīla wa-Dimna* in various ranges of difficulty according to their adabization. The process of adabization then can be thought of as the intellectual tuning system of the well-tempered reader. The analogy not only depicts texts and their readers, since it will be read by all types of readers; rather, the self-knowledge and awareness of this range, as I argue, is what separates the well-tempered reader from the not-so-well-tempered (or untuned) reader. The well-tempered reader is aware of the existence of the need for an adab-informed reading that would allow a realization of a range of reading, discourse, critique, and levels of meaning, and therefore is open to other readers and the adab sphere in a process of needing others, that is, other readers. An untuned reader is not an adabized reader. An untuned reader is disconnected from tradition, disengaged from a discursive tradition and other readers. The untuned reader will, by default, create dissonance.

In Homer's *Odyssey*, which retells the story of the adventures and eventual homecoming of Odysseus to Ithaca after leaving his wife, Penelope, and infant son, Telemachus, for seventeen years, an important account takes place in the first four books, known as the *Telemachy* or the *Paideia of Telemachus*. Telemachus, then seventeen, grew up without his father, Odysseus. He is unable to defend his house and property from the suitors of Penelope, who are only after his father's estate and the consuming of his resources. Athena, the goddess of wisdom, presents Telemachus with the choice to travel and meet with his father's friends and war comrades to learn more about his father and become educated. Telemachus expresses a sense of inadequacy for this venture because of a lack of knowledge in "dialogue" or "discourse." He does not know how to speak with people in general or elder people in particular:

> Telemachus replied, "But Mentor, how
> can I approach and talk to him? I am
> quite inexperienced at making speeches,
> and as a young man, I feel awkward talking
> to elders."[31]

The original Greek word used to describe Telemachus is *nēpios* (νήπιος). It does not mean "inarticulate" or "inexperienced" as such but "disconnected." Telemachus is characterized as a "clueless" young man; he is disconnected intellectually, morally, and emotionally.[32] It is quite easy to see why *nēpios*, "disconnected," would be understood and/or translated as "inexperienced" or "inarticulate." If someone is disconnected on all aforementioned levels, being inarticulate or lacking in experience becomes a plausible, even an inevitable, consequence to this disconnectedness. His disconnectedness evidently not only prevents him from being cognizant of the necessary tools to engage with people and derive meaning through understanding their stories but also prevents him from properly developing his future experiences.

MURŪ'A, ADAB, AND THE ADABIZED SUBJECT

I have thus far charted the map of terms and concepts and the framework for this book, which endeavors to further an understanding of what adab is rather than reinstate that adab is. In other words, the present study does not take previous definitions at face value, nor does it do away with them, but it attempts to see anew with fresher eyes and innovative links and patterns. As mentioned, the corpus of this study hails from various genres: animal fables that are also recognized as mirrors for princes such as *Kalīla wa-Dimna*; the philosophical-theological allegory of *Ḥayy b. Yaqẓān*; auto-commentaries and treatises of self-defense by al-Maʿarrī; an *urjūza* (pedagogical poem) by al-Suyūṭī; and a lexicon masquerading as a novel parodying novels by al-Shidyāq. By all means these works classify and understand themselves as works of adab, but this is not the only criteria of selection. The major criterion of choice, as mentioned and understood broadly, is reading. In this respect, as a corpus self-defining as adab, it offers an opportunity to examine how the texts performed adab as praxis and therefore how it transferred this praxis on the meta level to its readers. In other words, how do the grammar of adab and the values of murūʾa, as the amalgamation of all virtues, inspire the performance of adab, which legitimizes its own existence, and how do they simultaneously offer the reader a discursive and sustainable value of adab? Incontrovertibly, each text had a different set of questions and challenges and therefore performed adab differently through various derivatives of murūʾa, as shall be explained in due course. But despite these texts' differences and performances, they all performed through the grammar of adab that derived its syntax from the conception of murūʾa as the values contributing to the formation of the ideal human and the adabized subject.

THE WELL-TEMPERED READER: THE SUBJECT OF ADAB

This brief introduction has attempted to present, explain, and account for the title's keywords—well-tempered reader, adab, legitimization, Arabic literary tradition—and has put forth the central question of the book. In six core chapters, the book will further delineate the concepts introduced in the introduction and further chart the argument as each chapter, though different than the last, builds on the argument within as the work progresses.

Chapter 1: Adab *and/as* Murūʾa

In this chapter, I examine and analyze an early work on adab and murūʾa/humanism, hitherto undiscussed, by the eighth-century Ṣāliḥ b. Janāḥ, where I set out the ideals and conceptions of adab and murūʾa. I also discuss the subsequent, though less innovative, and only other available work on the subject of adab and murūʾa by Ibn al-Marzubān (d. 309 AH/921 CE). These discussions act as a framework that holds murūʾa as the conceptual reservoir of Arab-Islamic virtues defining humanism/the ideal human. Murūʾa in these works is conceptualized as an umbrella for various virtue-ethics that become the building blocks of the grammar of adab: hospitality, discourse, civility and decorum, will and resolve. In this respect, as per these early Arabic sources, the ways of being human, through these virtues, are the defining virtue-ethics of the ideal human, and simultaneously they are reflected in adab but also take adab as a vehicle to actualize them. The book understands humanism within the Arab-Islamic parameters of the definition of murūʾa as the ideal human who perfected an expression of this humanity through the exercising of murūʾa.

Chapter 2: Adab *as Hospitality*

This chapter considers the act of translation of *Kalīla wa-Dimna*, the first work of prose in Arabic, from the Sanskrit via Pahlavi by Ibn al-Muqaffaʿ as an act of adab qua hospitality toward the text but also readers. To add, Ibn al-Muqaffaʿ's own rationalization and defense of adab in his *al-Adab al-kabīr wa-l-adab al-ṣaghīr* (The Major and Minor Adab) advances the legitimization of adab because it encourages what he defines as "discourse" (*shuʿūb al-ḥadīth*), which he sees as conducive to the flourishing of mind and intellect but also society, hence the actualization of what he calls "the good life" and social *poiēsis*. This is reflected in his own exordium to the translated work *Kalīla wa-Dimna*, which, while acknowledging the work's figurative language as a crisis in understanding but also an exercise in multiple interpretations, he delineates through a typology of readers who will exhibit different levels of understanding across both horizontal and vertical times, thereby creating hospitable "conditions of understanding" and a hospitable reader. The hospitality shown to the reader by Ibn al-Muqaffaʿ as well encourages one to be imaginative and critical, which enables this social adabization through what I call the adab sphere, hence adab as praxis. The chapter also puts forth a comparison between Plato's and Aristotle's views of figurative language versus its conception in the Arab-Islamic context, taking into account the translation movement of Greek sources at the time and comparing the latter's attitude toward figurative language versus the Arabic.

Chapter 3: Adab *as Discourse*

The twelfth-century epistle *Ḥayy b. Yaqẓān* by Ibn Ṭufayl gives us ample room for displaying how a literary work can both represent a crisis in understanding and participate in resolving it, thereby acting as an interlocutor and allowing others to participate in what I identify as the adab sphere. On the macro level, the crisis in understanding refers to the remarks Ibn Ṭufayl makes in the exordium, which point to his own reading reception of other scholars' works, as well as other scholars' reception in general. The critique of available scholarship that went into his work, as evidenced by the citational exordium, points to these positive crises of reading experience. It refers to a crisis of understanding factored in time that Ibn Ṭufayl says he will rectify for the young disciple as a distillation of his own reading to act as an introduction. There are explicit references to crises of understanding, as Ibn Ṭufayl says that readers may have misunderstood some elements in al-Ghazālī's *Mishkāt al-anwār*, one of the book's sources. On the micro level, the narrative of *Ḥayy b. Yaqẓān* deploys the process of "understanding" itself as a perpetual crisis in the text, on the level of self and Ḥayy himself, to the absence of language at the beginning as an accepted vehicle of understanding and communication, until the narrative moves to the people of the island with Absāl and Salāmān and the diversity of understanding and reception of Ḥayy's teachings because of the "extralinguistic" nature of his experience that he attempts to convey. The inadequacy of language as a vehicle for expressing spiritual experiences is an argument that is emphasized in the epistle and it is one that is in a citational relationship with Avicenna's ideas on language as "mental content" rather than language as logic or grammar (as per the famous tenth-century debate between Abū Bishr Mattā and Abū Saʿīd al-Sirāfī). Lacking critical tools of adab because of their oppressive ruler, the people of the island's understanding, except Absāl's, borders on, and anticipates, Locke's "ideational theory," which attempts to reduce a metaphor to its archetype that stands in opposition to Ḥayy's "intellective reasoning" and the "extralinguistic." The disparity in the reception of the ideas advanced by Ḥayy evokes what Gadamer calls the "historical conditioning of understanding."

Chapter 4: Adab *as Critique*

Pursuing and building on what has been discussed in the previous chapters, this chapter takes al-Maʿarrī's (d. 449 AH/1057 CH) auto-commentary *Zajr al-nābiḥ* (Chiding the Barking Dog(s)), written in response to misreadings, misrepresentations, and falsifications about his poetry collection *Luzūmiyyāt*, also known as *Luzūm mā lā yalzam* (Unnecessary Necessity), as its case study. Acknowledging the deliberate misreading of his poetry, al-Maʿarrī utilizes an arsenal of rhetorical, grammatical, and poetic techniques in this auto-commentary to achieve the performative nature required in this work. Al-Maʿarrī does not treat this as a crisis in understanding and therefore an innocent misreading of his work, but as a deliberate injustice (*ẓulm*)—the same word used by Ibn Ṭufayl in referring to those that misread the works cited in his exordium. This therefore does not only become an attestation to a conception of both "ethical reading" and critique as *naẓar* but also points us to an incident in literary history where the poet's greatest achievement and authority are turned against him. Misreading as injustice was not lost on later historians like Ibn al-ʿAdīm (d. 660 AH/1262 CE) and literati like Yūsuf al-Badīʿī (d. 1037 AH/1662 CE), who both authored their own versions of defense based on a close reading of al-Maʿarrī's work and the latter's aforementioned auto-commentary. Both authors had no vested interest in al-Maʿarrī, nor were they his contemporaries. Rather, Ibn al-ʿAdīm titled his distinct monograph *al-Inṣāf wa-l-taḥarrī fī dafʿ al-ẓulm ʿan Abī al-ʿAlāʾ al-Maʿarrī* (The Righting and Investigation in the Elimination of Injustice against al-Maʿarrī) to refute the claims and fabrications against al-Maʿarrī. This act of "critical justice" (*inṣāf*) toward al-Maʿarrī therefore shows us that it was a most fundamental critical category of thought; critical justice acted as categorical "critique" for reliable versus unreliable narrators in ḥadīth studies; it is an ethical imperative. This also shows how the theoretical virtue of "justice" was transformed into a praxis proper that allows the formation of the critical subject qua the adabized subject.

Chapter 5: Adab *as Method*

If the threat or the actual act of insulting another is one that aims at dehumanizing the subject, ridiculing them, and stripping them out of their ontological status as human, socially and morally, how does one adabize an insult? In this chapter, I discuss an anecdote that relates how, on his way to al-Sharīf al-Murtaḍā's (d. 436 AH/1044 CE) court, al-Maʿarrī, the visually impaired poet, stumbles on a man. The man, flustered, formulates an insult in the form of an inquiry relegating al-Maʿarrī to a third-person bystander: "Who is this dog?" (*man hādhā al-kalb*). Al-Maʿarrī retorts quickly and tells the man, "A dog is someone who does not know seventy names for the dog" (*al-kalb man lā yaʿrif li-l-kalb sabʿīn isman*) and leaves it there in apparent philological victory. Al-Maʿarrī apparently not only returned the favor but insulted everyone for posterity, as al-Suyūṭī's (d. 911 AH/1505 CE) philological enterprise later attests. Four hundred years later, Egyptian scholar al-Suyūṭī does not leave it there. He takes this insult to heart and also to adab. He writes an *urjūza* titled *al-Tabarrī min maʿarrat al-Maʿarrī* (The Disowning of the Disgrace of al-Maʿarrī), which traces all the names of the dog he could find in lexicons and books to explain away the insult in a manner of an *explication de texte/mot* or a commentary (*sharḥ*) on "dogness." Al-Suyūṭī therefore shows us that he responded back to the insult in a methodology of adab that reflects the times he lived in where lexical and commentarial pursuits were prime. Adab as method therefore shows us how literati engaged and framed their work within the structures and logics of adab and not just a textual universe they alluded to. This crisis of the insult, spanning over four hundred years, was resolved, adabfully.

Chapter 6: Adab *as Resolve and Will*

This chapter discusses Aḥmad Fāris al-Shidyāq's (ca. 1806–87 CE) *Leg over Leg* in light of its unique genre-breaking oeuvre. The work combines several genres: autobiography, travelogue, lexicons, and premodern *maqāmāt*, among others. The chapter argues that al-Shidyāq's will and resolve to critique the novel's form and to author a book in the aesthetics and mannerism of premodern adab serve a double aim. The Arabic language and its literary constituents are, according to some, incompatible with the project of modernity and with commerce and administration, as al-Shidyāq relates to us. The Arabic tradition and language are thus seen as both an impediment and a threat to progress and one of the salient literary symbols of modernity and progress: the novel. In this work, al-Shidyāq questions and critiques these claims aesthetically through a nod to the premodern forms and language he adopts, thereby resisting the simplified form and language of the emerging Arabic novels of the time.

By adopting and declaring this position explicitly, he immediately posited himself as a critic of these views. He even goes further and calls modern Arab users of the language "foreign Arabs" who are unable to access the very language they use, a nomenclature he uses in the subtitle of his book. Al-Shidyāq's engagement with adab therefore shows how certain exploitative practices contributed to the loss of Arabic and in turn the subject's linguistic being, which thus limit their abilities to articulate the world, to imagine and conceptualize and achieve their maximum potential, as he shows us in *Leg over Leg*. The latter status is in a direct relationship to the intellectual virtues discussed throughout the book and which, as al-Shidyāq cleverly argues, become lost with the loss of language and the subject's access to adab. The restriction of adab and its concomitant intellectual grammar and language limited the subject's ability to articulate the world and turned the subject into a "restricted" reader and thinker.

Coda: The Sustainability of Adab

The coda ties together all the threads of this book's arguments. It also advances, delicately, that some acts of reading that are resistant to adab by modern literati may have, perhaps unwittingly, advanced the delegitimization of adab by creating certain historical conditions of understanding and different modes of reading, therefore creating a different type of reader than the premodern one. This not only raises the question on the meaning and function of adab versus literature in light of the book's argument—the legitimization of adab as practiced by premodern literati—but also the premodern versus the modern reader. That adab indeed held a social function, beyond the literary and pedagogical, in its privileging of the imagination and language skills, allows the adabized subject to move beyond the confines of the "literal" and "restricted" language and differentiate between reality and imagination, and also to develop "textual empathy" and become "connected" to temporal and textual others; the mediation of all these spaces is sustainable through adab; the absence of these space creates what I call a restricted reader and thinker. The restricted reader is one who exhibits restriction not only in terms of their inability to read with or within the tools of adab but one who is restricted temporally by not having empathy or access to their temporal others—and ultimately textually. The restricted reader is disconnected.

Through this complex and multilayered study, the book takes on five main tasks. (1) It first examines the relationship between adab and the conception of the ideal human through the investigation of murūʾa. Adab's very foundation rests on the pillars of murūʾa through the virtue-ethics that form murūʾa and hence its relationship to adab's ethical-intellectual constituents as developed by premodern scholars, chiefly Ibn Janāḥ (fl. 2nd century AH/8th century CE) in his *al-Murūʾa wa-l-adab* (Humanism and Adab). (2) The book then takes these delineated intellectual virtue-ethics as constituents of adab and puts forth the framework or grammar of adab as hospitality, discourse, critique, method, resolve and will. (3) Taking each virtue-ethic on its own, the book shows in respective chapters how these virtues are highlighted not just in the textual universe of adab but through the performativity of adab as reading and understanding, whether in a stable context or in a crisis-ridden one. (4) The argument then hones in on the criteria of selection as the instability of reading and understanding as "crisis" to be the focus of the chapters' examinations manifest in a crisis of reading/understanding. (5) Thereby we examine the aspects of the act of reading and the tools of adab itself and the types of readers adab cultivated.

The book therefore identifies the unadabized readers whose methods of reading, as I show, departed from the grammar of murūʾa and adab, and who also profiteered from what I identify as false readings and errorism to epistemically trade and profit and accumulate cultural capital. In each chapter, the issues of reading and understanding, meaning, figurative language versus literal language, and the tools of adab are raised; this is what holds the book together as it advances the argument on how adab was legitimized as the participants in this adab sphere saw the fundamental links between the cultivation of essential critical tools, hence one's humanity, and the intellectual and social virtues identified with the tools adab fostered. The pursuit of adab therefore cannot be said to be ancillary to activities, or gratuitous, or elitist. To say it is elitist would imply that the cultivation of the subject and human flourishing was regarded as a gratuitous activity and that the conception of the human exhibited as murūʾa qua hospitality, for instance, is understood by elites but not the average person. If adab is regarded as a means to the cultivation of human virtues, it justified its own necessary, not superfluous, existence. The conception of adab put forth in this book argues for more than the inculcation of refinement and moral excellence, which is an accepted definition of adab. The book posits that this adab sensibility becomes a framework for the adabized subject by providing critical intellectual tools required for reading, understanding, and literary production as well as for success in life, as premodern literati argue. The latter argument can be seen manifest in the ways the tools of adab encourage social poesies and the resolve of conflicts through the ideals of murūʾa and humanism.

1

Adab and/as *Murūʾa*

The Ways of Being Human

MURŪʾA AS THE HABITUS OF ADAB

It is very easy to discuss both murūʾa qua humanism and adab in positive abstract terms and build a framework *only* from very affirming sources such as manuals on murūʾa. However, a detour to manuals that are concerned with less positive moral qualifiers, circumstances, and environments may offer a rewarding venture regarding the comparative framework they present. In other words, it is expected that a book on humanism will offer a positive framework in an abstract theorization of these conceptions divorced from real crises or a social framework; for example, generosity is good, or veracity is respectable. Therefore, to speak about a habitus of adab in the Arab-Islamic context, it is imperative that a recourse to a form of crisis is present.

Habitus is understood as the manner in which individuals hold their social world but also interact with it. Adab thus indicates both a shaping and transformation of the habitus—and, by turn, individuals—through unconscious mimesis by following social norms and through pedagogic processes and virtue training. This pedagogical aspect of the habitus and its ethical context were where the earliest conceptions of habitus were formulated as per Aristotle.[1] Saba Mahmood notices the connection between the Aristotelian formulation of the moral formation and between its counterpart in select Islamic thinkers such as al-Ghazālī (d. 505 AH/1111 CE), Ibn Rushd (d. 595 AH/1198 CE), and Ibn Khaldūn (d. 808 AH/1406 CE). In explaining Ibn Khaldūn's use of the term *malaka*, Ira Lapidus argues that *malaka*, while often translated as "habit," is best translated as "habitus," which he defines as "that inner quality developed as a result of outer practice which makes practice a perfect ability of the soul of the actor."[2] Ibn Khaldūn maintains in *The*

Muqaddimah that "a habit[us] is a firmly rooted quality acquired by doing a certain action and repeating it time after time, until the form of that action is firmly fixed [in one's disposition]. A habit[us] corresponds to the original action after which it was formed."[3] Like the Aristotelian habitus in the Greek tradition, the Arab-Islamic habitus's "moral cultivation implies a quality that is acquired through human industry, assiduous practice, and discipline, such that it becomes a permanent feature of a person's character." In other words, "a habitus can be said to exist only when someone has actively formed it."[4]

In the context of the objects of theoretical faculty in Islamic philosophy, Majid Fakhry uses habitus as *malaka* as "the perfection of [certain] power."[5] The relationship between adab and power is one that I shall discuss in due course. But power need not be thought of as strictly perceivable or material; it can be thought of as influence, social capital, or a power of one's own *malaka* that they have inhabited. Lapidus discusses *malaka* within the realm of faith as "the acquisition, from the belief of the heart and the resulting actions, of a quality that has complete control over the heart so that it commands the action of the limbs and makes every activity take place in submissiveness to it to the point that all actions, eventually, become subservient to this affirmation of faith. This is the highest degree of faith. It is perfect faith."[6] When one inhabits this habitus of faith as per the example in Lapidus's discussion, or adab, or another intellectual institution, its power will take over the heart of said actor enforcing the unconscious submission to this habitus's unconscious praxis. This is a very apt explanation that is in keeping with the root *m-l-k* (to rule, to possess), which not only indicates the possession or the inhabitance in a certain habitus but that the habitus, in turn, possesses the individual, involuntarily and reciprocally; to possess and be possessed by the habitus. To possess adab is to be possessed by adab in praxis—it becomes second nature.

IBN JANĀḤ'S *AL-ADAB WA-L-MURŪʾA*

As a concept, murūʾa has had quite the development. Further studies may be able to diachronically trace, examine, and study this concept from its pre-Islamic understanding and conceptions until the present day. For the sake of our present discussion, it is prudent to focus on its concomitance with two things: ethics (*akhlāq*) and the conception of the human (*al-insāniyya*). The aforementioned relationship between ethics and murūʾa is traced in Prophetic ḥadīth: *wa-in kāna laka khuluq fa-laka murūʾa* (if you have ethics/virtues, you have murūʾa),[7] and in another ḥadīth: *lā dīn illā bi-murūʾa* (there is no religion without murūʾa).[8] It is thus not ethics or virtues, as such, but what the achievement of these virtues makes of one: the ideal human. Ibn Manẓūr (d. 710 AH/1311 CE) similarly tells us that it is *al-insāniyya*.[9] Al-Fīrūzābādī (d. 817 AH/1415 CE) defines this through the verb *maruʾa*, to have murūʾa and *insāniyya* (humanity).[10] He also mentions a form V of the verb, *tamarraʾ* (*fulān yatamarraʾ binā*), which means someone hopes to emphasize their own humanity through highlighting its perceived lack in someone else (*yaṭlub al-murūʾa bi-naqṣinā*).[11] This, of course, is a pretentious act of feigning humanity (*takalluf al-murūʾa*).[12] Al-Sharīf al-Jurjānī (d. 816 AH/1413 CE) tells us that murūʾa is a self-resoluteness that propels beautiful actions considered praiseworthy with a just cause (*quwwa li-l-nafs mabdaʾ li-ṣudūr al-afʿāl al-jamīla ʿanhā al-mustatbaʿa li-l-madḥ sharʿan wa-ʿaqlan wa-farʿan*).[13] Al-Zamakhsharī relates, in *Asās al-balāgha*, *m-r-ʾ* as the root for human being and explains it as follows: "He is a man/human of veracity (*imrūʾ ṣidq*), she is a woman of wickedness (*imraʾat sūʾ*), someone who has murūʾa is the ultimate culmination of manliness (*kamāl al-rujūliyya*)."[14]

In a more detailed eighth-century epistle titled *al-Adab wa-l-murūʾa* (Humanism and Adab), poet Ṣāliḥ b. Janāḥ al-Lakhmī charts in thirty-six concise chapters the moral ingredients of the titular epistle's ethical value: the relationship between possessing adab and perfecting one's humanity and ideal behavior (murūʾa).[15] Not much is available on Ibn Janāḥ's precise dates, but the sources tell us that he lived in the eighth century during the reign of Caliph Hārūn al-Rashīd (d. 193 AH/809 CE) and may have been one of al-Jāḥiẓ's tutors (d. 255 AH/868 CE), who was familiar with him and his writing.[16] Murūʾa is a concept that predates Islam and has been absorbed and assimilated after the advent of Islam. The concept of murūʾa (etymologically from *marʾ*: man/human) is sometimes cursorily translated as "manliness" to denote bravery, assisting those in need, chivalry, and courage. If generosity or hospitality (*karam*) is often regarded as the highest Arab virtue as it pertains to material giving; murūʾa can be considered the nonmaterial equivalent of the highest virtue; a generosity of spirit since it translates as the nonmaterial giving of oneself, exercising humanity to its fullest potential, and ideal behavior. It encompasses bravery, generosity, hospitality, defending the weak and less able, and a certain readiness and willingness to assist, defend, and serve. One who possesses murūʾa means one who has perfected being human, possessing ideal behavior and ethics, and is being true to the core of human values, and has achieved the highest level of humanity.

The concept is expansive in its all-encompassing nature as it becomes a moral amalgam for the highest Arab virtue and is not and should not be restricted to gender, which seems a rather modern misuse and misunderstanding. Al-Dhahabī (d. 748 AH/1348 CE) relates a brief biography of one female ḥadīth scholar, Zaynab bt. Abī Aḥmad ʿAbd al-Wāḥid (d. 740 AH/1339 CE), who had an *ijāza* (certificate) to narrate ḥadīth (*rawat bi-l-ijāza*); her brother describes her in a eulogy as *dayyina, khayyira, dhāt murūʾa wa-saʿat khuluq* (religious, generous, has murūʾa and forbearance).[17] Another is a certain Khadīja, the daughter of the judge of Mecca Shihāb al-Dīn b. Aḥmad, who is described as *dhāt murūʾa wa-khayr wa-ḥishma* (possessing murūʾa, generosity, and modesty).[18] Murūʾa, then, is used to convey a quality that paints a fully human picture of the ideal behavior of the entity described regardless of gender; in other words, etymologically, it is derived from the essence of the "human" or expressing "humanity" in its fullest. Litterateur Ibn Janāḥ further explains in his *al-Adab wa-l-murūʾa*:

> اعلم أن العرب قد تجعل للشيء الواحد اسمًا، ويسمى بالشيء الواحد أشياء فإذا سنح لك ذكر شيء فاذكره بأحسن أسمائه فإن ذلك من المروءة وإنما المرء بمروءته
>
> Know that Arabs may designate for one thing many names, and name one thing many names; if you are able to mention something, mention it with the best name it has, for this is indeed murūʾa, and a human being is made by their murūʾa.[19]

Ibn Janāḥ then defines murūʾa:

> فالمروءة اجتناب الرجل ما يشينه واجتنائه ما يزينه وأنه لا مروءة لمن لا أدب له، ولا أدب لمن لا عقل له، ولا عقل لمن ظن أن في عقله، ما يغنيه ويكفيه عن غيره
>
> Murūʾa is avoiding that which blemishes one and achieving and endeavoring to that which enhances one. There is no murūʾa for one who has no adab, and there is no adab without *ʿaql* (reason), and there is no *ʿaql* for one who deems that s/he is self-satisfied with their own *ʿaql* (reason) and thinks s/he can do without others.[20]

He maintains that adab and murūʾa are the culminating totalization of ethics (*jimāʿ al-akhlāq*) and the ultimate goal of virtues (*muntahā al-faḍāʾil*).[21] Ibn Janāḥ argues that murūʾa and adab are dependent on each other and that one cannot exist without the other. He then argues that adab and *ʿaql* are also commensurate and mutually dependent, thereby arguing that murūʾa and *ʿaql* are also reliant on each other via adab.

He then begins with a *via negativa* introduction to his discussion on murūʾa. The early pages discuss hypocrites and double-faced people (*dhū al-wajhayn*) without mentioning explicitly that they are devoid of murūʾa, though it is understood that they are exhibiting anti-murūʾa behavior and traits.[22] He then talks about disaffection and alienating people (*al-ṣudūd*), or antisocial behavior, as another anti-murūʾa trait.[23] In both negative examples, Ibn Janāḥ supports his discussion with poetry. Furthermore, as is expected, he discusses *ḥumq* (senselessness/foolishness) as another anti-murūʾa trait that affects not only the person in question but the people around them. He mentions that the company of a senseless person will inevitably be harmful, and even if some benefit appears in it, the harm outweighs the benefit.[24] He argues, in poetical verse, that foolishness is a trait that cannot be cured; it is an affliction: "[a] person gets a headache, and then it goes away / but idiocy has no cure."[25] Ibn Janāḥ then tells us, aptly, of the effects of caprices and vagaries (*al-hawā*) on human beings and the virtue of reason (*faḍl al-ʿaql*). On this particular topic, he does not offer an absolute opinion since he acknowledges that people are different. He maintains that sometimes they are left to their desires so they are blinded by them, while some actually begin to see; he advises moderation and self-control.[26] In this respect Ibn Janāḥ highlights the role of resolve and will as part of murūʾa. Another anti-murūʾa trait is what Ibn Janāḥ calls "transparent faces" (*al-wujūh al-shaffāfa*), which he describes as those who smile to your face when they need something but grimace when denied their requests.[27]

To be well prepared contributes to one's murūʾa. Ibn Janāḥ here advises being well prepared for anything given its own magnitude and nature; he likens the example of fighting someone who is outside one's league to one who goes out to kill themself. He advises that using acumen in testing one's own strength and the adversary's strength (or in any other situation) would allow the individual to measure the preparedness needed.[28] It may be argued that his inclusion of this trait and behavior is part of one's self-respect, social image, and standing in one's community as well, which, if threatened, dehumanizes the subject; this is why Ibn Janāḥ ties it to one's humanity. In the same vein, he discusses that reproachment (*ʿitāb*) can be detrimental to one's self-respect (*daʿawtahum ilā ihānatik*) if sought in those whom one should not reproach.[29] Ibn Janāḥ implies that understanding shared emotional intimacy with people is key here. He maintains that overestimating this intimacy with people who do not feel the same way about us is a dehumanizing act because it will lead us to ask from them emotionally, through reproachment, hence implying a closer emotional proximity than what is true, and that which they are not/cannot be giving or do not consider giving. All the measurements required of the individual toward their murūʾa entail balancing various difficult emotional and intellectual tools that can be at times paradoxical. For instance, murūʾa presupposes and indeed encourages hospitality, both material and emotional, since it shuns disaffection and alienating others but at the same time encourages restraints in demanding emotionally from others that which they cannot give. It can be argued therefore that to possess murūʾa and cultivate it, one is also cultivating and simultaneously possessing acumen, perception, and critique. It is impossible to assess the intricacies of these social nuances without the tools it demands cultivating and that are fostered gradually.

Ibn Janāḥ further argues that one is unable to truly know their friends without experiencing travel together. In this section, the discussion on the rights of friends (*ḥuqūq al-ikhwān*) centers on discourse and the etiquette of exchange.[30] This explains why Ibn Janāḥ highlights the role of travel as a factor that allows frank speech to take place. In travel, the novelty, ambiguity, and even sometimes indescribable events and culture shock (a) propel one to express one's experience of what they are going through frankly and engage with their friend(s) and allow differences and learn from each other; and (b) allow travel to be the test of this friendship should one need assistance in case of illness, theft, and so on. In both cases, there are tests of true character beyond the pleasantries and niceties that are required by social decorum in more comfortable settings. In a further section, Ibn Janāḥ discusses the traits of friends and enemies. He presses his readers to uphold the trait of *inṣāf* (critical justice) with themselves at all times and with their enemies (for more on *inṣāf*, see chapter 4). Similarly, Ibn al-Marzubān repeatedly cites *inṣāf* and *iḥsān* as the two supreme and umbrella virtues under which everything else is subsumed. He relates an anecdote that ʿAlī b. Abī Ṭālib passed by a group of people and asked them what they were doing. They answered that they were discussing and studying murūʾa (*kunnā natadhākar al-murūʾa*). He replied, "Aren't the words of God in the Qur'an enough for you? [referring to Q.16:90, 'God commands justice, doing good, and generosity,'[31] or *inna Allāh yaʾmur bi-l-ʿadl wa-l-iḥsān*] *ʿAdl* (justice) is *inṣāf*, and *iḥsān* (doing good) is *tafaḍḍul* (bounteousness)—what is left after this?"[32] ʿAlī b. Abī Ṭālib's definition is inspired by the Prophetic ḥadīth. It is reported that the Prophet asked a man from Thaqīf, "What is murūʾa for your people?" The man said, "Prophet of God, [it is] *al-inṣāf* (justice) and *iṣlāḥ* (reform)." The Prophet replied, "And it is the same for us" (*wa-hiya kadhālika fīnā*).[33]

The virtue of murūʾa (humanity) encourages the ethical subject to cultivate diplomacy and discernment in handling one's affairs rather than the use of brutal (verbal/physical) force and social violence in combating one's enemies. Ibn al-Marzubān lists one of the many views on murūʾa as gentleness with friends and complimenting them while subduing one's enmity to others with self-restraint (*al-tadhallul li-l-aḥbāb bi-l-tamalluq wa-mudārāt al-aʿdāʾ bi-l-taraffuq*).[34] In both books on murūʾa, there is a discouragement to openly face one's enemies with force or to engage in retaliation. It would appear that should one attempt to defend themselves, they are encouraged to pursue adabized modes of self-defense rather than forgoing decorum, which is discouraged in this discourse.

Ibn Janāḥ furthers his discussion by including hospitality, but he does not state the obvious by mentioning that murūʾa necessitates the virtue of hospitality; it is a given. He fine-tunes the virtue of hospitality by emphasizing to the reader that if one is hosting guests, one should make sure the people preparing the food are professional and hygienic and one should not shy away from drawing their attention to their mistakes or reproaching them if they err. The reason for this, he maintains, is that guests will attribute the blunder(s) to the host, not the helpers.[35] This extends to having clean water and clean garments and cloths and proper comportment. Ibn Janāḥ maintains that only fools (*al-ḥamqā*), whether men or women, will allow themselves to be seen in dirty clothes and it is indicative of their mindlessness (*balāda*).[36] Ibn Janāḥ's book is concerned with adab as ethics and comportment and technologies of the self, as well as adab as a corpus of texts among others, as he discusses poetry and wisdom in support of his view on the praxis of murūʾa. In this respect, the concomitance of the behavioral and textual parts of adab that are recognized in Ibn Janāḥ, as well as in Ibn al-Muqaffaʿ, could be considered foundational to the ethical refinement of what Joseph Sadan discusses as *al-adīb al-ẓarīf* (the refined litterateur).[37] Contextualizing Abū al-Ṭayyib Muḥammad b. Isḥāq al-Washshāʾ (d. 325 AH/937 CE) against this background may present a diachronic development of this conception.

Although *al-Muwashshā* (*al-Ẓarf wa-l-ẓurafāʾ*) is mainly known for its discussion on refinement, refinement is discussed within the context of adab and murūʾa. Al-Washshāʾ, student of al-Mubarrad (d. 286 AH/899 CE) and Thaʿlab (d. 291 AH/904 CE), maintains that murūʾa is the foundation of literatis and the apparatus of the rational ones (*ʿimād al-udabāʾ wa-ʿitād al-ʿuqalāʾ*). Like Ibn Janāḥ and other aforementioned scholars, al-Washshāʾ avers that adab needs murūʾa but murūʾa does not need adab (*al-adab yaḥtāj maʿahu ilā al-murūʾa wa-l-murūʾa lā yaḥtāj maʿahā ilā al-adab*).[38] In this respect, he sees murūʾa as the guiding principle of adab. In *al-Muwashshā*'s discussion of the characteristics of the refined (*ẓurafāʾ*), al-Washshāʾ delineates the four main elements of *ẓarf* (character refinement): *al-faṣāḥa* (articulateness), *al-balāgha* (eloquence), *al-ʿiffa* (purity/virtue), and *al-nazāha* (integrity).[39] The category of the *ẓarīf* (the refined), as al-Washshāʾ tells us, is concomitant with adab. James E. Montgomery reads this as "an intensification of certain features, intellectual, literary, social, and personal, that are held to characterize [the *adīb*]."[40] In addition to "elegance," "refinement," and "man of the world," Montgomery also uses the famous archetype of the "dandy," reminiscent of European—especially British and French—Romanticism, and "refined people," as another comparative category for *ẓurafāʾ*. Perhaps "refined" is more useful than the "dandy" in this comparison, given that the historical European eighteenth- and nineteenth-century dandies and their female counterparts were more often than not regarded as a "curiosity" by more conservative members of society. While they may share several traits with the *ẓurafāʾ*, like meticulous grooming, fashionable style, and trendsetting, wit, social grace, and influence, dandies of both genders were also often regarded as flirting with gender norms and what they perceive as outdated social conventions. Female dandy-like novelist George Sand (1804–76) was known to wear tailored male clothing and smoke cigars to challenge gender norms—imitating the male dandies in their own pushing of social norms through style. In this respect, dandies may have invited some curiosity at best or criticism at worst. This is not to discredit some similarities with the *ẓurāfāʾ*, but "dandyism" was not always regarded in a positive light, especially as it may have attracted critique of excesses; hardly comparable to the category of the *ẓarīf* and its investment in ethical and aesthetic refinement as explained by al-Washshāʾ. He defines *al-ẓarf* within the parameters of adab and murūʾa as follows:

يجب على المتأدب اللبيب والمتظرف الأريب المتخلق بأخلاق الأدباء والمتحلي بحلية الظرفاء أن يعرف قبل هجومه على ما لا يعلمه وقبل تعاطيه ما لا يفهمه تبين الظرف وشرائع المروءة وحدود الأدب، فإنه لا أدب لمن لا مروءة له، ولا مروءة لمن لا ظرف له، ولا ظرف لمن لا أدب له

The intelligent adabized person and the refined person who conducts themself in the ethics of *adībs*, and is adorned with the embellishments of the refined, must know finesse, the laws of humanity/murūʾa, and the limits of adab before attacking what s/he does not know, and before undertaking what s/he does not understand. There is no adab for one who has no humanity/murūʾa, and no humanity/murūʾa for one who has no *ẓarf*, and no *ẓarf* for one who has no adab.[41]

The concept of *ẓarf*, as is obvious from the above, is therefore one of three parts: the other two being murūʾa and adab. It should be noted that the archetype of the *ẓarīf* is also gender neutral; al-Washshāʾ relates many interesting anecdotes about refined women *ẓurāfāʾ* who perfected their adab and subsequently their *ẓarf*. The *ẓarīf* archetype is one who possesses adab but also humanity and, while these may seem abstract, the other dimension of *ẓarf* also has an aesthetic dimension of keeping up one's appearance and comportment and maintaining impeccable grooming and hygiene. One may argue then that the evolution of the concept of murūʾa is in itself a development of conceptualizing and understanding the "ideal human" across time diachronically. The pre-Islamic ideal human, who had many virtues but also waged vendetta and blood feuds (as part of murūʾa), is not the same ideal human of later times who gradually abandoned this practice but maintained murūʾa and developed it through other practices. The link between cultivating humanity and its relationship to the evolving civilizational concepts of adab and *ẓarf* is therefore fruitful to understand as diachronic.

Of interest to our discussion on adab is Ibn Janāḥ's section engaging *al-ʿaql wa-l-adab*. As he previously outlined foolishness/senselessness (*ḥumq*) and moral baseness (*luʾm*), he says that the foolish person, like the morally base, does not know their friend from their enemy or what is good for them. They also do not accept any advice or guidance.[42] In this respect, Ibn Janāḥ decidedly highlights the role of reason (*ʿaql*) as a factor in moral perfection, ideal behavior, and, accordingly, adab. Ibn Janāḥ uses several analogies to highlight this particular relationship. He says that *ʿaql* is a prince (*amīr*) and adab a vizier: without a vizier the prince weakens, and if there is no prince, no vizier is needed. He then highlights the relationship by saying that *ʿaql* and adab are like the sword (*al-sayf*) and its sharpener (*al-ṣayqal*); when the sharpener *takes* the sword, it *adds* to it (*idhā aʿṭā al-sayf akhadhahu*); the sword becomes beautiful (*fa-ṣaqalahu fa-ʿāda jamālan*) and reliable (*ʿaḍadan li-yuʿtamad ʿalayhi wa-yultajaʾ ilayhi*).[43] Ibn Janāḥ then elaborates that should adab find a rational faculty/reason like the sharpener finding the sword, it then becomes stronger and beneficial. He then tells of two people who undergo adab (education/refinement) together (*yataʾaddabān bi-adab wāḥid*): one of them becomes better than the other (*anfadh*) because of the aptitude of reason (*qudrat al-ʿaql*).[44] Ibn Janāḥ's book is concerned with adab as ethics and comportment of oneself and among others. In this respect, this part of adab could be considered as foundational to the ethical refinement al-Washshāʾ speaks about.[45] Contextualizing al-Washshāʾ against this background of Ibn Janāḥ, al-Jāḥiẓ's teacher, may offer us a diachronic development of this conception.

Ibn Janāḥ then cautions that there are threats to this ethical construct such as lying (*kadhib*), as it deprives one of their sense of modesty and makes them shameless. Expectedly, the presence of ignorance/bigotry (*jahl*) is one of the nullifiers (*nawāqiḍ*) of adab. Ibn Janāḥ's predecessor Ibn al-Muqaffaʿ (d. 142

AH/759 CE) worked within the same frame of adab and its ethical structure. For Ibn al-Muqaffaʿ, "the mind has its dispositions and characteristics with which it receives adab, and with adab the mind is improved and enhanced."[46] Ibn al-Muqaffaʿ discusses this within the arc of what he calls living "the good life in the here and hereafter," which he maintains is a common goal among people.[47] Living the good life in the here and hereafter, Ibn al-Muqaffaʿ avers, cannot be achieved without a sound mind and critical reflection with resolve and will; these he maintains cannot be acquired without adab. The path to this universal goal therefore is concomitant with ethical refinement; it is both an oral and written textual corpus and actions (see chapter 2).

Ibn Janāḥ is not the only author to write on murūʾa. Another well-known work is Ibn al-Marzubān's (d. 309 AH/921 CE) *al-Murūʾa*. Unlike Ibn Janāḥ's text, which is devoted to his reflections and thoughts on the topic, Ibn al-Marzubān's is a collection of epigrams from various poets, scholars, and notables. It does not represent his own thought but rather a collection of views on murūʾa. To this end, references to Ibn al-Marzubān will be made as they intersect with others here as necessary. Another successor to both authors, Ibn Ḥibbān (d. 354 AH/965 CE), in his *Rawḍat al-ʿuqalāʾ wa-nuzhat al-fuḍalāʾ*, devotes a chapter to discussing the encouraging (*al-ḥathth*) of the virtue of murūʾa, and he makes quite an admirable grammatical move by relating murūʾa in the plural as *murūʾāt*, acknowledging the richness of the definition. He maintains that one cannot say that murūʾa is one thing but rather many things and he lists numerous aforementioned virtues (generosity in money and spirit; justice qua *inṣāf* and defending the weak; veracity and earnestness; decency; gratitude; fortitude in the face of afflictions; resourcefulness; refinement in clothes, perfume, and comportment; holding charming conversations; wealth and offspring). He concludes by saying that to him murūʾa comprises two traits: avoiding what displeases God and Muslims in actions, and sticking to what pleases God and Muslims in behavior. He explains this as a byproduct of reason (*ʿaql*) and adduces as proof a ḥadīth relating that the Prophet said one's humanity (murūʾa) is their reason (*ʿaql*).[48] In another chapter, Ibn Ḥibbān encourages the learning of adab and the tools of eloquence (*taʿallum al-adab wa-luzūm al-faṣāḥa*). He begins by relating the famous analogy in the ḥadīth that some speech and eloquence are akin to sorcery in their ability to exert influence and power over people (*inna min al-bayān la-siḥran*). He further relates poetry by al-Bassāmī (d. 302 AH/914 CE) in support of his own legitimization of adab.

ليس المسود بالمال سؤدده . . . بل المسود من قد ساد بالأدب
لأن من ساد بالأموال سؤدده . . . ما دام في جمع ذا الأموال والنشب
إن قل يوما له مال يصير إلى . . . هون من الأمر في ذل وفي تعب

It is not with money that someone with power will exert their influence
But the influential is one who dominates with adab

The status of one who dominates with money
Will not last in gathering wealth
If their wealth decreased one day
They will face humiliation and stagnation[49]

The word used to describe one of the fruits of adab here is *suʾdud*, which can be thought of as social capital, influence, power, and status; it may also point to official sovereignty or leadership. In this respect, Ibn Ḥibbān relates adab to the social sphere and to power, to social capital, and ultimately polity. It is no longer a private affair that one should cultivate but one that may have ramifications on society and the polity. Ibn Ḥibbān then avers that eloquence is the best garment the reasonable person (*ʿāqil*) should wear and that adab is one's friend wherever one goes; it is a companion when there are none, a decoration in gatherings, an increase in reason, and a proof of one's humanity (*dalīl ʿalā al-murūʾa*).[50] The linking of the triptych—adab, murūʾa, and *ʿaql*—appears to be one that cannot be separated in these intellectual efforts to both explain adab in terms of its virtue clusters and simultaneously argue for the legitimization of adab from the point of view of the sociopolitical. Ibn Ḥibbān's understanding also advances how adab influences social relationships and how it can in itself become a resource, an asset, that can be factored in the development of human capital and hence society and the polity.

In his *al-ʿIqd al-farīd*, Cordoba-based Ibn ʿAbd Rabbih (d. 328 AH/940 CE) includes a brief discussion on murūʾa and on the merits of learning and adab (*kitāb al-yaqūlu fī al-ʿilm wa-l-adab*). He argues that education and adab are the poles (*quṭbān*) that life and religion orbit and they are what differentiate human beings from beasts. He maintains they are the substance of reason, the fire of the body (*sirāj al-badan*), the light of the heart (*nūr al-qalb*), and the foundation of the soul (*ʿimād al-rūḥ*). Ibn ʿAbd Rabbih argues that some things are the foundations of others and intergenerative of each other (*mutawallidan min baʿḍ*). He argues that deliberation (*rawiyyat al-fikr*) is the thrust for will (*al-irāda*) and that will in itself controls the drives of work (*asbāb al-ʿamal*).[51] However, instead of including the discussion on murūʾa under the general volume on adab and education, he includes it under the section (*bāb*) of *suʾdud* (power/influence); this makes for a peculiar choice worthy of discussion. He includes a brief discussion on murūʾa as a subtopic of power and governance (*suʾdud*). He begins this section by discussing governance and power among people, then he aptly concludes by discussing an individual's self-governance and autonomy or technologies of the self (*sawdad al-rajul bi-nafsihi*).[52] Ibn ʿAbd Rabbih appears to suggest, through the anecdotes related under this idea, that it is through the exercising of certain traits that an individual is capable of disciplining or mastering the self, thereby harnessing power and autonomy over it. Ibn ʿAbd Rabbih immediately follows this with a discussion on murūʾa where he charts its definitions and multiple traits. He begins with a ḥadīth, "[There is] no religion without humanity" (*lā dīn illā bi-murūʾa*), and he then relates various anecdotes and maxims pointing to the cluster virtues of murūʾa (generosity, decency, being an amiable companion, reading the Qur'an, frequenting the mosque, and purity). Honest living and work (*iṣlāḥ al-maʿīsha*) are obviously considered part of what constitutes one's murūʾa qua humanity.[53] The rest of the virtues related by Ibn ʿAbd Rabbih can be easily clustered under those related here since they fall under one or the other.[54]

Ibn ʿAbd Rabbih's rationale can be explained by a similar choice made by his predecessor Ibn Qutayba (d. 276 AH/889 CE) in his *ʿUyūn al-akhbār*. Ibn Qutayba's book has several subsections. He begins the first part with the Book of the Sultan (*kitāb al-sulṭān*), then the Book of War (*kitāb al-ḥarb*), and then the Book of Governance and Power (*kitāb al-suʾdud*). Subsumed under the latter are many subsections on the quiddity of governance, its sources, power, and influence through wealth, trade, religion, will, arrogance, praise, modesty, reason, forbearance and anger, opulence, humiliation and charisma, and then murūʾa to be followed by attire, jewelry (rings), perfumes, salons and conversations, the boorish (*al-thuqalāʾ*), houses and buildings, jesting and its limits, moderation in things, and the actions of notables and noble people. It appears that this section on *suʾdud*, evoking conceptions of governance and power, does not only point to the nature of power associated with office and governance as such but to social capital. Judging by Ibn Qutayba's subsections and their topics of discussion and the sources of *suʾdud* from wealth to modesty, reason, perfumes, attire, and murūʾa; *suʾdud* points to social capital akin to what we may describe as civility, decorum, and influence. A break in decorum is a break in *suʾdud*, which amalgamates the concept with civility rather than just influence—because some people with influence and power may indeed break social decorum, slowly putting their social capital in deficit. It may be argued that the relationship between adab and *suʾdud* is an expected sociopolitical development with the evolution of the nature of polity in the Arab-Islamic empire.

In this respect, *suʾdud* points to self-respect through the practice of certain technologies of the self that garner social esteem, respect, and admiration; it is a marker of civility and politesse. In his short chapter on murūʾa, under civility, Ibn Qutayba relates various anecdotes and epigrams that reiterate most ideas and definitions found in Ibn Janāḥ before him and those succeeding him. A thought-provoking delineation of murūʾa in Ibn Qutayba's work is his relating of a dictum by ʿUmar b. al-Khaṭṭāb (d. 23 AH/644 CE) that "learning Arabic increases one's murūʾa." ʿUmar b. al-Khaṭṭāb is a speaker of Arabic as are most of the people he is addressing. His urging his addressees to learn Arabic cannot be understood on the level of language, grammar, mechanics, and basic understanding but whereby one is able to discern the nuances of language and words and their multiple meanings. ʿUmar's argument that mastering the language and its intricacies increasing one's murūʾa goes beyond the obvious fact that language differentiates humans from nonhuman species but also allows the individual better understanding of others and a better expression of their self, which in turn increases their social capital (*suʾdud*) and contributes to social adab among members of one's society. ʿUmar also differentiates between evident murūʾa and unseen murūʾa, as he says that the seen murūʾa is clean attire (*al-thiyāb al-ṭāhira*), which indicates that one is observing social decorum. Similarly, al-Aṣmaʿī relates that three behaviors should be judged as possessing murūʾa: someone you saw riding (*rajul raʾaytahu rākiban*), or heard using proper grammar (*yaʿrib*), or smelled a pleasant whiff of (*shamamta minhu rāʾiḥa ṭayyiba*). Conversely, al-Aṣmaʿī says there are three you should judge as lowly (*taḥkum ʿalayhim bi-l-danāʾa*): someone reeking of wine in a gathering, someone you heard speaking Persian in Arabic-speaking lands (*yatakallam fī miṣr ʿarabiyya bi-l-fārisiyya*), or someone fighting their destiny on the curbside (*ʿalā ẓahr al-ṭarīq yunāziʿ al-qadar*).[55] In both ʿUmar b. al-Khaṭṭāb's and al-Aṣmaʿī's views of murūʾa, language use is a marker of civility and self-respect. To speak proper Arabic is indicative of self-respect and one's humanity altogether. Al-Aṣmaʿī's association of lowliness or anti-civility with speaking Persian in Arabic-speaking lands can also be read within the framework of the components of murūʾa. It has already been established that will and resolve and discernment are all components of murūʾa qua humanity. Al-Aṣmaʿī's lack of forgiveness for someone speaking Persian in an Arabic-speaking land draws attention to the lack of effort exerted on the person's part if s/he lives in an Arabic-speaking land but makes no effort to communicate in the people's language. While it is easy to read this as part of *shuʿūbiyya* propaganda, especially as there are several examples of hostility toward the Persian language as a marker of low murūʾa and anti-murūʾa such as in Ibn al-Marzubān's selections, it is more conducive to our discussion to look at this from the requirements of murūʾa/humanity and civility in a social setting as speaking clearly with people in their language or a language that most would understand. This is especially corroborated by Ibn Qutayba's sharing in this section Maslama b. ʿAbd al-Malik's statement that "murūʾa is influence and social capital (*al-riyāsa*) and eloquence (*al-faṣāḥa*)."[56]

ANTI-ADAB

In most discussions on adab as a cultivated virtue that is concomitant with and substantiating one's expression of humanity (murūʾa), the lack of adab does not cease at an accusation of lack of reason or lack of murūʾa; it often goes far and beyond to likening the person involved to a beast (*al-dābba*). Ibn Ḥibbān, under adab, uses the image of one who seeks to learn ḥadīth but does not have the tools of grammar as a beast carrying empty sacks (*al-dābba ʿalayhā al-mikhlāh laysa fīhā shayʾ*).[57] The devolving into the nonhuman status here does not only pertain to one's adab as learning and praxis, as decorum also receives the same treatment. In one of the more injurious lines between Jarīr (d. 110 AH/728 CE) and al-Farazdaq (d. 110 AH/728 CE), Jarīr lampoons the latter based on an anecdote that he harassed the women wherever he stayed as a guest and often left in shame.

وهَلْ كانَ الفرزدقُ غيرَ قرْدٍ . . . أصابتْهُ الصواعقُ فاستَدارا
وكُنْتَ إذا حلَلْتَ بِدارِ قَوْمٍ . . . رَحلتَ بخزْيةٍ وتركتَ عارا

Was al-Farazdaq but an ape?
Struck by thunderstorms, he regressed [became an ape again]!

When you stay at people's homes
You departed with humiliation and left a disgrace[58]

Jarīr tells us that al-Farazdaq was never a human being to begin with, hence the use of the word *istadāra* (to return/regress) to indicate that he returned to his previous form and that his semblance of humanity was perhaps never real; a simulacrum. The "thunder," functioning as a natural phenomenon but also a reference to his scandal, becomes a factor in the uncovering of his failure at maintaining his human status as the invective lines argue because it acted as the catalyst of his regress. Questioning al-Farazdaq's humanity here is predicated on the breaking of basic murūʾa and adab values with regard to his behavior toward said women as the second line insinuates. Similarly, Ibn ʿAbd Rabbih uses the beast analogy to signify a lack of adab when he says that if an adult has no education or adab, it is as if they have no reason (*ʿaql*), and if a child did not receive adab and was occupied with a book, the child becomes the most stupid of brutes (*ka-ablah al-bahāʾim*) and the most stray of beasts.[59] In the discourse on murūʾa, excessive *mizāḥ* (jesting) is often pitted against murūʾa and hence adab. It may very well be regarded as anti-adab. This should not be understood in the sense that it is opposed to adab but that it derives its tools from the lack of adab.[60]

While the previous examples may offer an enhanced view into the dichotomies of beast/human and anti-adab/adab, they also allow for a cursory interpretation since they mostly point to the pedagogical, with the exception of Jarīr and al-Farazdaq. In his *Tahdhīb al-akhlāq*, philosopher and historian Miskawayh (d. 421 AH/1030 CE) has a noteworthy discussion on adab within the section on the hierarchy of animals (*marātib al-ḥayawān*). He maintains that

> animals like to partner up, reproduce, and raise offspring through acts of caring, feeding as one would normally witness in mammals and birds to varying degrees, until they reach a status almost similar to that of humans' horizons (*ḥattā yaqrub min ufuq al-insān*). It is then that the animal accepts *taʾdīb* and with accepting adab it possesses a virtue (*faḍīla*) that sets it apart from other animals. This virtue increases in animals until it honors its possessor like horses (*al-faras*) and hunting hawks (*al-bāzī al-muʿallam*) until they gradually reach the animal that mimics humans on their own and imitates their ways without education or training like monkeys and their class; they are intelligent enough to acquire adab through mimicry of humans

> only and this is the ultimate teleology of animals' horizons, which, if they passed and crossed, they would depart their animal horizon and move into human horizon that accepts reason, exceptionality, speech, faculties, and so on. If they reach this stage, they would venture into knowledge and thirst for mastering disciplines (*ʿulūm*), and they would discover their power, habitus, and gifts given from God (*quwan, malakāt, mawāhib*) that would allow them to further ascend.[61]

Indeed, Miskawayh's reconfigurations can be traced further and reconsidered with other philosophers and scholars, such as by the subsequent Ibn Ṭufayl in *Ḥayy b. Yaqẓān* (see chapter 3). The feral child, animal-like at the beginning, without language, without adab, was able, on his own, in this allegorical narrative, to reach the status of what Miskawayh also identifies as the ideal or perfect human (*al-insān al-kāmil*) and gain knowledge about the universe, creation and creatures, and achieve his maximum potential (*ghāyat ufuqihi*). The "power, habitus, and gifts given from God" Miskawayh discusses can be thought of within nonmaterial spiritual parameters as divine providence and inspirations (*al-fayḍ al-ilāhī*).[62] This divine providence (the gifts) is materially observed in the knowledge and learning Ḥayy possesses and produces through his interaction with others.

MURŪʾA AND MODERNITY

Egyptian scholar Rifāʿa al-Ṭahṭāwī (1801–73) discusses murūʾa in the context of virtues necessary for what he describes as the driving force behind them that are indicative of modernity and urbanity. Al-Ṭahṭāwī views these virtues as revealing of the flourishing of society and state (*al-manāfiʿ wa-bayān mawāddahā al-aṣliyya wa-annahā dālla ʿalā al-tamaddun wa-l-ʿumrān*) in his *Manāhij al-albāb al-miṣriyya fī mabāhij al-ādāb al-ʿaṣriyya*. As evident from the title of the book, al-Ṭahṭāwī juxtaposes *al-ādāb* qua praxis and ethics with the "modernized," to highlight the compatibility of ideas and values in the institution of adab with the institution of modernity in the nineteenth century; he also approaches the topic from a practical and *fiqh*-inspired angle in what he terms as *manfaʿa* (benefit). An important feat exemplary of reformist thought during the time, al-Ṭahṭāwī's book delineates the salient role of education to all in progress. He does not see education's role in progress as a theoretical abstraction materialized in the reformed curricula; al-Ṭahṭāwī speaks about public morals within the context of social and moral reform as indicative of progress itself. It appears that the discussion on virtues has a private and public aspect, or at least al-Ṭahṭāwī deemed it necessary to examine both. Al-Ṭahṭāwī begins his book with the discussion on public morals before the discussion on private morals. In this respect, it could be argued that he views the public and social expression of adab as inseparable from the private expression of morality, where the former is indicative of progress but also justice. This explains al-Ṭahṭawī's emphasis on the need to fight corruption. This is because the relationship between public and private morals can be viewed as a feedback loop of a society's ethical reward and punishment systems; it is self-regulatory. A corrupt society, such as in al-Ṭahṭāwī's discussion, is not punishing negative moral output and may even be unwittingly rewarding it. This response to negative moral output gradually overturns and punishes the expression of positive moral output. Therefore, in al-Ṭahṭāwī's example, it could be extrapolated that while the ethical subject may possess murūʾa and adab privately, if the ethical subject is unable to exercise their virtues publicly or if these virtues are not socially promoted or rewarded because of policies promoting corruption instead, then the ethical subject will ultimately be alienated or ostracized at best or compelled to adopt the corrupt system's moral equilibrium point at worst unless they escape the corrupt moral order. In this regard, as al-Ṭahṭāwī intimates, negative public morals are symptomatic of corruption and a system that rewards anti-murūʾa; the lack of murūʾa is seen as antithetical to progress and ultimately the project of modernity, as al-Ṭahṭāwī maintains.

Al-Ṭahṭāwī calls murūʾa *ḥilyat al-nufūs wa-zīnat al-himam* (the crown jewel of the self and the embellishment of the will), and he defines it as the acquiescence of the self to its best of states (*mujārat al-nafs ʿalā afḍal aḥwālihā*).[63] While most aforementioned scholars conjoined *ʿaql* and murūʾa as concomitant and sometimes morally synonymous, al-Ṭahṭāwī presents a welcome advance; he argues that reason (*ʿaql*) pushes one to do the most useful (*yaʾmuruka bi-l-anfaʿ*), while murūʾa pushes one to do the most virtuous and noble (*taʾmuruka bi-l-arfaʿ*).[64] Indeed, the absence of a humanizing virtue to reason can leave it unchecked, cold, and even dangerous; adab and murūʾa can be thought of as humanizers of reason. It is unsurprising that Jalāl al-Dīn al-Rūmī (or Rumi) also argues, in the context of his theodicy and explaining Satan's refusal to bow before Adam (hence an intimation on the nature of evil as such), that Satan viewed Adam with one eye only, that of knowledge and cold reason; he is missing the other eye, according to Rumi, that of love.[65] Al-Ṭahṭāwī further explains that very few people choose murūʾa because it is a difficult choice (*thiqal takallufihā*), and only those who can overcome challenges and difficulties, because of their desire for honor, are able to pursue it; this is why, al-Ṭahṭāwī reasons, that the leader of people is the one most engaged in laborious pursuits (literally, "most distressed") (*sayyid al-qawm ashqāhum*).[66] Al-Ṭahṭāwī then corroborates his reasoning with a line from al-Mutanabbī (d. 354 AH/965 CE): "Were it not for hardship, everyone would be sovereign."[67] Following this reasoning, al-Ṭahṭāwī, perhaps unintentionally, provides an expounding commentary on both Ibn Ḥibbān and Ibn ʿAbd Rabbih, who argued that one of the fruits of adab is *suʾdud*. While it would not be erroneous to understand their reasoning as one that has tenor in the corridors of power and upward social mobility, al-Ṭahṭāwī's dissection of power from adab qua murūʾa explains the cause and not the effect that may or may not happen, according to Ibn Ḥibbān and Ibn ʿAbd Rabbih. Al-Ṭahṭāwī, similar to his predecessor al-Washshāʾ,

maintains that the very pursuit of murūʾa (qua adab as praxis) is a challenging activity, and should the ethical subject find courage in themselves to overcome difficulties (*istishāl al-ṣaʿb*) in holding on to murūʾa, it is because of their will (*ʿuluww al-himma*) and integrity (*sharaf al-nafs*).[68] Will, he argues, is a propellant for self-improvement and progress (*al-taqaddum*) and a call for specialization and professionalism (*al-takhaṣṣuṣ*). The vocabulary of the modernization project can be seen at work here. While the honor of the self and its integrity is its own adabization, its agreement is to accept adab and refinement (*al-taʾdīb wa-taqwīm al-tahdhīb*). If the self had integrity (*sharufat al-nafs*), it would seek adab (*kānat li-l-ādāb ṭāliba*) and virtues (*wa-l-faḍāʾil rāghiba*).[69] The adabized subject becomes a candidate for *suʿdud* because of ethical and aesthetic self-forming through adab and the qualities this self-formation cultivated: courage, will, integrity, and justice, that is, the praxis of adab. In this respect, it may very well be argued that adab was a cultural capital indicating more than the quantifiable sum of an individual's education or literary pursuits but also a qualitative measure of character traits. And while adab as praxis or text may often be thought of as belonging to the private pursuits of individuals, it is evident as a public convention and a normative decorum from premodern and early modern scholars, who viewed adab as fundamental in the social and the polity and the adabized subject as essential for a functioning society and the promoting of civic or public cooperation.

Al-Ṭahṭāwī argues that virtues are necessary for the progress of society and the individual and are often stretched between excess (*ifrāṭ*) and lack (*tafrīṭ*) and that true justice lies in the mean between the two limits. He further adds that these virtues need cultivating and are not inherent (*taʿyīn maḥall taʿallum al-faḍāʾil*) in order that the ethical subject does not conflate their opposites or anti-virtues (*tashtabih bi-aḍdādihā*).[70] It is implicit in this line of reasoning that the cultivation of virtues, genealogically, is left to adab and the adabization of the subject as per the Arab-Islamic tradition and history. Al-Ṭahṭāwī maintains that without adab and education people can use anti-adab tools for alternative technologies of the self to squirm through life.

It is related that Taha Hussein (d. 1973) asked Ahmad Amin (d. 1954) to conceive of an intellectual blueprint for a school of murūʾa where there is a specialization, curriculum, and people can learn murūʾa. Amin writes about this in an essay in his *Fayḍ al-khāṭir*, where, in exclamatory tones, he respectfully acknowledges Hussein's good intentions and relays that, according to the latter, if such a school existed it would produce people who are above all the trivialities and transcend all imperfections (*rijālan yartafiʿūn ʿan al-ṣaghāʾir . . . wa-yantahizūn ʿan al-naqāʾiḍ*).[71] But simultaneously after to-ing and fro-ing with the term-concept murūʾa and its history and diverse definitions, Amin concurs that it is an impossible task, exclaiming, "How does one teach people murūʾa?" However, he acquiesces that if he learned something new, he would modify the curriculum in the ministry of education. Hussein is correct in conceiving of murūʾa, like al-Ṭahṭāwī and their premodern predecessors, as something that needs to be taught. The rift between adab and murū'a as *a way of life* and its modern conceptions during Hussein's time is not a local or Egyptian phenomenon of modernity. It is part of a shift in the way fields of knowledge were regarded in modernity and the purposes they serve. Friedrich Nietzsche observes this shift and "laments the situation of philosophy in his day, which has been reduced to a study of its philological, historical, and cultural aspects rather than *as a way of life* that has practical implications."[72] Egypt, and most colonized Arab states, were, as Brockelmann maintains, "aligned with European culture" at the time. In this respect, the globally modern perceptible rift between knowledge production and fields of study can be practically observed when adab became literature.[73] Hussein's vision of a school of murū'a is a possible insight into the status of the discursive formation of the subject and the role of the Arab-Islamic discursive tradition at the time or lack thereof.

The idea of taught murū'a, whether communicated directly or intuited by the subject, was commented upon. Ibn al-Marzubān relates an anecdote by Faḍl b. Dalham that "they were taught murū'a in the army of Hishām b. ʿAbd al-Malik like one would be taught the Qur'an!" (*kunnā nataʿallam al-murūʾa fī ʿaskar Hishām b. ʿAbd al-Malik kamā yataʿallam al-insān al-qurʾān*).[74] The reference here is to the reign of the tenth Umayyad caliph (r. 105–25 AH/724–43 CE), whose armies fought at five frontiers at once: the Caucasus, Central Asia, Sind, North Africa, and Byzantium.[75] It thus appears that this conceptual institution of murū'a qua a culmination of humanity that has been inherited from pre-Islamic virtue-ethics saw its evolution as well during the Umayyad period as the anecdote informs us. It is difficult to ascertain what Faḍl b. Dalham exactly meant in this military education context, whether a definition of murū'a as courage and perseverance in battle, or murū'a as a culmination of all virtues through adab and a certain education, or both. The analogy used here, "like one would be taught the Qur'an," implies not only seriousness and commitment but the fundamental importance and authority of this institution of murū'a and adab, whether as militaristic resolve in battle, or edification and adab. And it has been recognized as an important virtue-ethic for the ethical subject, whether they self-identify as literati or as soldiers and officers engaged in the armies of the empire. It thus appears to have developed and evolved even before the famous Abbasid so-called cosmopolitanism, avant la lettre, and the *translatio studi et imperii*.

Algerian Tunisian Muḥammad al-Khiḍr Ḥussein (d. 1958), the grand mufti of al-Azhar (1952–54), was actively invested in issues of reform, like al-Ṭahṭāwī, as well as issues pertaining to the Arabic language and philology. In his collected works, *Rasāʾil al-iṣlāḥ* (Letters of Reform), which cater to his project on reform, he has an article on murū'a previously published in *Majallat al-hidāya al-islāmiyya* (The Magazine of Islamic Guidance), which he founded. Like the aforementioned Taha Hussein's request to Amin on murū'a and adab, Muḥammad Ḥussein's article speaks about what is amiss through the highlighting of what is at stake. In his discussion on murūʾa, he summarizes all previously mentioned views on murūʾa related by premodern scholars, which have been recounted here from Ibn Janāḥ, Ibn al-Marzubān, and others through anecdotes, maxims, and sayings. And it seems that he is aware that his readers may have encountered these views before, because he ends his summary by reiterating the purpose of his article as if he feels the need to justify repeating classical authors' views on murūʾa. He says:

> The purpose of this discourse (*al-gharad min hādhā al-ḥadīth*) is that we saw how murūʾa created and systematized high virtues (*intaẓamat al-murūʾa akhlāqan saniyya*) and luminous adabs (*ādāban muḍīʾa*), and we recognized that the establishment of these virtues and adabs inside oneself (*fī al-nafs*) needs patience and strife (*ṣabr wa-mujāhada*), perceptiveness (*diqqat mulāḥaẓa*), and healthy taste (*salāmat dhawq*). It behooves us that we raise our children to tend to this as soon as they are at an age of discrimination (*ʿahd al-tamyīz*) so that no vices and bad habits (*akhlāq ghayr naqiyya wa-ʿādāt ghayr raḍiyya*) come between them and these virtues, lest humanity cannot find its way to them (*lā tajid al-murūʾa ilā nufūsihim madkhalan*).[76]

Like al-Ṭahṭāwī, Ḥussein sees the link between adab, the social, and polity in the formation of the subject.

Al-Ṭahṭāwī also adds that human beings are urban by nature (*madanī bi-l-ṭabʿ*); they need a city (*madīna*) with a population (*khalq kathīr*) in order for their felicity and human happiness to be actualized (*li-tatimm lahu al-saʿāda al-insāniyya*).[77] Al-Ṭahṭāwī reasons that all human beings need others and social interaction and friendships and companionship; this is how others perfect and complete each other's humanity. Conversely, he criticizes *zuhd* (asceticism) as a virtue where seclusion and isolation are a preferred choice and mode of existence. He maintains that those who are isolated in the mountains or places of worship and want nothing to do with people do not exhibit the virtues of purity (*ʿiffa*), readiness to help (*al-najda*), magnanimity (*sakhāʾ*), and justice (*ʿadl*); these virtues are idle and dormant. This is because they are neither directed toward good or evil: if the virtues are idle (*muʿaṭṭala*) and have not exhibited their own actions, then the virtues do not benefit others, and so they become like non-sentient objects (*manzilat al-jamādāt*) or dead people (*al-mawtā min al-nās*); they think of themselves and are thought of as virtuous but they are not.[78] While al-Ṭahṭāwī might be harsh on ascetism as a personal choice, it must be acknowledged that it offers a possible solace for those who chose this way of life. It can be argued therefore that al-Ṭahṭāwī regards ascetism as devoid of enough moral and epistemic friction to activate and cultivate virtues as part of human experience and adab as praxis; to him, it appears that ascetism may offer a theoretical haven of virtues with an arguably conjectural protection and shield from the real world. But virtue and murūʾa, as discussed by most premodern scholars, cannot be realized except through crisis and strife. If it were that easy to actualize, al-Washshāʾ relates, then the most lowly of people would be able to possess it (*al-makārim lā takūn illā bi-l-makārih wa-law kānat khafīfa latanāwalahā al-safala bi-l-ghalaba*).[79] It is unsurprising that the word used here to indicate the sum of virtues is *makārim*, which is traced to the root of generosity (*k-r-m*), often within the context of hospitality. The perceptible crisis and strife in something like hospitality is arguably the tension between the practical realities of the feasibility of extending hospitality to others and the ethical ideal that it is a virtue that must be upheld. It is understandable therefore that the altruistic act should be a nomenclature for the sum of virtues and an attestation of murū'a because it proves that the perceived tension between practicality and ethics toppled in favor of ethics, in which case the other is perceived as wholly human; a practical approach would always view the other as less than fully human.

2

Adab as Hospitality

The Adab *Sphere: Reading* Mathal *and Discourse*

In 1968, Haifa-born writer Emile Habibi (1922–96) spoke about how he and his countrymen and women "lived in intellectual and cultural isolation from the Arab world (*munqaṭiʿūn ʿan al-ḥayāt al-thaqāfiyya wa-l-fikriyya fī al-ʿālam al-ʿarabī*). To save our heritage (*turāthunā*), we published *Kalīla wa-Dimna* at our own expense, despite being poor."[1] Habibi considered the text as popular since the time of its translation and dissemination. During Habibi's time and perhaps for posterity, he viewed it as an invisible invitation to cure what he defined as "isolation" and connect with temporal and geographical others across space and time. *Kalīla wa-Dimna* became the source of the unreceived but desired hospitality shown to Habibi and his fellow countrymen and women. It would not be far-fetched to propose that Ibn al-Muqaffaʿ could in fact, hypothetically and transtemporally, see in Habibi's gesture one of the legitimizations of adab he argued for.

About thirteen centuries ago, in Fars (Persia, today's southwestern Iran), which was then under Umayyad rule, a notable official responsible for the town's taxes was accused of embezzlement; the official was arrested. The governor had the official's fingers crushed, rendering them withered.[2] In Arabic, the noun associated with such a physical state, as lexicographers and philologists would not be at a loss of words to tell us, is *al-muqaffaʿ* (the man with shriveled fingers) from the verb *taqaffaʿa*. The man appears to have left Khurasan for Basra to attend to his son's future. The son acquired an Arabic nickname and became known as "the son of the man with shriveled fingers": Ibn al-Muqaffaʿ (106–42 AH/724–ca. 760 CE). Litterateur, translator, and scholar, born Rōzbih pūr-i Dādoēō, he became Abū Muḥammad ʿAbd Allāh Rūzbih b. Dādūwayh, or simply Ibn al-Muqaffaʿ. He is described as a talented litterateur with enviable prose, who authored, among many works, both *al-Adab al-kabīr* and *al-Adab al-ṣaghīr*. Sources tell us that he was of exceptional intelligence to the point that it was said that no Persian is smarter or more generous, humane, and loyal to his friends than Ibn al-Muqaffaʿ. His comment on an incident with ʿAbd al-Ḥamīd b. Yaḥyā al-Kātib summarizes his views on friendship: "You owe your friend your blood and money" (*ibdhul li-ṣadīqika damaka wa-mālaka*).[3] Of the original literary monographs, administrative epistles and works, and his translations, wit, generosity, and being a loyal friend, he is mostly known for two things: his translation of *Kalīla wa-Dimna* and his tragic, gory, and controversial death sentence with a false charge of heresy (*zandaqa*), a well-rehearsed smoke-screen accusation because he became a threat to those in the corridors of power.[4] Especially true when read against his letter of advice to the Abbasid caliph al-Manṣūr (r. 136–58 AH/754–75 CE) "recommending that the latter promulgate an official statement of the Islamic creed, adopt a uniform code of law, and pay the army regularly. The recommendations were not adopted, but the diagnosis of the state of the empire proved strikingly prescient."[5]

ADAB AND HOSPITALITY

By translating *Kalīla wa-Dimna*, Ibn al-Muqaffaʿ developed what I refer to as an enactment of adab characterized by murūʾa, which functions as a dual form of hospitality. He offered both internal or endogenous and external or exogenous hospitality to the text he translated, introducing what is considered the first work of prose fiction into Arabic and Arabic culture without state sponsorship. This external hospitality is shown to the foreign text translated into Arabic, while his internal hospitality is extended to the reader, which I shall explain in due course. The "enactment of adab" shown here extended beyond the realm of the literary, aesthetic, and/or stylistic where the context of *Kalīla wa-Dimna*'s translation exemplifies a habitus of adab.

Exogenous Hospitality

Ibn al-Muqaffaʿ was an active translator, often accused retrospectively of translating only what is perceived and labeled as heretical books either to bolster the official narrative of his mysterious death as make-believe or play his Persian heritage in the then ongoing Arab-Persian cultural wars (*shuʿūbiyya*). However interesting these questions, they are beyond the scope of this chapter. The translation of *Kalīla wa-Dimna* was not commissioned under the espousal of the Abbasid caliph al-Manṣūr or any other patron. It was a voluntary act that Abdelfattah Kilito reads as "strange," invoking the Persian ancestry of Ibn al-Muqaffaʿ.[6] In light of reading translation as an act of competition that is premised on imperial interests, following George Steiner, Kilito questions Ibn al-Muqaffaʿ's calculated generosity in translating and investing time and effort into the Arabic language, the language of those who conquered Persia, as Kilito maintains;[7] one might also add that it is the language of those who accused and deformed his father's hands. Kilito reads this translation investment, nonetheless, as a less than innocent act especially in light of Ibn al-Muqaffaʿ's preface to the work.[8] In the preface, the latter asserts that "reading and understanding this book [*Kalīla wa-Dimna*] would suffice; it collapses all other books (*iktafā wa-istaghnā ʿan ghayrihi*)."[9] Ibn al-Muqaffaʿ, Kilito reads, elevates this book from an ordinary translation to the extraordinary. It distills knowledge of all books into one book, or what Kilito calls "the supreme book" (*al-kitāb al-aʿlā*).[10] Scholars' and compilers' classification of *Kalīla wa-Dimna* indicates the nature of the work's reception and how it was literarily or adab-ly sustainable. Ḥājjī Khalīfa (d. 1067 AH/1657 CE) describes *Kalīla wa-Dimna* as a book concerned with the improvement of moral qualities and the refinement of character (*iṣlāḥ al-akhlāq wa-tahdhīb al-nufūs*).[11] In this respect, the book is read and received within the framework of "refinement of character" as a pathway to murūʾa, but it was also authored within this very framework of murūʾa as the habitus of adab.

Paul Ricoeur proposes a philosophical mediation, a solution of sorts to the paradox, between identity and alterity through the concept of linguistic hospitality (*l'hospitalité langagière*), "where the pleasure of dwelling in the other's language is balanced by the pleasure of receiving the foreign word at home, in one's own welcoming house" (*le plaisir d'habiter la langue de l'autre est compensé par le plaisir de recevoir chez soi, dans sa propre demeure d'accueil, la parole de l'étranger*).[12] Ricoeur speaks of "an ethos of translation whose goal would be to repeat on a cultural and spiritual level the gesture of linguistic hospitality" (*d'un ethos de la traduction, dont le but serait de répéter au plan culturel et spirituel le geste de l'hospitalité linguistique*).[13] The linguistic guests Ibn al-Muqaffaʿ brought home in the Arabic language are not only the heralding of the earliest fictive work in Arabic prose but also guests that held up a mirror for princes. In both the Arab-Muslim and European traditions, numerous definitions have been put forward concerning the term "mirrors for princes," and so distinguishing between the nuances of the definition as in Roberto Lambertini's explanation in the Western tradition might be helpful: "These terms can be used in a rather loose sense, referring to a very wide range of sources, even narrative or iconographic ones, or parts thereof, carrying notions concerning rulership, or in a stricter sense limited to independent works explicitly aiming at instructing kings and lesser rulers about the virtues they should cultivate, their lifestyle, their duties, the philosophical and theological meaning of their office. They usually follow standard conventions so that their teachings about royal justice, princely virtues, and the like tend to give the impression of a continuous repetition of commonplaces."[14] For Arab-Muslim works, the more general category of advice literature is applied to a variety of written texts provided they serve a counseling purpose. The idea that they must address a royal recipient is debatable given the case of *Kalīla wa-Dimna*, but this tendency can be applied to other works that self-identify as "*ḥikma* (wisdom), *mawʿiẓa* (moral exhortation), *akhlāq* (ethics, characteristically in the personal, domestic, and political setting), and *waṣiyya* ('testament,' usually of a father to his son(s) and successor(s))."[15]

Ibn al-Muqaffaʿ played an important role in the theorization of the polity during the reign of Caliph al-Manṣūr when he made clear the defects he saw in the administration and the potential threats that would undermine the stability of the government, as evident in his *Risālat al-Ṣaḥāba*.[16] It may also be argued that part of Ibn al-Muqaffaʿ's motivation is the similarity between aspects of the competitiveness of Indian and Sassanid court life that propelled the initial composition and translation of the work. Besides the book's mirroring qualities for princes, offering strategies for survival to the perplexed courtier, as allegorized in the work, may have indeed been useful for life in the Abbasid court.[17] While these are legitimate queries, it is more productive for the purposes of this chapter (and book at large) to situate the question of Ibn al-Muqaffaʿ's interest in translating *Kalīla wa-Dimna* within the context of his understanding and legitimization of adab rather than *only* his political career or the hermeneutics of suspicion, without rejecting that these are valid questions. Questioning the translator's motives is a recognized trope, especially retroactively, not only because of famous translator-spies in literary history, working as informants and/or against the culture of their source texts,[18] but also because it recognizes and situates the translator as a resident of two cultures: "A translator is a double agent, constantly playing two texts, two languages, two cultures, two readerships off each other in order to arrive at a truth that ultimately serves no master but his own exacting ideal of excellence."[19] This residency in two cultures that may at times have competing narratives was not lost on eighth- or ninth-century translators and scholars in Baghdad during the translation movement that Ibn al-Muqaffaʿ participated in. A century later, philosopher al-Kindī (d. 256 AH/873 CE), continuing the same position of intellectual hospitality, and anticipating critical voices, preempts the attacks with a sensible position on translation and foreign books: "We must not be ashamed to admire the truth or to acquire it, from wherever it comes. Even if it should come from far-flung nations and foreign peoples, there is for the student of truth nothing more important than the truth, nor is the truth demeaned or diminished by the one who states or conveys it; no one is demeaned by the truth, rather all are ennobled by it."[20]

It is not my intention, nor is it the purpose or within the capacity of this book, to discuss the philosophy of al-Kindī. Rather, I cite al-Kindī as an example of another polymath situated at the core of a translation movement. Perhaps he, too, is a possible later reader of Ibn al-Muqaffaʿ's translation that qualified—if one may use the word—as a bestseller for centuries to come. Al-Kindī holds the same position. The passage of al-Kindī participates in creating this social and intellectual climate of adab, or the adab sphere, as it creates what I would like to call *conditions of reading* based on this intellectual hospitality as a framework of adab. Even though al-Kindī anticipated criticism and attacks, the conditions of reading allow this to happen within a framework of social and intellectual adab. I use the word "conditions" in a *double sens* to mean both requests and an environment. These conditions act in the manner of more than an encouragement from the author to the reader or a "motivation" for them. It is an organic conceptual environment where the author appears to be in an intellectual consortium with trends and networks in their milieu; the author both participates in and creates these hospitable conditions through their prefaces, justifications, and explanations, thereby conditioning and/or fashioning readers. Al-Kindī creates what may now be called comparatively cosmopolitan conditions of reading, which are akin to Ibn al-Muqaffaʿ's hospitality conditions of reading, to value any contribution made to what he calls the correct views or a truth (*ṣawāb*), whatever its source or origin. According to him, philosophy, as a part of or a branch of knowledge, cannot be an individual enterprise. Al-Kindī, like his predecessors, realizes that all knowledge, philosophy included, is a collective enterprise. He discourages narrowness, which he explains as either stemming from envy or an estrangement from this collective enterprise of truth and knowledge. Al-Kindī says that "if one collects together the little that each one of these people has attained of the truth, the result is quite considerable." He continues:

> *On First Philosophy* §III.1–2 (AR 103–4, RJ 13–15): [We must] be on guard against the evil of the interpretation of many in our own time who have made a name for themselves with speculation, people who are estranged from the truth. They crown themselves undeservedly with the crowns of truth, because of the narrowness of their understanding of the ways of truth . . . [and] because of the filth of the envy that has mastered their bestial souls, whose veil of darkness cloaks the vision of their thought from the light of truth.[21]

Al-Kindī seems to be creating conditions to counter anticipated or possible adversarial readings, as he encourages his readers to be "on guard against the evil of interpretation." This, I read, as preempting violent reading conditions, which would propel and encourage predatory reading or as previously mentioned the "wolf intervals" that would create dissonance, which he cautions against, and also as an attempt to maintain good citizenship in social and intellectual adab.

Kalīla wa-Dimna, as evident from the preface, was not popular or publicly consumed in its two previous homes: the Indian and Sassanid courts; it is presented as a book with limited readership. As the preface maintains, it was a treasured work that the Indian sovereign Dablishim received from the sage Bidpai and never divulged its secrets. The Persians heard of the book and wanted to acquire it. Persian physician Burzūyah, through an act of ruse, managed to get hold of a copy for the Sassanid king Khosraw Anūshirvān.[22] And it was this Pahlavi copy on which Ibn al-Muqaffaʿ based his translation of *Kalīla wa-Dimna*. The most interesting fact here is that the book entered the Arabic tradition and literary canon intersecting with two other traditions, the Indian and the Persian, through what appears to be not a pure act of *translatio studi et imperii*—although it still remains one—but an individual effort. In his *Tārīkh al-adab al-ʿarabī*, ʿUmar Farrūkh summarizes three possible theories in answer to the question of whether *Kalīla wa-Dimna* was copied (*manqūl*) or authored (*mawḍūʿ*). The most widespread narrative is the one stated above; it entered the Arabic tradition through the Middle Persian text, which is a translation of the Sanskrit. However, other scholars maintain that the book itself is unheard of in ancient literatures and the names mentioned by Ibn al-Muqaffaʿ such as Dablishim the king and Bidpai the philosopher are temporally incongruent.[23] In other words, the sovereign Dablishim and philosopher Bidpai (or Pilpay) may have never been contemporaneous, if the latter is indeed a real person. The word "Bidpai" may very well have been a corruption from the Sanskrit विद्यापति Vidyāpati (विद्या *vidyā*: knowledge; पति *pati*: lord/master), therefore meaning "chief scholar or master of knowledge."[24] In the Sanskrit *Panchatantra*, the Indian sage used these fables in his courtly instructions to teach his sons. The introduction to the Indian frame tale tells of King Amarasakti "and his sore distress at his three moronic sons, some kind of drop-outs, who 'being hostile to education, are lacking in discernment.'"[25] All efforts to educate them fail so he entrusts them to the sage Vishnu Sharma, who will teach them "the art of living intelligently." This art happens to be in five books. The political philosophy of the *Panchatantra* (Five Treatises) is represented in discussions among animal characters, chiefly the Lion, the Bull, and the two famous jackals Karataka and Damanaka, who became Kalīla and Dimna, respectively, in Ibn al-Muqaffaʿ's rendition by way of Pahlavi. Ibn al-Muqaffaʿ jettisons human characters who tell stories about animals and instead opts for animal characters who tell stories about other animals. And thus, while in the Sanskrit version we have a narrator of stories about people and animals, the narrator is recognized as giving narrative agency to animals. In Ibn al-Muqaffaʿ's version, the blurred world of mediating linguistic beings gives complete agency to animal narrators. This can be read as Ibn al-Muqaffaʿ's creative use of indirect frank speech, a narrative technique where a character's thoughts or speech are presented indirectly or in the third person; in this respect they can share their views without speaking in the first person, and this indirect speaker does not need to explain their perspective by describing it plainly.[26] The absence of a narrator in Ibn al-Muqaffaʿ's *Kalīla wa-Dimna* further removes the burden of indirect frank speech off the narrator's shoulders by one remove. If *Kalīla wa-Dimna* would have had a narrator responsible for the indirect frank speech of *all* animal characters, the narrator's political burden may have been pronounced and visible, especially as a human character, as ventriloquizing his/her perspective through the animals. The diversity of animals and their views decentralize views.

It has been argued that even our notions of public sphere where direct frank speech takes place can be rethought as we consider Ibn al-Muqaffaʿ's *Kalīla wa-Dimna*. A public sphere, Jennifer London maintains, "is a forum where individuals use creative media to express their political views with others in the hope that it will help them learn about politics and make sound political decisions. Individuals can speak, write or read something written by themselves or by someone else (which can be either fiction or non-fiction)."[27] This designation situates *Kalīla wa-Dimna* in the domain of *only* the political and hence gives it the term public sphere where a discourse will influence political action. This is plausible. But what *Kalīla wa-Dimna* and adab do is create, engage, invite, and participate in what I call the adab sphere. This invitation to discourse and discussion, through the text as an interlocutor, is aimed to influence more than just political action, including the personal, social, intellectual, and internal lives of the subjects. It is precisely this adab sphere that lends itself to the technologies of adab to become more than text and therefore become praxis as well as technologies of the self.

Endogenous Hospitality

In showing hospitality to the reader, by orienting invitations to the adab sphere, Ibn al-Muqaffaʿ was still operating from the space of the "enactment of adab" as an act of hospitality in offering all types and levels of readers a visible welcome and a socially and intellectually identified space in the text. George Steiner speaks of *cortesia* (courtesy) on the part of the reader toward the text, but not the other way around; he emphasizes the necessary investment on the reader's part, where the "reader meets the book with a courtliness of heart (that is what *cortesia* signifies), with a courtliness, a scruple of welcome and entertainment of which the russet sleeve, possibly of velvet or velveteen, and the furred cloak and bonnet are the external symbols."[28] Indeed, this is the ideal reader that Steiner and many *adīb*s would dream up. But Ibn al-Muqaffaʿ offered us something entirely different and innovative, and arguably a measure that would allow the formation of this ideal reader. He offered a reading hospitality. There is a conceptual link between his conception of adab as a form of hospitality and its etymological and relational meaning of *maʾduba* (banquet) as "a banquet in which the good customs of hospitality are respected . . . [with] a host that respects good customs."[29] The book's intrinsic tolerance, through its author's preface, of the levels of readings and meanings showed the good customs of hospitality, while the author qua *adīb* in this respect observed these relations; s/he is cognizant of these ontological relationships between the abstract concepts of adab and hospitality.

Edward Said reminds us of the generosity involved in the act of interpretation that "makes a place in it for a foreign Other." He tells of how "to practice [understanding] was one that sympathetically and subjectively entered into the life of a written text as seen from the perspective of its time and its author (*eingefiuhling*) [*sic*]. Rather than alienation and hostility to another time and different culture, philology as applied to *Weltliteratur* involved a profound humanistic spirit deployed with generosity and, if I may use the word, hospitality."[30] Ibn al-Muqaffaʿ recognized the different levels of readers in his preface, whom he welcomed generously by identifying them as guests of the book; he equally acknowledged that these readers may not remain at one level of understanding, thereby acknowledging adab as a discursive practice. Their transformation process, the possibility to access the levels of meanings Ibn al-Muqaffaʿ speaks of, is proof of this. The legitimizing of adab here does not take its cue from the practice of literary writing; it becomes an adab toward the reader whose participation in this pluralistic manner of reading allows their understanding of other reading capacities. The recognition of the obstacles of understanding is not communicated as an obstruction from *meaning/truth* but rather a process toward *a* meaning/truth. The readers of Ibn al-Muqaffaʿ then realize that the *meaning* of the text might not be readily attainable or singular; the imagined community of readers of this text will not be united by its meaning; rather, they will be united over a discourse over its meaning(s). In this respect, as readers they recognized that, through an engagement of discourse, they need the other readers. They, like other readers, have something to offer to each other: *a* meaning, an additional understanding through what Ibn al-Muqaffaʿ calls *shuʿūb al-ḥadīth* or discourse. The reader thus will never think that their community of readers are intellectually dispensable, worthless, or distant. Disagreement will not be framed within the parameters of "worthlessness" or "ridicule." One is able to discern this beyond the text under discussion into the reception of this very text. For instance, *adīb* Abū ʿAbd Allāh Muḥammad al-Yamanī (d. 400 AH/1010 CE) voiced many a disagreement with what he perceived as pro-Persian sentiments in Ibn al-Muqaffaʿ's text, and mostly also the choice of prose over poetry, and the rising popularity of the book over Arabic poetry, as the pride of Arabs. Al-Yamanī, despite these disagreements, engaged in an adabized manner with the text; adab as method (see chapter 5) therefore becomes his hospitable engagement that is generative and not destructive, since he selected what he saw as similar parallels in meaning and therefore possible sources from Arabic poetry to *Kalīla wa-Dimna*.[31] In this respect, the performance of adab as hospitality engages readers in discourse, even if critical, which enables this social adabization through the adab sphere, hence adab as praxis.

SETTING THE READING STAGE: THE SIGNIFICANCE OF PREFACES

In the exordium to *Kalīla wa-Dimna*, titled *Bāb ʿarḍ al-kitāb* (On Presenting the Book) in modern editions, Ibn al-Muqaffaʿ takes some time to explain a few things to the reader that he deemed salient before venturing into the book in the manner of an introduction.[32] The function of the exordium in Ibn al-Muqaffaʿ's translation is quite striking. Questioning the preface, in this regard, is to ask what Jacques Derrida calls "a diabolically simple question."[33] Prefaces are not part of the main text; rather, they adorn it and present it to the world. In other words, they legitimize its existence. Gérard Genette tells us about prefaces' relationship to the text as they "surround it and extend it, precisely in order to *present* it, in the usual sense of this verb but also in the strongest sense: to *make present*, to ensure the text's presence in the world, its 'reception' and consumption in the form (nowadays, at least) of a book."[34] The preface in this respect is part of the intellectual and textual space of the condition of reading the author or translator lays out before their reader to orient them toward a certain reading or, like al-Kindī did, to resist another. This intellectual space creates a mode of many possible readings. Before venturing further, I would like to discuss the role of prefaces, introductions, prologues, and paratexts in general in the Arab-Islamic practice of reading and writing. The first to discuss paratexts as part of a book's introduction was philosopher al-Fārābī (d. 339 AH/950 CE).[35] This is not to say that authors did not pay attention to or write introductions and exordiums before that, as Ibn al-Muqaffaʿ's exordium would prove. Rather, al-Fārābī stressed that the purpose of a book and its benefits, divisions, genre, class, title, author's name, and pedagogical objectives are essential parts.[36] Similarly, ʿAlī b. Khalaf (d. ca. 414 AH/1023 CE), poet and chancery secretary, emphasized the role of the exordium in a book. He maintains:

أن يؤسس كلامه بمقدمات في صدره ليخرجه من حد النثار إلى حد النظام، فإن منزلة هذه المقدمات من كل كلام مُؤلف منزلة الرأس من الجسد، والأساس من البناء، وكما أن الرأس يضم أعضاء الجسد ويرأسها؛ كذلك المقدمة التي يقدمها المنشئ في صدر كلامه تضم ما تتبعه ويقع في ضمنه. وكما الباني لا بد له من وضع أساس لما يبنيه يعتمد عليه ويستند إليه، كذلك مؤلف الكلام لا يُغني عند تقديم مقدمة يتطرق منها إلى ما يروم التأليف فيه، لأن كل كلام لا يخلو من فرش يُفرش قبله غير داخل في حكم الكلام المنظوم، وإنما تخلو من المقدمات كتب الأخبار التي تضمن نصوص ما يخبر به، وما يدور بين الناس في العوارض والحاجات من الكلام المبتذل . . . ومن نظر في التصانيف الموضوعة في جميع أفانين العلم لم يكد يقع على كتاب خال من مقدمة يتطرق منها إلى ما بعدها ويرتقي عليها إلى ما يتلوها

To build one's discourse with prefaces at its introduction moves it from chaos to organization. For the status of those prefaces of every authored discourse is the status of the head to the body and the foundation in construction-building. And as a head gathers the rest of the organs and leads them, so does the introduction that an author presents at the beginning of their discourse; it includes what is found inside and included. And as a builder should lay down a foundation for the structure they are building such that they can rely upon it, so does an author where he introduces what he intends to discuss because every discussion must have a basis that is not inside the content of the text itself before delving into the discussion. But books of anecdotes (*akhbār*) that relate informative texts and what happens between people in events and needs of commonplace verbiage do not have introductions . . . and whoever looks into the authored books in all kinds of arts and sciences will almost always find no book without an introduction to walk them through it to what is after it and use it as a springboard for what is above it.[37]

Ibn Khalaf was not the only one. Several scholars like Yāqūt al-Ḥamawī (d. 626 AH/1229 CE) emphasized the role of prologues and introductions (*khuṭbat al-kitāb*) in the overall meaning of a book.[38] Scholars from various disciplines emphasized the role of the introduction and exordium in the overall cohesion of a book, such as al-Nawawī (d. 676 AH/1277 CE). Al-Nawawī even says that some authors leave these pages blank until they finish writing the book, then they attend to the introduction (*khuṭba*) so that it is in unison with what they have written, thereby acknowledging the organic nature of writing.[39]

LEVELS OF READING: *MATHAL* AND ITS HOSPITABLE READERS

It is imperative to highlight the rest of Ibn al-Muqaffaʿ's prefatory remarks to his readers. Ibn al-Muqaffaʿ underlines levels of reading through accentuating the allegorical nature of the text and its figurative language, *mathal*, which he pointed to in his preface. The designation *mathal* is used before the title of each of the stories instead of tale or story, *ḥikāya, qiṣṣa*, and so on—readily available designations, of course. It may be that Ibn al-Muqaffaʿ saw that the *mathal* lies not in its definition but in its function; that any story could become a *mathal* on the condition that the reader is involved and identifies with (*al-tamāhī*) characters and is able to understand, interpret, and apply what was understood.[40] *Mathal*, scholar Ibrāhīm al-Naẓẓām (d. ca. between 220 AH/835 CE and 230 AH/845 CE) maintains,

> يجتمع في المثل أربع لا تجتمع في غيره من الكلام: إيجاز اللفظ، وإصابة المعنى، وحسن التشبيه، وجودة الكناية، فهو نهاية البلاغة. وزاد ابن المقفع: والوسعة في شعوب الحديث
>
> has four elements that no other type of speech has: it is succinct, conveys the meaning effectively, features appealing metaphors and imagery, and has *kināya* where tropic and/or literal interpretations can be supported and this is the ultimate eloquence. And Ibn al-Muqaffaʿ added to this definition the presence of the width in the byways of speech [width of the scope of discourse] (*al-wisʿa fī shuʿūb al-ḥadīth*).[41]

It seems that *shuʿūb al-ḥadīth* is one of Ibn al-Muqaffaʿ's famous contributions that was not only quoted by al-Naẓẓām in his definition of *mathal* but also used by subsequent scholars like Sharaf al-Dīn al-Ṭībī (d. 743 AH/1342 CE) to explain the famous ḥadīth and maxim "there is a form of eloquence that has the effect of sorcery" (*inna min al-bayān la-siḥran*). Al-Ṭībī says that "this maxim is used when the reasoning and logical thought are plausible (*istiḥsān al-manṭiq*) and the advancing of compelling proof (*īrād al-ḥujja al-bāligha*), and this is what Ibn al-Muqaffaʿ means by the width of discourse (*al-wisʿa fī shuʿūb al-ḥadīth*)."[42] Al-Ṭībī, and expectedly his readers, therefore understood this unique expression of Ibn al-Muqaffaʿ as one pointing to a rich and enriching discourse where multiple and diverse competing but compelling proofs were presented. This structured exchange of arguments and ideas reflects a social and intellectual practice that seems literary on the surface (reading and interpreting tropically or literally using evidence-based reasoning and critical thinking) but at its heart this activity is a social practice where the diversity of perspectives teaches and promotes active listening and/or exchange of ideas, respect, and empathy. Ibn al-Muqaffaʿ's conception of discourse explains his classification of the imagined readers of *Kalīla wa-Dimna*.

Ibn al-Muqaffa‘'s understanding of the presence of levels of reading indicates this departure from several elitist and intellectual authoritarian, patronizing, authorial practices; chief among them is dictating how a book should be read (see chapter 3) or the claim to a single correct meaning of the text. This is not an idea that Ibn al-Muqaffa‘ presented, nor is it a sustainable idea in the Arab-Islamic reading tradition altogether. Ibn al-Muqaffa‘ differentiates between the obvious, literal meaning of a tale featuring animals, and other figurative, more intricate meanings—all valid, provided plausible reasoning. Emphasizing the levels of reading of the text would in turn acknowledge the existence of different readers of the text. Ibn al-Muqaffa‘ does not expect, nor is it rational to expect, that all readers would have an equal approach and understanding of the text and its multiple meanings, which he maintains that he accessed. Ibn al-Muqaffa‘'s discussion also acknowledges the fact that understanding and knowledge, as part of one's experience, character, and self-defined identity, is changeable and part of intellectual and social development. He relegates some of these facts to more than simply a binary of understanding/not-understanding; it is intellect, but also age, experience, and personal proclivities:

[هذا] كتاب كليلة ودمنة وهو مما وضعته علماء الهند من الأمثال والأحاديث، التي التمسوا أن يدخلوا فيها أبلغ ما وجدوا منا لكلام في النحو الذي أرادوا ولم تزل العلماء من كل أمة وأهل كل لسان يلتمسون أن يعقل عنهم ويحتالون لذلك بصنوف الحيل ويبتغون في إخراج ما عندهم من العلل حتى كان من تلك العلل وضع بليغ الكلام ومنمقه على أفواه البهائم والطير . . . فوجدوا منصرفا في القول وشعابا يأخذون فيها لهوا وحكمة فاحتمله الحكماء لحكمته والسخفاء للهوه والمتعلمون من الأحداث وغيرهم فنشطوا لعلمه وخف عليهم حفظه فإذا احتنك الحدث واجتمع له العلم وتدبر ما كان حفظ مما صار مقيدا مزبورا في صدره وهو لا يدري ما هو عرف أنه قد ظفر من ذلك بكنوز عظام

This book is a work of parables and stories composed by the people of India, who sought to incorporate into it the most eloquent speech they could find in the style they preferred. In order to make their intentions comprehensible, scholars of every nation and tongue have employed a variety of devices and means when presenting their arguments. One device was to put eloquent and elegant language into the mouths of animals and birds. This enabled them to accomplish a number of things: they found a way to speak indirectly and to communicate through implication [*shu‘ūban*, lit. byways]. Because such a book combined entertainment with wisdom, the wise would study it for its wisdom, and the simple for its value as entertainment; young pupils and others would be delighted to read it and it would be easy for them to memorize. When the young person reached maturity and grew in knowledge, he would ponder what he had memorized—as it had been recorded and inscribed in his heart without his knowing its true nature—and would come to realize that he had acquired a great treasure.[43]

Ibn al-Muqaffa‘ therefore identified various types of readers who would access the book according to the levels he mentioned previously. Various things are at play here. Ibn al-Muqaffa‘'s translation not only privileged its readers in acknowledging different levels of reading and types of readers, it removed the previous elitist restrictions placed on the book and its restricted readership in its previous homes. It is made accessible to everyone with different outcomes, where all the adabized outcomes of this reading are legitimate and valid (wisdom, entertainment, sheer memorization, etc.) through a scope of discourse (*al-siʿa fī shuʿūb al-ḥadīth*).[44] In other words, Ibn al-Muqaffaʿ's acknowledgment of the inevitability of diverse reading and understanding its stages is theorized into this typology. Each reader is left to their own reading journey. Ibn al-Muqaffaʿ, though claiming to have accessed *all* possible meanings, never closes the book for posterity and future readers and future interpretations. In this respect, he created and acknowledged reading autonomy and also prevented the possible conditions of creating "interpretative laziness" by virtue of preventing "reading laziness."[45] This is an antidote to the "lazy reader." Ibn al-Muqaffaʿ's reader does not need a controlling hand and is obliged to work and perfect their own reading and interpretative skills with no prior judgment on the book or its content. Ibn al-Muqaffaʿ fashioned an all-encompassing reading condition that is inclusive of several readings and readers; to read and reread the book with as many interpretations as there are readers within an evidence-based reasoning.

On the other hand, and by way of *mathal*, it is also useful to regard the typology of readers as a process of adabization. Ibn al-Muqaffaʿ includes several types, including young untrained readers, who may not access the meaning. He suggests that the young readers will hopefully, someday, be able to understand the other levels of the book, even if they now merely memorize it for fun. He mentions that by the time they grow up and gain experience, they will realize the treasure they possess. This is a progression to the wise ones he already mentioned, who may access further layers of the book. He ultimately refers to himself as having accessed the book, in reference to his status as an *adīb*. What is interesting here, in this juxtaposition of reader typologies, which is not unusual in premodern adab,[46] is that it offers a process of becoming. The typology of readers therefore operates on two levels: vertical and horizontal. A vertical line cuts through time in a process of evolution factored in adab, and a horizontal line amasses all readers in a single moment of time on its axis by degrees of adabization. Adab as a process can indeed offer this elevation from the literal level of reading associated with the young and/or unadabized in their precritical naivete, to the more adabized critical reader. The loss of reading credulity, critique, differentiated from the literal readings often associated with the youth as the preface purports, becomes then the condition of adab.

SPEAKING IN *MATHAL* AND THE LEGITIMIZATION OF ADAB

Does adab need legitimization? Did litterateurs theorize a function of adab beyond the pedagogic and recreational? Ibn al-Muqaffaʿ begins his preface to his *al-Adab al-ṣaghīr* (The Minor Adab) with a universal common denominator uniting readers but also humanity together:

> أما بعد، فإن لكل مخلوق حاجة، ولكل حاجة غاية، ولكل غاية سبيلًا. والله وقّت للأمور أقدارها، وهيأ إلى الغايات سبلها، وسبب الحاجات ببلاغها فغاية الناس وحاجاتهم صلاح المعاش والمعاد، والسبيل إلى دركها صحة العقل، وأمارة صحة العقل اختيار الأمور بالبصر، وتنفيذ البصر بالعزم
>
> Now, then, every creature has a need, and every need has a purpose, and every purpose has a means. God has set the destinies for events and circumstances, prepared for their purposes paths, and caused needs to be fulfilled. For the purpose and need of people is living the good life in the here and hereafter. And the means to achieving this is the sound mind, the proof of which is choosing things critically after reflection (*baṣar*) and executing critique with resolve/will (*ʿazm*).[47]

Ibn al-Muqaffaʿ begins his exordium with a universal purpose uniting all readers, and humans, across space and time: living the good life. He maintains that this legitimate need cannot be achieved without having a sound mind. Indeed, for the mind (reason) will guide the individual to this good life through making sound choices after critical reflection and possessing resolve. Ibn al-Muqaffaʿ uses *baṣar* to mean critical reflection. He explains further that one who seeks excellence and virtue (*ṭālib al-faḍl*) without critical reflection (*bi-ghayr baṣar*) is lost and confounded (*tāʾih ḥayrān*), and the one who discerns excellence without will and resolve is chronically ill and deprived (*dhū zamāna maḥrūm*). I translate *baṣar* as "critique via critical reflection" but, as I shall show in due course, it is much more complex and holds remarkable conceptual power.

Al-Farāhīdī (d. 170 AH/790 CE), an earlier lexicographer and contemporary of Ibn al-Muqaffaʿ, explains this in terms of insight and reverts the word to *baṣīra* (insight, perception) as a "name for that which is believed in one's heart from religion or truth of a matter" (*ism li-mā uʿtuqida fī al-qalb min al-dīn wa-ḥaqīqat al-amr*).[48] He maintains that *baṣar* is a certain perception in the heart (*nafādh fī al-qalb*), which can be understood as insight.[49] Ibn Fāris (d. 395 AH/1004 CE) relates to us that *al-baṣīra* is proof (*al-burhān*).[50] Al-Farāhīdī, as well as Ibn Fāris, also adds an interesting nuance to *baṣīra* as the shield (*dirʿ*) to anything that one wears, such as a shield from artillery (*mā lubisa min al-silāḥ fa-huwa baṣāʾir al-silāḥ*).[51] Al-Ṣaghānī (d. 650 AH/1252 CE) furthers this trope of weapons, stating that the verb *baṣara* also means to cut (*baṣarahu bi-l-sayf*: to cut/kill s.o. with the sword).[52] With cutting proof in mind, it is not surprising then to see Ibn Manẓūr (d. 711 AH/1311 CE) later clarify, after explaining the word's literal meaning as relating to the "eye" and "sight," that *baṣar* also means *ʿibra* (lesson, understanding), *ʿilm* (knowledge), and reflection and identification (*tabaṣṣur: al-taʾammul, al-taʿarruf*).[53] This view is also shared by Fīrūzābādī (d. 817 AH/1414 CE), who tells us that *baṣar* is defining and explicating (i.e., theorizing) (*al-tabṣīr: al-taʿrīf, al-īḍāḥ*).[54] Similarly, he mentions that *baṣīra* is *ḥujja* (proof, presentation of proof).[55] Additional metaphorical meanings (*majāz*), as al-Zamakhsharī (d. 538 AH/1143 CE) tells us, include the active participle (*baṣīr*) of the root verb *baṣira*, which is to be a watcher and a witness (*raqīb, shāhid*).[56] Likewise, Fīrūzābādī relates this meaning in the context of Q.75:14–15 ("Truly, man is a clear witness against himself, despite all the excuses he may put forward"): an individual will be a proof against themself (*ḥujja ʿalā nafsika*).[57] This is an interesting image where the Qur'anic discourse presents the individual as unwilling to face the evaluation of their work or deeds, in a state of involuntary auto-critique (*bal al-insān ʿalā nafsihi baṣīratun*) for failure or unwillingness of self-critique (*wa-law alqā maʿādhīrahu*), self-critique necessitating getting outside of oneself. The Qur'an's allusion to the failure of self-critique is remarkable in that Q.75:15 covers past and present temporalities. In other words, it tells us that self-critique will be replaced by excuses at the temporal moment defined in the verse, the hereafter, but also extends this failure to a temporal past in the here in an astounding manner where also lack of self-critique becomes the cause of this moment and its effect. Al-Zabīdī (d. 1205 AH/1791 CE) relates additional information in relation to *al-mustabṣir* that is worth mentioning. According to a Prophetic ḥadīth, "Does not a road [company] bring together the merchant and the traveler; the insightful and the *majbūr*? [i.e., all sorts of people]" (*alaysa al-ṭarīq yajmaʿ al-tājir wa-ibn al-sabīl wa-l-mustabṣir wa-l-majbūr*).[58] In other variations of the ḥadīth, there is no mention of the merchant and sometimes the *barr* (virtuous) and *fājir* (odious) appear at the beginning before the listing of the other typologies. *Majbūr* is explained variously. Most lexicons maintain that it refers to the one who has been compensated (*man jabart*), not the one who is oppressed (*ajbart*). In sources pertaining to the ḥadīth and its commentaries, the reference is to the second meaning of oppressed (*majbūr* as *makrūh*).[59] The explanation of the ḥadīth is a reference to people's intentions (*niyyāt*), hence the relating of people's diverse character types and typologies. In keeping with the above explanation, it can be inferred that the use of *majbūr*, as per ḥadīth commentaries, is an antonym for *mustabṣir*. Similarly, in the world of jurisprudence if the term and the act of *taqlīd* is accepted as conceptually in an antonymic relationship to *baṣar*, *taqlīd* is also a form of intellectual oppression toward others and the self in certain cases. As George Makdisi maintains, the layman's right to practice *taqlīd* was commendatory when applied to them. *Taqlīd* "was, on the other hand, a term of disapprobation when applied to the mufti, the jurisconsult. A mufti had no right to 'clothe with authority' the opinion of another mufti. Therefore, in his [jurisprudent] case, *taqlīd* was considered 'servile imitation.'"[60] A servile mufti, Makdisi argues, has relinquished his authority because he is violating his mission that would lead to a practice of consensus, and eventually he will lose his reputation and no longer be considered an authority. The mufti's authority rests on his personal original research, "an activity called technically *ijtihād* (literally: the unsparing exertion of one's effort, the doing of one's utmost)."[61] The servile imitation here can be considered a form of intellectual servility due to voluntary will or by intellectual oppression; *ijtihād*, conversely, while attesting to personal innovation, is an activity that requires will and resolve.

This is very helpful in explaining Ibn al-Muqaffaʿ's astute use of will and resolve (*ʿazm*) as prerequisites to the application of *baṣar* as critique. In charting out a genealogy of the term *baṣar*, it becomes clear that Ibn al-Muqaffaʿ considers the valance and meanings of the language as understood by his readers. It is not surprising that Ibn al-Muqaffaʿ should define adab as such. His conception of adab is an institution that offers a sustainable relationship with the intellectual tools of adab but also its grammar: critique and an environment for the production of knowledge through discourse. Discourse as both an intellectual tool of adab but also a social one; it encourages and supports the act of intellectual affluence, of reading more, seeing more, and hearing more from oneself and others. In other words, Ibn al-Muqaffaʿ's use of *naẓar* and *baṣar* involves a certain awareness that discourse only arises when individuals have "more" to say. That is, if all people were reading the same text and saw and read the same way—i.e., one thing—why should there be discourse if all are in agreement? Why should people living in the same country engage in discourse if they can all see the same thing? The elimination of "more" is precisely the elimination of the potentiality for discourse. Controlling ways and access of seeing to eliminate the "more" for the people is about eliminating both the ontology and the ability of seeing "more" as a concept or an idea. People under this interpretive understanding regime of seeing are normally referred to as "oppressed," the *majbūr*. But that oppression is not only from outside; it is also a way of seeing and conditioning. The antonym is not just about those who are free but, as the aforementioned anecdote maintains, it is those who can "see more" and thus be critical and insightful (*mustabṣir*) and engage in discourse versus those who are oppressed by their own intellect and insight.

ADAB AND DISCOURSE

With these philological insights into *baṣar*, I would like to discuss the terms also used by Ibn al-Muqaffaʿ here; "critical reflection" (*baṣar*) and its relationship with the exemplifying parable he uses to illustrate his point, as it becomes clear that he links this willful *baṣar* to reading and adab. This emphasis on *ʿazm* is enlightening as it highlights Ibn al-Muqaffaʿ's indirect emphasis on intellectual courage and independence. This emphasis on intellectual independence is stressed later in the twelfth century by al-Ghazālī and Ibn Ṭufayl (see chapter 3). Ibn al-Muqaffaʿ then immediately follows this section, by way of explanation, with one that begins with the sentence "Adab cultivates the mind" (*al-adab yunammī al-ʿuqūl*).

الأدب ينمي العقول

وللعقول سجيات وغرائز، بها تقبل الأدب، وبالأدب تسمى العقول وتزكو
فكما أن الحبة المدفونة في الأرض لا تقدر أن تخلع يبسها، وتظهر قوتها، وتطلع فوق الأرض بزعوتها وزيعها، ونضرتها ونمائها، إلا بمعونة الماء الذي يغور إليها في مستودعها، فيذهب عنها أذى اليبس والموت، ويحدث لها بإذن الله القوة والحياة، فكذلك سليقة العقل مكنونة في مغرزها من القلب: لا قوة لها، ولا حياة بها، ولا منفعة عندها، حتى يعتملها الأدب، الذي هو ثمارها، وحياتها، ولقاحها.

Adab cultivates the mind.

For the mind has its dispositions and characteristics with which it receives adab, and with adab *the mind is improved and enhanced.*

> Just like a seed buried in the earth cannot shed its dryness, reveal its strength, and emerge above the ground with its vegetation and distribution, its brilliance and growth, without water that penetrates deep into its recesses to save it from detrimental aridness and death, and bring about for it, by God's permission, power and life; so too the nature of the mind (reason) is concealed in its roots from the heart—powerless, lifeless, and useless until it is polished by adab, *which is its fruit, life, and fertilizer.*[62]

Ibn al-Muqaffaʿ creates a link to this universal aim that unites all peoples with adab: a pursuit not necessarily shared by *all* people, thereby legitimizing adab not only in itself for its intrinsic qualities but for the universal aforementioned aims of having a sound mind to enable a good life. He then uses an allegorical image to explain his analogy to the conception and function of adab. Ibn al-Muqaffaʿ's image utilizes the vocabulary and image of fecundity and productiveness. Interestingly, this allusion is juxtaposed against the aforementioned image of chronic illness and the vocabulary of privation that cloaked his description of the absence of a sound mind, critique, and resolve. Ibn al-Muqaffaʿ here sees adab as both the fruit of the mind and its water. It is a two-way relationship, or better yet an auto-relationship. The works of adab cannot be generated without adab itself. This idea is expressed in his *al-Adab al-kabīr* (The Major Adab). He begins by saying that our ancestors and predecessors had bigger bodies. They were anatomically larger and they were more intelligent to the extent that they would be in a secluded, arid area and leave all their knowledge on rocks, preempting death and hating that it would escape those who come after them. Ibn al-Muqaffaʿ sees this gesture as "parental," as if a parent in all their love and compassion tries to secure their children's future and ensure they lack nothing.[63] Ibn al-Muqaffaʿ is similarly telling us that our litterateur parents have almost left us nothing new to say, echoing an earlier pre-Islamic warrior-poet, ʿAntarah b. Shaddād (525 AH–608 CE), in his *muʿallaqa* (hanging ode), who questioned if there was anything left to say or a meaning yet unexhausted by poets: "Did poetry die in its war with the poets?" (*hal ghādara al-shuʿarāʾu min mutaraddamin*).[64]

Equally interesting is Ibn al-Muqaffaʿ's choice of a parable (*mathal*) to highlight his conception of adab as "the food of the mind" in the allegory of the seed and its fecund growth. Ibn al-Muqaffaʿ continues that the allegory/parable is logically clearer (*al-mathal awḍaḥ li-l-manṭiq*). He maintains that if speech (*kalām*) were made in the form of *mathal*, it would be logically clearer (*awḍaḥ li-l-manṭiq*), more lucid in meaning (*abyan fī al-maʿnā*), and wider in the scope of discourse (*awsaʿ li-shuʿūb al-ḥadīth*).[65] *Shuʿūb al-ḥadīth*, as Ibn al-Muqaffaʿ elaborates further, refers to the different types of discourse and its diverse nature (*mutafarriquhu wa-mutanawwiʿuhu*).

When Ibn Sīnā was explaining how mimesis (*muḥākāh*) works he held that it is dependent on *amthāl* (allegories) and *qiṣaṣ* (stories) and that it is *not* poetry. The only example of *mathal* as prose he gave was *Kalīla wa-Dimna*.[66] Ibn Sīnā considers the function of books like *Kalīla wa-Dimna* as *ifādat al-ārāʾ*.[67] He defines the very term *ifādat al-raʾy* (pl. *al-ārāʾ*) in this context as conclusions (*natāʾij*) and experiences (*tajārib*) applied to nonexistent things or hypothetical situations (*tunsab ilā umūr laysa lahā wujūd*).[68] This he explains as the purpose (*gharaḍ*) of *mathal* and defines as outcomes from nonexistent situations.[69] Matthew L. Keegan reads this as "conveying pieces of advice" within the "poetics of virtual experience."[70] While it is indeed a purpose and a result of *Kalīla wa-Dimna*, naturally categorized under the *speculum principis* genre, or the mirror for (the Muslim) prince(s) genre and similar works, as Ibn Sīnā avers that a benefit of these *amthāl* is counsel (*al-mashūra*), I understand Ibn Sīnā's *ifādat al-ārāʾ* expansively in this context as the discourse the *mathal* generates by virtue of its diverse opinion-inviting nature. To illustrate this further, Ibn Sīnā defines *raʾy* elsewhere as the reasoned opinion or judgment that could either be effective or rejected/avoided, depending on the persuasive power of said cause (*ʿilla*) in said opinion/judgment:

> وأما الرأي فإنه قضية كلية، لا جزئية، وهى في أمور عملية، ومن جهة ما يؤثر أو يجتنب. والتفكير الرأيي قريب من المستنتجة التامة. ونتائج الآراء، إذا أخذت بانفرادها، هي أيضا آراء، كما أن مقدماتها آراء، لكنها إنما تكون تفكيرا إقناعيا، إذا قرنت بها العلة، مثل قولنا: إن معرفة الأحداث بالحكمة فضول. فهو رأى، ونتيجة رأى. وهو أنهم حينئذ يكونون مدخرين ما لا ينتفعون به. لكنه إذا أخذ الرأي الذي هو نتيجة وحده، لم ينتفع به، لأنه لا ينفع، إذ ليس مقبولا بنفسه، إذ القبول يناله بعد قبول مقدمة، هي علة

> As for the opinion/judgment, it is a universal proposition, not partial, and it is in practical issues, where it could be effective or rejected. Deliberative thinking is close to deductive reasoning and the results of the opinions/judgments if taken on their own. These, too, are opinions/judgments, in the same manner that their premises are opinions/judgments. But they are persuasive thinking if they are considered with their cause, such as when we say: "knowing events through wisdom is superfluous." This is an opinion/judgment and a result of the opinion/judgment. And it is then they are saving what they are not benefiting from. But if one takes the hypothesis that is a conclusion on its own, he will not benefit from it, because it is not beneficial, for it is not acceptable on its own. Acceptance is granted after accepting a premise that serves as its cause.[71]

Ibn Sīnā defines *raʾy* and uses it as a qualifier of a mode of thinking (*al-tafkīr al-raʾyī*), which can be translated as "deliberative thinking," thereby rendering *raʾy* itself as "reasoned or considered opinion."[72] *Raʾy*, as a term, could also mean "judgment," "theorem," "concept."[73] As per Ibn Sīnā's explanation, not every judgment can be considered valid; an opinion is reasonable after accepting its proposition(s). This explains his statement on opinions, and therefore discourse, that can be transformative and effective (*mā yuʾaththir*) or avoided and rejected (*yujtanab*). Similar to Ibn al-Muqaffaʿ's intimation of the discourse-inviting *mathal* where deliberation happens over possible meanings, Ibn Sīnā's *raʾy* as reasoned opinion explains the workings of *shuʿūb al-ḥadīth* to us. In a deliberation over meaning, if someone avers that the meaning of a certain story in *Kalīla wa-Dimna* is such and such, this is reasoned thinking as a premise of an opinion and a result. According to the above, neither Ibn Sīnā nor Ibn al-Muqaffaʿ would accept the manner of this result without the premises leading to this opinion, which may or may not be convincing and therefore can be modified by others and built on (effective/*mā yuʾaththir*), or rejected for lack of persuasive power, hence inviting the *shuʿūb al-ḥadīth* and expanding it. The *mathal*'s interpretation is therefore always inviting and hospitable in itself; this is what Ibn al-Muqaffaʿ proposes as *shuʿūb al-ḥadīth*. In the terminology of Ibn Sīnā therefore the understanding of *ifādat al-ārāʾ* extends beyond the immediate experience of the reader and considers the implications as not only pertaining to the literary and the imagination but also the social. The private reading experience of the reader and their "virtual experience" is one outcome where as a reader they accept/reject premises of an opinion critically, adabfully. But *ifādat al-ārāʾ* also applies to the public sphere and social practice of contributing reasoned opinions; a practice that in itself is socially and intellectually edifying.

This understanding of *raʾy*'s role in reading and critique explains Ibn al-Muqaffaʿ's legitimization of adab as the food of the mind, relating adab to the critical and social skills of making a good living in life and the spiritual fruits of life's activities in the here and hereafter. Ibn al-Muqaffaʿ links adab to reason and reasoning, critical thinking and critique, discourse, and resolve, regarding these as mediators of a successful and fruitful life beyond the literary. He describes the absence of adab in the rhetoric of illness and privation. The metaphor extends to social failure since it explains that a mind (*salīqat al-ʿaql*) without the "process of adabization" (*ḥattā yaʿtamilahā al-adab*) is incapable of contributing in any meaningful way (*lā quwwa lahā, wa-lā ḥayāt bihā, wa-lā manfaʿa ʿindahā*).[74] This is because the individual lacks both the social and intellectual skills, tools, and power. In this respect, the individual would not be able to either cultivate or achieve *suʾdud* (empowerment and influence) by way of adab and would be regarded as lacking murūʾa, hence lacking social and intellectual success for Ibn al-Muqaffaʿ. His preference for figurative language, the *mathal*, as logically clearer and more lucid in meaning, is adduced by his theorization of adab as enhancing to the mind. This would cultivate adab, hence *suʾdud* and murūʾa. Figurative, rich language that is deceptively simple works on two levels. On the one hand, it forces the reader to think about the language itself and its connection to the meanings at hand; the relationship between *lafẓ* (utterance) and *maʿnā* (meaning) beyond the literal. On the other hand, the nature of this multivalent language invites multiple meanings (*taʿaddud al-maʿānī*) and hence discourse through plausible reasoned opinions that must be logically defended as Ibn Sīnā maintains, which Ibn al-Muqaffaʿ identifies in his defense of *mathal* as "wider in the scope of discourse." Ibn al-Muqaffaʿ's theorization and defense of adab and *mathal* as inducive of and conducive to discourse proposes to us that both understanding and interpretation are a process that is always in progress; it is unfinished. In other words, it wards against the hubris of certainty that comes with a false sense of intellectual closure and the belief of the possibility of acquisition of *all* knowledge. The latter intellectual posture can only birth intellectual dogmatism and hegemony of absolute meanings, bordering on the mathematical, which naturally begets prejudice and intolerance to any truth claim, which comes with the closure of interpretation, hence possible meanings. It is important to also regard what Ibn al-Muqaffaʿ calls *shuʿūb al-ḥadīth* as not only the discussion of a topic but also the creation of and the possibility of creating novel topics and ideas. The forking of different conceptual paths (*shuʿūb*) in no way restricts this definition to a discourse about a designated topic. Rather, it is an invitation to pursue topics that are also born out of this discourse through an adab sphere and hence become a force of a generative and creative power as opposed to the sterility and bareness of closure.

The articulated conditions of possibility of understanding and this adab sphere therefore rest on adab; adab is a condition of possibility. The defense of *mathal* reverts full circle to Ibn al-Muqaffaʿ's parable of the seed enjoying a fecund growth as it takes in water in the form of adab and gives back fruits in the form of adab. Ibn al-Muqaffaʿ's example is reminiscent of the image of the "word as a tree" in Q.14:24–25 in Abdel Haleem's translation: "[Prophet], do you not see how God makes comparisons (*mathalan*)? A good (*ṭayyiba*) word is like a good tree whose root is firm and whose branches are high in the sky, yielding constant fruit by its Lord's leave—God makes such comparisons for people so that they may reflect—but an evil (*khabītha*) word is like a rotten tree, uprooted from the surface of the earth, with no power to endure." The tree, al Rāzī explains, has four qualities. The first is being good, which could mean aesthetically and visually, olfactorily or gustatorily good, or simply good because it is beneficial and useful in some way. The second quality of this tree is its firm root (*aṣluhā thābit*), which presupposes its longevity. Then the third quality is the tree's tall branches reaching the sky (*farʿuhā fī al-samāʾ*). Finally, the last quality of the tree is its perpetual state of fruitfulness: its fruits are ripe at all times (*tuʾtī ukulahā kulla ḥīnin*).[75] Next, al-Rāzī tells us that this fruit is knowledge (of the divine). Like knowledge, there is pleasure in its acquisition and dissemination; conversely, the evil tree, according to al-Rāzī, is ignorance (of the divine).[76]

MATHAL AND GREEK/WESTERN PHILOSOPHY

It might be tempting to question Ibn al-Muqaffaʿ's linking of adab, especially in his defense of the use of *mathal*, to wisdom and reason in light of Greek influences at the time, all the more since he was close to the translation movement. However, as the disciplines of classics, philosophy, and literature tell us, Plato was against the idea that poetry teaches wisdom, let alone imparts reason. Plato's famous attack on poetry in the *Republic* was against its performative nature as well as its ethical doctrines. The initial scenes from the *Republic* 1–2 show us clearly the unreliability of poets as possible or reliable sources of wisdom or knowledge. He believed that poetry, as a mimetic practice, has almost a material and physical effect on the body, and therefore it has the power to effect a change in the body and soul, especially among the youth, which was his concern. In this respect, "Plato is so relentless—and so literal-minded—in censoring them."[77] Not only that but allegoresis was categorically denied as a method because it was considered dangerous. The poets' license to "riddle" was not tolerated by Plato. In the *Republic*, a poet's license to use another word for a literal one was regarded as simplistic, according to Socrates. The latter argues that the poet should have used the "intended" word without "riddling" (*Republic* 322b–c).[78] In the *Phaedrus*, Socrates "faults allegoresis because it does not result in certain interpretations" (229e–230a); "Plato's Socrates argues on several occasions that no form of poetic exegesis can get around the fact that the text of old poets can be construed in various ways and, unless one has the poets at hand to cross-question, one cannot be certain that the meaning construed from a text is what the poet 'meant.'"[79] These discussions and attitudes toward allegoresis are contradictory when juxtaposed with Plato's own use of the allegory of the cave in the *Republic* (514a–b), and similarly, to Socrates of the *Phaedrus*, who uses allegoresis "to reinterpret a story about divine impropriety but in the end turns away from the method for a different, social reason."[80] But perhaps the use is not so contradictory if we were to view it in light of what Plato and Socrates "meant" by the "intended" or "certain interpretations," as the canonical meaning of their own allegories might attest, especially when viewed in light of the Socratic method in Socrates's dialogues with his students as a guided conversation toward an "intended true meaning" or a "certain meaning"—since Socrates declares that he "consider[s] such things [allegoresis] elegant and amusing (*kharienta*), but an occupation suited for someone who is formidably clever (*deinos*) and painstaking (*epiponos*) and not altogether enviable" (*Phaedrus* 229d).[81]

However, an important point of entry of the metaphor and imagery into philosophy comes through the Egyptian-born Roman philosopher Plotinus (ca. 204–70 CE), who is widely considered the founder of Neoplatonism as it developed and grew in Alexandria. Plotinus blended Platonism as well as concepts from Judeo-Christianity emphasizing that all existence emanates from one source and the possibility that individuals can unite with this source. In developing his philosophy, he fashioned myths, metaphors, and images that have been influential to philosophers and theologians in various religious traditions.[82] Although Neoplatonism's presence in the Islamic tradition has been thoroughly treated in excellent scholarship, it is helpful to consider that that "which we might call 'Neoplatonism' has been rethought and reconfigured so often, in fact, that concepts from it have become" what Cyrus Ali Zargar calls "a thoroughly integrated 'Islamic' way of thinking about the cosmos, the soul, and existence—one sometimes only faintly resembling the Plotinus strain in its DNA, especially when that strain is found in Sufism."[83] The embracing of the metaphor and figurative in Neoplatonic thought may be owed to Plotinus's borrowing of concepts and images from Judeo-Christianity where the ineffability of the One and the limitations of human language necessitate the use of figurative language. Naturally, the literary community discusses allegoresis today as an essential part of a conversation on layered meanings and extended metaphors in texts, but allegoresis as such, as Andrew Ford maintains, "did not enter the *Poetics* [of Aristotle]," the seminal and earliest treatise on literary theory.[84] The dominant and foundational voices from Greek antiquity (Socrates, Plato, and Aristotle) that were against allegoresis and figurative language altogether were not the only ones in the intellectual and/or literary history of Western literary criticism and thought; this intellectual position makes a strong comeback in the seventeenth century in *An Essay Concerning Human Understanding* (1690) by British empiricist John Locke (1632–1704), heralding the ideational theory of meaning (see chapter 3). Recent scholarship, such as Thomas Bauer's *Die Kultur der Ambiguität* (translated from German as *A Culture of Ambiguity*, 2021), has also critiqued Western modernity for its low tolerance of what Bauer calls "ambiguity," which he sees as characteristic of premodern Islam's understanding and acceptance of different perspectives. Bauer faults colonization's erasure of the epistemic frameworks that birthed this culture of "ambiguity" in classical Islam and introduced, in the name of modernity, a "fear of ambiguity and obsession with truth" that Bauer sees as symptomatic of what he describes as some reformist thought and Salafist groups.[85] Bauer's diagnosis in itself is hardly refutable. However, this book does not understand premodern Islam in terms of "ambiguity" as such, nor do I see that the complexity and sophistication of classical Islam owes itself to a nonchalant attitude to what modernity identifies as "Lockian archetypes as truths." Rather, this book advances an understanding that is more attentive to the cultural grammar of the formation of the subject, to which adab as praxis and application is an attestation. The adabized subject's acceptance of multiple perspectives betokens a more intricate intellectual and social lived experience that is supported by intellectual institutions (adab as example) than a Weberian "ideal type" (*Idealtypus*) of "ambiguity" as a defining feature of the social and cultural phenomenon of tolerance and accepting multiple perspectives.[86] The virtue-ethic murūʾa, or the ideal human, demonstrating its immanent structure in premodern Arabic culture, and the formation of the subject, regarded adab as a literary, analytical, and cultural force owing to its participatory role in knowledge systems. The embracing of multiple discourses and the ability to accept and entertain other perspectives can also be regarded within the framework of an ethos of collective knowledge construction and production. Islam's keen fascination with knowledge and learning may have regarded all its epistemic others, even adversaries, as potential contributors to personal but also collective human effort in universal knowledge conceivably owing to the ethos of Q.49:13; even if the epistemic other is not an active contributor through scholarship and intellectual life, passive contribution through epistemic otherness is still a contribution through the recognition of the human in the other.[87]

A TRADITION OF READING

To presuppose that there is a tradition of reading means that reading is more than an act or an activity whether done privately or publicly or in a group. Rather, it is bound by a tradition. Tradition, Talal Asad maintains, "consists of discourses that seek to instruct practitioners regarding the correct form and purpose of a given practice that, precisely because it is established, has a history. These discourses relate conceptually to *a past* (when the practice was instituted, and from which the knowledge of its point and proper performance has been transmitted) and *a future* (how the point of that practice can best be secured in the short or long term, or why it should be modified or abandoned), through *a present* (how it is linked to other practices, institutions, and social conditions)."[88] In this respect, a tradition, according to Asad, is "discursive." It is very much alive as it evolves while it negotiates with and interrogates the past, present, and future. A tradition's engagement with the past is not an imitation; rather, it is a conception of what the practitioners perceive, in Asad's term, as an *apt performance*.[89] In other words, what constitutes an appropriate and correct performance of the practice; "[a] discursive tradition does not interpret its foundational texts in a literalist way, nor is it characterized by blind imitation of predecessors without any consideration of temporality and change."[90]

The (Arabic-)Islamic reading tradition, then, is singular in the way it is built around an interactive text: the Qur'an. The figurative language that comprises most of the Qur'an demands engaged and close readers. It may seem surprising to us now that the allegorical language of the Qur'an left it open to criticism during the time of the Prophet. The critics, in fact, satirized the Qur'an, saying that "the God of Muḥammad is using flies and mosquitos to draw parables."[91] Peripatetic al-Zamakhsharī (d. 538 AH/1144 CE), who traveled across the Islamicate (born in Khwarazm and studied in Bukhara and Samarkand before arriving in Baghdad), calls these critics "ignorant and weak-minded" (*jahala wa-sufahā'*).[92] Al-Zamakhsharī tells us this in the context of explaining the term *amthāl* (sing. *mathal*) as allegory in Q.29:43.

وتِلْكَ الأمْثالُ نَضْرِبُها لِلنّاسِ وما يَعْقِلُها إلاَّ العالِمُونَ

Such are the comparisons We draw for people, though only the wise can grasp them.

Al-Zamakhsharī explains the second half of the verse, "though only the wise can grasp them [metaphors, allegories, examples, similitudes]," as follows:

أَيْ لَا يعقل صِحَّتُهَا وَحُسْنُهَا وَفَائِدَتُهَا إِلَّا هُمْ، لِأَنَّ الْأَمْثَالَ وَالتَّشْبِيهَاتِ إِنَّمَا هِيَ الطُّرُقُ إِلَى الْمَعَانِي الْمُحْتَجَبَةِ فِي الْأَسْتَارِ حَتَّى تَبْرُزَهَا
وَتَكْشِفَ عَنْهَا وَتَصَوِّرَهَا لِلْأَفْهَامِ

> That is, none can comprehend their correctness, beauty, and benefit except them, because examples and similes are only paths to meanings hidden behind veils until they are brought out, revealed, and depicted for the minds.

Al-Zamakhsharī posits that this type of language using *amthāl* would require a certain reception from the audience/reader to ascertain their correctness (*ṣiḥḥatuhā*), beauty (*ḥusnuhā*), and benefit (*fāʾidatuhā*). He argues that allegories and figurative language are the way to hidden meanings, which can then be unveiled to the intellect.[93] It is interesting to note here that the critics' point of entry to satirize and mock the language of the Qur'an operated from an anti-literary vantage point. I say anti-literary and not nonliterary because the community around the Prophet Muḥammad was indeed one with a high and developed literary sensibility and a recognized competence for poetry. This is indisputable. Their anti-literary reception of the nature of the *mathal* therefore is one that rejected to read the imagery of the language and instead opted for a linear reading that only saw the perceived irrelevance of "flies" and "mosquitoes." This related reception of the *mathal* focused on the literal rather than conceptual power of the metaphor for a more complex intellectual engagement. The linear reading focused on the sizes and nature of insects, which they saw as incommensurate with their perceived conception of the divine. In this respect, their reception is anti-literary because it was conscious of the literary nature of the parable as a device and yet it read the parable literally. An earlier exegete, Baghdad-based al-Ṭabarī (d. 310 AH/923 CE), explains the *mathal* in the same context of Q.29:43 as *al-ashbāh wa-l-naẓāʾir*, which indicates that al-Ṭabarī was thinking in terms of similitudes and resemblances. He does not explain the term, which is an established one in Qur'anic studies and therefore accessible to the adabized reader, but he gives a clarifying example from the poetry of al-Aʿshā for his reader.[94] In a similar vein, the Nīsāpūrian al-Thaʿlabī (d. 430 AH/1038 CE) defines the *mathal* as *al-ashbāh wa-l-awṣāf* in the manner of an idiomatic phrase (*qawl sāʾir*) that likens the second to the first.[95]

In his *tafsīr*, one might expect the powerhouse of rhetoric ʿAbd al-Qāhir al-Jurjānī (d. 471 AH/1078 CE) to deploy all the rhetorical calisthenics he showcased in his seminal works on *balāgha*, but he seemed reticent to offer so much as an interpretation or anything beyond the obvious word meanings, synonyms, and historical contexts. In the *mathal* of light in Q.24:35 ("God is the Light of the heavens and earth"), for example, he distinctly says that God's description using the light is of the *mutashābihāt* (allegorical verses) and should not be interpreted (*taʾwīlahā*) after recognizing and believing that God is above being similar (*mujānasa*) to the sun or the moon.[96] This is understandable given that the *mathal* refers to the nature of divine light. Al-Jurjānī does the same thing in all the verses that use figurative language, such as in Q.22:73:

> يَا أَيُّهَا النَّاسُ ضُرِبَ مَثَلٌ فَاسْتَمِعُوا لَهُ ۚ إِنَّ الَّذِينَ تَدْعُونَ مِن دُونِ اللَّهِ لَن يَخْلُقُوا ذُبَابًا وَلَوِ اجْتَمَعُوا لَهُ ۖ وَإِن يَسْلُبْهُمُ الذُّبَابُ شَيْئًا لَّا
> يَسْتَنقِذُوهُ مِنْهُ ۚ ضَعُفَ الطَّالِبُ وَالْمَطْلُوبُ

> You people, here is an illustration, so listen carefully: those you call on beside God could not, even if they combined all their forces, create a fly, and if a fly took something away from them, they would not be able to retrieve it. How feeble are the petitioners and how feeble are those they petition!

He does not offer any explanation but instead says that the verse is from the *mutashābihāt* and therefore one must derive its *ḥukm* from the *muḥkamāt* (*mutashābiha fa-wajaba iltimās ḥukmihā min al-muḥkamāt*).[97] Al-Jurjānī differentiates between clear and decisive verses that are obvious in meaning, and he does not use figurative language as opposed to the metaphorical and allegorical verses that require a literary interpretation. The Qur'an speaks of these differences in Q.3:7: "It is He who has sent this Scripture down to you [Prophet]. Some of its verses are definite in meaning (*muḥkam*)—these are the cornerstone of the Scripture—and others are ambiguous (*mutashābih*). The perverse at heart eagerly pursue the ambiguities in their attempt to make trouble and to pin down a specific meaning of their own: only God knows the true meaning. Those firmly grounded in knowledge say, 'We believe in it: it is all from our Lord'—only those with real perception will take heed."

As the verse maintains, the Qur'an then does not prevent readers from offering interpretations on the allegorical parts. However, it cautions against abusing the allegorical nature to offer misleading interpretations and ultimately says no one knows its interpretation except God. Al-Jurjānī refrained from offering any interpretation for the allegorical verses in his *tafsīr*. When compared with the way he used the Qur'an in his other works, it seems that he opted not to offer an interpretation of the allegorical verses, unlike his other works of *balāgha*. A similar position on this is noticeable in al-Suyūṭī (d. 911 AH/1505 CE), in Egypt, who refrained from defining *mathal*, relying instead on the reader's understanding as he jumps to say "those in the Qur'an," that is, parables in the Qur'an.[98] Al-Suyūṭī even explains the verse of light ("God is the Light of the heavens and earth") as "He is illuminating them with the sun and moon" (*munawwiruhumā bi-l-shams wa-l-qamar*).[99] It is not possible to ascertain as to why both al-Jurjānī and al-Suyūṭī, well-known litterateurs, refrained from offering a literary reading of allegorical verses. That they could not read the allegorical or proffer an interpretation is untenable. Equally implausible would be that they were not aware of previous exegetes' efforts in offering explanations and readings for these allegorical verses, which are by far superior to theirs in these instances.

Damascene historian and exegete Ibn Kathīr (d. 774 AH/1373 CE) offers a particularly interesting anecdote related to Q.29:43. He relates ʿAlī b. al-Ḥusayn as saying that reading a verse that he does not understand makes him sad because of the Qur'an's statement that only those with knowledge understand the *amthāl* of the Qur'an. The belief that these *amthāl* require additional effort and ultimately an engagement with one's intellectual others in person or through texts as interlocutors to be able to understand them is not lost on premodern scholars and adabized readers.

حَدَّثَنا عَلِيُّ بْنُ الحُسَيْنِ، حَدَّثَنا أحْمَدُ بْنُ عَبْدِ الرَّحْمَنِ، حَدَّثَنا أبِي، حَدَّثَنا ابْنُ سِنانٍ، عَنْ عَمْرِو بْنِ مُرَّةَ قالَ: ما مَرَرْتُ بِآيَةٍ مِن كِتابِ اللَّهِ لا أعْرِفُها إلّا أحْزَنَنِي، لِأنِّي سَمِعْتُ اللَّهَ تَعالى يَقُولُ: ﴿وتِلْكَ الأمْثالُ نَضْرِبُها لِلنّاسِ وما يَعْقِلُها إلا العالِمُونَ﴾

ʿAlī b. al-Ḥusayn narrated to us, [from] Aḥmad b. ʿAbd al-Raḥmān, who narrated to us, [from] my father, who narrated to us, [from] Ibn Sinān who narrated to us, on the authority of ʿAmr b. Murra, who said: "I never encountered a verse from the Book of God that I did not know except that it made me sad, because I heard [through the Qur'an] God the Most High say: 'Such are the comparisons We draw for people, though only the wise can grasp them.'"[100]

Polymath and scientist Niẓām al-Dīn al-Nīsāpūrī (d. 850 AH/1446 CE) offers a sophisticated approach and exegesis with regard to Q.24:43 as he engages other scholarship. He relates multiple interpretations, from the usual recounting of previous scholarship and reasoned opinions beginning with Ibn ʿAbbās's reading, to several others including a reference to al-Ghazālī's (d. 505 AH/1111 CE) work on the allegory of light in his *Mishkāt al-anwār* (The Niche of Lights). Of interest to us here is al-Nīsāpūrī's nuanced discussion of the layers of light in the parable and his problematizing of sensory and empirical perception versus discursive perception. He compares sight with insight, stating that the latter is more powerful than the former.

وَلَا شَكَّ أَنَّ الْبَصِيرَةَ أَقْوَى مِنَ الْبَصَرِ لِأَنَّ الْقُوَّةَ الْبَاصِرَةَ لَا تُدْرِكُ نَفْسَهَا وَلَا تُدْرِكُ إِدْرَاكَهَا وَلَا تُدْرِكُ آلَتَهَا وَهِيَ الْعَيْنُ، وَأَمَّا الْقُوَّةُ الْعَاقِلَةُ فَإِنَّهَا تُدْرِكُ نَفْسَهَا وَتُدْرِكُ إِدْرَاكَهَا وَتُدْرِكُ آلَتَهَا فِي الْإِدْرَاكِ وَهِيَ الْقَلْبُ أَوِ الدِّمَاغُ، وَالْإِدْرَاكُ الْحَسِّيُّ غَيْرُ مُنْتِجٍ لِأَنَّهُ لَا يَصِيرُ سَبَبًا لِإِحْسَاسٍ آخَرَ، وَالْإِدْرَاكُ الْعَقْلِيُّ يَصِيرُ سَبَبًا لِإِدْرَاكَاتٍ أُخَرَ حَتَّى تَجْتَمِعَ عُلُومٌ جَمَّةٌ

There is no doubt that insight is stronger than sight, because the visual faculty does not perceive itself, nor does it perceive its perception, nor does it perceive its instrument, which is the eye. As for the rational faculty, it perceives itself, perceives its perception, and perceives its instrument in perception, which is the heart or the mind/brain. Sensory perception is not productive because it does not become a cause for another sensation, and rational perception becomes a cause for other perceptions until many sciences come together.[101]

This is because, al-Nīsāpūrī maintains, sight (*baṣar*) is unaware of itself, its cognizing of its function, and its instrument (the eyes), whereas insight (*baṣīra*), which he calls a "rational faculty" (*al-quwwa al- ʿāqila*), is aware of itself and the active nature of its own thinking/reflection (*tudrik idrākahā*) and its instrument in this cognizance (*ālat idrākihā*), which is the heart or the mind/brain (*al-qalb aw al-dimāgh*). Al-Nīsāpūrī therefore highlights the vocabulary of experience and the shortcomings of empiricism not because it relies on the material and sensory experience but because he sees it as less generative, or unproductive. He observes that it cannot cause another sensory experience; it cannot reproduce itself. Al-Nīsāpūrī contends that empirical perception does not produce anything outside itself; it is a closed circuit. It is also uncritical since it is not generative. Alternatively, he sees insight as the rational force that is more generative since it produces more insights. In this respect, he is closer to al-Ghazālī's idea of the "intuition" (*ḥads*), which is similarly generative.[102] Al-Ghazālī highlights the importance of the purity of the self (*nafs*) and heart (*qalb*) as faculties that can receive divine insights or intuitive understanding. The idea is explored in Ibn Ṭufayl's *Ḥayy b. Yaqẓān* (see chapter 3).

Mathal by default privileges the realm of insight and flashes of intuition in its discourse-generating nature. In this respect, situating Ibn al-Muqaffaʿ's privileging of *mathal* as an aesthetic site of generating hospitable discourse and his defense of it, as understood from his choice to translate *Kalīla wa-Dimna* and his legitimization of adab in light of an Arabic-Islamic tradition of reading, should be rewarding. Ibn al-Muqaffaʿ's privileging of *mathal* could be understood in light of this working framework of adab that he gave us. This mechanism of the give and take of the same element, of adab as water penetrating the seeds, and simultaneously the fruit of the seed itself, as the parable of the seed shows, is the *act of discourse* itself, which yields the growth Ibn al-Muqaffaʿ speaks about. However, this *act* requires a certain type of reader: the adabized reader is the one who employs critical reflection (*baṣar*) and performs critique with courage and resolve/will (*ʿazm*). The adabized reader is therefore engaged courageously and shows resoluteness (*ʿazm*) with a will to read and then critique independently without crippling or self-imposed intellectual dependency, or overbearing guidance and authority—sometimes in the form of guided prefaces. In this respect, adab becomes discourse that is not only performed by adabized readers—it also simultaneously fashions these readers. In the realm of adab as text, the textual consequences are innovation and literary excellence. However, Ibn al-Muqaffaʿ did not separate adab from the social context. The engagement in this discourse by the adabized reader creates what I have discussed as the sphere of adab as praxis. This sphere bridges the textual and social realms, where the grammar of adab is applied beyond written texts, transforming them into tools for self-cultivation but also as technologies of the self.

This social success that Ibn al-Muqaffaʿ speaks of extends beyond making a good life. It also involves the intellectual circulation of texts that simultaneously compete with each other through critique, such as the aforementioned example of al-Yamanī and many others who are beyond the scope of this chapter. These adabizing technologies of the self allowed the social accommodation of counter-discourse, such as in the case of al-Yamanī, within the realm of adab. It therefore established itself as critique through adab and thus a form of social praxis that is focused on social *poiēsis*: the maintaining and making of harmony through adab even in disagreement. It is the generative act of making and creating "something" through an adabized means; the choice to critique, in a literary form, other works (for their artistic, political merits or shortcoming) is one that shows by example the *praxis* of both agreement and disagreement.

The generative force of adab at large, and *mathal* in particular, invites participatory reading. Reading then becomes a praxis that partakes in the textual and the social as it encourages and generates different readings through active learning by oneself, or with others, or against them but yet engaging with or against them within the frame of murū'a and adab. While engaged in this discourse readers are simultaneously competing for different human truths in these literary engagements and ultimately for literary power but also literary richness. Much like the image of the tree in the Qur'an that keeps growing out of a single word, the multiple growths are incremental and collective knowledge that are built on top of each other with and against others.

Adab as a framework, as a mode of reading, allows us to understand the intricacies of this intellectual and social institution beyond clichés. It opens a horizon where our theorization of the grammar of adab reveals these conceptual networks between the theoretical and the practical and how certain practices can allow individuals to develop technologies of the self and effect transformations on themselves and by extension on the ecology of knowledge production within this adabized and adabizing sphere.

3

Adab as Discourse

Text(s) as Interlocutor(s)

ADAB AS INTERLOCUTOR(S) AND THE ADAB SPHERE

It may appear from chapter 2 that discourse, as Ibn al-Muqaffaʿ's *shuʿūb al-ḥadīth* through reasoned opinion as Ibn Sīnā's *ifādat al-ārāʾ* demonstrate, would only be related to interpretative possibilities of the figural and the *mathal* universe of *Kalīla wa-Dimna*. Beside these interpretive possibilities, *Ḥayy b. Yaqẓān* should also act as a case in point of how a text can function as an interlocutor in the adab sphere: an aesthetic site of critique and discourse. In this respect, an interlocutor is not passive but synergistic. Ibn Ṭufayl's epistle gives us ample room for displaying how a literary work can both represent a crisis in understanding and participate in resolving it, thereby acting as an interlocutor and allowing others to engage in the adab sphere. On the macro level, the crisis in understanding refers to the citational activity Ibn Ṭufayl performs in the exordium, which points to his own and others' reading, reasoned opinions, and judgments (*raʾy*) hence critique of said authors. It refers to crises of understanding factored in time, which Ibn Ṭufayl says he will rectify for the young disciple as a distillation of his own reading as an introduction. There are explicit references to crises of understanding, as Ibn Ṭufayl mentions that readers may have misunderstood some elements in al-Ghazālī's *Mishkāt al-anwār*, as one example. On the micro level, the narrative of *Ḥayy b. Yaqẓān* deploys the process of "understanding" itself as a perpetual crisis in the text: from the level of self and Ḥayy's understanding of his difference from the animals, to the absence of language as an accepted vehicle of understanding and communication from the beginning, until he reaches the people of the island with Absāl and Salāmān, where Ḥayy encounters the diversity of understanding and reception of his teaching and counter-critique and counter-discourse. The text as interlocutor therefore shows the critical stances of the conception of discourse, critique, and understanding both in itself and toward other texts, as well as the historical conditions of discourse and what Hans-Georg Gadamer calls the historical conditioning of understanding.[1]

DISCOURSE: TEXT AS INTERLOCUTOR

Ibn Ṭufayl's twelfth-century *Ḥayy b. Yaqẓān* has an intertext. The physician and philosopher Ibn Sīnā wrote a short epistle titled *Risālat Ḥayy b. Yaqẓān* (The Epistle of Ḥayy b. Yaqẓān), related by an unnamed narrator. The epistle revolves around an elderly, well-traveled, handsome man with a certain air of authority about him. This man, named Ḥayy, meets the narrator, who is traveling with three other people. The three travelers represent mendacity, violence, and licentiousness, in this order.[2] Like the narrator and his company, Ḥayy, too, is traveling. The latter appears wiser than the narrator as he warns him that he is surrounded by evil company that could and will have detrimental effects on him. The man in question, the narrator, seems to agree with Ḥayy's reading of the situation and his judgment of his company. The narrator, as Ibn Sīnā seems to be telling us, is rational thought (reason), and upon meeting Ḥayy, who represents the active intellect (*al-ʿaql al-faʿʿāl*) and the seat of understanding, the narrator realizes how these human desires and inclinations are not conducive to his journey.[3]

A century later, rather than anticipating a Kerouacian literary work with Ḥayy meeting characters while traveling as Ibn Sīnā did, Ibn Ṭufayl takes another approach to the idea. Ibn Ṭufayl mentions Ibn Sīnā in his introduction, paying homage to the philosopher. Though strangely, according to Murad Idris, "he may or may not have known these other texts. Because his allegory is very different from Ibn Sīnā's two stories."[4] According to Dimitri Gutas, these particular works of Ibn Sīnā were unknown in Andalusia during Ibn Ṭufayl's time, though Ibn Ṭufayl might have read other works by Ibn Sīnā including *Remarks and Admonitions* and *The Book of Healing*.[5] He did not seem to have read the latter's epistle in full. It appears, then, according to Gutas, that he came across a paraphrase of the story.[6] Ibn Ṭufayl geographically situates his epistle and its characters and events on an unnamed island. The island is uninhabited by other humans except for the infant Ḥayy, whose birth origins are given some etiological options by the author. Two birth origins are proposed by the author:[7] the first is that Ḥayy's mother puts him in a chest to float on the river until he reaches the island randomly, which evokes the Qur'anic story of the infant Moses and his mother, as she tries to protect him from the despotism of Pharaoh by putting him in a chest to float on the Nile in Egypt, as attested in Q.28:7–8 ("We inspired Moses's mother, saying, 'Suckle him, and then, when you fear for his safety, put him in the river: do not be afraid, and do not grieve, for We shall return him to you and make him a messenger'") and Q.20:38–39 ("We inspired your mother, saying, 'Put your child into the chest, then place him in the river. Let the river wash him on to its bank, and he will be taken in by an enemy of Mine and his.' I showered you with My love and planned that you should be reared under My watchful eye"). The other option is Ḥayy's spontaneous generation from the earth, which could be read as an imaginative fictionalization of the creation narrative and the origin of humankind from clay or earth (Q.23:12: "We created man from an essence of clay"). And although Ḥayy was alone on the island, he felt a compulsory need to cover himself. He did so using tree leaves as Adam and Eve did in the creation story after the Fall (Q.7:22: "Their nakedness became exposed to them when they had eaten from the tree: they began to put together leaves from the Garden to cover themselves"). The other reading of the spontaneous generation is an interpretation that leans more toward the natural sciences as some scholars, premodern and modern, maintained. As Peter Adamson describes, the commitment to the spontaneous generation was not lost on Ibn Ṭufayl's contemporaries and those after him. It was not an anomaly. "A couple of generations later, al-Marrākushī went so far as to claim that Ḥayy is intended 'to explicate the origins of the human race according to the school of thought of the [natural sciences].'"[8]

In the epistle, a doe finds Ḥayy and breastfeeds and raises him. As all mortal beings must, the doe dies. Ḥayy thus learns about death and the soul when the doe, his mother, dies. He then dissects her body to discover the cause of death.[9] Ḥayy is following what is known as the scientific methodology or what Ibn Sīnā mentioned in his treatise *al-Burhān* (On Demonstration) of his book *al-Shifāʾ*. The method of scientific inquiry is summarized in the question "How does one acquire the first principles of a science?"[10] In this case, how does Ḥayy, or the scientist, "arrive at the initial axioms or hypotheses of a deductive science without inferring them from some more basic premises?"[11] "The ideal situation, Ibn Sînâ tells us, is when one grasps that a *per se* relation holds between the terms, which would allow for absolute, universal certainty. Ibn Sînâ then adds two further, perhaps more interesting, methods used by ancient and medieval scientists for arriving at first principles. These are Aristotelian induction (Arabic *istiqrâ'*, Greek *epagôgê*) and examination or experimentation (Arabic *tajriba*, Greek *empeiria*)."[12]

Through the scientific method Ḥayy discovers death. He not only becomes perplexed with the logistics of death and burial, as Cain did upon killing his brother Abel when he was inspired by the crow (Q.5:31: "God sent a raven to scratch up the ground and show him how to cover his brother's corpse and he said, 'Woe is me! Could I not have been like this raven and covered up my brother's body?' He became remorseful")—he also becomes preoccupied with death on a metaphysical level. "Death," Marwa Elshakry and Murad Idris maintain, "therefore was the first lesson of metaphysics."[13] He then becomes absorbed in reflection, meditation, observing plants, animals, celestial bodies, and the universe at large to finally arrive at the conclusion, using reason, that everything must originate from a First Cause. After much contemplation and investigation, at the age of fifty, he reaches illumination and becomes capable of "beholding the divine."[14] Ḥayy's discovery of the First Cause is reminiscent of the story of Abraham (Ibrāhīm) in Q.6:74–79.

> Remember when Abraham said to his father, Azar, "How can you take idols as gods? I see that you and your people have clearly gone astray." In this way We showed Abraham [God's] mighty dominion over the heavens and the earth, so that he might be a firm believer. When the night grew dark over him he saw a star and said, "This is my Lord," but when it set, he said, "I do not like things that set." And when he saw the moon rising he said, "*This* is my Lord," but when it too set, he said, "If my Lord does not guide me, I shall be one of those who go astray." Then he saw the sun rising and cried, "*This* is my Lord! This is greater." But when the sun set, he said, "My people, I disown all that you worship beside God. I have turned my face as a true believer towards Him who created the heavens and the earth. I am not one of the polytheists."

The Qur'an relates that Abraham was able, through reflection alone, to realize that there is a First Cause. Scholar and exegete al-Rāzī also relates that most exegetes recount a story about Abraham's childhood as follows: the king at the time, where Abraham's family lived, had a dream. It was interpreted that a boy would be born who would threaten the king's reign and dominion. The king ordered that all newborn boys be killed. Abraham's mother, though pregnant, did not disclose this pregnancy in public. When the time came to give birth, she went to a distant cave and delivered Abraham and left him there, coming every day to breastfeed him until he grew older and started questioning her, saying, "Who is my Lord?" She said, "I am." He then asked, "And who is your Lord?" "Your father is." He then asked his father, "And who is your Lord?" The father replied, "The king is." It is related that Abraham was not satisfied with these answers, so he then went outside the cave to look at the stars and celestial bodies until he cognized that there is a First Cause, or a Creator, for everything.[15] While Ibn Ṭufayl did not read Ibn Sīnā's aforementioned allegorical *Epistle of Ḥayy b. Yaqẓān*, it could be argued that the Qur'anic references to the creation story, Adam and Eve, and the stories of both Moses and Abraham are all part of the Islamic narrative repository and register. He might also have been familiar with the backstories circulating in select exegeses, although this is difficult to prove, since it cannot be ascertained which works of exegesis he had access to. Abraham's background is not mentioned in the Qur'an; it is only in exegeses that this story is mentioned. However, Moses's story, which shares a similar infanthood with Ḥayy, is related in the Qur'an.

Ibn Sīnā's late-ninth-century tale in Baghdad was perhaps popular or became appropriated and summarized in other texts and also circulated orally in scholarly gatherings in the adab sphere such that it reached Ibn Ṭufayl in twelfth-century Spain. The tale itself did not stop at Ibn Ṭufayl. The twelfth-century philosopher al-Suhrawardī, who became an eponym of the Illuminationist (*ishrāqī*) philosophical tradition, also wrote an epistle in the form of a story based on Ibn Sīnā's short epistle titled *al-Ghurba al-gharbiyya* (Occidental Exile) in intellectual admiration but also as a form of participation in an ongoing discourse identified by al-Suhrawardī as belonging to spiritual allusions. Al-Suhrawardī acknowledged the story of *Ḥayy b. Yaqẓān*'s novel ideas and its author's talent and proposed to add what he thought would be another take, perhaps complementary, on aspects of Ibn Sīnā's story.[16]

> أَمَّا بَعْدُ، فَإِنِّي لَمَّا رَأَيْتُ قِصَّةَ حَيِّ بْنِ يَقْظَانَ صَادَفْتُهَا، مَعَ مَا فِيمَا مِنْ عَجَائِبِ الْكَلِمَاتِ الرُّوحَانِيَّةِ، وَالْإِشَارَاتِ الْعَمِيقَةِ؛ مُتَعَرِّيَةً عَنْ تَلْوِيحَاتٍ تَشِيرُ إِلَى الطَّوْرِ الْأَعْظَمِ، الَّذِي هُوَ الطَّامَةُ الْكُبْرَى الْمَخْزُونَةُ فِي الْكُتُبِ الْإِلَهِيَّةِ[17]

> To begin: When I saw the tale of *Ḥayy ibn Yaqẓān*, I found it, despite its wonderful spiritual sayings and profound allusions, devoid of intimations which beckon towards the Greatest Experience which is the Great Overwhelming ([Q.]79:34), treasured in the Divine Books.[18]

Another literary response, but to Ibn Ṭufayl's *Ḥayy b. Yaqẓān*, not Ibn Sīnā's, is the thirteenth-century physician Ibn al-Nafīs's epistle *Fāḍil b. Nāṭiq* (Virtuous Son of Rational) or *al-Risāla al-kāmiliyya*.[19] Mostly famous for his work in describing the pulmonary circulation of the blood, Ibn al-Nafīs also responded to the epistle with a changed name for the protagonist and represented him as the feral child turned theologian (The Self-Taught Theologian, or *Theologus autodidactus*, as known in translation) on the unnamed island and added new elements, such as medicine.

Theoretically, it is enriching to observe the many literary responses to the different tales of *Ḥayy b. Yaqẓān*. In poetry, critics would normally call this *mu ʿāraḍāt* (imitations); however, this term in translation lacks the inner workings of its critical mechanism. A poem that engages in an act of *mu ʿāraḍa* is not an imitation as such but can be also an engagement in discourse and critique in the sphere of adab and often of its paternal poem. It is engaging in a discourse with an interlocutor. Looking at these texts in consortium, then, it would appear that they had their own agreements/disagreements with the engaged text; these engaged texts become textual interlocutors. The aforementioned literary responses are creative endeavors, not imitations; they are a creative critique of the work they are engaging with. Ibn Ṭufayl himself is engaging with the various texts he cited at the exordium on the level of micro critique of theories of perception, intuition, thought, and language. While they are part of a wider adab sphere, it is useful to consider these engagements as discursive critique. This is because while they are engaging in a discourse (*shu ʿūb al-ḥadīth*) inspired by a textual interlocutor, they are simultaneously applying critique to the text through response, agreement, and/or disagreement, in part or whole.

Ibn Ṭufayl uses the exordium to chart an answer to a question that readers are not privy to but may intuit from the map he offers to his interlocutor of his own readings, background, sources, and the trajectory of readings from Ibn Sīnā, al-Fārābī, Ibn Bājja, al-Ghazālī, Sufi poets, and Greek philosophy, to mention a few. Ibn Ṭufayl does not list descriptively but rather charts critically his intellectual journey through the corpus of these scholars and philosophers and provides his critique. He maintains that he did not find their ideas wholly convincing or intellectually satisfying. He avers:

> وَلَا تَظُنَّ أَنَّ الْفَلْسَفَةَ الَّتِي وَصَلَتْ إِلَيْنَا فِي كُتُبِ أَرِسْطُوطَالِيسَ وَأَبِي نَصْرٍ وَفِي كِتَابِ الشِّفَاءِ تَفِي بِهَذَا الْغَرَضِ الَّذِي أَرَدْتَهُ، وَلَا أَنَّ أَحَدًا مِنْ أَهْلِ الْأَنْدَلُسِ كَتَبَ فِيهِ شَيْئًا فِيهِ كِفَايَةٌ
>
> Do not think that the philosophy that reached us through the books of Aristotle and Abū Naṣr [al-Fārābī] and in [Ibn Sīnā's] *The Book of Healing* is enough for this purpose that I want; and do not think that anyone in Andalusia who wrote anything on it has sufficed.[20]

Ibn Ṭufayl criticizes al-Fārābī's philosophy and calls it skeptical (*kathīrat al-shukūk*) and defines this skepticism with a paradox he found in al-Fārābī's writing. Ibn Ṭufayl faults al-Fārābī for saying that the evil souls will remain in eternal pain after death in his *Doctrine of the Virtuous City* (*Ārā ʾ ahl al-madīna al-fāḍila*), but then al-Fārābī contradicts this opinion in his *Political Regime* (*al-Siyāsa al-madaniyya*). Ibn Ṭufayl adds that al-Fārābī in his commentary on Aristotle's *Ethics* talks about happiness as a pursuit that is only concerned with this world and any talk of the hereafter is old people's tales (*khurāfāt ʿajā ʾiz*).[21] Ibn Ṭufayl objects to this, saying that this thought can lead people to despair and to give up on God's mercy if the virtuous and the evil are both regarded as equal and have the same state. He maintains that this is a mistake that should not be uttered (*zalla lā tuqāl*). Ibn Ṭufayl also criticizes what he calls al-Fārābī's bad belief on the issue of prophecy (*sū ʾ mu ʿtaqadihi fī al-nubuwwa*) and al-Fārābī's preference for philosophy over prophecy.[22] With respect to the last point, it is an apt juncture to clarify some misunderstandings about Ibn Ṭufayl's own position on prophecy and religion in general and in the epistle. Some scholars read the epistle as a refutation of the need for religion and prophecy altogether, that "Ḥayy does not see the relevance of any revealed religion. But once he comes into contact with other men in society, he realizes that a revealed religion is perhaps the lesser evil."[23] As Asad Q. Ahmed maintains, the world that came after al-Ghazālī had the same attitude toward reason well into the late nineteenth century in several fields. These scholars were neither marginal nor on the fringes of society but operated in fields of Qur'anic studies, exegesis, ḥadīth, mathematics, astronomy, and so on. Therefore, as Ahmed argues, "the simple and naive binaries of reason vs. revelation, rationalist vs. scripturalist, Golden Age vs. Dark Ages, and philosopher vs. *mulla*, must be simply discarded—to say of course nothing of the conceptually ill-equipped and displaced categories such as orthodoxy, cleric, and seminary in the Muslim context."[24] In the same vein, Emilio González-Ferrín also maintains that it is "essential to give up the monolithic understanding of philosophy as poised against religion especially when dealing with medieval thought in general, and with Jewish/Muslim/Christian thought in particular."[25]

Ibn Ṭufayl seems to intellectually admire Ibn Sīnā. He praises his commentary on Aristotle and says that Ibn Sīnā added more than what reached us from Aristotle. This is not surprising since Ibn Ṭufayl seems to have responded to a paraphrase of Ibn Sīnā's short epistle, albeit never reaching him, bearing the same title: *Ḥayy b. Yaqẓān*, as previously mentioned. Ibn Ṭufayl's admiration of and affinity with Ibn Sīnā has been explained in terms of "theoretical Sufism" (*ahl al-naẓar*) but not "experiential Sufism" (*ahl al-dhawq*), that is, those who tasted and experienced the spiritual and intellectual states they describe. In this respect, it can be argued that both Ibn Sīnā's and Ibn Ṭufayl's representation of mysticism can be considered as a *taqlīd*, or perhaps abstract and theoretical, but not a lived practical experience of mysticism.[26] Ibn Ṭufayl describes Ibn Sīnā's *al-falsafa al-mashriqiyya* as the truth that is without confusion (*al-ḥaqq al-ladhī lā jamjama fīhi*).[27] He also does not critique Ibn Sīnā like others. While Ibn Sīnā commented on Aristotle and explained his philosophy in *al-Shifā'* (The Healing), he added original ideas to it through the commentary in what Ibn Ṭufayl identified as the parts that are not found in Aristotle, in other words, Ibn Sīnā's original thought, and the work he calls *al-falsafa al-mashriqiyya*.[28]

Ibn Ṭufayl then concludes with al-Ghazālī's scholarly views that he finds plausible in parts but not so much in others. He maintains that al-Ghazālī's views suffer from contradiction and indecisiveness because sometimes his book confirms one idea then he contradicts it in another book. Ibn Ṭufayl also takes him to task because of his classification of views into (a) that which is common with the majority of people and is shared with them; (b) that which depends on the addressee and/or students; and (c) that which one only keeps to oneself and shares with like-minded people.[29] But Ibn Ṭufayl also seems to include this classification in the epistle as evident in the meeting between Ḥayy and the people of the island, who can be categorized into what al-Ghazālī describes as *ahl al-salāma* (people of safety) or *al-ʿawāmm* (the common people). Extremely intellectually sheltered, in fact, the people of the island's ruler forbids activities that may encourage acts of intellectual courage and intellectual independence. Al-Ghazālī also mentions the other type of people as *al-khawāṣṣ* (the distinctive ones) or *ahl al-dhakā' wa-l-baṣīra* (people of intelligence and insight). Absāl is an example of this type. The final type al-Ghazālī mentions are the sophists or *ahl al-jadal*, who are an offshoot of the distinctive intelligent ones and who argue for the sake of argument or making a show, because in reality they hold prejudices and are not interested in the truth.[30] Ibn Ṭufayl then quotes al-Ghazālī's pedagogical framework where the latter says, "if after all this culminated in nothing but contributing to your doubt and skepticism in your inherited beliefs, it is enough as a benefit (*yushakkik fī iʿtiqādika al-mawrūth la-kafā bi-dhālika nafʿan*). He who does not doubt (*yashukk*) does not critique/critically reason (*yanẓur*), and he who does not critique/critically reason (*yanẓur*) does not see/comprehend (*yubṣir*), and he who does not see/comprehend will remain in blindness and confusion (*al-ʿamā wa-l-ḥīra*)."[31] Ibn Ṭufayl further adds a couplet by al-Mutanabbī (d. 354 AH/965 CE), cautioning against *taqlīd*, which al-Ghazālī uses to adduce his idea:

خُـذْ مـا تَـرَاهُ ودَعْ شَـيئاً سَـمِعْـت بِهِ
فِي طَلعَةِ الشَّمْسِ مَا يُغنِيكَ عَنْ زُحَلِ

Take what you see and leave what is passed down through hearsay
In the bright sunlight, what suffices against Saturn.

PERCEPTION, INTUITION, AND THE "E" WORD

Ḥayy b. Yaqẓān's perceived "empiricism," perhaps read through Ibn Sīnā's perceived "empiricism" as well, which is often compared to John Locke's, can be read inaccurately if one is not careful. There is not a simple answer as to whether the aforementioned claim is true or false despite efforts to peg Ibn Sīnā as an empiricist, retrospectively, in the Lockean sense.[32] The principal problems this claim faces include Ibn Sīnā's epistemology regarding celestial bodies, unseen things, immaterial substances, and God. With no help of sense perception and only through "intellective reasoning," "experience" is "unnecessary for the origination of these conceptions."[33] "This 'empiricist' reading primarily aims at defeating a previously standard reading of Avicenna according to which 'Avicenna is a rationalist,' believes in 'a priori concepts,' and uses them to construct 'a priori proofs' for the existence of God."[34] Ibn Sīnā's epistemology is constructed on "*maʿānī* as conceived and mental states and attitudes."[35]

Admittedly, while Ḥayy relies on sense perception, he relies largely on "intellective reasoning" for the unseen and the immaterial, which is represented as "understood" or "perceived" but "inexpressible." The very language of "sight" and the pedagogical influence of both Ibn Sīnā and al-Ghazālī can be seen in Ḥayy's experience after his doe mother dies; his thought process, mental content, and experience are described in the narrative using the verbs of sight such as when the boy first *saw* his dead mother (*raʾāhā*). Then he started to *look at* and *examine* (*yanẓur*) her ears and eyes and body to see if there is a perceptible cause of death till the end of the famous body dissection until he realizes that it was an internal organ that failed and caused the death. The verb used here to describe his thought process through intellective reasoning is "he discerned/intuited" (*waqaʿa fī khāṭirihi*).[36] The description of the process of understanding, from a crisis of understanding to plausible interpretation and analysis, is related as having culminated in an insight; the flash of intuition (*ḥads*) with which an idea is perceived. This is one of al-Ghazālī's influences on Ibn Ṭufayl. So renowned was this intellectual contribution of al-Ghazālī, the prophetic intuition that comes as a flash of lightning, that it can also be seen in Dante's (d. 721 AH/1321 CE) *Paradiso*: "Se non che la mia mente fu percossa / da un fulgore in che sua voglia venne" (33.140–41) (But then my mind was struck by light that flashed / and, with this light, received what it had asked).[37] The flash of light (*fulgore*) here refers to intuition with which the poet received his wish. Dante's knowledge of al-Ghazālī, which is confirmed by his mentioning him in his work *Convivio*, comes mediated through the Latin translation of Albertus Magnus or Albert the Great (d. 679 AH/1280 CE).[38]

However, Ibn Ṭufayl also criticizes al-Ghazālī's pedagogy as cyphered, full of symbols, and only accessible to a select few who have the aptitude or who were taught its meaning.[39] He then points to a misreading in the reception of al-Ghazālī's *Mishkāt al-anwār* where some attributed a gross misinterpretation of al-Ghazālī's words related to the Oneness of the divine (*al-waḥdāniyya*). Ibn Ṭufayl treats these as "misreaders," whom I should like to call "errorists" (see chapter 4). Ibn Ṭufayl identifies them as (intellectual) oppressors (*ẓālimūn*) not only against the divine but against al-Ghazālī.[40] He then tells us that he studied the corpus of al-Ghazālī and Ibn Sīnā and checked them against each other (*ṣarafa baʿḍahumā ilā baʿḍ*) in addition to the circulating views of his time until he arrived at a correct view, through research, disputations, and critique (*al-baḥth wa-l-naẓar*).[41] The latter is a major contribution by al-Ghazālī as shown in his *Iḥyāʾ ʿulūm al-dīn* (The Revivication of Religious Sciences) and his reasoning and methods that "developed requiring *naẓar*, speculation in philosophical theology as the means of access to salvation."[42] Ibn Ṭufayl's act of intellectual *inṣāf* (see chapter 4) or giving due intellectual justice can only be performed through the propelling force of critique as *naẓar*. Only then, he says, was he able to present in the epistle what he could attribute to himself. Ibn Ṭufayl then cautions his addressee that if he disclosed all the results of his research and the conclusion explicitly (*ghāyāt mā intahaynā ilayhi*) without the addressee reviewing its introductory foundations (*tuḥakkim mabādiʾahā*), it would not benefit them any more than if it was an imitation (*amr taqlīdī mujmal*). Ibn Ṭufayl adds that the mastering of scholarship requires time, effort, and motivation. Serious study demands the sincerity of the addressee's will (*ʿazm*).[43] However, he tells his addressee that what he offers now is a simple glimpse (*lamḥa yasīra*) to whet the appetite (*al-tashwīq*) and to motivate the addressee on entering this path.[44] He says this is in his description of the story of *Ḥayy b. Yaqẓān*.

LANGUAGE, CRITIQUE, AND LINGUISTIC BEINGS

One interpretation of the absence of language in Ḥayy's life is that human beings are able to reach divine truths and other truths through reason without the influence or inculcation of social conditioning mediated through language. I propose an alternative reading that problematizes the absence of language, such that it was made absent not to emphasize the role of reason alone but to comment on both the inadequacy of language in the context of divine truths and the nature of language itself.

It appears then that Ibn Ṭufayl, like Ibn al-Muqaffaʿ, coated the ideas and concepts he mentioned in the introduction in a figurative language and, according to him, simplified them in an interesting manner. On the one hand, this is their legitimization of adab. On the other, the use of figurative language gives an instance of the aforementioned crisis of understanding in relation to al-Ghazālī's views as well as those of others and especially where language is concerned. Ibn Ṭufayl deliberately points that there is more to the concepts his addressee asked about where the mystical experiences are concerned: "[They] cannot be put into a book. . . . For, clothed in letters and sounds and brought into the perceptible world, it [mystical experience] cannot remain, in any way, what it was. . . . But on the other hand you may desire a discursive, intellectualized introduction to this experience. And this—God honor you with His intimacy—is something that can be put into words and set down in books."[45] Ibn Ṭufayl here makes a reference to the inadequacy of language. This is also a nod to the Ghazālian concept of what Ebrahim Moosa identifies as the "extralinguistic,"[46] where the verbal expression or representation of divine truths is concerned. In *al-Munqidh min al-ḍalāl* (Deliverance from Error), al-Ghazālī speaks about his struggle to make sense of phenomena and experience that go beyond the range of our usual instruments of perception. He discusses mystical experiences as follows: "Language will be narrow for these experiences (*darajāt yaḍīq ʿanhā al-nuṭq*) . . . anyone who attempts to express (*yuʿabbir*) these [experiences], his words will contain some blatant errors (*khaṭaʾ ṣarīḥ*), which cannot be avoided (*lā yumkinuhu al-iḥtirāz ʿanhu*)."[47] He maintains that to attain unmediated "presence" to experience the truth one must expand one's discursive apparatus so that it includes the intelligibility of symbols. In the end, al-Ghazālī concedes that linguistic references to God must by necessity be viewed as a product of metaphoric expression and figurative expansion.[48]

Ḥayy's nonexistent language and speech throughout dramatizes his thought process not on the level of speech but on the level of logic and mental content. This evokes the tenth-century debate between al-Ṣirāfī (d. 368 AH/978 CE) and Ibn Mattā (d. 328 AH/940 CE) on whether logic or grammar was the way to think.[49] By the time Ibn Ṭufayl wrote his epistle in the twelfth century, he would have been exposed to the various views on this debate, especially as a reader of philosophy and theology as he himself attested, explicitly naming Ibn Sīnā as one of his sources. In his book *al-Shifāʾ*, Ibn Sīnā investigates the debated issue of the extent to which the logician must be concerned with the features of language: "An investigation of vocal form is a matter of necessity, and yet vocal forms are not something that the logician qua logician should concern himself with, unless [he is simply using them] in conversation or discussion with others. If it were possible to study logic through pure thought with only the mental contents themselves observed, then that would be enough. If the logician were to be able to apprise his interlocutor of that which is in his soul through some contrivance, then he would be able to dispense with vocal forms."[50]

Ḥayy's mental contents and intuition are outside language as a vocal vehicle but not language as an abstraction and mental content as Ibn Sīnā would tell us. This is also evident when Ḥayy meets Absāl for the first time.[51]

> وَجَعَلَ يَسْتَعْطِفُهُ وَيَرْغَبُ إِلَيْهِ بِكَلَامٍ لَا يَفْهَمُهُ حَيُّ بْنُ يَقْظَانَ وَلَا يَدْرِي مَا هُوَ، غَيْرَ أَنَّهُ كَانَ يُمَيِّزُ فِيهِ شَمَائِلَ الْجَزَعِ. فَكَانَ يُؤَنِّسُهُ بِأَصْوَاتٍ كَانَ قَدْ تَعَلَّمَهَا مِنْ بَعْضِ الْحَيَوَانَاتِ وَيَجُرُّ يَدَهُ عَلَى رَأْسِهِ يَمْسَحُ أَعْطَافَهُ
>
> Ḥayy tried to calm Absāl with sounds he had learned from the animals and by patting his head. He stroked his cheeks and smiled at him until, eventually, Absāl regained composure and realised that Ḥayy meant him no harm.[52]

The encounter between Ḥayy and Absāl reveals to us it is not so much the linguistic exchange that occurred between them, or would have occurred if Ḥayy possessed language, but rather the respective mental contents of Ḥayy and Absāl. Ḥayy was communicating in a medium other than one readily available for human comprehension. Absāl understands the mental contents of Ḥayy, the literal voices of Ḥayy, which are symbolic, as he uses, or rather borrows, animal voices from nature, to communicate friendliness. The process of understanding in the narrative here is not represented as a crisis but rather as an argument, even a critique of some positions on logic and philosophy. "The relationships with which Avicenna was concerned were between mental contents more than they were between mental content and vocal form. Language comes into the logical picture only as an accident, by accident. To understand the relation between 'human' and 'not-human' is to understand the implications of one piece of mental content for another piece of mental content, not one bit of language for another bit of language."[53]

Ḥayy eventually learns language with Absāl as his teacher, who is represented as a philologist of sorts. We are told he has a passion for hermeneutics and interpretation, which perhaps explains the drive and passion to speak most languages (*li-maḥabbatihi fī ʿilm al-taʾwīl qad taʿallam akthar al-alsun*).[54] However, as they exchange notes on various concepts, Ḥayy comes to the conclusion that the people's understanding of certain concepts that he had arrived at earlier, extralinguistically, is and has become literal. He uses imagery of beasts to describe their state alluding to the simile in Q.25:44 ("They are just like cattle—no, they are further from the path").[55] Although the people of the island are described as kind and virtuous (*muḥibbīn li-l-khayr*), they are unable to understand Ḥayy. Their lack of understanding is diagnosed as a lack in *fiṭra* (*naqṣ fiṭratihim*),[56] which is the Islamic understanding of "uncorrupted natural disposition" as the pure state of human beings at birth in alignment with the divine (inclined toward the good always hence fully "human," inclined toward the rational and beautiful, and accepting monotheism naturally).[57] Ḥayy's diagnosis may be the effect not the cause of their understanding since we are told a few lines earlier that the ruler of the island, Salāmān, prohibited isolation and individual time and forced people to stay in groups and never be alone: "Salāmān, averse to contemplation and personal choice, urged commitment to society."[58] The ruler of the island therefore inhibits the full development of murūʾa of its inhabitants, which the narrative diagnosed as *naqṣ fiṭra* or a lack in proper expression of humanity and human nature; it has been corrupted. Through the hermeneutic encounter with Ḥayy, the people of the island were unable to exercise what has been discussed earlier as the *baṣar* and *naẓar* or to offer a critical exchange and approach Ḥayy from a liminal perspective. At the end of the epistle, when Ḥayy becomes convinced that the discourse with the people of the island is futile because they cannot seem to understand his ideas, the narrator tells us, "When he understood people's nature and that the majority of them are like the nonspeaking animal . . ." (*fa-lammā fahima aḥwāl al-nās wa-anna aktharahum bi-manzilat al-ḥayawān ghayr al-nāṭiq* . . .).[59] The reference to speech as a differentiator here between humans and nonhumans is intriguing, since the people of the island do talk. It is reminiscent of ʿUmar b. al-Khaṭṭāb's (d. 23 AH/644 CE) motivation to people to learn Arabic to increase their murūʾa, hence humanity. It is not that people around ʿUmar did not speak Arabic, but it is understood that it is an incentive to learn the nuances of the language or what is understood as the "width/richness of Arabic" (*siʿat al-ʿarabiyya*). This is reminiscent of what philologist al-Anbārī (d. 577 AH/1181 CE) called the "secrets of Arabic" (*asrār al-ʿarabiyya*), partaking in the titular genre of unlocking the secrets of language by using the title "secrets," after al-Jurjānī's (d. 471 AH/1078 CE) groundbreaking *Asrār al-balāgha*. The learning of Arabic and its "secrets" is therefore believed to remove the individual from the confines of narrow meanings, which would beget narrow thinking, and instead allow access to wider meanings and thinking. It is worth reiterating that Absāl, the only one able to understand Ḥayy and probably transcend the draconian intellectual molds of Salāmān to devote time to study, is the one who studied adab: hermeneutics, interpretations, and languages. In other words, Ibn Ṭufayl is doubly legitimizing adab through the fictive character of Absāl as an example of the adabized interlocutor qua adabized reader.

Ḥayy becomes an undesirable stranger because the people of the island do not think they are necessarily obligated to him in their process of understanding or self-understanding in particular. The people of the island operate from a sense of certainty that communicates a material truth that is hard to shake: this perceived world is attainable. What Ḥayy challenges therefore is the idea of "the unattainability of the world" as such or a world beyond the senses to which the only means is the extralinguistic. In this respect, the narrative offers us a more complex tale beyond the binaries that the people of the island represent "religion" as a category and Ḥayy represents "freethinking" and "secularism" as another. This is inaccurate. In other words, language as a carrier of the conceptualizations and mental contents of Ḥayy as well as the people of the island does not make either one of them less true in their attempt to express "divine truths" of their faith. The latter tests the reliability and limits of language, not the other way around. Language use in this case becomes a theophanic vehicle. It attempts to present a perceptible manifestation of the divine to humanity. Ḥayy offers a narrative that is deeply entrenched in the language of the Qur'an as it tells us of both the unattainability and uncertainty of this world. In Q.57:20, the Qur'an explains that this world is illusory in nature ("Bear in mind that the present life is just a game, a diversion, an attraction, a cause of boasting among you, of rivalry in wealth and children. It is like plants that spring up after the rain: their growth at first delights the sowers, but then you see them wither away, turn yellow, and become stubble"). The people of the island treat life and everything about it with a worrisome certainty. Ḥayy attempts to explain the unattainability of this certainty; indeed, like the *mathal* of the plant in the verse, certainty is unsupported because of the very nature of transience and the illusory nature of the world as a "game." The language of Ḥayy, figurative as it is, points to the nature of this world; it reveals the limits of language not the limits of faith. The people of the island materialized the language into concrete things. Al-Ghazālī "had to concede that all linguistic reference to God must by necessity be viewed as a product of metaphoric expression and figurative expansion."[60] Ḥayy's experience of the divine was what al-Ghazālī would define as extralinguistic, and unlike the people of the island, his experience was not a crisis of understanding and language; rather, it is an experience that is ineffable. "For the great mystics, this crisis of language is defined not as crisis but as ecstasy; a possession by the Divine which renders the subject (the mystic) speechless through total communion or union—which requires a total erasure of identity, of self."[61]

What the people of the island fail to show is critique and independent thinking or a little courage as Absāl's etymology shows. This intellectual habitus was manufactured, imposed on them by the ruler, whom we are told had little time for interpretation and thus preferred literal meanings or that the latter were simpler and easier. Critique and independent thinking are both definitions of murūʾa as *baṣar* and *naẓar*, which is the framework of the epistle as Ibn Ṭufayl related in his exordium, and as established in the earlier chapters. The absence of critique and independent thinking and their expression removes the person from the status of human to nonhuman, not because of the absence of language as such but because of the absence of these tools, the grammar of adab (courage, critique, independent thinking, reasoning, etc.), as constituents of murūʾa.

The difference between Absāl and the people of the island is that the former allowed Ḥayy a theoretical space. As an adabized interlocutor, we are told that Absāl is trained in languages and hermeneutics. The praxis of his adabization, as an interlocutor, is by offering this theoretical space. The "fanatic interlocutor" qua "fanatic reader," like the people of the island, is unable to occupy what al-Ghazālī conceptualizes as the theoretical *dihlīzī* space.[62] The *dihlīz* (threshold) is a space in between, a liminal space that allows its occupant to be both inside and outside as a vestibule of intellectual liminality. It should not be thought of as a threatening space but rather a welcoming and hospitable one, as one would welcome their guest, thereby embodying the virtues of murūʾa. The *dihlīz* can also be a locus of epistemic enunciation.[63] The people of the island were unable to understand the speculative and figurative nature of Ḥayy's language because it offers a narrative of a world that is unimaginable through their linguistic horizon, even in theory, or abstractly. It is thus not only a matter of a differing worldview that is disagreeable but also a matter of a language that imagines and describes a world that is inaccessible to the other. The other is unable to theoretically entertain or engage or even imagine the idea. The epistle's use of figurative language is a prompt in the direction of the dangers of literalism and the singular, even oppressive, world it builds, or rather circumscribes, as it destroys possible imaginative horizons through language. This in turn obstructs this theoretical liminality and hence possibilities. It is worth mentioning a prime example from Q.40:29, the encounter between Moses and Pharoah; the latter, in an attempt to dissuade people from following the message of Moses, told them, "I have told [or *showed*] you what I think; I am guiding you along the right path" (*mā urīkum illā mā arā wa-mā ahdīkum illā sabīl al-rashād*). Pharoah's statement can be understood to mean he only shows them what he sees and therefore prevents them from seeing other possibilities because this is the correct path, as any tyrant would decree. It can also be understood to mean he told them what he thinks and believes. The idea here is that he prevented the people from the hermeneutic encounter with Moses as "a possibility," to see differently or imagine a different world—a staple in the rhetorical regime of all tyrants.

The people of the island showed us the limits of the hermeneutic encounter with Ḥayy. They could not be moved to understand Ḥayy's horizon; not because they are intellectually incapable, for Absāl, the one person who opened up to Ḥayy, is the one who benefited from him. Absāl approached Ḥayy from a perspective of liminality, what Moosa explains as the Ghazālian *dihlīz*. He represents to us a reader in an interrogative mood. Al-Ghazālī's liminality may be attributed to what he practiced and taught as "learned ignorance," to practice skepticism or the *docta ignorantia* developed later by Nicholas of Cusa in the fifteenth century. It is the belief that certainty through scholastic ratio is unattainable, especially that about the quiddity of God. It is not possible to limit God to a definition because God has no limit or definition.[64] This "learned ignorance" about God encourages a healthy lack of certainty unlike what is practiced by the people of the island. The healthy liminality and "learned ignorance" are aware that the very fabric of language will never be able to ascribe a definition in the economy of certainty about the quiddity of God. Absāl's experience, like all transformations, involves a loss and a gain. It may be said that his loss of what may be perceived as the precritical naivete and childlike innocence of "literalism" involved a gain in the capacity to conceive of others' worlds in other language(s): those of Ḥayy. Metaphorically, Absāl can never return to who he was before; and in the epistle, this was proven true as he left his old "world" for that of Ḥayy when they departed the island—the island of literal interpretations, so to speak. Absāl's relationship with Ḥayy also explores the conditions of possibility of understanding and highlights its discursive nature in their exchange. The exchange between the two characters has a powerful explanatory power. Ibn Ṭufayl's appropriation of al-Ghazālī's thought was indicated in the book's preface. Ibn Ṭufayl's understanding, engagement, and representation of al-Ghazālī's *dihlīz* in Absāl's *dihlīzī* posture treated this idea as a condition of possibility. This condition of possibility can be a factor in determining the fashioning of the types of readers and the reading habitus in general and of certain texts in particular.

CONDITIONS OF (IM)POSSIBILITY

In all the epistle's critical renditions and responses, the hypothesis is that the text is a critical interlocutor. Does it remain a critical interlocutor outside its conditions of reading? In the case of Ibn al-Muqaffaʿ's hosting of *Kalīla wa-Dimna*, the text preserved its literary nature and allowed the readers space for discourse and critique. Did *Ḥayy b. Yaqẓān*, a text that advocates for independent and critical thinking and relinquishing self-imposed infancy, engage this very condition of reading and understanding? If a text legitimizes adab, reasoning, discourse, and critique, is it enough? Or is an ecology of legitimization necessary? By an ecology of legitimization, I mean the intellectual climate, including the reception and scholarship surrounding the text itself, that would allow the text and its readers full conditions of possibility that come with the text. To explain this point further, a discussion of the reception of *Ḥayy b. Yaqẓān* in Britain is useful.

Ḥayy b. Yaqẓān has been a very popular text since its inception, and the history of its translation attests to that.[65] Of interest to our discussion are the translations of the text into English in the seventeenth century by Edward Pococke and then Simon Ockley. The first publication of Ibn Ṭufayl's *Ḥayy b. Yaqẓān* in Britain dates to 1671 in Arabic with Latin translation and then in English in 1674.[66] It was translated by Edward Pococke, son of the first Laudian Professor of Arabic at the University of Oxford, although much of the actual work was carried out by his father, Edward Pococke Sr.[67] It is described as a translation that gleans with his "learned brilliance," giving an accurate account of Ibn Ṭufayl's life and the vast reach of *Ḥayy b. Yaqẓān* among readers and philosophers, both Arab and Jewish. The translation is justified by "invoking the European race to increase and improve the quality of Arabic studies, remarking that despite strong competition on the continent, too little had been done in England until Archbishop Laud and Thomas Adams created chairs of Arabic at Oxford and Cambridge respectively."[68] Pococke also tries hard to explain to the reader that the book may be intellectually threatening without fully alienating them.[69] "In view of the radical potential of Tufayl's fable, Pococke takes pains to explain that the author is in fact presenting a new method for attaining knowledge of higher things but that it does not necessarily displace or obviate the need for revelation: indeed, it merely underlies the limitations of human reason. Pococke encourages the reader to make an individual judgment about the purpose and meaning of Hayy ibn Yaqzan, taking account of the differences between twelfth-century Spain and seventeenth-century England."[70] Pococke therefore points out the context and geography of the text and allows the reader to make their own judgment within a framework that is relatively intellectually sober compared to what would follow a few years later.

In 1708, Simon Ockley, a fellow of Jesus College and vicar of Swavesey, produced a translation based on the original Arabic text with the addition of engravings of Ḥayy's coming of age as well footnotes addressed to readers unfamiliar with the Qur'an.[71] In 1711, he was chosen as Adams Professor of Arabic at Cambridge University. He dedicated this translation to the younger Edward Pococke. It should also be mentioned that Ockley's translation is quite independent of Pococke's.[72] Ockley's version in the English language owes itself to the growing interest in the topic espoused by the epistle: the role of reason and insight and the self-improvement of individuals, seventy-six years before Immanuel Kant's posing or rather responding to the famous question "What is Enlightenment?" in 1784. "The nature of the work probably explains why it remained unpublished in the middle of the seventeenth century, and why, on the other hand, it became popular towards the end of that century. It is concerned with the self-improvement of man in the state of nature, a topic congenial to western European thought in the late seventeenth and eighteenth centuries."[73]

Ockley's translation is titled *The Improvement of Human Reason Exhibited in the Life of Hai Ebn Yokdhan*. Toward the end of the preface, he alerts the reader to some elements that are to be encountered in due course in the book. "I have here and there added a Note, in which there is an account given of some, great Man, some Custom of the Mahometans explain'd, or something of that Nature, which I hope will not be unacceptable. And lest any Person should, through mistake, make any ill use of it, I have subjoin'd an Appendix, the Design of which the Reader may see in its proper place."[74] Ockley stipulates that there is a correct way of reading the book and handling the text as he justifies this explanation to buffer against "mak[ing] any ill use of it." In the appendix, he elaborates more on the ways of reading the book and how readers should approach it because there has been "a bad Use made of this Book before."[75] Ockley maintains that some readers are unable to discern for themselves and therefore he is justifying this intervention because some readers, in his words, are "weak" or are suffering from the prejudices of "bad Education." He says: "Lest otherwise, that Book, which was by me design'd for the Innocent, and not altogether unprofitable Diversion of the Reader, might accidentally prove a means of leading some into Error, who are not capable of judging aright; and of confirming others in their Mistakes, who, through their own Weakness, or the Prejudice of a bad Education, have the Misfortune to be led out of the way."[76]

He then decides the epistemic trajectory of the reader by letting the reader know precisely why this book must be rejected. It is specifically because it contains errors. "There are a great many Errors both in his *Philosophy* and *Divinity*: And it was impossible it should be otherwise, the one being altogether *Aristotelian*, the other *Mahometan*."[77] "Mahometan" being a strictly European invention, "the imaginary spatial formation that lent itself to popular consumption through its seeming disconnect with English society" was also associated with the declining influence of Aristotle as another dissimilarity, at the time at least.[78] Ockley performed on his readers the necessary epistemological immunization against the insalubrious consequences of reading *Ḥayy b. Yaqẓān*. He created the underlying conditions of future understandings by providing what Gadamer calls a fore-understanding (*Vorverständnis*) and/or prejudice (*Vorurteil*).[79] Readers are then guided not by their critical questions and understanding but by a preunderstanding of the text, an intellectually premasticated guidance to feed readers unable to break it down for themselves. What conditions of understanding, might one ask, would drive Ockley to reduce an entire text to an idea, or indeed, as Muhsin al-Musawi rightly notes, reduce literary texts into "documents" in the context of his discussion of the *Thousand and One Nights*?[80] The ready-made answer today would be "Orientalism." However, it is arguable that Orientalism is an intellectual symptom of an ecology of legitimization that has paved the epistemological foundation for it. The difference between the two scholarly translations of a very popular text may alert us to another popular text that was the theoretical framework of the times.

In his seminal work *An Essay Concerning Human Understanding* (1690), John Locke (1632–1704) resolves what he perceives as the incompatibility of empirical thinking with figurative language by rejecting the metaphor:

> —that men who have a great deal of wit, and prompt memories, have not always the clearest judgment or deepest reason. For wit lying most in the assemblage of ideas, and putting those together with quickness and variety, wherein can be found any resemblance or congruity, thereby to make up pleasant pictures and agreeable visions in the fancy; judgment, on the contrary, lies quite on the other side, in separating carefully, one from another, ideas wherein can be found the least difference, thereby to avoid being misled by similitude, and by affinity to take one thing for another. This is a way of proceeding quite contrary to metaphor and allusion; wherein for the most part lies that entertainment and pleasantry of wit, which strikes so lively on the fancy, and therefore is so acceptable to all people, because its beauty appears at first sight, and there is required no labour of thought to examine what truth or reason there is in it. The mind, without looking any further, rests satisfied with the agreeableness of the picture and the gaiety of the fancy. And it is a kind of affront to go about to examine it, by the severe rules of truth and good reason; whereby it appears that it consists in something that is not perfectly conformable to them.[81]

Locke's importance in this discussion is evident: "Locke rules the thought of his own and the coming period because he interpreted so completely the fundamental beliefs which had been worked out at this time. He ruled, that is, by obeying."[82] Locke describes metaphor and allusion as requiring no "labor of thought" and he calls it an affront to examine it by the rules of truth and good reason. It is not surprising that the *Essay*, popular as it is not just in Britain but Europe as well judging by Voltaire's comments on it, earned the wrath of Romantic poets such as William Blake (1757–1827), who regarded it with "Contempt and Abhorrence."[83]

Locke's rejection of figurative language, or what he calls the "Poetick Vein," stems from his renunciation of metaphor for pragmatic concepts of language. In his view, what he calls "Wit" is situated in an "assemblage of ideas" to make these pleasant pictures, as he describes it. "Judgment," on the other hand, requires separating the assemblage of these ideas one from the other in order to avoid being misled by what he calls "Similitude." To Locke, then, the literary image must be carefully reduced to an *Idea*. Some of our ideas are adequate, Locke observes, while others are inadequate; the adequate "perfectly represent those archetypes which the mind supposes them taken from: which it intends them to stand for, and to which it refers them."[84] Figurative language therefore is by default inadequate unless we reduce it to its simple idea which it must refer to: the archetype.

In this respect, it could be argued that this becomes the specter that haunts modern thought, where "the truth of the object determines the truth of discourse that it describes, leading to positivism," or where "the truth of the philosophical discourse constitutes the truth of the phenomenon, leading to a form of discourse that Foucault calls 'eschatological.'"[85] This "attempt to settle the fluctuation by combining eschatology and positivism will only end in being both at once, and thereby lapse into a pre-critical naivety."[86] Indeed, Ockley's preface to the work and his treatment of his readers attests at best to a preference of this precritical naivete and at worst to the historical conditions of what I would like to call and identify as the fanatic or literal reader.

Later in his *Essay*, Locke provides the remedy to what he deems as the imperfections and abuse of words and language. Among these remedies, for instance, is providing definitions for ideas used or naming objects by which one of its qualities signifies this idea. Imagination and Wit are considered a misusing of words.

> Wit and imagination get a better welcome in the world than dry truth and real knowledge; so people will hardly think that the use of *figurative language and literary allusion* constitutes an imperfection or misuse of language. In contexts where we seek pleasure and delight rather than information and improvement, such ornaments are indeed not faults. But if we want to speak of things as they are, we must allow that all the art of rhetoric (except for order and clearness)—all the artificial and figurative application of words that eloquence has invented—serve only to insinuate wrong ideas, move the passions, and thereby mislead the judgment; and so they are perfect cheats. . . . It is evident how much men love to deceive and be deceived, since rhetoric—that powerful instrument of error and deceit—has its established practitioners, is publicly taught, and has always been highly regarded. No doubt I will be thought rash or oafish to have spoken against it.[87]

Certainly, for someone who was a professor of Greek, whose library included seventy-three works of English literature, including Donne and Milton, and who composed poetry himself including his own epitaph,[88] Locke is aware of how these views might sound as shown by his disclaimer-like final line. However unpopular the views may be, the popularity of Locke's *Essay* is often compared to Newton's *Principia* (1687, translated into English in 1728). Locke was obeying the times, for he speaks of language in terms of achieving a morality analogous to mathematics: "That is why I venture to think that morality is capable of demonstration, as well as mathematics."[89] Romantic English poet William Blake (1757–1827), in his own assessment of this period, writes:

> I turn my eyes to the Schools and Universities of Europe
> And there behold the Loom of Locke whose Woof ranges dire
> Washed by the Water-wheels of Newton[90]

Blake, of course, describes the technological progress but also the popularity of both Locke's and Newton's ideas as intellectual shapers of eighteenth-century European discourse. As Leslie Stephen observes, for the following century, "Locke's philosophy blends spontaneously with the ordinary language of all educated men."[91] An educated man, Ockley was obeying the historical conditions of understanding and reading but simultaneously failed to show hospitality or adab to the text or the text's own message. Ockley maintains that it should be rejected. One may ask, Why was it translated in the first place and who are the readers qua beneficiaries? Or better yet, How do these receptions affect our understanding of instances of world literature? Did the Lockian framework itself affect the interpretive discourse on *Ḥayy b. Yaqẓān*, through an ecology of legitimization, conditioning readers to interpret it as an example of "Enlightenment" rather than its own enlightenment or even a source for Enlightenment?

If we seek to understand and identify the presence of an early modern and Enlightenment world literature, we can, as Srinivas Aravamudan argues, "make visible the traces of what vertical national histories have subsequently obscured. We need multiple historical cosmopolitanisms anchored in the past to contextualize our singular global modernity, whether this would mean Sinicizing, Africanizing, Americanizing, or Islamicizing it."[92] A principal example of both Enlightenment and Orientalism, Aravamudan argues, *Ḥayy b. Yaqẓān* forces "a reconsideration by eighteenth-century scholars as an Islamicate instance of World literature that is adduced as a source—rather than just as a product—of the Enlightenment."[93]

If Ockley's preface and appendix are an example of the "advancement of good literature by bringing to light much knowledge which as yet is locked up in that learned tongue," it unfortunately created the conditions for a patronized, infantilized reader, who read literally for the *Idea*, for the archetype, becoming an intellectual captive of religious, aesthetic, and literary differences.[94] In Ibn Ṭufayl's language, this is a gross injustice as he was telling us about misreading al-Ghazālī and eventually his own act of intellectual *inṣāf* (see chapter 4). Indeed, this act of intellectual *inṣāf* or giving due intellectual justice can only be performed and actualized through the propelling forces of critique and reasoning as *naẓar*; a reader without *inṣāf* is a fanatic reader. Ockley could not meet the alterity of his text's interlocutor. Instead, he seized control over the readers of his translation as he reduced them epistemologically into cognizable categories of incomprehensibility. Oblivious to his participation in an ecology of delegitimization, Ockley is (perhaps) unaware how nihilistic his hermeneutic move was. It betrays critical readings and instead privileges noncritical, "fanatical," readings. It did not produce novel worldviews or values, but instead reproduced its own image. An "understanding" would entail that Ockley was able to garner a semblance of useful insights from this encounter, to generate knowledge. The intellectually barren hermeneutical move is nihilistic because it closes interpretation and insights for posterity after reducing the horizon of the text to its own. Contrary to this nihilistic move is the generative adabful reading of British writer and poet Alexander Pope, who is a later reader of both Ockley and Locke. In May 1713, Pope published an essay in a London broadsheet called *The Guardian* condemning the way certain local pastimes involved the abuse of animals.[95] In this essay, Pope laments the cruelty shown toward animals in Britain at the time, which he deems "a distinguishing character of our own nation, from the observation which is made by foreigners of our beloved pastimes, Bear-baiting, Cock-fighting, and the like." To construct his argument, Pope appeals to several literary, historical, and religious authorities to make a case against this behavior. Among the figures and authorities invoked, in order of reference in the essay, are English poet John Dryden (1631–1700); French essayist Michel de Montaigne (1533–92); English philosopher John Locke (1632–1704); Monsieur Fleury (1639–85), a French lawyer turned actor and writer who wrote plays that satirized society;[96] Seneca (ca. 4 BC–AD 65), Roman Stoic philosopher, statesman, and also a dramatist; Plutarch (ca. AD 46–120), Greek biographer and essayist famous for his *Moralia* or *Moral Essays* and *Parallel Lives* of Greek and Roman military leaders and statesmen; Cato the Elder or the Censor (*Censorius*, 234–149 BC), a Roman soldier, senator, and historian who was also the first to write history in Latin. Pope then makes a reference to the "Arabian author" and his protagonist "The Self-Taught Philosopher." He then quotes Ovid (43 BC–AD 17/18), a Roman poet during Augustus's time, famous for his *Metamorphoses* and the *Heroides*. Pope also references *The Persian Fables of Pilpay*, also known as *Kalīla wa-Dimna*. Afterward, he quotes John Dryden (again) and then finally concludes with a story from the book of Jonas and the book of Deuteronomy from the Bible.[97] Pope wanted to reach out to every single reader and the only mediating tool possible is what is perceived as the foundational texts in the humanities. "The privilege of the reader's perspective is predicated on the distance or gap between the past and the present, but the classical, Hans-Georg Gadamer argues, overcomes the very idea of historical distance. . . . It implies a . . . continuous historical mediation between the past and the present."[98] This in turn means that the work's power to address us is "fundamentally unlimited."[99]

History tells us of a wise and polite nation that rejected a person of the first quality, who stood for a judiciary office, only because he had been observed in his youth, to take pleasure in tearing and murdering of birds. And of another that expelled a man out of the senate, for dashing a bird against the ground which had taken shelter in his bosom. *Every one knows how remarkable the Turks are for their humanity in this kind: I remember an Arabian author, who has written a treatise to show, how far a man supposed to have subsisted in a desert island, without any instruction, or so much as the sight of any other man, may, by the pure light of nature, attain the knowledge of philosophy and virtue.* One of the first things he makes him observe is, that universal benevolence of nature in the protection and preservation of its creatures. In imitation of which the first act of virtue he thinks his *self-taught philosopher* would of course fall into is, to relieve and assist all the animals about him in their wants and distresses.[100]

The work referred to in Pope's letter is Ibn Ṭufayl's twelfth-century epistle, which is the *locus classicus* of the feral child in philosophy.[101] The book was so popular that "the identification of the *Hayy ibn Yaqzan* . . . had become widespread enough to be how the editor of a 1757 edition of the letters of Alexander Pope glossed a passing reference to it."[102] The effortless juxtaposition of these references forces us to question a few things, as Aravamudan intimates, with regard to conceptions of world literature avant la lettre, canon, and circulation of Arabic literature and its uses and value, and the tools of critique, all great and important questions but outside the scope of this discussion; but most importantly for us it shows how Pope used the text as an interlocutor to engage in discourse, in an English adab sphere, so to speak. Pope was arguably going against routine discourse in British culture where certain attitudes toward animals are concerned, as he acknowledges in the letter. It would not be inaccurate to describe him as the exceptional discourse, among the earliest advocates where animal rights were concerned at the time.

In this respect, as Sanjay Subrahmanyam advises, if we were to go about big global intellectual and/or literary histories, then other parts of the world cannot simply be used as a foil or reflection to some other parts, or a comparison alone as well, but there must be a focus on connections and intellectual contacts.[103] By doing so, we would be able to regard texts as interlocutors and therefore they can show us the critical stances of both the text itself toward the conception of discourse, critique, and understanding in itself and toward other texts but also the historical conditions of discourse and the nuances between routine discourse and exceptional discourse (to which we now turn).

4

Adab as Critique

*Reading as Critical Justice (*Inṣāf*): al-Maʿarrī's* Zajr al-nābiḥ *and a Typology of Negative Readers*

INṢĀF AS AN ISLAMIC IMPERATIVE AND THE EPISTEMOLOGY OF ETHICAL READING IN ADAB: AL-MAʿARRĪ'S *ZAJR AL-NĀBIḤ*

This chapter situates the critical responses to al-Maʿarrī's (d. 449 AH/1057 CE) auto-commentary *Zajr al-nābiḥ* (Chiding the Barking Dog(s)), written in response to misrepresentations and falsifications about his poetry collection (*dīwān*) *Luzūm mā lā yalzam* (Unnecessary Necessity), within a discourse of "ethical reading" under the critical category of *inṣāf*. Acknowledging the deliberate misreading of his poetry, al-Maʿarrī's utilization of rhetorical, grammatical, and poetic techniques in this auto-commentary achieves the performative nature required of the agon between him and his opponent(s) and situates the adversaries as non-adabized readers.

The book's dialectical nature was not lost on later literati and/or historians like Ibn al-ʿAdīm (d. 660 AH/1262 CE) and Yūsuf al-Badīʿī (d. 1037 AH/1662 CE), who both authored their own versions of critique based on a close reading of al-Maʿarrī's work and the latter's aforementioned auto-commentary. Both authors had no vested interest in al-Maʿarrī, nor were they his contemporaries. Rather, Ibn al-ʿAdīm authored a distinct monograph as *al-Inṣāf wa-l-taḥarrī fī dafʿ al-ẓulm ʿan Abī al-ʿAlāʾ al-Maʿarrī* (The Righting and Investigation in the Elimination of Injustice against al-Maʿarrī) to refute the claims and fabrications against al-Maʿarrī. Translating *inṣāf* as "righting" may not do it justice but it is a springboard to our discussion on this important Islamic ethical imperative. Considering al-Maʿarrī's auto-commentary and the two subsequent works in its support allows us to achieve a better understanding of ethical reading and the critical category of *inṣāf* as an Islamic imperative within the context of the agon presented.

Zajr al-nābiḥ is a product of, and a reply to, misreading and malicious intent according to al-Maʿarrī.[1] Al-Maʿarrī's rival in this book is unknown. He is never addressed by name and al-Maʿarrī never tells us if it is one individual or many. It is likely that al-Maʿarrī had one person, not several, in mind in the context of this agon.[2] This is not to rule out that al-Maʿarrī did not have rivals and critics who attacked his poetry verbally or critiqued him. Rather, there is indication in *Zajr al-nābiḥ* that al-Maʿarrī was referring to textual evidence, not an amalgam of hearsay or a verbal criticism. The textual evidence therefore must have belonged to an author, naturally. It is unfortunate (for us) that al-Maʿarrī never named him. There are several examples of this textual evidence that will be mentioned in due course. In the most condemning one, for instance, al-Maʿarrī describes how this person performs deliberate poetry (mis)reading. He maintains that this objector conjoined a line of poetry with another couplet that should not be conjoined and read them as one (*wa-min jahl hādhā al-muʿtariḍ annahu waṣala bi-hādhayn al-baytayn baytan lā yadkhul maʿhumā wa-ẓanna annahu yajūz ann yūṣal ilayhumā*).[3] Al-Maʿarrī tells us that misreading here exceeds the boundaries of miscomprehension to the boundaries of deliberately doctoring the text but also that this misreading cherry-picks in some places to conjoin couplets in another place to falsify their order and therefore alter their meaning completely in a clear move of textual disfigurement and violence. The intellectual diagnosis of al-Maʿarrī for this action is a fault in character and an unsound mind and intellect (*gharīza nāqiṣa wa-lubb laysa bi-thābit*),[4] deliberate ignorance (*jāhil*), resistance to knowledge, or prejudice (*mutaḥāmil*), which he classifies as malicious falsification (*mummawih, mutaqawwil, mutakharris*), and epistemic trading (*mutasawwiq*).[5] In this diagnostic anatomy of *jahl*, we are given a conceptual map that dissects *jahl* through the many ways of misreading: the objector is ignorant, feigning ignorance, prejudiced, a liar, a forger, epistemic broker (*mutasawwiq*). The category of the epistemic trader, *al-mutasawwiq*, is also part of al-Maʿarrī's lexicon in his *Luzūmiyyāt*, where it is used in the same capacity (*wa-lā taqbalū min kādhib mutasawwiq taḥayyul fī naṣr al-madhāhib wa-ḥtajja*):[6]

> Do not accept from a liar, an [epistemic] trader, their artifice in
> Rallying for their ideas (*madhāhib*); object [resist]

The accusation therefore is presented as part of an epistemic warfare aimed at leveraging cultural capital at the expense of another or pushing certain agendas against others. Nowhere does al-Maʿarrī consider these acts of misreading here as misunderstanding, unexcused ignorance, inexperience, or honest mistakes; they are considered falsification proper. He classifies them as assaults (*jahl wa-iʿtidāʾ*).[7] Similarly, as mentioned in chapter 3, Ibn Ṭufayl classified the misreading of and attacks on al-Ghazālī in the same category as oppression and injustice (*ẓulm*) and those who performed them as unjust (*ẓālimūn*). This assault al-Maʿarrī diagnoses morally as depravity that is propagated by base people (*al-sāfila*) for whom lying became a habit (*wa-man jarā ʿādatahu bi-l-kadhib*).[8] Reading here is diagnosed as an activity that can be morally marred by the unsoundness of character and action and malicious intentions. This counterargument, one of many in the book, on al-Maʿarrī's part points to an awareness of an existing written text of the latter's doctored poetry that is circulating and was brought to his attention.

ANTI-*INṢĀF* AND NON-ADABIZED READERS

Forged (*mawḍūʿ*) or inauthentic, fabricated (*manḥūl*) poetry attributed to al-Maʿarrī may have appeared first (or was made to appear) in a potent manner in Ibn al-Jawzī's works (d. 597 AH/1201 CE); this is from Ibn al-Jawzī's *al-Muntaẓim*, as an example:

إن كانَ لا يَحْظَى بِرِزْقِكَ عَاقِلٌ وَتَرْزُقُ مَجْنُونًا وَتَرْزُقُ أَحْمَقًا
فَلا ذَنْبَ يا رَبَّ السَّمَاءِ عَلَى إمْرِئٍ رَأَى مِمَّا يَشْتَهِي فَتَزَنْدَقَا

If the reasonable is not favored with Your subsistence,
While You give subsistence to the senseless and the foolish,
Then, O God of Heaven, there must be no blame for him
Who receives from You what he does not desire
And then becomes an unbeliever (*tazandaqa*)[9]

Ibn al-Jawzī relates these couplets with a chain of transmission (*isnād*) that Ibn Nāṣir related them to him personally on the authority of Abū Zakariyyā (d. 502 AH/1109 CE), that al-Maʿarrī said these lines. Ibn al-Jawzī invokes the authority of his teacher Abū Zakariyyā al-Tabrīzī, since the latter was al-Maʿarrī's student, which makes Ibn al-Jawzī al-Maʿarrī's student one generation removed.[10] Ibn al-Jawzī's work is replete with forged poetry for unknown reasons other than what Tahir al-Garradi identifies as an "obsession with maintaining, through every means possible, the negative image of al-Maʿarrī."[11] Al-Maʿarrī is not the only target of the famous polemics of Ibn al-Jawzī. The latter has a famous maxim that became a quoted stigma in almost all subsequent books. He maintains that "the heretics of Islam (*zanādiqat al-Islām*) are three: Ibn al-Rawandī, Abū Ḥayyān al-Tawḥīdī, and Abū al-ʿAlāʾ al-Maʿarrī; the most malicious is al-Tawḥīdī because the other two were open about it but he hid it."[12] As Ibn al-ʿAdīm confirms to us repeatedly, these couplets, which first appear in Ibn al-Jawzī's work, are not to be found in any of al-Maʿarrī's *dīwān*s and cannot be authenticated; Ibn al-ʿAdīm calls them *mawḍūʿ* (forged).[13] If we entertained the thought that they were indeed said in private to al-Tabrīzī or to his students as part of an aside or a whimsical thought during a discussion as insinuated by Ibn al-Jawzī; the poetry's stylistics do not match al-Maʿarrī as previously indicated. Indeed, it is even believed that they were composed by al-Rawandī, whom Ibn al-Jawzī includes, not al-Maʿarrī, since Ibn al-Rawandī has similar poetry carrying these ideas, as does Ibn al-Rūmī according to al-ʿAqqād.[14]

Al-Tabrīzī, as one of al-Maʿarrī's close disciples, never insinuated the purported allegations raised by Ibn al-Jawzī. These couplets were later copied and imitated by including the attribution to al-Maʿarrī. These couplets were attributed to al-Maʿarrī despite the fact that they do not appear in his work. Ibn al-ʿAdīm maintains that not only is this bad, lowly, and tasteless poetry (*fī ghāyat al-suqūṭ wa-l-nuzūl wa-l-hubūṭ*), it committed the one who composed it to ignorance and disbelief (*yaqḍī ʿalā nāẓimihi bi-l-jahl wa-l-ʿamah wa-l-kufr*).[15] These are not the only forged couplets Ibn al-Jawzī relates for al-Maʿarrī, and Ibn al-Jawzī is not the only one to do so. Scholars Yāqūt al-Ḥamawī (d. 574 AH/1229 CE), al-Qifṭī (d. 646 AH/1248 CE), Qizughlī (Sibṭ Ibn al-Jawzī) (d. 654 AH/1256 CE), and Ibn Kathīr (d. 774 AH/1373 CE) similarly cite such lines. With the exception of Ibn Kathīr, the other scholars predated Ibn al-ʿAdīm, who offered a critical review of the accusations against al-Maʿarrī, which these authors seemed to have copied from each other. Ibn Kathīr, though, is an interesting case since he comes after Ibn al-ʿAdīm and quotes him in several places in his books. Despite this, he opted to copy from others and relate the forged poetry. He repeats the opinion of Ibn al-Jawzī and quotes him in several places. He even rejects those who apologize for al-Maʿarrī. He maintains, "He [al-Maʿarrī] authored many works, mostly poetry, and some of his poetry contains evidence of atheism and depravity (*zandaqa wa-inḥilāl*) and some people argue against this apologetically to say that he was indeed a Muslim but he said this in the manner of poetry (*kāna fī al-bāṭin musliman wa-innamā yaqūl dhālika bi-lisānihi*)."[16] Ibn Kathīr only mentions apologetic defense that may rely on emotions or aesthetic and stylistic defense arguing for poetic licenses but Ibn al-ʿAdīm indeed provided evidence against the forgeries circulating in the very books Ibn Kathīr is quoting from. Ibn Kathīr, in fact, does not provide a convincing reason against Ibn al-ʿAdīm nor does he present this case to argue against it. Rather, he quotes Ibn al-Jawzī throughout and it seems that the latter's authority, despite the mistakes and inaccuracies, is far more authoritative to Ibn Kathīr than the compelling evidence provided by Ibn al-ʿAdīm's *Inṣāf*. Ibn al-Jawzī was labeled the Imam of his time but, according to other scholars, his books contained many mistakes (*kathrat aghlāṭihi fī taṣānīfihi*). This may be attributed to his prolific nature, since he worked on many books simultaneously.[17] Although Ibn al-Jawzī has indeed made many important and monumental contributions not only in *fiqh*, ḥadīth, *tafsīr*, and *waʿẓ* but also adab, he was noted for praising himself in his work and considering himself above others (*wa-naẓartu ilā ʿuluww himmatī fa-raʾaytuhā ʿajaban. . . . khuliqat lī himmāt ʿāliya taṭlub al-ghayāt*).[18] And it was attributed to him that he described himself as a "compiler and not an author" (*anā murattib wa-lastu bi-muṣannif*).[19] It would not be inaccurate to argue that the forged poetry attributed to al-Maʿarrī in the aforementioned scholars' works may be the first, and perhaps only, point of entry to al-Maʿarrī's presumed poetry for some readers. This rather unfortunate introduction can explain the persistence of the allegations against him.

THE TEXT WITHIN THE TEXTS

It is imperative to ask at this juncture two questions: Why, despite al-Maʿarrī's authoring *Zajr al-nābiḥ* to defend himself and his poetry, do the accusations persist as seen in the aforementioned scholars' works? Do the doctored or patched-up couplets that appear in the works of the abovementioned scholars rely on each other without resorting to the primary source (i.e., *taqlīd*) or on the defamatory book mentioned by al-Maʿarrī at least at the first instance of copying the doctored verses? It seems that within the corpus of these prominent scholars, the poetry of al-Maʿarrī is corrupted. This suggests that the authors are either copying from a similar independent primary source (the defamatory book) or that they relied on each other at some point without consulting al-Maʿarrī's works. Copying from the defamatory book seems unlikely because that would imply they all owned copies of the book or consulted it, but it is more logical to conjecture that these authors read each other; Ibn Kathīr read Ibn al-Jawzī, and it is more probable that the former would have read someone in his field rather than a secondary or tertiary source on one poet that is not the focus of his scholarship. That said, on the one hand, it is a mark of inadequate scholarship and also a case of bad *taqlīd* and, on the other, it shows a prejudice against the corrective evidence presented, which Ibn Kathīr and others after him still rejected.

Premodern litterateurs point to a single book that was specifically written as an attack on al-Maʿarrī by one Abū Manṣūr al-Khawāfī (d. 480 AH/1087 CE) titled *Rajm al-ʿifrīt*,[20] or *Rajmat al-ʿifrīt* (The Stoning of the Demon, or The Tombstone of the Demon).[21] This work is mentioned by Yāqūt al-Ḥamawī[22] and al-Ṣafadī (d. 764 AH/1363 CE).[23] Al-Khawāfī was a scribe (*kātib*), a keeper of accounts (*ḥāsib*), and a composer of poetry as well.[24] A contemporary of al-Maʿarrī, he lived and worked in Baghdad, while al-Maʿarrī did not leave his hometown in Maʿarrat al-Nuʿmān in Syria or his house with the exception of the nineteen-month journey to Baghdad to visit the library of Dār al-ʿIlm (House of Knowledge) and his return back in 400 AH/1009 CE.[25]

Al-Khawāfī has another book titled *Kitāb khalq al-insān muratabba ʿalā ḥurūf al-muʿjam* (The Creation of Man Arranged in a *Luzūmiyyāt* Manner). In other words, he is exhibiting the highest form of flattery, not only toward al-Maʿarrī, in imitation, by arranging a book lexically, but also to al-Aṣmaʿī and others in the topic and title of choice.[26] The sensational and catchy title, *Rajm al-ʿifrīt*, may explain Ibn al-Jawzī's and others' scathing criticism against al-Maʿarrī and the relating of all the doctored verses in some of their selections of al-Maʿarrī's poetry and why Ibn al-Jawzī, for instance, calls him "the damned al-Maʿarrī" (*al-Maʿarrī al-laʿīn*), with different variations on this name-calling in his books. One should add, this does not preclude Ibn al-Jawzī from citing and quoting from al-Maʿarrī's poetry in a positive tone alongside al-Mutanabbī's in his book *al-Mudhish* to corroborate his argument for asceticism, *al-Mudhish* being, of course, a book concerned with guidance and leading a life of spiritual wellness (a genre of *waʿẓ wa-irshād*).[27] Since *Rajm al-ʿifrīt* is not available to us, it is difficult to ascertain its content.[28] In other words, we are constructing its content based on al-Maʿarrī's agon in his *Zajr al-nābiḥ* and his selections of couplets and responses.

THROUGH A BOOK JUSTLY: THE METRICS OF *INṢĀF*

Ibn al-ʿAdīm (d. 660 AH/1262 CE) and Yūsuf al-Badīʿī (d. 1037 AH/1662 CE) both authored their own versions of *critical justice* works (*inṣāf*) based on a close reading of al-Maʿarrī's work and the author's auto-commentary. The two books by Ibn al-ʿAdīm and al-Badīʿī are united by more than their subject matter. Though separated by four centuries, they both engage in a unique type of scholarship that I would like to call critical justice scholarship. I use the word justice, although other terms may be available, such as corrective or testimonial. This is based on the authors' identification of the type of work they do. Ibn al-ʿAdīm used the words *inṣāf* and *taḥarrī*, justice and (information) pursuing, to defeat injustice in the matter of al-Maʿarrī: that was the title of his book. *Inṣāf* loosely means justice (*ʿadl*) as an abstract concept. But its original acceptation refers to giving the half (*niṣf*) of something to someone. *Inṣāf* can then be safely regarded as distributive justice but can only be applied after investigative critique—how else is one to determine the nature or magnitude of the missing part? Ibn Manẓūr (d. 711 AH/1311 CE) tells us that *inṣāf* is giving someone their right (*iʿṭāʾ al-ḥaqq*).[29] In this respect, it is quite fruitful to think of this image as giving someone their right by presenting the missing part (half) of the argument that may be deliberately hidden, or as Ibn Khaldūn would say "artificially distorted."[30] Ibn Manẓūr's definition implies that the right may be owed by person A to person B and therefore it should be given. This is certainly the case; however, as both Ibn al-ʿAdīm and al-Badīʿī show us, they are giving the right to al-Maʿarrī though they do not directly owe it to him in the sense of a direct right but rather of a moral right. *Inṣāf* therefore implies an obligation and a commitment to the abstract notion of justice at large for which the injustices against people, even strangers, or temporal and historical others such as al-Maʿarrī in our case, may be universally owed this justice. We are morally owed and owe *inṣāf*. In other words, *inṣāf* becomes an imperative to uphold. I argue also that this imperative derives its legitimacy not only from a commitment to justice as an ethical abstraction but also from a commitment to truth; the veracity of knowledge and its production; and the justice of understanding, which I shall explain in due course. As previously mentioned, both authors had no vested interest in al-Maʿarrī, nor were they his contemporaries. Considering this allows us a better understanding of ethical reading and *inṣāf* as an Islamic imperative and a critical category of thought within the context of the agon presented.

The jurisprudent of Aleppo Ibn al-ʿAdīm studied the entire corpus of al-Maʿarrī. In addition to giving the detailed information about the physical structure of the book, Ibn al-ʿAdīm maps the epistemic valence of these allegations and the types of characters behind them. Beside stating the obvious that these claims are baseless lies, he distinctly describes their perpetrators as "without conscience" and without respect for human sanctity itself (*ḥurma*), not only because they find it easy and normative to violate al-Maʿarrī's reputation with baseless and harmful allegations, but also because they have no respect for his scholarship.

> وَقَدْ وَضَعَ أَبُو الْعَلَاء كِتَابًا وَسَمَّاهُ بِزَجْرِ النَّابِحِ، أَبْطَلَ فِيهِ طَعْنَ الْمُزْرِيِّ عَلَيْهِ وَالْقَادِحِ. وَبَيَّنَ فِيهِ عُذْرَهُ الصَّحِيحَ، وَإِيمَانَهُ الصَّرِيحَ، وَوَجْهَ كَلَامِهِ الْفَصِيحِ. ثُمَّ أَتْبَعَ ذَلِكَ بِكِتَابٍ وَسَمَّاهُ بِنَجْرِ الزَّجْرِ، بَيَّنَ فِيهِ مَوَاضِعَ طَعَنُوا بِهَا عَلَيْهِ بَيَانَ الْفَجْرِ. فَلَمْ يَمْنَعْهُمْ زَجْرُهُ. وَلَا اتَّضَحَ لَهُمْ عُذْرُهُ. بَلْ تَحَقَّقَ عِندَهُمْ كُفْرُهُ. وَتَجَرَّأُوا عَلَى ذَلِكَ وَدَامُوا، وَعَنَّفُوا مَنِ انْتَصَرُوا لَهُ وَلَامُوا. وَقَعَدُوا فِي أَمْرِهِ وَقَامُوا. فَلَمْ يَرْعَوُا لَهُ حُرْمَةً، وَلَا أَكْرَمُوا عِلْمَهُ، وَلَا رَاقَبُوا إِلًّا وَلَا ذِمَّةً، حَتَّى حَكَوْا كُفْرَهُ بِالْأَسَانِيدِ، وَشَدَّدُوا فِي ذَلِكَ غَايَةَ التَّشْدِيدِ، وَكُفْرَهُ مَنْ جَاءَ بَعْدَهُمْ بِالتَّقْلِيدِ

> Abū al-ʿAlāʾ wrote a book and titled it *Zajr al-nābiḥ* wherein he invalidated the claims of those who attacked him and explained his correct defenses, correct faith, and his eloquent speech. He then followed it with a book and titled it *Najr al-zajr* wherein he pointed out their claims as false. His chiding did not stop them, and they did not want to see his explanation. Indeed, they were even more convinced in his disbelief (*kufrihi*). That is how impudent they were. And they continued with this and even intimidated those who sided and supported him [Abū al-ʿAlāʾ]. Fixated as they were with him, they never let the matter drop. They never heeded that they were violating his human sanctity (*lam yarʿū lahu ḥurma*), they never recognized his knowledge and scholarship (*wa-lā akramū ʿilmahu*), they were not cognizant of any limitations or even their own conscience (*wa-lā rāqabū illā wa-lā dhimma*), so much so that they narrated and propagated the allegation of his atheism with chains of transmission (*ḥakaw kufrahu bi-l-asānīd*) and were extremely rigid and fixated about it. Thus, those who came after them accused him of blind imitation (*taqlīd*).[31]

Ibn al-ʿAdīm also interestingly sheds light on the problematic issue of blind imitation in scholarship (*taqlīd*), where he calls those who followed suit blind imitators. He also indirectly insinuates that they are weak as well, since they cowered before the intimidation (mainstream opinions resulting from peer pressure of the doxa) of those who wish to defame al-Maʿarrī. He debunks the false allegations of those who accused him of parodying the Qur'an and atheism.

The other litterateur who mentions *Zajr al-nābiḥ* is Yūsuf al-Badīʿī (d. 1037 AH/1662 CE) in his book *Awj al-taḥarrī ʿan ḥaythiyyat Abī al-ʿAlāʾ al-Maʿarrī* (The Apex of Tracking the Context of Abū al-ʿAlāʾ al-Maʿarrī), where he maintains:

> وَقَدْ أَلَّفَ أَبُو الْعَلَاء كِتَابًا فِي الرَّدِّ عَلَى مَنْ نَبَّهَ إِلَى مُعَارَضَةِ الْقُرْآنِ وَالْجَوَابِ عَنْ أَبْيَاتٍ اسْتَخْرَجُوهَا مِنْ نَظْمِهِ، وَرَمَوْهُ بِسَبَبِهَا بِالْكُفْرِ وَالطُّغْيَانِ. وَسَمَّى الْكِتَابَ (زَجْرَ النَّابِحِ). رَدَّ فِيهِ عَلَى الطَّاعِنِ فِي دِينِهِ وَالْقَادِحِ
>
> Abū al-ʿAlāʾ authored a book defending himself against those who accused him of parodying the Qur'an. The reason for this accusation of atheism and [intellectual] despotism was some verses that he composed. He called the book *Zajr al-nābiḥ*, in which he responded to those who accused him in his religion and disparaged him.[32]

INṢĀF AND KNOWLEDGE PRODUCTION

Arab-Islamic intellectual history is not short on discussions on the nature, definition, and essence of knowledge (*ʿilm*) and its concomitant relationship to truth. Franz Rosenthal's study on knowledge offers a helpful examination of the subject and the ways disciplines and fields regard knowledge: from its conception and use in poetry in pre-Islamic times and the Qur'an, to definitions by several scholars in fields like theology, religious science, Sufism, and philosophy. Therefore, to say that there is one standard definition across the board would be inaccurate. To say that exegetes and ḥadīth scholars defined knowledge in the same manner or held the same definition for all disciplines of life would also be erroneous. Both aforementioned literati, Ibn al-ʿAdīm and al-Badīʿī, are dealing with what is generally described in Western academe as a secular topic: the poetry of al-Maʿarrī. Their approach to this poetry as an object of knowledge may be influenced by their training but it remains within the confines of adab. That said, Rosenthal suggests that as of the ninth century, some scholars authored books with chapters devoted solely to knowledge and its merits "in a secular sense and thus have stood close to the beginnings of a long chain of literary effusions in praise of knowledge."[33] In this respect, the accuracy demanded in religious fields can be observed in secular topics, and the pursuit of knowledge was not restricted to certain fields over others. The purported allegations and the forged poetry dealt with different aspects of the definitions and essence of knowledge. In the realm of facts and factual knowledge, for the adversaries to say al-Maʿarrī *is* or *is not* an atheist would simply entail, as Ibn Ḥazm would tell us, a "certain cognition"; "Knowledge is certain cognition (*tayaqqun*) of a thing as it is."[34] That certain cognition and certainty (*yaqīn*) is a definition that points to a different set of skills on the acquisition of this knowledge and the tools of actualizing this certainty/*yaqīn*. While Ibn Ḥazm offers a theoretical definition, al-Ibshīhī offers a more practical one as he advises a recourse to both the traditional and intellectual. He says that it is "the perception of the realities of things through traditional and intellectual channels (*masmûʿan wa-maʿqûlan*)."[35]

But might one ask how the subject ascertains the type of knowledge acquired after applying themselves to the "traditional and intellectual"? How do Ibn al-ʿAdīm and al-Badīʿī and al-Dhahabī, for instance, *know*, without mistake or error, that they have achieved a certain *yaqīn*? How did Ibn al-Jawzī or Ibn Kathīr assess their knowledge of al-Maʿarrī? The application of skills also therefore points to a method of either copying one's predecessors, as some of the aforementioned scholars did, or viewing the material afresh with the sole purpose of knowing and examining. This leads us to al-Tahānawī's general definition that perhaps traverses disciplines, where knowledge "is definite and firm (*thâbit*) belief that conforms to actuality (*al-muṭâbiq li-l-wâqiʿ*)."[36] "Understanding," as a term, is used when the steps of knowing are "combined, coupled with epistemic justification, and placed in a broader, coherent, cognitive context."[37] In this respect, one can say, accordingly, *understanding* al-Maʿarrī, or any subject, involves several elements and channels of the "traditional and intellectual" that need the application of skills to actualize this knowledge (*tayaqqun*) by going through the entire corpus, such as the case of Ibn al-ʿAdīm and al-Badīʿī. This is what the two authors did: in their exposition of al-Maʿarrī's defense or *inṣāf*, Ibn al-ʿAdīm and al-Badīʿī list his works. These lists indicate both the facts and the direct firsthand experience as a way of knowing. The skill that they are displaying in the work to the readers is their method. To say that al-Maʿarrī *is*, in other words, to produce knowledge about al-Maʿarrī, requires the method displayed by the two authors in their books. Al-Badīʿī's imitation of Ibn al-ʿAdīm's method attests to the discursive nature of this knowledge as skill by *how* he imitated, not only the genre of justice and defense scholarship in the method displayed. This methodology of *inṣāf* also points to the significant nature of this critical category of thought. In his *Masālik al-abṣār fī mamālik al-amṣār*, Ibn Faḍlallāh al-ʿUmarī (d. 749 AH/1349 CE) quotes Ibn al-ʿAdīm on his own method and book in defense of al-Maʿarrī:

إِنِّي وَقَفْتُ عَلَى جُمْلَةٍ مِنْ مَصْنَفَاتِ عَالِمِ مَعَرَّةِ النُّعْمَانِ أَبِي الْعَلَاء أَحْمَد بْنِ عَبْد اللّٰه بْنِ سُلَيْمَان الْمَعَرِّيِّ فَوَجَدْتُهَا مَشْحُونَةً بِالْفَصَاحَةِ وَالْبَيَانِ مَوْدَعَةً فُنُونًا مِنَ الْفَوَائِدِ الْحَسَانِ، مُحْتَوِيَةً عَلَى أَنْوَاعِ الْأَدَبِ مُشْتَمِلَةً مِنْ عُلُومِ الْعَرَبِ عَلَى الْخَالِصِ وَاللُّبَابِ. لَا يَجِدُ الطَّامِحُ فِيهَا سَقْطَةً وَلَا يُدْرِكُ الْكَاشِحُ فِيهَا غَلْطَةً. وَلَمَّا كَانَتْ مُخَصَّصَةً بِهَذِهِ الْأَوْصَافِ مُمَيَّزَةً عَلَى غَيْرِهَا عِندَ أَهْلِ الْإِنْصَافِ قَصَدُوهُ جَمَاعَةً لَمْ يَعُوا عَنْهُ وَعْيَهُ وَحَسَدُوهُ إِذْ لَمْ يَنَالُوا سَعْيَهُ، فَتَتَبَّعُوا كُتُبَهُ عَلَى وَجْهِ الْاِنْتِقَادِ وَوَجَدُوهَا خَالِيَةً مِنَ الزَّيغِ وَالْفَسَادِ، فَحِينَ عَلِمُوا سَلَامَتَهَا مِنَ الْعَيْبِ وَالشَّيْنِ سَلَكُوا فِيهَا مَسْلَكَ الْكَذِبِ وَالْمِينِ. وَرَمَوْهُ بِالْإِلْحَادِ وَالتَّعْطِيلِ وَالْعُدُولِ عَنْ سَوَاءِ السَّبِيلِ، فَمِنْهُمْ مَنْ وَضَعَ عَلَى لِسَانِهِ أَقْوَالَ الْمُلْحِدَةِ وَمِنْهُمْ مَنْ حَمَلَ كَلَامَهُ عَلَى غَيْرِ الْمَعْنَى الَّذِي قَصَدَهُ، فَجَعَلُوا مَحَاسِنَهُ عُيُوبًا وَحَسَنَاتِهِ ذُنُوبًا، وَعَقْلَهُ حَمْقًا وَزُهْدَهُ فِسْقًا، وَرَشَقُوهُ بِأَلِيمِ السِّهَامِ وَأَخْرَجُوهُ عَنِ الدِّينِ وَالْإِسْلَامِ، وَحَرَّفُوا كَلِمَهُ عَنْ مَوَاضِعِهِ وَأَوْقَعُوهُ فِي غَيْرِ مَوَاقِعِهِ

I studied the corpus of al-Maʿarrī and I found it to be charged with eloquence and clarity, a repository of various forms of beneficial arts, containing several types of adab, comprising the knowledge of the Arabs. The faultfinder will not find in it any mistake. And since it was characterized by all these unique qualities, on a niche of its own as the fair-minded and just people (*ahl al-inṣāf*) would concur; a group of people who could not achieve his aptitude became resentful and envious that they could never accomplish what he did. So, they scoured through his books and could not find any sign of corruption in them. Knowing that, they opted instead for lying and twisting facts and accused him of atheism . . . some of them attributed false quotes to him and some interpreted his words in a different way than what they purport. . . . They cast him with the most painful of arrows, ousted him from religion and Islam . . . twisted his words from their meaning.[38]

Ibn al-ʿAdīm therefore presents for us his methodology; he maintains that he *studied* the works of al-Maʿarrī and not only did he study the ones available to him, but he went to great lengths to find books that were under-copied or rare. He gives us the exact locations of where copies were to be found. In reference to *Kitāb al-hamza wa-l-radif*, for instance, he maintains that it was rare because of its huge volume and the only copies available were at the Niẓāmiyya library and in Egypt in the collection of al-Malik al-Ṣāliḥ Ayyūb inherited from al-Qāḍī al-Ashraf and his father before him.[39] Al-Maʿarrī authored numerous works, as Ibn al-ʿAdīm's comprehensive list attests, but unfortunately not all of them have reached us. Al-ʿUmarī, a reader of Ibn al-ʿAdīm's critique and his methodology, further relates Ibn al-ʿAdīm's critique that reminds the reader that even the Qur'an, as a sacred and an inimitable text, was subject to deliberate allegations and misinterpretations from those whom he classifies as "falsifiers" (*ṭāʿinīn*, sing. *ṭāʿin*). He says that these people attempted to deceptively offer twisted interpretations to serve their own interests but they did not succeed (*fa-mā aḥsanū fī dhālika wa-lā ajādū*).[40] He then says, "Why should we be surprised that a regular person's words (human beings who are all prone to error) would be subjected to these claims? Even though his [al-Maʿarrī's] expertise and depth of language elevated him to a place no other could attain; the resentful ones deliberately twisted his words out of their meaning."[41] Al-ʿUmarī employs the commonly used word in Arabic for those deliberately misinterpreting and misreading to serve their own interests: *ṭāʿin* (*ṭ-ʿ-n*, lit. "s.o. who stabs with a sharp object"). The violent etymology of the verb explains its conceptual semantic meanings as also "abusive, libelant, calumniator." It is also a reminder of the previously mentioned idea of predatory reading commensurate with the image of dissonance as "wolf intervals." The etymology and the aforementioned meanings interestingly further explain to us the conceptual links between the false allegations against someone (*ṭaʿn*), and another variation of the verb as the plague (*ṭāʿūn*), not just in its obvious material meaning as an eminent lethal attacker that will end life indiscriminately but in its nonmaterial meaning as an entity with circulation, transmission, and negative influence.[42]

Al-Badīʿī took his cue from Ibn al-ʿAdīm's title and also wrote in the same genre. Writing in this genre, the two authors were operating from a paradigm of justice not only in relationship to al-Maʿarrī as a human being, a person, scholar, and poet, but also from the perspective of justice to knowledge and knowledge production. But unlike Ibn al-ʿAdīm, the Damascene poet and literatus al-Badīʿī includes a particular exordium to justify the composition of his book such that its title may be taken for its raison d'être.[43] In keeping with his titular methodology of inquiry (*taḥarrī*), he begins with al-Maʿarrī's biography and comparatively inserts the strength of memory for al-Mutanabbī (d. 354 AH/965 CE) and then, defying chronology, Abū Tammām (d. 231 AH/845 CE). Al-Mutanabbī may have indeed been al-Maʿarrī's favorite poet, and according to some premodern scholars, it was not difficult to see the specter of Abū Tammām in some of al-Mutanabbī's poetry.[44] But more than the spectral ghosts of past poets, there is an anecdote that relates the relationship between the three poets that may explain al-Badīʿī's choice of writing on these three or linking them. Al-Maʿarrī was once asked which of the three has the most poetic craft (*ashʿar*). Al-Maʿarrī replies, "al-Mutanabbī and Abū Tammām are sagacious (*ḥakimān*) but the poet is al-Buḥturī."[45] Ibn al-Athīr relates an even more superlative image about how he is poetically fulfilled (*iktafayt*) with these three poets over others. He described the three poets as the deities of Arabic poetry for their technique, craft, and the incorporation of innovative techniques of modern poets (*gharābat al-muḥdathīn*): "and these three are the Lāt of poetry and its ʿUzzā and Manāt" (*wa-hāʾulāʾ al-thalāthatu hum lātu al-shiʿri wa-ʿuzzāhu wa-manātuhu*).[46] The triptych of nonanxious influences was not lost on al-Badīʿī, who devoted two books to two of the three poets, the other two being *al-Subḥ al-munbī ʿan ḥaythiyyat al-Mutanabbī* and *Hibat al-ayyām fīmā yataʿallaq bi-Abī Tammām*. Al-Badīʿī's methodology, as evident from his chapters' selections, relies for the most part on relating biographical anecdotes on al-Maʿarrī's interactions with various people, his travels, what people say about him, and the controversy surrounding his poetry and faith from secondary sources. Even when he discusses the controversial opinions and the confirmation of al-Maʿarrī's faith he depends on secondary sources with no personal input on his part. Even in the section titled "Criticism against al-Maʿarrī" (*al-ashyāʾ al-muntaqada ʿalā Abī al-ʿAlāʾ*), al-Badīʿī relates what Yāqūt al-Ḥamawī had said and allows other scholars and authors to present their critique against al-Maʿarrī's poetry in a poetic dialogue-like presentation. He begins with Yāqūt al-Ḥamawī, then mentions al-Maʿarrī's lines and the counter-lines or critique by other scholars in a conversational style. For instance, al-Badīʿī writes "so the Judge al-Qazwīnī said," "the Judge Abū Muḥammad al-Yamanī replied," "and so replied al-Dhahabī."[47] The larger part of the book is devoted to selections from al-Maʿarrī's works. While al-Badīʿī is engaged in his neutral investigation, critique was not lost on him. His arrangement of the scholars responding to al-Maʿarrī or critiquing his poetry is in fact an attestation to (a) *inṣāf* to the responding scholar, al-Maʿarrī, as well as the reader and (b) an implicit understanding of the virtue of *inṣāf* on al-Badīʿī's part. Even if al-Badīʿī strategically placed himself outside critique by almost muting his critical voice and maintaining a neutral position subsumed under a methodology of "investigation" or an "inquiry," the work still operates under the ethics of *inṣāf*. Thus, while it may seem that al-Badīʿī is copying from secondary sources uncritically and engaging in *taqlīd*, the title itself communicates to the reader that the result of neutral investigation would lead to similar results. The same thing is true of Ibn al-ʿAdīm, who said in the exordium that he "studied the corpus of al-Maʿarrī . . . the faultfinder will not find in it any mistake nor would the spiteful adversary catch a mistake."[48] The critical stance therefore is in al-Badīʿī revisiting the secondary literature on al-Maʿarrī anew and cross-referencing critique as well as studying the corpus of al-Maʿarrī as evident in the selections offered in the book.

It may be worth asking why al-Badīʿī picks up the controversy nearly four centuries after Ibn al-ʿAdīm's book. Logically, it may appear tied to his literary interest in both Abū Tammām and al-Mutanabbī. However, the investigative stance of al-Badīʿī allows us to expand this conjecture that his is perhaps a critique of certain methodologies of *taqlīd* and/or rivalry and malice masked as attacks on faith. Ibn al-ʿAdīm envisioned his critique for a *future* he could imagine to be partially remedied of misunderstandings and attacks, that is, set right by his act of *inṣāf*. This is not what happened. The future discourse on al-Maʿarrī was not free of the same allegations Ibn al-ʿAdīm endeavored to expose through his critique. Ibn al-Wazīr al-Yamānī (d. 840 AH/1436 CE), who authored *Naṣr al-aʿyān ʿalā sharr al-ʿumyān* (The Victory of the Sighted over the Evil of the Blind), tells us that some ignorant people became taken by the poetry of al-Maʿarrī and "this poetry is so despicable to be even documented and it is far too base and insignificant to be even mentioned" (*aḥqar min an tusṭar wa-ahwan min an tudhkar*).[49] Another such work is *Kitāb al-muṭāwīl* by Muḥammad b. ʿAlī al-Qāmghār, known as Ibn al-Khaymī (d. 642 AH/1286 CE), which, according to al-Suyūṭī and al-Maqrīzī, responds to al-Maʿarrī in places where he erred (*al-radd ʿalā al-Maʿarrī fī mawāḍiʿ sahā fīhā*).[50] It is not possible to ascertain the content of this book or how Ibn al-Khaymī responded, but it is categorized under the general umbrella of responding to al-Maʿarrī.[51]

INṢĀF AS A CRITICAL CATEGORY OF THOUGHT

The viral copying of authors from each other and the deliberate ignoring of al-Maʿarrī's own self-defense invokes what Shahab Ahmed cautioned against: "When Muslims claim to be speaking and acting as *Muslims*, that is, to be speaking and acting in *Islam*, we need, as an analytical and conceptual matter, to take them *at their word*."[52] Perhaps playing one's own devil's advocate, if we postulate that *inṣāf* is a moral imperative, why does *inṣāf* wait two centuries after al-Maʿarrī's death to show itself in the form of these two works? Was the critical category of thought, *inṣāf*, unknown before? What are the epistemic sources of its critical value?

Concomitant to the categories of justice and truth, *inṣāf* is not a stranger to Islamic thought as an abstract concept fundamental to knowledge production and the understanding and the interpretation of empirical experience. While al-Maʿarrī was being inundated with false accusations in the eleventh century, Muslim scholars were beginning to write in the category of *inṣāf*.[53] One of the earliest works to employ *inṣāf* as a critical category of thought is by eleventh-century scholar and theologian Ibn ʿAbd al-Barr (d. 463 AH/1071 CE), the judge of Lisbon who authored *Kitāb al-inṣāf* about the various opinions and differences between scholars on the issue of saying the *basmala* before reading *al-fātiḥa*.[54]

To see the seeds of this intellectual fruit, it is rewarding to highlight what Ibn ʿAbd al-Barr relates elsewhere in a chapter devoted to *inṣāf*, in which he describes "the thriving and blessing of knowledge and its decorum (*ādāb*): impartiality/intellectual sobriety (*al-inṣāf fīhi*). One who is not impartial, does not understand and does not seek understanding" (*min barakat al-ʿilm wa-ādābihi al-inṣāf fīhi wa-man lam yunṣif lam yafham wa-lam yatafahham*).[55] *Inṣāf* here becomes the framework for the ethics of differences and disagreement. Ibn ʿAbd al-Barr relays the various views and disagreements among scholars in an attempt to arrive at an impartial judgment. *Inṣāf* therefore becomes a virtue-ethic as it regulates these differences and our interpretation of them.

The critical value was not a matter of personal proclivity or reasoned opinion of said scholar. Being a member of an epistemic community, the formulation of *inṣāf* as an ethical framework is arguably the result of deliberated discussions, efforts, and debates but also problems and issues that may have sparked solutions in the form of critical values, within the epistemic community. The genealogy of *inṣāf* may be argued therefore in terms of what was conceived as a critical category of thought, albeit abstract, and can also be seen in praxis in the birth and development of the science of criticism and praise (*al-jarḥ wa-l-taʿdīl*) since the early days of establishing the sciences of ḥadīth transmission concerning the evaluation and criteria of the reliability and unreliability of transmitters of ḥadīth. But it took shape by the eleventh century with the increase of untrue transmissions and conflicts. With the science of criticism and praise, *inṣāf* becomes an intellectual virtue proper, aimed at arriving at the truth of transmission. One would find here anecdotes about family members who testify against each other in favor of intellectual veracity. With regard to reliability of chains of transmission (*isnād*) of ḥadīth, for instance, once ʿAlī b. al-Madīnī was asked about his father, and he replied, "Ask someone else." They said, "We ask you." He looked down then lifted his head and said, "This is the religion: My father is weak [in ḥadīth narration]."[56] Transmitters of ḥadīth then applied the category of weak (*ḍaʿīf*) as it pertains to ḥadīth studies to their fathers, sons, and brothers regardless of their kinship or emotional ties. This practice, or rather praxis, is a direct application of Q.4:135 ("You who believe, uphold justice and bear witness to God, even if it is against yourselves, your parents, or your close relatives"). *Inṣāf*, then, can be seen to be applied as a critical category of thought that is used for the purpose of critique and rational judgment despite ties of kinship. The Qur'anic discourse places a prime importance on justice and critical justice as the utmost value to be held even if it is against oneself. *Inṣāf* as an imperative virtue is communicated as stronger than any perceived blood tie.

Ḥadīth scholar Abū Dāwūd al-Sijistānī (d. 275 AH/889 CE), well known for his *Sunan Abī Dāwūd*, called his own son a "liar."[57] In this respect, this science has constructed strict and unique rules for reliability that elevated *inṣāf* as a criteria for its methodological framework because it is an Islamic imperative. *Inṣāf*, as already established, is a requirement of murūʾa (the perfecting of being human or *humanism*).[58] Murūʾa is a quality that describes the fully human or the ideal human picture of the requisite behavior of the entity described regardless of gender; in other words, etymologically, it is derived from the essence of the human or expressing humanity in its fullest. In their discussion on murū'a, scholars stressed *inṣāf* as that which reigned supreme among other virtue-ethics.[59] It is reported that the Prophet asked a man from Thaqīf, "What is murū'a for your people?" The man said, "Prophet of God, *al-inṣāf* (justice) and *iṣlāḥ* (reform)." The Prophet replied, "And it is the same for us" (*wa-hiya kadhālika fīnā*).[60] The fields of ḥadīth and *fiqh* are not only showing us the place of this ethical imperative and its praxis as an intellectual virtue in Islamic intellectual history; these relationships also propose, indeed offer, conceivable intellectual connections between the fields of Islamic sciences and other fields as well as show their interrelated roles in mutual advancement and progress of these unique sciences (criticism and praise). Ḥadīth's framework for what constitutes reliable *isnād* proffered what can also be seen as the redefining of the intellectual virtuous subject who possesses *inṣāf*. If Abū Dāwūd, for instance, calls his son a "liar" where the authenticity of transmission is concerned, this heightens the imperative nature of *inṣāf* as a virtue and a critical category of thought as a foundation to epistemic justice. His love for his son is independent of his son being an unreliable ḥadīth transmitter. This does not only show us a slice of intellectual history and a footnote in the Islamic conception of justice but also sheds light on an unprecedented moment of emotional depth and maturity in accepting someone (even a family member) and at the same not being blinded by their shortcomings and failings, not letting their human faults affect one's acceptance of them. This stance—which may seem paradoxical to some—underscores a salient slice in the history of emotions with regard to not only the compartmentalization of emotions but the compartmentalization of emotions and acceptance of different colors in a relationship, even that of father-son. These examples impart on us lessons of emotional depth and tolerance as they also shun nepotism and favoritism that beget corruption, fanaticism, and societal decline. If this praxis of *inṣāf* is a prerequisite to murū'a, it is obvious that acknowledging the shortcomings of others but not letting that infringe on professionalism is an attestation of true expression of humanity. The Qur'an's choice of words is apt. In a perceived moral dilemma of choosing between justice and not threatening blood ties; the Qur'an urges to choose justice always. The perceived micro-chaos caused by privileging justice over blood ties sees the fierce instrument of morality as a threat, when in fact had that very instrument been upheld at all times, it would act as a buffer against the imminent and incremental macro-chaos and tyranny should justice be overthrown by the corrosiveness of weak morality. These strict and perhaps unique rules for reliability that elevated *inṣāf* as an intellectual virtue show not only the place of this ethical and intellectual virtue in Islamic intellectual history but also propose conceivable connections between the advancement and progress of these unique sciences (criticism and praise, *jarḥ wa-ta'dīl*) and the discourse on *inṣāf*. This theoretical discussion of *inṣāf* participates in the redefining and shaping of the intellectual virtuous subject. The desire, conscious or unconscious, to exercise *inṣāf* and the understanding of human biases and also weaknesses and the attempt to highlight them cannot be dissociated from adab and murūʾa. *Inṣāf*s imperative nature confronts these biases a priori within. The individual's will to *inṣāf* is an attestation of imperative justice, and, by extension, the sensibility of *inṣāf* will be the intellectual maturity that is also underlined with emotional maturity. The praxis of *inṣāf* is conceived as a practice of forming and epistemically evaluating something to arrive at a truth or knowledge that is "justified" via justice and therefore is a just truth. *Inṣāf*, then, is not just a critical category of thought that was and could be used as a *critique* of something. The historical moments in *fiqh* and ḥadīth where possessing *inṣāf* was a key to epistemic credibility and trustworthiness is therefore part of this intellectual tradition and ethical community even if they are not within the realm of *fiqh*. Aside from the theoretical value of this discussion, what this cross section of intellectual history shows us is a different form of social and relational tolerance in personal relationships. The son's admitting his father is weak or unreliable in the chain of transmission or the father's admitting his son's unreliability compartmentalized the personal from the professional. These individuals' *inṣāf* attests to their emotional and intellectual maturity and their own and others' humanity, which by far exceeds one who cannot accept the humanity or the flaws of their parents/children and would sacrifice professionalism for personal ties.

INṢĀF AND THE VIRTUOUS SUBJECT

This forces us, if we are to practice *inṣāf*, to shift the focus of discussion to others who did not generate the appropriate critical link and slipped into the *routine* interpretative habits such as Yāqūt al-Ḥamawī, Ibn al-Jawzī, Ibn Kathīr, and others. Is it appropriate to morally blame them for lack of *inṣāf*? Or is it more appropriate to practice what some moral philosophers call "resentment of disappointment," which encourages us to contest thinking of and challenge discourse that sees a culture's moral discourse as a "finite monolith"?[61] This is because a disappointment in general is based on the belief that it "*was* historically possible, in our newly extended sense, for [our distant/historical others] to have made a better judgment."[62] This blame cannot stand because in addition to the routine discourse, there is also the exceptional discourse, which may or may not have been within the ethical subject's reach. Is it possible to blame them for not making some exceptional leap of moral insight that was within their reach?[63] Is our blame stemming from questioning the epistemic tools and resources available to them at that historical moment or from knowing, in posterity, that they could do better? Can we think of these scholars as individuals only or as part of a structure, as they all read each other and operated within a field, hence the injustice toward al-Maʿarrī is more of a structural one rather than an individual one? Using these insights therefore when we are focused on what is perceived as *routine discourse* of this historical moment or that culture or this literary figure, we are viewing Arabic literary history as a *monolith* and also abandoning and not considering the *exceptional discourse* offered, which is not only exemplary of its historical moment but one that has utilized all moral and intellectual resources available to it.[64] To consider all discourses is *inṣāf* on our part. Therefore, there are two options offered to us as readers of these historical others presented in this chapter: to blame historical others like Ibn al-Jawzī and Ibn Kathīr, among others, for failing to realize what was obvious and available to Ibn al-ʿAdīm and al-Badīʿī, or to situate *inṣāf* as an imperative and embrace the discursive nuance in the one discourse as one pointing to contingencies; some are easier than others to discern. Ibn al-ʿAdīm attacks these people espousing the routine discourse using two categories: intellectual and ethical. He accused them of blind imitation and having no respect for al-Maʿarrī's scholarship and being without conscience. Ibn al-ʿAdīm relates to us that the majority of al-Maʿarrī's students "were imams, judges, scholars, literati, narrators of ḥadīth. They all learned and benefited from him and no one said anything about him that would tarnish his reputation or character."[65] Al-Maʿarrī himself, Ibn al-ʿAdīm maintains, is *musnad*; he narrated ḥadīth.[66] To add, Ibn al-ʿAdīm repeatedly and through various anecdotes shows us how close to the elite al-Maʿarrī was. He was known and favored by very powerful people in the corridors of power who asked him to author books for them, and some of them repeatedly offered to give him more money than his allotted allowance to subsist comfortably but he refused.[67] Within the framework of *inṣāf*, Ibn al-ʿAdīm therefore removed the accusers, who are outside the ethical and intellectual economy of *inṣāf*, into a deficit of credibility. To put it more clearly, to embrace the knowledge offered outside the imperative of *inṣāf* is to offer an interpretation of the work and the world without the complete hermeneutical tools and critical categories available and thereby would warrant that the reading is falling into grave errors, chief among which, as Ibn al-ʿAdīm tells us, is blind imitation.

It is unsurprising that Ibn al-ʿAdīm authored this book. Trained in ḥadīth, Ibn al-ʿAdīm possessed and forged the aforementioned intellectual links propelled by ḥadīth studies where *inṣāf* as a critical category of thought is put to practical use in the sciences of ḥadīth in particular. The abstract concept of *inṣāf* as an Islamic imperative is transformed into praxis and a genre of writing as Ibn al-ʿAdīm engages through *inṣāf* with the corpus of al-Maʿarrī. Ibn al-ʿAdīm authored his book in defense of al-Maʿarrī in what appears to be a scholarly genre of *inṣāf* paving the way for people outside the field of ḥadīth centuries later, like al-Badīʿī, to partake in the genre. The aforementioned intellectual tools presented by ḥadīth and *fiqh* offer the ethical subject a "tradition" of *inṣāf*, whereby the subject is epistemically socialized through this heritage from the ethical community to "generate an appropriate critical link between the traditional moment in which [they] gained their primary ethical socialization and the experiences that life offers [them]."[68] It appears then to us that the exceptional interpretative moment, the *inṣāf* of Ibn al-ʿAdīm and al-Badīʿī's books, offers us a link between the traditional moment exemplified in the Islamic imperative of *inṣāf* when faced with a life experience or a crisis, so to speak, of writing about al-Maʿarrī.

The opponent, to whom al-Maʿarrī is responding, wants us to believe that he performed critique on al-Maʿarrī's poetry and arrived at the conclusion that al-Maʿarrī and his poetry are outside Islam, adab, and the Arab-Islamic tradition. Al-Maʿarrī performed an adabized critique using the *iḥāla* of Arab-Islamic literary, historical, and social resources. The framework of regulating the adab of critique, so to speak, must rely on a recognized referent. Relying on speech (i.e., the content of his proof) al-Maʿarrī utilized the Arab-Islamic history, poetry, and idioms. In this respect, we have a difference between the two agons: the opponent is one who is disconnected from this history, while al-Maʿarrī practices what Andalusian poet, philologist, and literary critic Ḥāzim al-Qarṭājannī (d. 648 AH/1285 CE) calls *iḥāla*,[69] which is referring, but also, in a sense, a commitment to the reference. Referring indicates an allusion where a reader is invited to an understanding of a literary relationship by way of language and symbols. This invitation in itself carries a commitment of association. In other words, a noncontextual reading or a decontextualized reading, such as in this case, that overlooks all references and allusions cannot be classified as an adabized reading. This is the reason al-Maʿarrī depicts this reading as failed and errorist. Thus, a reference to history in a poem, or in al-Maʿarrī's agon, is more than an allusion or a reference to history to remind, represent, and compare, as al-Qarṭājannī lists some of the uses. It is a committing in the sense of obligating the other party to a framework of critique and reading through shared intellectual/historical institutions that cannot be escaped because it is (a) shared history and (b) a shared memory used to read the poem. By using this frame, al-Maʿarrī shows that if a reader is going through a hermeneutical crisis of understanding, it is because the reader does not have a critical, theoretical, and/or cultural frame. The reader is disengaged; although al-Maʿarrī and his readers know that the crisis is a fabricated hermeneutic crisis. In this respect, there is a difference between the two agons: the opponent is one who is disconnected from this history, cannot commit to *iḥāla*, and refuses the intra-linguistic reality of al-Maʿarrī's poetry or what Stefan Sperl calls "semiological mimesis,"[70] while as noted above al-Maʿarrī practices *iḥāla*. Constructing the opponent's speech/text through al-Maʿarrī's responses would indicate to us that his premises did not abide by any of the rules mentioned above. In this respect, in its own attempt in persuasion, besides being a lie, it rhetorically ignored the rules of persuasion and usurped what al-Qarṭājannī calls the committing referent (*iḥāla*), which al-Maʿarrī used. The opponent's text and accusations, as constructed through al-Maʿarrī's relating of the critical response, would fall under what I identify as an errorism that al-Maʿarrī tells us attempts to epistemically trade and profit. The errorist, whom al-Maʿarrī calls *jāhil* (ignorant), is not in need of a few lessons in adab or so al-Maʿarrī would have addressed him as a potential *adīb*. The errorist is intentionally misreading. Al-Maʿarrī therefore does not address the *homo ignorans*. Rather, he refers to him as if absent or in the third person. The *Zajr*'s grammatical shift (*iltifāt*) offers a posture away from the opponent; it evokes what Suzanne Stetkevych calls the *Luzūmiyyāt*'s "poetics of disengagement."[71] It disengages not only from the vital signs of life but arguably also from the reader as it constantly challenges them with ambivalence, an ambivalence couched, contradictorily, in a tyrannical, conformist lexical pattern.[72] The point of contention here is that this predatory reader, the errorist, is framing their critique of al-Maʿarrī's work using *jahl*-inducing frameworks and attempting to universalize this reading. He is engaging in the hermeneutics of *jahl* while al-Maʿarrī disengages and addresses the adabized, well-tempered reader. The intellectually scandalous dialogical exposure of said opponent is unenviable but also points us to adab as a critical method in itself. The act of critique is therefore granted to all parties; however, the soundness of critique is not.

The routine discourse of al-Maʿarrī that relates his alleged skepticism or atheism is not only an uncritical view but one that has adopted a routine discourse uncritically and abandoned a framework that took the full virtues in question. In other words, a critique that is not based on the cognizance of ethical imperatives is questionable, as it fails to embody complete integrity. The refusal to see these discursive nuances therefore is a refusal to see the discursive efforts within the one tradition. This ultimately highlights a tendency to adopt one narrative rather than the other—cherry-picking. Embracing the routine discourse only is a choice on the reader's part, past and future readers, which points to an embracing of literary and critical judgments based on subjects who, according to the culture's intellectual and ethical imperative, have not applied full virtue-ethics. In the aforementioned examples, the achievement of full virtue-ethics depended on generating a critical link between the tradition in an ethical continuum with the tradition in a moment of hermeneutical crisis. And contrary to common beliefs, the critical link with the tradition allows readers to intellectually savor a nuanced view of al-Maʿarrī as opposed to the monolithic, fanatic, intellectually amputated views that are severed from any critical links save for themselves.

5

Adab as Method

Philological Retaliation and the Seventy Names for a Dog: al-Maʿarrī's Insult and al-Suyūṭī's Exoneration

LITERARY CHAGRIN AND THE FOUR-HUNDRED-YEAR-OLD INSULT

From Argos the faithful dog of Odysseus, the dogs of Exodus 11:7, Laylā's dog that led Majnūn to her, and Toto in *The Wizard of Oz* to Emmanuelle Levinas's Bobby the stray dog as "the last Kantian in Nazi Germany," dogs have never ceased to occupy and enrich people's lives and imaginations. Nor have they ceased to be the referent of slurs. Even with a literary tribute like Ibn al-Marzubān's (d. 309 AH/921 CE) *Faḍl al-kilāb ʿalā kathīr mimman labisa al-thiyāb* (The Virtue of Dogs over Many Who Wear Clothes)—worthy anecdotes of pre-Kantian dogs—the slurs did not stop.[1] The threat or the actual act of insult aims at dehumanizing another, ridiculing them, and stripping them of their ontological status as human, socially and morally. It can be considered an anti-adab act if viewed abstractedly, but adab devoted part of its pursuits to the poetic mode of *hijāʾ* (invective poetry). *Hijāʾ* often preoccupies itself with criticism of what appears to be a failure in perfecting a conception of the ideal human and murūʾa and the failure in keeping up acceptable behavior; accordingly, even with *hijāʾ*, there was an ethical criterion and framework.[2] An insult is conceivably both an emotional and a moral crisis. It is not just about humiliation and the very understandable visceral emotional pain involved but also the moral question of the desire for retaliation. Retaliation does not need to follow suit; it does not need to equally insult the other party. Literati and *adībs* are not removed from these unenviable situations. However, they may have engaged with innovative methods for adabful retaliation.

An anecdote relates that on his way to al-Sharīf al-Murtaḍā's (d. 436 AH/1044 CE) court, al-Maʿarrī, the visually impaired poet, stumbles on a man. The man, flustered, formulates an insult in the form of an inquiry relegating al-Maʿarrī to a third-person bystander, "Who is this dog?" (*man hādhā al-kalb*). Al-Maʿarrī retorts quickly and tells the man, "A dog is someone who does not know seventy names for the dog" (*al-kalb man lā yaʿrif li-l-kalb sabʿīna isman*), and leaves it there in apparent philological victory. It seems al-Maʿarrī not only returned the jibe but almost insulted everyone, as al-Suyūṭī's (d. 911 AH/1505 CE) later philological enterprise attests. Four hundred years later, Egyptian scholar al-Suyūṭī does not leave it there and takes this insult to heart.

In a manner of an *explication de texte/mot* or a *sharḥ* of "dogness" al-Suyūṭī writes an *urjūza*, a poetic form on the *rajaz* meter, on dodging al-Maʿarrī's insult, titled *al-Tabarrī min maʿarrat al-Maʿarrī* (The Exoneration from al-Maʿarrī's Humiliation). He claims that after consulting philology books and lexicons, he compiled over sixty names for the dog, maintaining that his purpose for compiling this poem is to benefit his readers, as most people would not happen to just know seventy names for a dog—but it is assumed that al-Maʿarrī did. Since al-Suyūṭī managed to compile a list short of seventy, he asks leniency from his readers. It is interesting that he is not only inviting his readers to participate in this enterprise but that there also seems to be a double participation therein. Al-Suyūṭī did not treat al-Maʿarrī's eleventh-century anecdote as a representation of wit and erudition to silence disrespect, passed down from one book to another as an example of what Everett K. Rowson calls "Alexandrian qualities."[3] The "Alexandrian" character of the literary culture reflected in these works emphasized the centrality of erudition for these authors and their audiences. Everyone was conscious of a massive and substantial tradition behind contemporary literary efforts, which they acknowledged. However, there is little to no evidence for this tradition being perceived in any way as a burden—compared to some later *nahḍa* and modern literati, for instance. As Rowson maintains, "The 'anxiety of influence' becomes acute only when originality is prized in a way that would be completely foreign to our authors. What we seem to find instead is a real delight in influence."[4] For Mamluk writers, it can be argued that "intertextuality was what literature is all about; and the more of a past one has to deal with, the more one can glory in reproducing, ringing changes on, and playing with that past, to the ongoing enrichment of the Arabic literary tradition."[5] Identifying the names of precursor writers can be a deliberate act carried out by the learned successors, who are proud to have their work at the center of attention by virtue of being mentioned.[6] The tradition-centered pride is not stagnant; rather it is an engagement that reimagines and recrafts both the tradition and itself. In this respect, this is an invitation to understand the accomplishments of adab in the Mamluk period, an assessment on the basis of which will offer us a less "'jejune' and 'derivative' (in an assumed negative sense) than the consensus of past scholarship would insist was the case."[7]

The anecdote becomes a participatory invitation where al-Suyūṭī invited himself to add to this piece of tradition from the eleventh century.[8] He imagined himself, as well as his readers, and everyone in the history of adab, for that matter, to be held to disgrace by the insult "not knowing seventy names for a dog," hence the title. In this respect, he imagined an adab sphere with participants, players, and agents. It is a crisis that happened in the eleventh century to one man but al-Suyūṭī acknowledges its ripples in a trans-temporal continuum. The allusion in the *urjūza* does not become derivative or unimaginative in this case—a rehashing of a four-hundred-year-old anecdote; it becomes a means of communication with the past but also an appropriation of it to the present aesthetics. Mamluk aesthetics engaged in the "use of literary texts for pragmatic communication as well as the creation of pragmatic texts in a literature guise."[9] The use of verse as a pedagogical medium has a literary form that is employed for pragmatic communication. Famous earlier *urjūzas* include the *Mulḥat al-iʿrāb* of al-Ḥarīrī (d. 516 AH/1122 CE), the *Alfiyya* of Ibn Mālik (d. 672 AH/1274 CE), and its antecedent, the *Alfiyya* of Ibn Muʿṭī (d. 638 AH/1231 CE).[10]

Al-Suyūṭī is not unique in remodeling and reworking these models from the past and engaging with older texts. This is a Mamluk exercise par excellence. For instance, al-Ṣafadī (d. 764 AH/1363 CE) equally dwells on a debate that took place between Mattā b. Yūnus (d. 329 AH/940 CE) and Abū Saʿīd al-Ṣīrāfī (d. 368 AH/979 CE). This is an event that is dated to 330 AH/932 CE. Al-Ṣafadī inserts himself into these debates of logic and rationalist philosophy as part of his resistance to traditionalist modes of reading.[11] Through these revivals and adaptations of works of the past, Mamluk authors did not attempt to re-create past models or build on variations of Abbasid themes, "nor did they aspire to revive a 'golden age.'"[12] Rather, as Thomas Bauer maintains, these intertextual references fulfilled several purposes. They served as a means to define their relationship with the past, to engage with a dialogue with foundational texts, to present their ideas and theses into contemporary discourse, and to acclimatize this discourse to the then prevailing sensibilities. This is not to exclude the fact that in some other cases, this engagement may be chiefly a validation of ability and *technē* in remodeling an older text, an act that essentially participated in the shaping of the cultural memory of the times.[13]

PHILOLOGICAL RETALIATION: AL-MAʿARRĪ'S INSULT AND COUNTER-INSULT

It is useful to highlight the sources or the textual relations that al-Suyūṭī engages as he repurposes and reconstructs the anecdote. The anecdote is related in several sources. For example, in al-Anbārī's (d. 577 AH/1181 CE) *Nuzhat al-alibbāʾ fī ṭabaqāt al-udabāʾ*.[14] In his *Irshād al-arīb ilā maʿrifat al-adīb*, Yāqūt al-Ḥamawī (d. 626 AH/1229 CE) also relates the anecdote,[15] as does al-Ṣafadī (d. 764 AH/1363 CE) in *Nakt al-himyān fī nukat al-ʿumyān*[16] and al-Damīrī (d. 742 AH/1404 CE) in his *Ḥayāt al-ḥayawān al-kubrā*.[17] Not all scholars who came after al-Suyūṭī mention the *urjūza*. Kâtip Çelebi or Ḥājjī Khalīfa (d. 1068 AH/1657 CE), the Ottoman polymath, mentions the *urjūza* in his *Kashf al-ẓunūn ʿan asāmī al-kutub wa-l-funūn*. He says that al-Suyūṭī mentions it in his *Dīwān al-ḥayawān*.[18] However, in his *Maʿāhid al-tanṣīṣ ʿalā shawāhid al-talkhīṣ*, Egyptian ʿAbd al-Raḥīm al-ʿAbbāsī (Abū al-Fatḥ al-ʿAbbāsī) (d. 963 AH/1556 CE) relates al-Maʿarrī's anecdote along with copious others about his life, but he does not refer to al-Suyūṭī's *urjūza*.[19] The *urjūza* can be considered to exemplify the position of scholars of language toward synonyms (*al-tarāduf*).[20] Al-Labābīdī (d. 1318 AH/1900 CE) observes that scholars often boasted about learning and memorizing synonyms. Beginning with an anecdote related by Ibn Fāris, Caliph Hārūn al-Rashīd (d. 193 AH/808 CE) asks al-Aṣmaʿī (d. 216 AH/828 CE) about some poetry by Abū Ḥizām al-ʿUklī, which the former then proceeds to explain. The caliph, apparently pleased, tells al-Aṣmaʿī that "the strange (*al-gharīb*) for you is not strange (*ghayr gharīb*)."[21] Al-Aṣmaʿī replies, "And how should it be otherwise, when I have memorized seventy names for the stone (*ḥajar*)?"[22] It appears then that al-Maʿarrī's frame for the "seventy names of something" had a precedent, as seen in the anecdote of al-Aṣmaʿī.

Similarly, in his *al-Ansāb*, al-Samʿānī (d. 562 AH/1166 CE) relates an anecdote about poet Muḥammad b. al-ʿAbbās al-Khawārizmī (d. 383 AH/993 CE), who al-Samʿānī attests was unique in his mastery of the Arabic language and poetry. The anecdote relates that al-Khawārizmī enters the *majlis* of al-Ṣāḥib b. ʿAbbād (d. 385 AH/995 CE) wearing shabby clothes. He advances in the *majlis*, despite being a latecomer and disruptive to the already seated people, and so the attendants become dismayed. Thinking that al-Khawārizmī does not speak Arabic, an attendant exclaims, "Who is this dog?" Al-Khawārizmī retorts, "A dog is someone who does not know twenty names [in twenty dialects] for a dog (*ʿishrīn lugha*)." So everyone becomes silent and they commend him.[23] The anecdote becomes an antecedent variation on the subsequent narrative of al-Maʿarrī. In both anecdotes, the insult is always about an action perceived as anti-adab but the response is often more injurious than the perceived action in an adabful method. In this case, the anecdotes take adab as a moral decorum. The insulting person perceives a slight and acts accordingly. In al-Khawārizmī's case, advancing in the *majlis* was perceived as an anti-adab act. The anecdote also emphasized the shabby clothes since being well dressed is also a requirement of possessing adab as part of self-respect and one's humanity.[24] In al-Maʿarrī's case, it is stumbling over someone, perhaps a blunder in comportment, to be swiftly rectified by excusing oneself, but it may very well be involuntary. The insulting person in this case did not give al-Maʿarrī the benefit of the doubt in the first place and failed to understand that al-Maʿarrī is visually impaired. In both anecdotes, the narrative gives us two strings of competing performances of adab: the moral one where dress, manners, and speech are concerned, and the literary string of adab. The anecdotes tell us that the insulting *adīb* is representing one definition of adab as decorum and character, which the *adīb* sees violated by the insulted *adīb*. The latter, who may be excused, as is the case of al-Maʿarrī, is perceived as lacking adab but the counter-insult shows us that this is not the case. It represents the definition of adab as corpus and erudition and enables the *adīb* to reaffirm his adab status and to triumph through his own adab. It not only reiterates a definition of adab in this case but it presents a way in which the performance of the two foci of adab is deemed critical.

In *al-Maqāma al-shiʿriyya* by al-Ḥarīrī (d. 516 AH/1122 CE), al-Sarūjī and his son fabricate a story about a dispute among themselves over plagiarism or repurposing poetry (*sariqa*)—a prominent topic in premodern literary criticism—to dupe the judge and abuse his kindness.[25] After they are done, al-Sarūjī tells Ibn Hammām about the ruse and instructs him to let the judge know how easy it was to swindle him. When the judge hears this, he says that if it were not for al-Sarūjī's adab and its sanctity, he would have chased after him until he caught him.[26]

In this respect, we have a similar attitude here toward an action that is deemed anti-adab and the individual in question deemed talented enough to be superlatively impressive and labeled as a "golden boy" to the extent that what are represented as unacceptable actions are deemed less significant or sometimes pardonable next to his talent and adab. In this case, the judge, whether saving face over his failure of discovering the ruse or being truly sincere in his proclamation of the sanctity (*ḥurma*) of al-Sarūjī's adab, is also operating within the aforementioned dichotomous frame of adab as praxis and corpus.

How should we read al-Maʿarrī's retort in light of the context of his career and adab as both aesthetics (text) and ethics (morals and decorum)?[27] Al-Maʿarrī never insulted the man but pointed out his lack of adab as a literary sensibility and as a moral decorum. Had he been an *adīb*, he would not have insulted al-Maʿarrī or anyone for that matter—at least not explicitly. Had he been an *adīb* in the literary and scholarly sense, he would have known the seventy names for a dog or at least how to find them. "Correct Arabic . . . was both the condition of entry to and distinguishing mark of the elite."[28] While the man pointed to al-Maʿarrī's perceived lack of adab as decorum, al-Maʿarrī also pointed to the man's lack of adab in both the ethical and literary senses and quantified this moral lack in the parameters of knowledge. The certain absence of knowledge for seventy names of a dog is a certain absence of adab in the pedagogical sense for the insulting man, which is what al-Maʿarrī aimed at delivering. The attempt at humiliating al-Maʿarrī and thereby morally excluding him through humiliation as part of the inner workings of this incident explains his clever retort. Al-Maʿarrī mirrored the act of exclusion by using the registers of language and adab as a medium for insults by accusing the man of incompetence. "Accusations of defective and ungrammatical language," Michael G. Carter maintains, are "ipso facto attempts to exclude a person from that elite."[29] The man's exclusion from language competency, an important social and cultural capital, is even more injurious as the anecdote takes place in the court of an established person. It was therefore the man who was excluded from being a member of an elite group of litterateurs and from respect, not al-Maʿarrī.

In the realm of adab, the man insulting al-Maʿarrī, in calling him a dog, attempted to strip him of his *adīb* status metaphorically since "by virtue of adab man is distinguished from the rest of animals."[30] The question of murūʾa, hence humanity, exceeds the boundaries of the biological, chemical, and anatomical definitions of the human being, which the insult aims at. Al-Maʿarrī's comeback quickly established him as an *adīb* and solidified his murūʾa beyond the biological and as a moral definition of the human, as it presented the man with an epistemic crisis in his ignorance of that which is used: language. The rhetorical battle that probably lasted a few seconds was a power struggle over the ownership of language. Carter observes that Islam is a "logocentric" civilization and by extension any "criminal trial is essentially a ritual to determine whether a certain name can lawfully be applied to be the accused."[31] While not a criminal legal trial, insulting and humiliating someone is also an attempt to work within this logocentrism and rhetorically apply a "name" or an "adjective" to another person and create a relationship between them essentially to humiliate the person in question through that accusation. It endeavors to ontologically change the status of the entity and hence our perception of said entity. An attempt to classify al-Maʿarrī's insult and retort as a *hijāʾ* would fail, since al-Maʿarrī did not resort to a rally to return the man's invective. In this case, al-Maʿarrī diverted the genre of the battle from verbal abuse or *hijāʾ* and ended the rally with a single lob over the man's head. Engaging in *hijāʾ* would confirm the man's mastery and ownership of language, since it would confirm that both the man and al-Maʿarrī use the same language and understand each other and the words used and therefore they can communicate and understand each other perfectly. Even if this exchange occurred in the realm of *hijāʾ* as an institution, it remains an implicitly agreed-upon institution, where there is a consensus stipulated by subscribing to participating in the genre to exchange insults willingly, but also artistically, and therefore would privilege the man's status as a potential *adīb* or even a proper user of the language. It would thus relegate al-Maʿarrī as a user of *this* language that was used as a vehicle to deliver the blow and confirm the insult's veracity. Rather, stripping the man of linguistic legitimacy rendered the insult invalid. The man thus becomes an incapable user of the language. The man's insult utilized the dog as a descriptor of a human thereby stripping the dog of its lexical meaning, as per the insult or any insult for that matter and al-Maʿarrī's ontological reality. Al-Maʿarrī's redefining of the dog from the realm of animals as an insult used against him to the realm of abstraction as an entry in the lexicon showcased what is known as *ṣarf al-lafẓ ʿan muqtaḍāhu*, turning the word away from its course of patterned or modeled use (*muqtaḍāhu*) by expanding the meaning of a certain word (*iṭlāq al-lafẓ*). He emptied it of its patterned meaning as an insult in this context and expanded or loosened it to another meaning. In this respect, al-Maʿarrī offered a new meaning for the word in this context. He thereby widened the semantic range of "dog," which is a Maʿarrian enterprise par excellence. In the context of al-Maʿarrī's poetry, meanings are multiplied in a wider semantic range. This is what Suzanne Stetkevych identifies as the "poetics of engagement."[32] In addition to the lexical dog that is misused to become an insult, the dog will also be someone who does not know seventy names for a dog. This is also what al-Qarṭājannī emphasized in his discussion of *al-ighrāb* (defamiliarization) as a salient component for the poetic image. He maintains that the purpose of an unfamiliar mimetic image (*muḥākāt al-aḥwāl al-mustaghraba*) would be either affective and rousing (*inhāḍ al-nufūs*) or as an exemplum (*iʿtibār*) or used to solicit a task to be done or deter from it altogether because of its strangeness (*ḥamlahā ʿalā ṭalab al-shayʾ wa-fiʿlihi aw al-takhallī ʿan dhālika maʿa mā tajiduhu min al-istighrāb*).[33] Al-Maʿarrī's counter-mimetic move took the mimetic cue from the man insulting him (man = dog) but offered a defamiliarizing definition for the dog that solicited something so strange that it is intrinsically deterred. Al-Maʿarrī's *ighrāb* or defamiliarization, though considered a speech-act, is therefore also what al-Qarṭājannī subsumes under any deductive analogy speech (*aqāwīl qiyāsiyya*) that builds on image-evoking (*takhyīl*) and contains mimesis (*muḥākāt*). Its premises may be apodictic/discursive proof (*burhāniyya*), dialectic (*jadaliyya*), oratorial/rhetorical (*khaṭābiyya*), conclusive (*yaqīniyya*), common (*mushtahira*), or probable (*maẓnūna*).[34]

Al-Maʿarrī indeed roused the man by asking him to know something he was not able to. The power struggle can only be won through knowledge of all lexicons, an encyclopedic knowledge for this matter, as al-Suyūṭī exemplified in his *urjūza*. Al-Maʿarrī continued the same rupture created by the man in the system of signs (man = dog) but the name expanded and transformed as an accusation of ignorance of what the man perceives as this system. The man cannot associate the name of the dog with the meanings of the dog in the prompted classification supplied by al-Maʿarrī. The latter supplied the potential knowledge that acts as the bond to associate the lexical dog with the meanings of dog together. Al-Maʿarrī's retort not only expanded the lexical dog to compete with the man's using the same framework but also implied the man's self-ignorance (a dog who does not know seventy names for dogs) and by extension overall ignorance. Al-Maʿarrī therefore expelled the man outside both the systems of knowledge and language.

LEXICOGRAPHICAL POETRY: AL-SUYŪṬĪ'S EXONERATION AND THE PHILOLOGICAL LIMITS OF THE DOG

In titling his work as such, al-Suyūṭī entered into a contract with readers and, as al-Musawi contends, in such a "response to a horizon of expectation and need, the writer may have wanted his production to be compatible with current needs and demands. In these titles we encounter resonance, assonance, intonation, paronomasia, antithesis, contrafaction, and also referents that send us to the body of the text and its intertexts and subtexts."[35] In this, al-Suyūṭī informed his readers of the antecedent literary forefather of this work and the time travel involved. In an *urjūza* made up of thirty-seven lines, divided into two hemistiches each, al-Suyūṭī relates the history and reasons behind the writing of this work. He then lists a little over sixty names for a dog from line 10 onward. In lines 2–5, he relates that the incident was transmitted through reliable chains of transmission thereby attesting its veracity but also an awareness of similar prior anecdotes. Al-Suyūṭī refers to the verbally insulting man as *al-mujjahal* (the one made ignorant), the man who verbally insulted al-Maʿarrī and said: "Who is this dog who did not see?" (*man dhālika al-kalb al-ladhī mā abṣara*).

The manner in which al-Suyūṭī refers to the insulting man is grammatically telling. He uses the passive participle (*mufaʿʿal*) of form II (*faʿʿala*) of the root *j-h-l* (ignorance, lack of reason). Form II usually describes the action of the verb intensely; it adds power and intensity to the verb. In this case, the man is described as being the passive recipient of an intense action of ignorance (*jahhala*), thereby being *mujahhal* (pronounced or instructed in ignorance). The passive recipient of *jahl* is an interesting take on the constituents of *murūʾa* and *adab* as will and resolve (*ʿazm*). Here is an indication that the man lacks will even for *jahl*; he is passively receiving it. This usage evokes form II of *d-r-s* (to teach) and its passive participle of *mudarras* (taught) and equally form II of *a-d-b* (to educate and instruct) and *muʾaddab* (one who is instructed in the manners of adab, possessing adab). The insulting man is therefore referred to in the grammatical parameters of teaching, instruction, but using the diction of anti-adab. Al-Suyūṭī saw through al-Maʿarrī's comeback and is proud of al-Maʿarrī's retort as he describes it as *qawl jalī* (lucid/polished words) (see the appendix for the full *urjūza*).

Al-Suyūṭī then tells us about his own research in the *urjūza*. He relates that he consulted numerous volumes but they fall short of seventy and for this he asks leniency from his prospective readers/critics:[36]

وقد تَتَبَّعتُ دَواوينَ اللُّغَه . . . لَعَلَّني أجمعُ من ذا مَبَلَغه

فجئتُ منها عددًا كثيرًا . . . وأرتجي فيما بقي تيسيرا

> In the vast oceans of our blessed language I dove
> Seeking to gather these names, a treasure trove

> I thus amassed numerous findings indeed
> While in what remains, I seek divine ease to proceed

It must be noted that the lexical pursuit in itself was not a static and inorganic scholarly activity. Lexicons started as a specialized enterprise to set the standard for correct usage and a way to preserve the purity of language beyond not only intrusion but idiolects and transmutation. And while there was not a dearth of lexicons in the formative period and during the developing stages of lexicons in the tenth century, they were regarded as insufficiently important, a position that al-Musawi argues was seriously revised in the thirteenth and fourteenth centuries when "lexicons turned into custodians of an Islamic narrative."[37] Indeed, al-Suyūṭī's *urjūza* attests to these changed sensibilities toward lexicons as a display of Mamluk times.

In line 10, al-Suyūṭī relates that *al-bāqiʿ* is a name for the hyena (*al-ḍabʿ*); the term also describes a person who is very cunning (*dāhiya*) and is derived from the spotted skin of the hyena (*al-baqaʿ*), as explained by Ibn Manẓūr, al-Ṣaghānī,[38] and al-Zabīdī.[39] They also refer to poet al-Akhṭal's (d. 92 AH/708 CE) line:

كُلو الضَّبَّ وابْنَ العَيْرِ والباقِعَ الَّذي يَبِيتُ يَعُسُّ اللَّيْلَ بَيْنَ المَقابِرِ

Eat the lizard and the mule of donkeys
and the dog (*al-bāqiʿ*) that spends the night vigilant between graveyards

In line 10, he lists *al-wāziʿ*, *al-kalb*, *al-abqaʿ*, and *al-zāriʿ*. Al-Ṣaghānī relates the names of the dogs quoting Ibn Durayd (d. 321 AH/933 CE) as *awlād dhāriʿ*, *awlād zāriʿ*, and *awlād wāziʿ*.[40] Ibn Manẓūr and al-Zabīdī are more convincing in giving us an etiology as they explain that the dog is called *wāziʿ* (deterrent) because it intimidates wolves from attacking mixed herds or a group of livestock. In the four names above, *al-abqaʿ* (spotted) does not seem to be a name or epithet (*kunya*) for the dog but rather the proper way of describing the spotted dog. Ibn Manẓūr tells us that all spotted animals (black and white) have a proper descriptive name.[41] In line 11, al-Suyūṭī lists *al-khayṭal* (the swaggerer), *al-suḥām* (darkness), *al-asad* (lion), *al-ʿurbuj* (small coachman), *al-ʿajūz* (the old one). Like *al-bāqiʿ*, *al-khayṭal* also refers to a very shrewd person and is a synonym for the dog.[42] This is a positive simile reservoir of dogs. *Al-suḥām* refers to a quality of hair or fur, soft and beautiful. *Al-suḥām* (darkness) was then not used as a name of a dog but more of a description of a dog with dark coat. Al-Suyūṭī tells us that *al-asad* (lion) is also one of the names of the dog despite al-Jāḥiẓ relating the objection of some people in using the lion and dog interchangeably: "The dog is not one of the names of the lion and neither is the lion one of the names of the dog" (*laysa al-kalb min asmāʾ al-asad ka-mā an laysa al-asad min asmāʾ al-kalb*), except if you were to compliment someone's dog and liken it to a lion.[43] Interestingly, Damascene al-Labābīdī lists "the dog" (*al-kalb*) as one of the names of the lion.[44] That said, al-Jāḥiẓ adds that the dog can only be called a lion interchangeably if it is a rabid one (*ʿaqūr*).[45] He relates that lion and dog bites should be treated similarly, referring to the fatality of both.[46] Despite being the favorite prey of the lion, as al-Jāḥiẓ maintains, it is possible that calling an uncontrollable dog a lion is a semiotic move that corresponds to the dog that has become violent or rabid, that is, no longer fitting the description of a dog as a domesticated animal, humans' helper, and/or companion.[47] Alternatively, *al-ʿurbuj* (a big hunting dog) is like *al-thamtham* (hunting dog) (line 21); both refer to hunting dogs of bigger sizes.[48] *Al-ʿajūz* is a curious and witty use on al-Suyūṭī's part; it can mean both the dog and the jackal.[49] Following the hunting dog name, he completes the image with a possible reference to the part of the sword referred to as *al-ʿajūz* (meaning "the old one" but also "the blade");[50] *al-ʿajūz* is also another name for war (*al-ḥarb*).[51] The sword and war are concomitant and immemorial, hence *al-ʿajūz* (the old one). The name may have little to do with dogs except with reference to the part of the sword with the aforementioned name located beside the part known as *al-kalb* (literally, "the dog," which, according to al-Labābīdī, is the nail (*mismār*) in the grip of the sword), and they are often explained together in lexicons.[52] The hunting dog in the *urjūza* is therefore explained within the framework of the lexical entry meaning both: the hunting dog and the sword parts. The similarity of functions loaned the homonymic purchase.

Because the dog curls its tail up often, it is called *al-aʿqad* (the curled). The poet al-Farazdaq (d. 114 AH/732 CE) used the simile to describe a certain walk (*mashyat al-jādhif al-aʿqad*, "the walk of a brisking trot") as if they are walking affectedly.[53] A later lexicon like al-Zabīdī's tells us that the dog that has a little white in its neck would be called "the one with a neck."[54] Earlier, Ibn Manẓūr defines *al-aʿnaq* differently and does not involve the dog, even though it was previously mentioned as such in Andalusian Ibn Sīdah's (Ibn Sayyidihi) (d. ca. 458 AH/1066 CE) *al-Mukhaṣṣaṣ* and in the Yemeni linguist and literatus Nashwān al-Ḥimyarī's (d. 573 AH/1178 CE) *Shams al-ʿulūm*, for instance.[55] Further, al-Suyūṭī relates *al-dirbās* (rabid dog), which is a common name, with lions too,[56] as is *al-ʿamallas*, which is a common name shared with the violent wolf and the ferocious dog.[57] Then, *al-quṭrub*, which are little puppies; *al-furnī* is a reference to a large or thick mass, which al-Zabīdī uses to refer to both a big dog and a big man.[58] In his *Mukhtār al-ṣiḥāḥ*, al-Rāzī explains *al-furnī* also as a thick type of bread that is oven-baked, hence named after the oven (*furn*).[59] *Al-falḥas* is also used to describe a dog since it refers to qualities of attentiveness (*ḥirṣ*) and tenacity (*ilḥāḥ*).[60]

In line 13, *al-thaghim* is explained as the fierce dog (*al-ḍārī min al-kilāb*), and the reference here is to the dog's mouth as the source of fierceness. It is the same verb used for kissing (*muthāghamat al-marʾa*, i.e., *mulāthamatuhā*).[61] *Al-ṭalq* (the set loose) is a description used for the hunting dog for being set loose (*muṭlaqan*).[62] *Al-ʿawwāʾ* means "the howler" in reference to the sound some dogs make;[63] interestingly, al-Suyūṭī onomatopoeically points to the way the word is pronounced with either *madd* (prolongation/extension) or *qaṣr* (shortening), phonetically mimicking the aural references to the "howl" in stretching or shortening the vowels (either long or short). Al-Hamadhānī (d. 398 AH/1007 CE) uses the same word for dog in his *al-Maqāmāt* in *al-kūfiyya*:[64]

وغَرِيبٌ أوقِدَتِ النّارُ عَلى سَفَرِهِ، ونَبَحَ العَوّاءُ عَلى أثَرِهِ

> An exile after whose departure the fire of banishment was kindled, in whose wake the howling (*al-ʿawwāʾ*) dogs have barked[65]

The same root is used again in line 25 for the female dog as *muʿāwiya*.[66] Shortly after the nod to the usage of al-Hamadhānī in line 13, al-Suyūṭī makes a reference to al-Hamadhānī's successor al-Ḥarīrī (d. 516 AH/1122 CE) in his use of *al-baṣīr* (the seeing one) as the name for the dog as he says it was part of a riddle by an expert (*khabīr*). The usage *baṣīr* is also featured in Majnūn Laylā's (Qays b. al-Mulawwaḥ) (d. 68 AH/688 CE) poetry as "dog" (I see the campfire of Laylā or her *baṣīr* (dog) sees me), as Ibn Fāris (d. 395 AH/1004 CE), Ibn al-Jawzī (d. 510 AH/1116 CE), and al-Zabīdī (1205 AH/1790 CE) maintain.[67] Al-Ḥarīrī's riddle/pun goes as follows:

أَيُسْتَبَاحُ مَاءُ الضَّرِيرِ؟ نَعَمْ وَيُجْتَنَبُ مَاءُ الْبَصِيرِ

> *Q:* Is [a] washing-water provided by a *ḍarīr* better than [a] washing-water provided by a *baṣīr*?
> [*Ḍarīr* means blind but also edge of a wadi (valley); *baṣīr* means sighted but also dog]
>
> *A:* Yes, and you can take that to the bank.[68]

The following two lines are merely the names of the dog as indicators of generosity when strangers are hosted, as usually the host's dog would be the first to spot the stranger and alert the host: *dā ʿī al-ḍamīr* (the caller of conscience), *hānī ʾ al-ḍamīr* (the gladdened of conscience), *dā ʿī al-karam* (the caller of generosity), *mushayyid al-dhikr* (the builder of reputation), *mutammim al-ni ʿam* (the culminator of blessings). These names refer to the dog's ability to spot strangers and guests or lost people in the desert, facilitating the act of hospitality.[69] Another word from al-Suyūṭī's list is *kālib* (with dogs, *dhū kilāb*).[70] *Hibla ʿ* is a loud, fast hunting dog referred to as *al-salūqī*, after Salūq, a village in Yemen (Saluki, often referred to as the Arabian hound).[71] The adjective Salūqī also refers to certain types of shields (*durū ʿ*) after the same village,[72] as Ibn Sallām's manual of weaponry explains the philological nomenclature and types of weapons used by Arabs in pre-Islamic and Islamic times. *Mundhir* (the alarmist) is the one who warns and alarms. *Hijra ʿ* is a light and agile Saluki dog according to al-Farāhīdī.[73] *Kusayb* is defined as a generic dog.[74]

Al-Suyūṭī then includes *al-qalṭī*, a short dog, and the Saluki, both of which resemble the Chinese (*al-ṣīnī*) dog as described.[75] He then tells us that *al-mustaṭīr* is used to describe a raging dog according to the author of *al- ʿUbāb*, in reference to al-Ṣaghānī. *Al-mustaṭīr* (enflamed) is a dog (male or female) in heat. It is also used for camels during their mating cycle.[76] In line 21, he mentions the common *jarw* and *al-dirṣ* as puppies. According to Ibn Sīdah, *al-dirṣ* is the offspring of rats, hedgehogs, rabbits, cats, and dogs.[77] Most other renowned lexicons such as al-Zabīdī's *Tāj al- ʿarūs* mention *al-dirṣ* as the offspring of several animals but do not explicitly mention the dog; it is inferred, as al-Zabīdī says, among other animals, rabbits, cats, and the like. Interestingly, al-Suyūṭī himself, in his *al-Muzhir fī ʿulūm al-lugha wa-anwā ʿihā* (The Luminous, on the Sciences of Language and Their Types), only defines *al-dirṣ* as the offspring of jerboas, referring to *Tāj al-lugha wa-ṣiḥāḥ al- ʿarabiyya* by al-Jawharī (d. 393 AH/1003 CE).[78] Although Ibn Sīdah makes this reference and al-Suyūṭī includes the scholarship of the former in his book, al-Suyūṭī does not include the explanation of *al-dirṣ* made by Ibn Sīdah comprehensively with the "dog" reference he makes in his *urjūza*. It could be concluded that he wrote *al-Muzhir* before the *urjūza*. The date given for the composition of *al-Muzhir* is around 900–906 AH/1495–1501 CE, while the *urjūza* does not have a known date.[79] Al-Suyūṭī nonetheless mentions a predator-hybrid (*sabʿ murakkab*), a wolf-dog hybrid, as *al-simʿ*. Al-Suyūṭī defers to al-Ṣūlī (d. 335 AH/946 CE) as the source for this explanation and he defines the term using the teknonym (*kunya*) Abū Khālid. We see the use of Abū Khālid as a *kunya* for the dog attested in the work of poet Ibn al-Rūmī (d. 283 AH/869 CE). He does not directly call the addressed a dog but simultaneously the father and son of a dog (hence dog). The addressee was named Khālid, which makes the use of Abū Khālid as an insult even more injurious. The line might refer to this hemistich:[80]

أخَالِدٌ لَا تَكْذِبْ وَلَسْتَ بِخَالِدٍ . . . هُنَالِكَ بَلْ أَنْتَ الْمُكَنَّى بِخَالِدِ
وَلِلْكَلْبِ خَيْرٌ مِنْكَ وَلُؤْمُكَ شَاهِدٌ . . . عَلَيْكَ وَمَا دَهْرِي بِإِبْعَادِ شَاهِدِي

O Khālid! Don't lie! You are not *khālid* [immortal] there
But you are the one with a teknonym [of Abū] Khālid
For the dog is better than you, and your meanness is a witness against you
And my Time does not a witness oust

In lines 23–24, al-Suyūṭī introduces *kasba* (dog) and *kasāb*. He then tells us that people adopted the use of the noun *al-ruhdūn* (also *al-rahdūn*), which refers to a bird that walks in a circular motion, and also to liars, and applied it to dogs.[81] Al-Suyūṭī then continues about the *kasāb* in the *muʿallaqa* of the poet Labīd (d. ca. 41 AH/661 CE) where he describes the wild cow avenging her calf. Labīd relates that the arrows of the hunting men could not get the oryx cow. Perhaps in a calculating move, the men then sent two hunting dogs referred to as *kasāb* and as *sukhām* (also *suḥām*) to facilitate hunting her. The oryx cow mustered enough strength to kill them both and the hunters.[82]

فتقصّدت منها كساب فضرّجت
بدم وغودر في المكرّ سخامُها

Kasábi bears down on her
He is smeared in blood,
And Sukhám, in his place of attack,
is left to die[83]

In a lexicographical move, al-Suyūṭī then invokes the phonetics of the name *kasāb* to *qaṭām* as well and consequently to Qaṭām bt. Shinja, a Kharijite whose brother and father were killed in the battle of Nahrawān fought between the caliph ʿAlī b. Abī Ṭālib and the Kharijites in 38 AH/658 CE. Qaṭām used her reportedly exceptional beauty to her advantage and agreed to marry Ibn al-Muljam on the condition that he kill ʿAlī b. Abī Ṭālib. The former struck ʿAlī with a poisoned sword on his head.[84] Naturally, al-Suyūṭī's rhetorical move invokes Qaṭām phonetically to assess her historically in a *hijāʾ*-like maneuver. Al-Suyūṭī does not stop there. He continues in the following lines as he relates the names of female dogs and begins with "take to her" (*khudh lahā*) with no explicit indication on the identity of the object pronoun "her" except Qaṭām. It thus appears that while al-Maʿarrī attempts to wittily expand and change the signification (*waḍʿ*) of the dog as an insult, al-Suyūṭī still recycles the insult with its original signification when referring to Qaṭām as an actor in a deciding chapter in Islamic history.

Both *al-ʿusbūra* and *al-khayhafʿā* are hybrid dogs from a she-wolf.[85] Al-Suyūṭī continues with crossbreeds of dogs with wolves and foxes like *al-daysam*.[86] He then moves to a different species, sea dogs or seals (*kilāb al-baḥr*). He indicates that there is *qiyās* (syllogism) in this move that should be applied to whatever resembles that (*wa-qiss fardan ʿalā mā shākalahu*). Al-Suyūṭī then includes the synonyms for sea dogs: *al-harākila*, *qundus*, which lexicographers correct as *kundus* but also explain its Persian origin as a loanword from *qunduz*. Then, *quḍāʿa*, Ibn Manẓūr, relates, is the sea dog.[87] Al-Suyūṭī relates that closer to a dog's family (*min jinsihi*) is the Asiatic jackal (*ibn āwā*) and all synonyms derived from the verb (*d-ʾ-l*), which implies "walking, or going, with short steps, and in an unusual manner, as though heavily burdened, or overburdened," in this case stealthily in a deceiving manner to hunt a prey.[88] *Al-dhuʾalān* is the wolf. *Al-ʿilwaḍ* or *al-laʿwaḍ* is the jackal in the language of Ḥimyar (an ancient kingdom, a polity, in the southern highlands of Yemen),[89] and in the same language it is *al-ʿillūsh* as the wolf.[90] *Al-nawfal* is a male hyena and also another name for the jackal.[91] Al-Ṣaghānī reports, after al-Aṣmaʿī, that some Arabs call the jackal *al-surḥūb*.[92] Similarly are *al-waʿʿ* and *al-waʿwaʿ* for the jackal,[93] as well as *al-shaghbar*.[94] So what is presented here is a case of synonyms according to different dialects. Of these names, *al-waʿwaʿ* has an onomatopoeic edge evoking the howling of wolves and dogs but it is also a name for the jackal according to most lexicographers, although al-Zabīdī relates a possible meaning as fox.[95] Similarly, *al-waʾwāʾ* is the cry of the jackal.[96] Finally, al-Suyūṭī concludes with a couplet indicating that this is what he collected from books.

QIYĀS AND THE PHILOLOGICAL AND ONTOLOGICAL LIMITS OF THE DOG

As established, al-Suyūṭī tells us that he collected more than sixty names for the dog. In a hemistich that shows a complete faith in language, he tells us that he asks for leniency from readers with the rest (*wa-artajī fīmā baqā taysīrā*). How does al-Suyūṭī know that there are still more? How does he know that his readers know that there are *really* seventy and that it is not merely an exaggeration? Is the remainder in this case an indication of faith in an infinite possibility of "dogness" in Arabic including all dialects, rare and common usages, and strange words, hence an absolute faith in language?

In his *al-Muzhir*, al-Suyūṭī, like other scholars before him, relates the impossibility of acquiring all knowledge of the Arabic language. He attests that, according to scholar and jurisprudent al-Shāfiʿī (d. 204 AH/820 CE) in his *Risāla*, "The Arabic language is the most wide-ranging and has the most vocabulary. We do not know a person who has the most knowledge of it except a prophet. But if anything escapes the average person, this knowledge would certainly be available among others. Knowledge of the Arabic language for Arabs is like knowledge of the *sunna* among jurists. No one person knows all the Prophetic *sunna* but if he collects all the knowledge of those jurists, he then has knowledge of the *sunna*."[97] He maintains that only a prophet can have total mastery and knowledge of the Arabic language (*kalām al-ʿarab lā yuḥīṭ bihi illā nabī*).[98] In like manner, al-Suyūṭī resorts to collecting what is available among others as al-Shāfiʿī's analogy intimates. In this respect, there is an implicit faith in the language that it would indeed serve and fulfill the number seventy, whether the number was used in earnest on al-Maʿarrī's part or idiomatically as exaggeration. In other words, "seventy" is not only an exaggeration for those who know the idiomatic usage of the language but a real number that could even be broken by new records.[99]

Al-Suyūṭī, however, promised us names (*asmāʾ*, sing. *ism*) for dogs. The *urjūza* delivered synonyms as names for the most part but as it gradually progressed, the *urjūza* moved to purported hybrid dog breeds, sea dogs, wolves, jackals, hyenas, and foxes. One could hardly say that these are names or synonyms as the initial section asserted even if they are members of the same Canidae. There are two ways of reading this: either al-Suyūṭī used *qiyās* or both al-Maʿarrī and al-Suyūṭī understood *ism* as a name/noun in a certain way.[100]

From a *qiyās* perspective, al-Suyūṭī and his readers are aware that all the breeds presented share the same family, but they cannot be grouped under "dog" syllogistically. In his *al-Muzhir*, al-Suyūṭī himself appears to have reservations about *qiyās* as he relates previous scholarship on the subject and then concludes with his opinion. The most famous example of *qiyās* is the *khamr* (wine) and *banj* (anesthetic). *Al-khamr* is an intoxicant and may render one unconscious and *al-banj* may lead to similar results. Nevertheless, one may not refer to *al-banj* as *khamr* or the other way around. They do not share the same name, characteristics, or interchangeability through *qiyās*.[101] In his *Kitāb al-ḥayawān*, al-Jāḥiẓ (d. 255 AH/868 CE) has a chapter on what looks like a dog but is not. In a section he titled "Naming types of animals as 'dogs'" (*tasmiyat anwāʿ min al-ḥayawānāt bi-l-kilāb*), al-Jāḥiẓ reports that "some people claim that jackals, foxes, dogs, and hyenas are all dogs and that is why they mount one another (*tusāfid*) and conceive (*wa-tulāqiḥ*)." Al-Jāḥiẓ continues that others object to this, saying if people want to use these names interchangeably as a metaphor, then other animals could be "dogs" for a reason or two. However, there are more differences than similarities, so it is not permissible (*hādhā mimmā lā yajūz*). Al-Jāḥiẓ not only disagrees to likening these animals to dogs but he expresses disbelief in their alleged interbreeding and relegates these stories to desert lore. He maintains that "we are yet to see the offspring of these crossbreeds." Al-Jāḥiẓ then expresses this skepticism, saying, "How else would any story be more interesting or wondrous, if it is equally known to everyone?" (*fa-kayfa yaddaʿūn mā huwa aẓraf wa-l-ladhī huwa aʿjab wa-arghab ilā mā yastawī fī maʿrifatihi jamīʿ al-nās*).[102] Al-Jāḥiẓ here is referring to alternative metasemantics of "dog," or the etiological foundations of the meaning of the name "dog," which has given the value of dogness to animals that are not dogs, whose name range is determined by accounts that he referred to as desert lore that offered the features that determined these semantic facts and/or values. In other words, "the referent is the referent (or the range is the range) because it satisfies a particular condition, but that condition amounts to consistency with past use, rather than encapsulating the meaning of the expression."[103] The related references to "dog" are therefore established by consistent use. The refutation of the value of "dog" in al-Jāḥiẓ's model questions the veracity of these anecdotes as they become dog for most people because they satisfy certain conditions and these conditions appear to have a history of being taken for granted.

A *SHARḤ* BY ANY OTHER NAME

But if al-Suyūṭī is likely aware of this objectionable use, why then does he go to great lengths to simply exonerate himself, and everyone, accordingly, from an insult that is more than four hundred years old? Why not stop at the synonyms and not venture to other linguistically shifty members of the Canidae, as al-Jāḥiẓ cautions? It could be argued that even though al-Suyūṭī was writing to exonerate himself and everyone from the insult, he was writing in the genre of *sharḥ* (commentary) even though he structured his piece as an *urjūza*. In other words, this is a commentary in the form of *urjūza* not only to explain away an insult but to explain it in the manner of adab and thereby respond to the insult in a framework and method of adab that is an adabized technique. In the genre of commentaries, an author is expected to explain and demystify language usages in a simple manner for their readers. It can be argued that this *urjūza* is an encyclopedic commentary. The philological undertaking of tracing the names of the dog to all usages in the lexicons adabizes the insult and takes it away from its context of discord to what Elias Muhanna recognizes as the "encyclopedic ethos" of the Mamluk period.[104] As Muhsin al-Musawi maintains, *sharḥ* can take many forms, "as commentary, explication, marginal notes, and annotations. It can add, emend, explicate, and expand on the original. . . . The *sharḥ* often turns into another encyclopedic enterprise with a plan and strategies of explication, along with erudite annotations that touch on other works."[105]

Al-Suyūṭī engaged in a Mamluk enterprise par excellence by gathering knowledge from different disciplines and discourses to explain or rather offer a commentary on a word and engaging encyclopedically with it, in the same manner as Mamluk scholars. But by invoking his giant predecessor, al-Maʿarrī, he is presenting himself as the adabized and learned descendant of the institution of adab, its methods and tools, and therefore was also sustaining "a vigorous presence for [himself]."[106] Al-Suyūṭī provides all usages: common, uncommon, strange, and even unacceptable usages for one word as commentaries would, as a well-tempered reader, not merely as an author.

In his *al-Muzhir*, al-Suyūṭī tells us more about *qiyās* and differentiates between two uses: the juristic (*al-sharʿī*) and the linguistic (*al-lughawī*). He responds to those who think it is permissible to do linguistic *qiyās* on the basis of understanding the meaning (*fahm al-maʿnā*), as in legal rulings (*al-aḥkām al-sharʿiyya*). They say if the meaning is *one* then *qiyās* is permissible in jurisprudence; by extension linguistic names (*al-asāmī al-lughawiyya*) can therefore be subject to *qiyās*. Al-Suyūṭī says this is incorrect (*bāṭil*).[107]

Al-Suyūṭī therefore argues that the meaning in the juristic *qiyās* is applied with an agreement with common and constant usage (*muṭrid*), while linguistic *qiyās* is not an agreement with an analogy or a constant usage (*ghayr muṭrid*). He argues that language is fixed not by *qiyās* but by transmission from Arabs' usage (*naqlan ʿan al-ʿarab*). Al-Jāḥiẓ's objection to calling the aforementioned animals dogs first related the counterargument through a *qiyās*. Those who entertained the interchangeable names of the dog with other members of the Canidae said that it might be for one or two reasons (*ʿilla*) as a metaphor but the differences are more. As per the jurist al-Shāfiʿī, who explains *qiyās* as a measure of explanations of similarities (*qiyās ʿillat al-ashbāh*), it is a measure for the cause (*qiyās al-ʿilla*).[108]

Al-Suyūṭī thus does not offer a personal or an individual view on these names like al-Jāḥiẓ does. Otherwise, he would have omitted the unlikely names that he relates. He does not present these names as part of the average person's common knowledge or his own knowledge. The names of the dog are presented as part of what the opposite of *mujahhal* (instructed in ignorance) would know according to both common and uncommon usage. The *muʾaddab* (one who is instructed in the ways, praxis, decorum, and texts of adab) is the one who would know the names of the dog in the Arabs' usage of the language as transmitted. The collection of the names is part of adab, lexicons, poetry, and desert lore's usage to varying degrees and explanations. It also demonstrates nuances in the uses of names and Arabic's expansive, metaphorical, and real usage of language, which are part of its meaning as per Ibn Jinnī.[109] Ibn Jinnī gives an example where he maintains that the Prophet Muḥammad is related to have once described a horse (*faras*) as sea (*baḥr*). Ibn Jinnī here refers to the actual name of one of the Prophet's horses (*al-baḥr*, lit. the sea), which Ibn Jinnī reads as a description also.[110] Ibn Jinnī says three meanings are actualized in this use: expansiveness (*ittisāʿ*), adducing what linguists and philologists understood as *siʿat al-lugha* (the expansiveness of the [Arabic] language), because it is an addition to the names of the horse; metaphorical, because of the way horses sprint and run like bodies of water; and emphatic (*tawkīd*), because the expression likened the accident (*ʿaraḍ*) with the essence (*jawhar*) and this is more effective on people's sentiments (*athbat fī al-nufūs*).[111] Like the horse in this example, the adabized reader is invited to think about the dog's expansive, metaphorical, emphatic, and real names. In the same vein of Ibn Jinnī, in his *al-Lāmiʿ al-ʿazīzī*, al-Maʿarrī offers a *sharḥ* (commentary) for al-Mutanabbī's *dīwān*. He relates one of al-Mutanabbī's panegyric lines as follows:

الشَّمْسُ مِنْ حَسَادِهِ وَالنَّصْرُ مِنْ قُرَنَائِهِ وَالسَّيْفُ مِنْ أَسْمَائِهِ

> The sun is among the envious of him; and victory / is a peer, and the sword is of his names.[112]

He then explains it as follows, invoking Ibn Jinnī (d. 392 AH/1002 CE):

يَعْنِي اللَّفْظَةَ دُونَ جَوْهَرِ السَّيْفِ؛ لِأَنَّ الْحَدِيدَةَ لَا تَكُونُ مِنَ الْأَسْمَاءِ، وَإِنَّمَا يَكُونُ اسْمُهَا؛ لِأَنَّ الاسْمَ عَرَضٌ، وَالْحَدِيدُ جَوْهَرٌ، وَلَا يَكُونُ أَحَدُ الْجِنْسَيْنِ مِنَ الْآخَرِ، وَعَلَى ذَلِكَ فَسَّرَهُ أَبُو الْفَتْحِ بْنُ جِنِّي

Al-Maʿarrī does not go over every word in al-Mutanabbī's line. He only explains what he sees as a strange or uncommon use: the part of "the sword is of his names." The philosophical bent in his commentary on al-Mutanabbī is evident.[113] In the passage prior, he says that it means "the word (*lafẓa*) without the essence (*jawhar*) of the sword because iron (*al-ḥadīda*) is not one of the names, but rather its name. For the name is an accident (ʿ*araḍ*), and iron is an essence, and the two [essence and name] are not derived from each other. And it is on this basis that Abū al-Fatḥ Ibn Jinnī interpreted it." Ibn Jinnī explained this in his book *al-Khaṣāʾiṣ* within his discussion on reality and metaphor (*al-ḥaqīqa wa-l-majāz*).[114] Indeed, "every shift in form," the powerhouse of rhetoric al-Jurjānī (d. 471 AH/1078 CE) tells us, "entails a shift in meaning."[115]

The dog becomes more than an insult. In al-Suyūṭī's micro-commentary, it is an opportunity to comment and reflect on language and adab through one word.

CONCLUSION

In both anecdotes involving the dog insult, al-Khawārizmī's and al-Maʿarrī's, there seems to be a display of mastery over language in attaining names of dogs. "The model litterateur (*adīb*) was—if not a walking encyclopedia—certainly an individual who had something apposite and witty to say about nearly any topic."[116] Al-Khawārizmī, a master *adīb* of his time as the anecdote suggests, was nonetheless defeated by the then rising star al-Hamadhānī (d. 398 AH/1007 CE) in a famous *munāẓara*. The wonder boy of his time was said to have wanted to be in the spotlight.[117] Al-Hamadhānī, who also purportedly stated, tongue in cheek, that he is the Jāḥiẓ of his age in his *Maqāmāt* and that every age has its Jāḥiẓ, may have been operating from a place of rivalry and competition with the prodigious adab masters. While al-Hamadhānī's literary dispute was with al-Khawārizmī, his contemporary, he was operating from a Jāḥiẓian index to overcome not one but two, if not more, towering figures. Al-Jāḥiẓ created an index of excellence, as Abdelfattah Kilito observes, to the extent that Ibn al-ʿAmīd (d. 360 AH/970 CE) was dubbed "the second Jāḥiẓ" or "the last Jāḥiẓ" as a substantiation of his skill.[118] While it is true that al-Hamadhānī, Ibn al-ʿAmīd, and even al-Tawḥīdī may have had a Jāḥiẓ complex, and were operating within this anxiety of influence, al-Suyūṭī, a litterateur of the Mamluk period, was operating from a different paradigm. The centrality of an anxiety-of-influence figure like al-Jāḥiẓ who acted as a specter of sustainable invitation for envy and one-upmanship for subsequent literati does not extend to the Mamluk period in the same capacity.[119] Mamluks, it could be argued, were more open to the world. For instance, considering Egyptian poet Ibn Nubāta's (d. 768 AH/1366 CE) comment on the issue of plagiarism (broadly allusions) among scholars, he maintains: "I have seen how the by-products of people's thoughts [*natā'ij afkār al-nās*] are no more than progeny passed on from one to another and from nations whose poetries originate side by side on this earth."[120] As al-Musawi argues, there are links and transference between the nature of governance and state and cultural output but also outlook.[121] It may be argued that the nature of the Mamluk state, compared to the earlier Abbasid and Umayyad polities, did not inspire the kind of obsession seen in literary predecessors with a central figure of excellence. This is not to say that there was no competition. On the contrary, it is arguable that competition grew in both horizontal and vertical trajectories across time, with one's contemporaries but also predecessors, in equal fierceness. The result was a vigorous cultural output, encyclopedic in ethos but also in size, that closely rivals the zenith of Abbasid productivity.[122] By extension, the concept of adab itself has witnessed an expansion in the Mamluk period as Muhanna observes. It became "maximally expansive, encompassing topics and forms of discourse once deemed beyond its purview."[123]

The competition across layers of time can be measured through the mastery of the quantification by the number of dogs; first twenty names for a dog in different dialects in the tenth century and then seventy in the eleventh century. The relationship between knowledge and power, as discussed by Franz Rosenthal, is one where there is a concomitance of *'ilm* (knowledge) with *ri'āsa* (power and leadership).[124] Indeed, as mentioned in chapter 1, there is an established relationship between adab and power, where *su'dud* (influence) is regarded as one of its fruits. Power here need not be thought of in negative terms. Indeed, it can be nonmaterial influence, such as social capital, for the good in general or for the enhancement of the subject's life in material and nonmaterial terms. Thus, al-Suyūṭī's *urjūza* is actively competing with antecedents in the manner it resolves an unresolved issue using the tools, forms, conventions, and ethos developed by Mamluk literati while simultaneously asserting its literary power in the manner it amassed and disseminated knowledge in a way no antecedent or contemporary could. There was no need to overthrow the specter of al-Jāḥiẓ, or any other, as every individual is their own specter.

Al-Suyūṭī's adabization of the insult therefore offers a case in point of how adab as method works. The framework of response to this insult is structured in adab. This is not to say that adab as method or technique is a Mamluk enterprise or a feature of this time only. In the same manner, Ibn Qutayba (d. 276 AH/889 CE) titled his book *Adab al-kātib* (The Adab [i.e., adabized technique and method] of the Scribe), which is a manual or guide for scribes; it conceptually combined the text and praxis and the virtue-ethic into a method of adab for scribes, how to write and document but also how to do so in an adabized manner. What this difference in thinking means for us when we study Ibn Qutayba's book, or any other, is that instead of regarding it as solely a manual for scribes, or regarding al-Suyūṭī's poem as just an obscure *urjūza* on dogs, we are presented with an opportunity to regard the manner in which authors framed their work. The existence of conceptual and ethical frameworks for composition rested on a foundational structure of adab.

6

Adab as Resolve and Will

The Philological Gadfly and the Lexical Ark

I am the gadfly of the Athenian people, given to them by God, and they will never have another, if they kill me. And now, Athenians, I am not going to argue for my own sake, as you may think, but for yours, that you may not sin against the God by condemning me, who am his gift to you. For if you kill me you will not easily find a successor to me, who, if I may use such a ludicrous figure of speech, am a sort of gadfly, given to the state by God; and the state is a great and noble steed who is tardy in his motions owing to his very size, and requires to be stirred into life. I am that gadfly which God has attached to the state, and all day long and in all places am always fastening upon you, arousing and persuading and reproaching you. You will not easily find another like me, and therefore I would advise you to spare me.

—*APOLOGY OF SOCRATES*

Part One of the Book Leg over Leg Regarding al-Fāriyāq *ends here and will be followed by Part Two once the author through God's favor and generosity has been stoned and crucified. Amen.*

—*LEG OVER LEG*, 4:427

Aḥmad Fāris al-Shidyāq's (1805–87) *Leg over Leg* (1855) is unique in that it is caught in a condition of both resistance to linguistic and epistemic infiltrations but also implicit and explicit engagement with world texts by Rabelais, Cervantes, and Byron, to name a few. The author adopts this posture in the epilogue of the book (*khātima*), where he acknowledges the unpopularity of his opinions and what the book has to offer. Al-Shidyāq begins the book with an exordium telling the reader that there are two purposes for composing the work. The first is to underscore the strange and the rare in the Arabic language (*gharāʾib al-lugha wa-nawādiruhā*) and the characteristics of letters and language where each letter has its own unique qualities that affect meaning (*kull ḥarf yakhtaṣṣ bi-ma ʿnā min al-ma ʿānī dūn ghayrihi wa-huwa min asrār al-lugha al-ʿarabiyya al-latī qall man tanabbah lahā*).[1] The second purpose is to show the ascendence of women in knowledge pertaining to their environment as he gives the example of the narrator's wife, al-Fāriyāqiyya, who, we are told, comes to debate people of critical outlook and experience and astutely critique political and social conditions in the countries visited (*tujādil ahl al-naẓar wa-l-khibra wa-tantaqid al-umūr al-siyāsiyya wa-l-aḥwāl al-ma ʿāshiyya wa-l-mu ʿādiyya fī al-bilād al-latī ra ʾathā aḥsan intiqād*).[2] Al-Shidyāq adds afterward that her language is impeccable and there were never any strange words uttered by her. There is an emphasis here on the obvious role of education al-Shidyāq highlights with respect to women in particular and the critical subject in general. Al-Fāriyāqiyya, as the adabized subject, shows development as a reader. Salient to this critical stance, which he himself adopts, is the use of language, and which is by turn among the subjects of his book. The relationship between language, concepts, and thinking or the production of knowledge was highlighted elsewhere by al-Shidyāq. In an 1869 article in the newspaper *al-Jawā ʾib*, he comments on a scientific general committee that will meet to translate useful books from all languages to Arabic. He questions this endeavor's ability as an activity that could hold potential in alleviating people's daily hardships. Al-Shidyāq accuses the translation movement of damaging the Arab knowledge-producing power. He saw this movement as a purely commercial enterprise that is submerging the Arabic language with ideas, terms, and foreign cultural products without producing or exporting something equivalent in terms of ideas. In this respect, al-Shidyāq's reservation stems from this lack of equality in the then current traffic.[3]

Pursuant to this spirit of gadfly critic, al-Shidyāq opens his book with the chapter "Raising a Storm" (*ithārat riyāḥ*), which begins with onomatopoeic imperatives urging the reader to be still and stop what they are doing (*meh*) and be quiet and shut up and listen (*ṣeh!*) ("Gently! Hush! Silence! Quiet! Cock an ear! Listen up! Hold your tongue! Quit talking! . . .").[4] He then situates himself with "following in the footsteps (*aqfū*) of that company of men who have rendered their reputations white by covering pages in black (*al-ladhīna bayyaḍū wujūhahum bi-taswīd al-ṭurūs*), for if they did well, then I too may be considered to have done well (*fa-in kānū qad aḥsanū fa-anā u ʿaddu ayḍan min al-muḥsinīn*), and if they did badly, it may be that one more book is needed to add to their efforts (*takmila*)."[5] In both cases, al-Shidyāq regarded his predecessors, and himself, as correct in their enterprises. Anticipating both proponents and opponents of premodern adab, he nodded to the opponents by saying that even if literary predecessors are thought of as antiquated, his book has the ability to be in a renewed dialogue with this tradition. In fact, he sketches the hermeneutical map for interpretation (*ta ʾwīl*) of his work. Al-Shidyāq reminds the reader that should they find some indecorous words (*fāḥish*) or expressions, they are to employ interpretation and not take it literally and remember Abū Nuwās. Al-Shidyāq's observation on the waning of understanding of literary language as such and the disappearance of the consideration of the "poetic persona" in interpretation and the disappearance of genres and modes from Arab writings such as *ars erotica* in the nineteenth century, for example, are telling, as he conjoined the gradually disappearing tools of adab but also some modes of adab at the time.[6]

> If you were to say that its expressions are so explicitly clear, it needs no interpretation or hermeneutics; I say to you that only yesterday you were making mistakes, mispronouncing, and maledicting, uttering solecisms and stuttering, erring and aberring, speaking randomly and raggedly, misspeaking and randomly mouthing off, rambling and roaming, raving, ranting, and talking irrationally, faltering and floundering, babbling like foreigners, bumbling as though you had plums in your mouths and mumbling as though your mouths were covering, dragging out your words and wagging your tongues mischievously (and at great length too), stammering, yammering . . . so at what point did you acquire the knowledge that would allow you to understand it?[7]

Interesting is the juxtaposition of "interpretation" or exegesis as *taʾwīl* and al-Shidyāq's listing of forty-five synonyms of "error" as crises in understanding. The listings imply not only the many ways a word could be understood, or rather misunderstood, but also the many ways an error could be made. He is consciously situating his book in the adab compendium and pleading that should it not be accepted among adab literature, considering it a thesaurus would suffice (*wa-la ʿamrī law lam yakun min shāfiʿ li-qabūlihi wa-ijrāʾihi ʿinda al-udabāʾ wa-ʿindakum antum ayḍan majrā kutub al-adab suwā sard alfāẓ kathīra min al-mutarādif la-kafā*).[8] Al-Shidyāq is reminding us, befittingly, not only of the many ways we could say "error" but of more than forty reminders of "error" to signal the impossibility of notions of epistemic certainty next to interpretation as *taʾwīl*.[9] That words could mean more and have more synonyms disrupts the simplistic and unreflective use and reception of language, hence interpretation. Al-Shidyāq broke the relationship between the word "error" and the thing "error"; in other words, contra John Locke, who would tell us that a word needs to point to a thing, an archetype, approaching reading with mathematical precision, al-Shidyāq shows us the possibilities of interpretation but also error. Like his premodern predecessors, al-Shidyāq is also telling us the aforementioned words are not exact synonyms with surgical precision, even if they point to the phenomenon of error, and that they point to many nuanced meanings. In this respect, he dismantles the facile conceptual relationships induced by language; he is bringing not only language into question but the conceptual world it conjures. Perhaps also indirectly, al-Shidyāq tells us how complex the mind and imagination are in the way they express themselves in the synonyms of words; the multitude of words do not indicate that language failed at accuracy or that al-Shidyāq is taking after the alleged pedantry of premodern litterateurs who had plenty of time on their hands, but they orientate us to observe that it is precisely accuracy that was a concern. Perhaps far-reaching but premodern litterateurs also understood that the imagination and intellect are not one-dimensional to accept the limited range of word-meaning, the simplified language that would stifle them, and so al-Shidyāq created what Leo Spitzer calls a formulation of a phenomenology of language. Spitzer, in his famous essay "Linguistic Perspectivism in *Don Quijote*," argues that Cervantes, through his representation of things not as they are unto themselves but as objects of language and thought, formulated a phenomenology of language.[10] This he proves through an examination of the "polyetymology" and "polynomasia" in the novel. The variety of names assigned to some characters, and the polysemy of single words, Spitzer argues, are not lapses or mistakes where Cervantes is losing control over his work but rather full stylistic and aesthetic devices that reflect the perspectivist worldview.[11] "Spitzer demonstrated that Cervantes was acutely conscious of the fact that '*el mundo, tal como se ofrece al hombre, es susceptible de varias inter-pretaciones, exactamente igual que los nombres son susceptibles de varias etimologias*' ('the world, as it offers itself up to humankind, is susceptible to various interpretations, just as the names are susceptible to various etymologies')."[12] Al-Shidyāq warns us that his condition for reading this book is not to think that these synonyms share the same meaning. They might be similar, or close in meaning indeed, but they are not identical. He tells us that had they been identical, Arabs would not have a name for each item that would indicate these differences.[13] If the reader does not espouse this opinion, or think that they are identical, it is because we are at a distant temporal point from them (*wa-li-buʿd ʿahdihim ʿannā taẓannaynāhā bi-maʿnā wāḥid*) al-Shidyāq forbids the reader to read or enjoy the book (*lā ujīz lahu muṭālaʿatahu wa-lā uhanniʾahu bihi*).[14] There is an important reference here to more than being temporally distant from premodern philologists and their use of language and the temporal coordinates of al-Shidyāq and our own at this point in time. The reference is more about the habitus as "habit of mind" rather than the habitus as a temporal throw. The author, al-Shidyāq, describes himself as holding this book under his arms ready to defend it against critics, Orientalists, and everyone even if he were burnt or crucified as a result, he tells us; a rather extreme maneuver of his resistance but it also speaks of the prevailing intellectual climate, a habitus of mind. *Leg over Leg* argues, while holding the book tenaciously, that the reading tradition witnessed in the premodern Arabic tradition, like *Kalīla wa-Dimna* or *Ḥayy b. Yaqẓān*, for instance, is now lost and contaminated. The tools required to read or visit the Arabic literary tradition may no longer be available. So, the temporal throw of the nineteenth-century reader is also a result of a habitus of mind that has transformed the intellectual climate.

Al-Shidyāq, as his work attests, cannot be stifled, nor can language. The success of the philological tactics of al-Shidyāq does not simply rest in the way they retrieve the past linguistic tradition but in the way they pose pressing, timeless, and universal questions about language qua language and also about the Arabic language and adab as an institution in particular and a habitus. Erwin Panofsky defined habitus as "habits of mind" and it can be understood as the "habit forming force" that constitutes inclinations and intent, evaluative perspective and reaction. While Panofsky argues that these actions are repeated regularly through practice, Bourdieu maintains that they are exercised ordinarily as part of everyday life; they both can be said to agree that habits of mind are imparted through family, school, and society until they are almost second nature.[15] Al-Shidyāq's initial conceding that should his book not be accepted among adab books, and thus considering it a thesaurus, would be the solution for the non-adabized reader or the failed reader in al-Shidyāq's view. The non-adabized reader's horizon, in al-Shidyāq's view, was ossified in a presentist temporal point of time that is unable to move past itself because the non-adabized reader regards the past as dead. As Alasdair MacIntyre maintains, "So when an institution—a university, say, or a farm, or a hospital—is the bearer of a tradition of practice or practices, its common life will be partly, but in a centrally important way, constituted by a continuous argument as to what a university is and ought to be or what good farming is or what good medicine is. Traditions, when vital, embody continuities of conflict. Indeed when a tradition becomes Burkean, it is always dying or dead."[16] The *nahḍa* debates revolved around two issues: "Was literary modernity a European import, foreign to the Arabic literary tradition, or was it the outgrowth of an indigenous literary past? Al-Shidyāq rejects both of these as mutually exclusive options."[17] Al-Shidyāq would not be the only scholar and/or litterateur satirizing and cautioning against what Stephan Guth identifies as "Euromania" in his discussion of the similarly positioned literary works of the nineteenth century.[18] Al-Shidyāq, unlike some "modernists" of the *nahḍa*, who may have wanted nothing to do with tradition, left it to ossify or pretended that it was ossified and therefore had no place in their time; or in MacIntyre's terms, they left it to the Burkeans (conservatives) as they had a different project.[19] The different project need not to have been naturally born. As Jeffrey Sacks maintains, Arabic literature during the *nahḍa* emerged as a discipline linked to colonial and methodological practices that sought to domesticate language and impose new temporal and historical categories, where "the terms of the institutionalization of a literary object in relation to the legacies of Orientalism and the juridical violence of the colonial state . . . imparts the destruction and loss of *adab*."[20]

In his *al-Jāsūs ʿalā al-qāmūs*, al-Shidyāq describes his motivation behind composing the book. He first informs us that this is a book on language; it contains all the words that "were used by literati and writers and whoever authored a book" (*shāmilan li-l-alfāẓ al-latī istaʿmalahā al-udabāʾ wa-l-kuttāb wa-kull man ishtahara bi-l-taʾlīf*).[21] Al-Shidyāq then engages in praising the Arabic language and says that it ought to be the tongue of those with wisdom and precision (*fa-ajdarahu bi-an yakūn lisān al-ḥikma wa-l-iḥkām*).[22] However, he sees a predicament to this because of foreign influences either through hegemony or colonization at the time (e.g.,

Ottoman, French, British). He maintains that the foreign tongues competed with it (Arabic) at this age: they almost scumbled their language over the language of its people (*illā anna alsinat al-ajānib zāḥamathu fī hādhā al-ʿaṣr fa-kādat taḥlaʾ ʿanhu ahlahu*).[23] Al-Shidyāq gives his diagnosis for this from a linguistic and structural perspective; he says that it may be that their (foreign) language is easier than Arabic, it is also easier to learn, with fewer roots/words, and the definitions of their words do not include that many differences in their denotations.[24] In his *al-Jāsūs*, al-Shidyāq then argues that lexicons should be structured alphabetically as European dictionaries rather than the unique arrangements of premodern lexicons, beginning with al-Khalīl b. Aḥmad's *Kitāb al-ʿayn* in the eighth century and its articulation or emission points of letters to alphabetical arrangements like Ibn Sīdah's *al-Muḥkam* in the eleventh century, where an emphasis on root arrangement was observed and where thematic arrangements were observed in Ibn Sīdah's *al-Mukhaṣṣaṣ*. Premodern lexicographers, before al-Shidyāq, constantly developed the types of lexicons that obeyed the intellectual needs of the time.[25] Instead of ossifying the lexical tradition or leaving it to ossify, while being faced with those who already abandoned the language for its difficulty, al-Shidyāq offers a solution. He is aware of the discourse surrounding the uphill battle of Arabic in favor of Ottoman and European languages. Al-Shidyāq maintains that those who are in commerce (*yataʿāṭūn minnā al-tijāra*) and those in power and decision-making leadership (*yaḥmilūn ʿibʾ al-imāra*) "claim that Arabic is unfit in this age for these two purposes" (*lā taṣluḥ fī hādhā al-zaman li-hātayn al-khiṭṭatayn*), and therefore one must seek the assistance of the language of the foreigners (*kalām al-ajānib*) even if it leads to two disgraces and humiliations (*ḥiṭṭatayn*).[26] Al-Shidyāq criticizes this heavily and holds that to say Arabic is unfit is a complete lie and falsification (*mā barrū wa-lā ṣadaqū*), and they unwittingly have joined those who shamed themselves (*bi-l-ladhī ʿāb nafsahu laḥiqū*).[27] Those who say this, al-Shidyāq tells us, are only doing so because they are incompetent in Arabic. Indeed, this is a position al-Shidyāq adopts in *Leg over Leg* as he satirizes those who have numerous difficulties with the Arabic language as he capitalizes on mistakes for comic relief; he spares no one in this satire: Arabs, non-Arabs, and Orientalists alike.

Al-Shidyāq incorporated voices that spoke to him and his readers from the past, whose voices were employed using philological tactics to pose questions; to answer and engage with these questions, we must posit ourselves as recipients of these questions and begin to ask the questions, not reject them. To say that *Leg over Leg* is a satire of the daunting Arabic grammar and language betrays al-Shidyāq's own project and intellectual questions posed at the preface and elsewhere. It is an ossifying reading that engages in the *hijāʾ* of the literary tradition; the *hijāʾ*, however, becomes "satire," befittingly. The framework of satire as critique, in fact, does not tell us much beyond the terms of this critical judgment; in other words, to say *Leg over Leg* is a satire of aspects of the tradition does not offer anything beyond those terms since this critical judgment is not interested in a dialogue with the work but rather an opposition. In this respect, by positing itself in an adversarial stance, this critical judgment emptied the work of its value to imbue it with a different set of values: the values deserving of subsequent *hijāʾ*, hence abandonment.

Al-Shidyāq criticizes religious and political leaders (*ruʾasāʾ al-dīn wa-l-dunyā*) of being complicit in their subjects' ignorance; and he sees that this was done deliberately. This criticism comes also in the context of al-Shidyāq's frustration with poor Bible translations, which was an issue he critiqued. He wonders, "How is it that religious and political leaders' blood does not yearn for elegant words and eloquence?"[28] It appears then from the start that the purpose of the book, as al-Shidyāq tells us, is to critique a certain status quo that he deems endemic at the time and detrimental to the Arabic language and by extension learning and intellectual life. He sees this as a threat not only as structural on the political level, which he expressed before, but also manifest on the level of reading and interpretation of his book, and by extension other books, and the critical subject's makeup. He treats the interpretation of his book as a microcosm of the failure of the praxis of language (with forty-five synonyms for "error"). Al-Shidyāq tells us that his is a book of adab, which requires effort and interpretation. Therefore, to simply treat *Leg over Leg* as a lexicon would be the least sophisticated way of reading this work and is only reserved for the failed reader, who may very well be in need of this education, or as al-Mutanabbī would say, "I sleep like a baby unconcerned with poesy's complications (*anām milʾa jufūnī ʿan shawāridihā*) / and people lose sleep over its meaning and dispute each other (*wa-yashar al-khalq jarrāhā wa-yakhtaṣim*)."[29] Al-Mutanabbī also recognized the un-adabized and failed readers of his time on a scale of adab and mastery of language that he placed himself at the top of as indicated by the quality of sleep.

TAʾWĪL AND AL-SHIDYĀQ

Al-Fāriyāq, al-Shidyāq's narrator-character, posits himself as both a failed reader and interpreter when his employer, after assigning him the role of dream interpreter, calls on him to interpret a dream. In the dream the man mounts a horse and his head grows six horns; he then loses the horse saddle and with every day spent in town the horse loses an organ until it is no more and the man has to walk home on foot. Al-Fāriyāq attempts to interpret the dream and tells him that the horse is a woman (*al-faras kināya ʿan al-marʾa*) and the saddle is her manners and decorum (*al-sarj kināya ʿan adab al-marʾa*) and his fatigue from walking on foot is his bachelorhood (*wa-l-mashī wa-l-iʿyāʾ kināya ʿan al-ʿuzūbah*).[30] The man objects to this reading and tells him that he is mistaken on several points. First, unlike other interpreters, he is succinct, and second, the horse is not a metonym for a woman; his interpretation should be based on their terms/terminology/framework (*iṣṭilāḥunā*), not al-Fāriyāq's framework (*iṣṭilāḥukum*). Al-Fāriyāq is taught a lesson in the horizon of reading and thus meaning; his received horizon of meaning operated as a will to method in its attempt to decipher the man's dream. It is a nondialectical encounter that did not engage with possible aspects of language, hence possible meanings. His inability to establish a relationship between the dream and the world around him, of the man, resulted in this failure, even though they are communicating in the same language. As the hermeneutic encounter fails, the man urges al-Shidyāq to get ready for the second dream's interpretation, but he must exert some effort in his editing/checking and flow (*ijtahid fī al-taḥrīr wa-l-ishāb*).[31]

In the second dream, al-Fāriyāq's employer has his notebook mysteriously filled with eloquently composed speeches the moment he brushes his wife's hair. When he delivers this speech to the audience, they are very pleased. And as per his wife's advice, he should devise a way to speak to them abroad since there is little opportunity for giving speeches where he is. When the man attempts to do so, the pages carrying this mysteriously added speech all become blank except for the letters he jotted down himself. Trying to connect them together, they yield nonsense. And so he descends from the pulpit in shame unable to give his speech.

Al-Fāriyāq told the man that his speech only worked in his country and that is why the pages were blank and he was unable to connect the letters (*kalāmuka al-ladhī ʿujiba bihi qawmuka lam yaṣluḥ fī ghayri bilādika*).[32] The man, furious, told him that this interpretation was far worse than the first. Though al-Fāriyāq was motivated by what the man had initially proposed in the first dream, that interpretation should rely on emic terminology and not extraneous ones; his reading of the second dream did not prove successful in the man's eyes or the man did not like the interpretation. Al-Shidyāq here, through al-Fāriyāq, ridicules the will to method. His employing of the exact method, instructed by the man, without critique or resolve, invoked the man's anger as a sign of this encounter's failure.

The latter seems to be the case as the man's third dream features him ascending a pulpit. He begins by saying, "Praise be to God, who commanded the erection of this staircase and found it pleasing to serve as His Throne."[33] Indeed, it is not surprising to see one member of the audience question the mental soundness of the man and describe him as "out of his mind" (*maʿtūhan*).[34] The people start leaving as they hear him, and with each step of the pulpit ascended, he gives a speech to the people and they leave one by one until he is left alone at the top. Deeming himself closer to God and the heavens, after a hundred steps, the man is elated—until a poet sees him and asks him to spare himself from ridicule and being the laughingstock of everyone. The man is oblivious to the poet's pleas, until the poet dismantles the pulpit, whereupon the man and his book fall on the poet and they are both battered. Al-Fāriyāq interprets this to mean that the orator must not be loquacious because if he is, he is bound to fall hard and break his neck.

Inspired by the naming tradition witnessed in *Ḥayy b. Yaqẓān* (lit. Alive Son of Awake), al-Fāriyāq's employer, Dhāhūl b. Ghāfūl (Overwhelmed Son of Neglectful), is aptly named for being a failed interpreter and reader. Like the king who could not interpret his dreams in *Kalīla wa-Dimna* and sought the wisdom of sages until he was forced to learn how to interpret, this employer is depicted to be at a loss as well. Like the objects of his criticism in his first chapter, this presumed leader lacks any foundation in eloquence or common sense. The distance between the man and the people grew wider as he ascended the pulpit. The Shidyāqian nod to adab's salvific qualities in the figure of the poet is telling. The poet, a user and a proponent of literary language, adab, and an advocate of the open-endedness and discourse that language inspires, is a savior figure in the man's dream. As designated by his name (Overwhelmed Son of Neglectful), the man's perpetual state of confoundedness takes on the metaphysical quality of undecipherable dreams. Dreams, by their very nature, belong to another world, another language. The man is unable to engage with the language of dreams; he is unable to imagine a nonliteral world through deciphering those dreams. Al-Fāriyāq may be a good reader but the critique of the inadequate hermeneutic encounter that exposes al-Fāriyāq's incompetence as well makes the poet the only savior in this encounter, not al-Fāriyāq. However, the hope for the poet as savior is but a Blochian "disappointable hope."[35] The poet can and has the power to save the incomprehensible orator in the dream, and thus the man who will eventually become a better reader, but the orator is disinclined and in turn falls and hurts both himself and the poet. Al-Shidyāq's overall mood of "disappointable hope," as mentioned earlier, is felt throughout and expressed not only in his loss of language but also in his aforementioned criticism of religious and political leaders who are happy to see people left in ignorance.

THE CRITIQUE OF POOR LANGUAGE AND THE POETICS OF MALADIES

After this series of dreams, al-Shidyāq follows with the chapter "On the Curing of Bad Breath" (*fī iṣlāḥ al-bakhr*). *Bakhr*, lexically, refers to a medical condition known for its symptom of bad breath. Al-Fāriyāq tells us that he was employed to interpret dreams but also to fix these cases of bad breath that are endemic on this island. He relates that the people's breath is so bad that no one understands a word they are saying.[36] Al-Shidyāq employs bad breath as a metaphorical device that obstructs intelligibility. The image and attributes carrying this weight of comparison could be explained by Ibn Sīnā's (Avicenna) analysis of the medical condition as resulting from rotten mixtures in the respiratory organs (*akhlāṭ ʿafina fī aʿḍāʾ al-tanaffus*).[37] The concept al-Shidyāq refers to here is normally called *al-ʿayy* (lack of intelligibility) and it is one that Ibn Ṭabāṭabā (d. 322 AH/934 CE) lists as a quality necessitating criticism (*hijāʾ*) in his *ʿIyār al-shiʿr*.[38] Al-Shidyāq borrows the idiom *awwal al-ʿayy al-ikhtilāṭ*[39] (the beginning of unintelligibility is the mix-up [in the mind/emotions; also meaning anger]) to build this extended metaphor. The transferring of emotional and mental mix-ups (*akhlāṭ*) as grammatical mix-ups (*laḥn*) that have a medical mix-up effect reproduces the abstract concept of language errors in the register of maladies. These images flow with the other hygienic practices and technologies of the self that are related in the rest of the chapter and indeed the book. Relating grammatical mistakes to disease is perhaps one of Ibn Qutayba's (d. 276 AH/889 CE) unique features of his *akhbār*-cum-information, as he says in his *ʿUyūn al-akhbār* (The Wellsprings of Information) that "grammatical mistakes in speech are uglier than smallpox in the face" (*al-laḥn fī al-kalām aqbaḥ min al-judarī fī al-wajh*).[40] The quote conjoins bodily viral diseases with linguistic diseases manifest as grammatical mistakes. The latter, aurally and visually recognizable in both oral and written communication inasmuch as smallpox pustules, are also visible. Interesting, however, is this comparison because the scars that may be left by smallpox, Ibn Qutayba insinuates, can be an aftermath of bad grammar. The word *aqbaḥ* (uglier) in this instance not only carries aesthetic and moral connotations but also grammatical.[41] In other words, it is also painful (on several levels) to listen to bad grammar, he tells us. The failure to master a language compared to an infectious disease, even a plague, is an image that was conjured by al-Shidyāq; the latter is no stranger to the classical works of adab, as the analogy becomes viral in his *Leg over Leg*.

The chapter begins with al-Fāriyāq unable to interpret a dream related to him about a monster with six horns, numerous tails, many patterns, and spots on its body. Certain that the dream's image of the monster is literal and cannot be interpreted (*lā taḥtamil al-taʾwīl*), he complains to his wife, who offers us the clue to the entire chapter. The wife laments that some of her fellow Christian women of both Egyptian and Levantine origins are unable to truly get to know their husbands before marriage and believe that they are created to solely please men in bed and serve them and their household. She complains that husbands neglect their appearances and do not prioritize looking *presentable*, while they paradoxically focus on their wives' appearance lest their wives' hair is not coiffed and her appearance is unkempt. Al-Fāriyāqiyya continues complaining that these husbands ask their wives to wash their feet before bed or massage them until they fall asleep while blinking, dozing off, yawning, and stretching. The man may very well be a slinking wolf (*sayyid ʿamallas*).[42]

In a paradiegetic move to introduce her point, the wife goes on a digression to emphasize various repulsive practices that are not only off-putting, analogous to the bad breath al-Fāriyāq spoke about, but also diminish the murūʾa of said husband(s) as humans and make them comparable to wolves in al-Fāriyāqiyya's pun. The tacitly expressed demands, on the husbands' parts, conveyed by the wife above matches the punning of *sayyid* (master) but *sayyid* also means "wolf" or a "master of villainy/wolves" (*sayyid ʿamallas*). While the bad breath is used as a metaphor for unintelligibility, it is fitting among the repulsive improper hygienic practices listed above. Al-Fāriyāq refers to eloquence and possessing correct language in the same urgency of practicing the necessary hygienic technologies of the self. His wife refers to a compendium of practices (hygienic, emotional, sexual) that are also listed as part of the technologies of the self and are concomitant with a healthy and successful marital relationship. The marriage metaphor is elevated in their conversation to a marriage of words (*zawāj al-alfāẓ*).[43] The wife's interpretation of the dream, and al-Fāriyāq's acceptance of this interpretation, depends on the marriage of words, a relationship that was not possible in his earlier interpretation of his employer's dreams, where every dream interpretation is met with rejection. The wife's understanding of the metaphorical language of the dream, its ambiguity and multiple meanings, allowed her to participate in an adabized reading of this dream and create a reading through social *poiēsis* to reinstate murūʾa; adab as praxis here involves the creative production of desired and adabized social conditions. The act of creating an *exemplum virtutis* (a model example of virtue) out of a bad dream that was deemed literal and employ it in a critique that had both a direct and indirect effect places the wife as an ideal, adabized reader. To add, her very act of reading (interpreting) the dream is effecting a technology of the self, through employing the figurative aspect of language, to contribute to her well-being. Her husband, al-Fāriyāq, was able to understand the underlying meaning beyond her literal message in the form of dream interpretation. It is this "marriage of words," as they called it, which enabled the transformative *poiēsis* of the situation. The wordplay on the un-adabized man/husband (*sayyid*) being *sayyid ʿamallas* (a *kunya* for the slinking [*khabīth*] wolf) is illuminating for the monster image encountered before; here is also the binary divide between the adabized/un-adabized as human/beast. Al-Fāriyāqiyya, the wife, relates several other lamentable conditions beyond manners, hygiene, and redefining emotional and sexual equality. Al-Fāriyāq engages his wife in this interpretation of the monster, as he comes to realize this reading by asking a probing question at the end. He asks his wife whether she insinuated that he ought to fix his hair and clothes to look more presentable; his wife replies that he is not yet doing this but will be soon.

WRITTEN UNDER AN ARCHIVE STAR: FROM ARCHIVE TO META ARCHIVE

The famous title of al-Shidyāq's book, *Kitāb al-sāq ʿalā al-sāq fī mā huwa al-fāriyāq*, is supplemented by a subtitle, *Ayyām wa-shuhūr wa-aʿwām fī ʿajam/ʿujm al-ʿarab wa-l-aʿjām* (Days, Months, and Years [Spent] in the Erroneous Speech of Arabs and Non-Arabs). The title also read "Erroneous Speech of Foreign Arabs (*ʿajam al-ʿarab*) and Non-Arabs" or "The Erroneous Speech of Incorrect Arabic (*ʿujm al-ʿarab*) of Arabs and Non-Arabs" depending on how al-Shidyāq vocalized *ʿajam/ʿujm al-ʿarab*; and it may very well be that the polysemy is intentional.[44] Al-Shidyāq also utilizes the classical Arabic genre of *ayyām al-ʿarab* (the days of Arabs); this expression of "days" refers to what is accepted as *waqāʾiʿ* (events) involving the historical incidents, battles, and cultural and literary life during the Jāhiliyya or pre-Islamic Arab period. Al-Shidyāq then underscores these two titles with a couplet of poetry:

The writings of Zayd and Hind these days speak more to the common taste
Than any pair of weighty tomes
More profitable and useful than the teachings of two scholars
Are what a yoke of oxen from the threshings combs.[45]

Al-Shidyāq alludes here to the proliferation of the novel genre as he refers to the commonly accepted way in Arabic to refer to John and Jane Doe, anonymously alluding to the two protagonists (male/female) as Zayd and Hind, in place of somebody in the masculine *fulān* and feminine *fulāna*. He says that writing and reading (novels) about Zayd and Hind are becoming more popular than reading two comparatively larger books (insinuating that the novels he had in mind are smaller in size) and generally easier to read; he also points to the fact that these novels are more profitable (to authors and publishers) than teaching in general, which was his profession. There is an indication here to two things that may be related: the changing perception of time and its concomitance with labor and profit as part of the evolving economic landscape across eighteenth-century Europe and by extension in the "greenhouse modernities," forced to sprout violently, brought on by colonialism in the Middle East.[46]

The eighteenth-century reading landscape in Britain, for instance, also transformed as a result of the changing perceptions of time, industrialization, and modernity, and thereby the creation of many types of readers. In his *Dictionary of the English Language* (1755), Samuel Johnson includes many of the moral quotations from his friend Samuel Richardson's popular novel *Clarissa* (1751), which had, innovatively, an index organized by category and quotations to save time for the "busy young men." *Clarissa* was not often praised for its plot but rather for the lessons it imparted. There were two types of readers in the eighteenth century: the "deep or shallow, intensive or extensive, passionate or uninvolved."[47] Readers who were immersed in the books and entered their worlds, and those who picked and chose from books rather expansively. Not everyone could afford or was able to become a professional reader. There was a growing fear that people would become too interested and immersed in a book and "forget to do [their] job."[48] It is related that three or four days before his death, Johnson spoke "of the little fear he had of undergoing a chirurgical operation, 'I would give one of these legs for a year more of life, I mean of comfortable life, not such as that which I now suffer';—and lamented much his inability to read during his hours of restlessness; 'I used formerly, (he added,) when sleepless in bed, to read like a Turk.'"[49] Turk, of course, refers to the totality of Muslims and also the Ottomans. Johnson never explained what he meant by reading "like a Turk." The expression was left to later commentators. John Black, for instance, traces the expression to another: "To work like a Turk," a common expression in Britain at the time. Black maintains, "The saying might however have been introduced when people were exceedingly active. To *fight* like a Turk seems to have been the original expression."[50] But Johnson's usage of the image of the Turk seems to suggest both a certain fierceness akin to Johnson's own reading but also a sense of being a stranger or an alien on both psychological and social levels; Johnson seems to be defending a position that runs counter to the current norms of the reading habits of his time.[51] Of note is the transference of the fierceness of fighting with the fierceness of reading as perhaps Johnson articulated what Edward Said observed about reading as *ijtihād*.[52] *Ijtihād* (lit. exerting oneself), a term born out of Islamic sciences proper, also has a *double sens* meaning that can be noticed from its etymology since it originally means physical or mental effort expended in a particular activity.

Was the novel, in its language and form, in al-Shidyāq's opinion, an easier read than the larger tomes he refers to? Was it less time-consuming? It is clear that al-Shidyāq is not a stranger to the novel form either in translation or in the original languages he may have read on his travels. Despite this familiarity and his own critique of the novel as he mentions at the beginning, the desire to peg his work as the first Arabic novel betrays al-Shidyāq's own vision of his work and the indigeneity of the form(s) he chose. It unwittingly also betrays the critique of the novel that he declares at the beginning of the book and his ongoing critique of the mutual overlapping of power and knowledge in his other writings. Note, for instance, that not all *nahḍa* intellectuals were cognizant of this relationship or viewed it through the same lens. Rifāʿa al-Ṭahṭāwī (1801–73), "the first Arab intellectual to become acquainted with modern Europe through travel and study . . . failed to recognize the mutual imbrication of power and knowledge, which had crystallized merely three decades earlier in the French Expedition in Egypt. For Tahtawi, Europe was only a rival with expansionist tendencies . . . [it] did not constitute an imperial threat; rather, it was perceived as offering an opportunity for cultural and civilizational revival in the Arab world."[53] This was the tenor of the general discourse of the *nahḍa*. It is possible to understand this, in one way, through the lens of looking beyond the hegemony of the Ottomans, who, as al-Shidyāq repeatedly told us in various works, marginalized the Arabic language; despite the fact that the Ottomans "derived the legitimacy of their rule from their posture as an Islamic state—a posture that secured the support of the traditional religious establishment within the Arab world."[54]

The prevalence of these views confirms al-Shidyāq's own critique. To some Arab critics and scholars, such as Muhammad Yusuf Najm (1925–2009), al-Shidyāq's is not a first novel but a failed novel. Najm maintains that "al-Shidyāq is the biggest literary talent that was wasted at the beginning of our *nahḍa*. While his *Leg over Leg* boasts of narrative maturity to a large degree, he did not utilize it. This book is just an autobiography of his own life written in a pleasant narrative style (*uslūb qaṣaṣī fannī ṭarīf*) and in some chapters it reaches the status of some World literary masterpieces."[55] Najm continues to say that al-Shidyāq's inclusion of the *maqāmāt* shows some innovation in the art of the *maqāma* since he departed from the linguistic pretentiousness and rhetorical absurdity (*al-takalluf al-lughawī wa-l-ʿabath al-bayānī*) to the *maqāma* that deals with some social issues (*mawḍūʿan ijtimāʿiyyan*). He also writes that were it not for al-Shidyāq's inclusion of *maqāmāt* by al-Fāriyāq's narrator, al-Hāris b. Hithām, and fashioning it stylistically in the manner of *saj*ʿ and adorning it with poetry in a *maqāmāt* frame as it was known by its earliest writers, "we could have considered this a good start for the short story (*uqṣuṣa*)."[56] Najm adds that had al-Shidyāq not been involved in politics and journalism, he would have written the "story" on its modern critical terms (*bi-shurūṭihā al-naqdiyya al-ḥadītha*). It is tempting to ask, What were the set of practices that characterized literary discourse and standardized its features over time? What was the definition of the short story for Najm, writing in the 1950s? Rashad Rushdi, who published a study on the "short story" in 1959, introduces us to the history of this genre, beginning with what he calls the "factory of lies" (*maṣnaʿ al-akādhīb*), which he maintains was a room in the Vatican, where every night the papal secretaries gather for entertainment in the form of short stories. Rushdi refers here to the Bugiale, which was a club started by papal secretary Poggio Bracciolini, who was a collector of jocular tales; he published the first Renaissance jestbook, the *Facetiae*, in 1470.[57] Rushdi also relates to us Giovanni Boccaccio's (1313–75) *Decameron*, ending with Guy de Maupassant (1850–93) as the ultimate father of the short story and his literary children Anton Chekhov (1860–1904), Luigi Pirandello (1867–1936), Katherine Mansfield (1888–1923), and Ernest Hemingway (1899–1961). In this introduction, no attempt was made by Rushdi to engage any Arabic sources or comparisons. He later only cites an excerpt from "The Tale of Sindbad" from the *Thousand and One Nights* as an example of realistic dialogue between characters who, according to him, "speak like real people" and not in the elevated language of classical Arabic texts. He criticizes contemporary authors who use this style of what he calls "the outdated conception of literature that rests on stylistics and language" (*al-mafhūm al-qadīm li-l-adab al-ladhī yaqūm ʿalā al-ṣiyāgha al-lafẓiyya*) and deems it "an anomaly in our part of the world [in the Arabic language]" as opposed to any other part of the world.[58] The Arabic language is indeed an anomaly in this part of the world, as Emile Habibi observed. Habibi argues that the Arabic language is the primary art that the Arab-Islamic civilization developed and that its treasures (*kunūz*) are a sea (*baḥr*). Habibi likens the Arabic language to music (*mūsīqā*) and drawing (*rasm*), and he speaks of language and *turāth* (heritage/tradition) as resistance to the hegemonic erasures.[59] It would not be inaccurate to agree with Habibi, bearing in mind the linguistic achievements of premodern adab, whether in the genre of the *maqāmāt*, which is a celebration of language in and of itself, or in Arabic poetry.

The failure of al-Shidyāq's *maqāmāt* to *become*, a verb of the *progress* narrative, the short story, according to Najm and those with similar views, would be relegated to the restrictive paradigms Rushdi placed as an evaluative model. In other words, the typical narrative of progress suggests that the models Najm and Rushdi invoke establish a benchmark that the rest of the non-Western world, including their readers, students, and audience, should strive to meet. This invitation to participate and meet the criteria of said literature rests on the belief that the value of Rushdi's literary examples is concomitant with the historical movement of progress. This posture essentially questions the roles of everyone in this purported progress narrative based on a comparison between societies, cultures, and periods. Rushdi's devaluation of adab, premodern Arabic literature, and perhaps even the totality of Arabic literature to the role of a useless participant rested on the view that classical Arabic is inadequate for modern literary expression (an anomaly) in his opinion, compared to other perceived successful models. Najm's and Rushdi's views as authority figures in the Arab world of education and culture, writing in the post-decolonization period, evoke the potent words exchanged between the Mamur and the narrator about Mustafa Sa'eed in Tayeb Salih's novel *Season of Migration to the North* (1966). The Mamur questions: "Has not the country become independent? Have we not become free men in our own country? Be sure, though, that they will direct our affairs from afar. This is because they have left behind them people who think as they do."[60] Salih reiterates what Frantz Fanon tells us, "Colonialism is not satisfied merely with holding a people in its grip and emptying the native's brain of all form and content. By a kind of perverted logic, it turns to the past of the oppressed people, and distorts, disfigures, and destroys it. The work of devaluing pre-colonial history takes on a dialectical significance today. When we consider the efforts made to carry out the cultural estrangement . . . to convince the natives that colonialism came to lighten their darkness."[61]

On the form of the short story, Egyptian writer and novelist Gamal al-Ghitani (1945–2015) tells us in an interview shortly before he passed that he was astonished when he read the history and definition of the short story in the aforementioned study by Rushdi. He maintains that the latter offered a definition for the short story that is in concert with the European tradition (*ta'rīfan li-l-qiṣṣa muttasiqan ma'a al-turāth al-ūrūbī*). He maintains, "I felt that these techniques do not express what I feel inside. I felt that I needed techniques that would grant me greater freedom during the strict censorship at the time" (*sha'artu anna hādhihi al-taqniyyāt lā tu'abbir 'ammā fī dākhilī, kuntu ash'ur annī fī ḥāja ilā asālīb tuḥaqqiq lī ḥurriyya akbar, fī ẓill al-riqāba al-ṣārima li-l-adab ānadhāk*).[62] In this respect, it could be argued that there are two competing narratives: one that regards *Leg over Leg* as heading *toward* the novel as known in its conventional form.[63] The other narrative, supported by al-Shidyāq's own writing, regards his work as a continuum but also an innovation of adab and a unique and indigenous form in itself. Al-Ghitani articulates what Mikhail Bakhtin previously theorized in his study on the novel on the relationship between form and ideology. Bakhtin wanted to challenge the separation between the abstract "formal" approach and the similarly abstract "ideological" approach. He insists that "form and content in discourse are one" and that "verbal discourse is a social phenomenon."[64] If the conventional novel form that was available to both al-Shidyāq and al-Ghitani, and several other writers, did not seem to offer the necessary aesthetics that would assist them in what both viewed as a more expansive freedom of expression and resistance—cultural amnesia in al-Shidyāq's case, and censorship, globalization, and imperialism in al-Ghitani's—then it stands to reason that theirs is a project that was a continuation and innovation of, rather than a break with, tradition and the past. Both authors offered unconventional literary forms. The will to resolve, to challenge readily available forms, and therefore an impetus to originality and creativity (observed in both al-Shidyāq's and al-Ghitani's works) in order to express what truly is human, showcases the essence of murū'a as a framework for adab for both authors. Theirs was not only a crisis with their surroundings or their sociopolitical throw but a crisis of the readily available aesthetic forms that they had to negotiate.

THE *MAQĀMĀT* AS AN AESTHETIC CRISIS

The *maqāmāt*'s inclusion in al-Shidyāq's magnum opus attests to an important reality; the *maqāmāt* threatens the then modern linguistic sensibility, hence safety, and therefore understanding and meaning of the *maqāma* world, inside the work, and by mimetic extension, life. These timed interruptions, every thirteenth chapter in every volume of the four volumes, perform consistently and predictably, only to threaten the reader's sense of certainty and their situatedness in their linguistic being by aesthetically interrupting the world created by the other "safer" narratives and chapters, which to the modern reader are not so aesthetically and linguistically threatening; they disturb the habitus of the mind. The thirteenth chapter(s) signals to the reader what they are afraid of but also would like to archive, keep hidden, locked away in a coffer of deserted things.

The first *maqāma* refers to the pursuit of happiness and the state of anxiety that Ibn Ḥazm, who is invoked, speaks of. The narrator invents fictitious book titles that allude to real ones: *Kitāb muwāzanat al-ḥālatayn wa-muwāzanat al-ālatayn* (The Book of Balancing the Two States and Comparing the Two Straits), in reference to the genre and method of *muwāzana* and the *Kitāb al-muwāzana* of Abū al-Qāsim al-Āmidī (d. 370 AH/980 CE) (in full: *Kitāb al-muwāzana bayna Abī Tammām wa-l-Buḥturī*), whom the *maqāma* narrator confuses with another (Sayf al-Dīn) al-Āmidī (d. 631 AH/1233 CE), an important jurist of the Shāfiʿī school and, as the narrator acknowledges, an "honored sheikh and productive scholar of great virtue."[65] Al-Fāriyāq's narrator does not give us the name of this purported author of the book yet but he goes on to say that the author is Abū Rushd (d. 595 AH/1198 CE) "Brains" Ibn Ḥazm (d. 456 AH/1064 CE) in a clear reference to, though conflation and conglomeration of, Ibn Rushd and Ibn Ḥazm. The former is intellectually from a different philosophical and theological school than the latter. The "Masher, son of Pulverizer" mashed and mixed books that he tells us that he has read but al-Shidyāq's narrator's solecisms in pronunciation betray him. In his depiction of al-Hāris the "Masher," al-Shidyāq is in dialogue with al-Jāḥiẓ's theorization of solecism (*lathgha*) as a marker of incorrect Arabic (in the context of non-Arabs speaking Arabic), which he differentiates from involuntary lisping.

He says, "the most important symptom of this is the substitution of *sīn* for *thā ʾ* and *ṭā ʾ* with *tā ʾ* and the *ḥā ʾ* with *hā ʾ*."[66] Al-Shidyāq here nods to an important aspect of language or rather a critique of language use. Al-Shidyāq's narrative is not only a satire on the disease of language loss; it is an outright mockery of pronunciation. The name of the narrator is a play on normally mispronounced letters of Arabic by some native and nonnative speakers: *ḥā ʾ* as *hā ʾ* and *thā ʾ* as *sīn* (*ḥārith* becomes *hāris*, which bespeaks mispronunciation and is also a nod to the title of his book). Hishām becomes Hithām and the verb "narrated," *ḥaddatha* (to relate something), becomes *ḥaddasa*, to speculate or seek to learn of something, or more potently as al-Zabīdī says to have false impressions on the meaning of discourse (*al-tawahhum fī ma ʿānī al-kalām*).[67] The correct pronunciation of these names would take the reader back to both al-Hamadhānī's and al-Ḥarīrī's *maqāmāt* and their famous narrators ʿĪsā b. Hishām and al-Ḥārith b. Hammām, who both "relate" their stories, while al-Shidyāq's narrator is seemingly relating but also seeking the information by virtue of turning *ḥaddatha* to *ḥaddasa*; he is making inquiries or in need of information and knowledge. The linguistic maneuver on al-Shidyāq's part retained the spirit of the unreliable narrator of the ancestral *maqāmāt* narrators but added another layer of unreliability. The narrator is seemingly telling us a story but simultaneously seeking information from al-Fāriyāq and/or us, as he repeatedly shows. The inversion of the role of the narrator to the role of the seeker of information, while al-Fāriyāq, including us, as the audience, becomes the supplier and also the editor/corrector of this information, is concomitant with the narrator's name, also to be read literally as Masher, son of Pulverizer; it speaks to this predicament.[68] For he is constantly presenting corrupt information that needs revision on our part.

It is presumed that since Masher is a user of the language, that language would be readily available to him as it would to al-Fāriyāq or to the reader. His use is juxtaposed to that of al-Fāriyāq and to the reader, who would recognize the aspects of this critique. But Masher's use of the language shows us that there is a certain subjectivity as a result of Masher's own interaction with language, or lack thereof. His is not just a problem of articulating himself eloquently using the correct titles of the books; it is a deeper problem that the *maqāma* highlights comically at first as a *lathgha*, a marker of incorrect usage of Arabic, or corrupt language. This would in turn, according to al-Shidyāq's critique, induce incorrect thinking altogether. The conflation of book titles, authors, and ideas are not presented as endearing absentmindedness but rather as a consequence of adopting incorrect language that birthed incorrect thought. Al-Shidyāq's aesthetics concurrently highlights the problem as it presents Masher's inaccurate problems in reading and understanding and simultaneously diagnoses its reasons. The aesthetic placement of this inside the *maqāma* is a nod to the *maqāma* not just as a literary genre but as an institution of pride for the Arabic language, and of adab. Litterateurs used the *maqāma* as an aesthetic site to compete, ostentatiously, without shame, about not only their perfect Arabic but all their knowledge of poetry, history, and intellectual life, rhetorical devices, and the ability to include strange and unheard words and utilize the language to come up with inversion (*qalb*) or linguistic reversal (*al-'aks al-lafẓī*)—meaning a sentence/letters can be read from right to left and also left to right, sometimes giving the same sentence and meaning and others giving the opposite meaning depending on the intention of the use.[69] The *maqāmāt* were used pedagogically as a creative tool to teach students the intricacies of Arabic language; it is thus more than an "outdated" genre or a literary form. "The incommunicability of *adab*," Sacks avers, "mirrors its loss."[70] It should not be surprising that the *maqāmāt* of al-Ḥarīrī were among the translated literary works under British colonialism; it comes years after the translation of Ibn Mālik's *Alfiyya* (*La quintessence de la Grammaire arabe*) by Silvestre de Sacy in 1833. It was translated as the *Makamat of Rhetorical Anecdotes* in 1850.[71] The Royal Asiatic Society's translations were conducted through the Oriental Translation Fund. In other words, translations were funded based on a rationale to be discussed before a subvention was awarded. Translations served a purpose that was often regarded as important for the colonial administration, naturally. The Society, founded in 1823, was keen on translating, among other literary texts of other Asian languages, *turāth* and classical Arabic texts to further "the investigation of subjects connected with and for the encouragement of science, literature and the arts in relation to Asia."[72]

The investigation of subjects connected with the encouragement of literature as per the colonial translation funds did not seem too keen to support a continuation of the mastery of Arabic in literature and arts. In 1883, one year after coming to Egypt, Sir William Willcocks, a British missionary and civil engineer, advocated for the supplanting of Standard Arabic (*fuṣḥā*) with the Egyptian colloquial dialect (*'āmmiyya*) in all forms of written and spoken life. Along with these propositions were of course the attempts to render the Bible and the Qur'an in the Egyptian *'āmmiyya*. Willcocks argued that dispensing with *fuṣḥā* and opting for *'āmmiyya* would allow Egyptians to be more creative and express themselves freely and become more innovative in all forms of life; *fuṣḥā*, he alleged, was stifling the conceptual and thinking capacities of Egyptians and the Arab people.[73] How strange are the similarities between Willcocks's views and the aforementioned Rushdi's frustration with the Arabic language and its Modern Standard Arabic (MSA) and *fuṣḥā* anomalies in Arabic literature, which he would like to exchange for colloquial? It is unclear if being creative and innovative to freely express oneself would be possible using the knowledge and world of more words learned in *fuṣḥā* versus the very limited world of the colloquial and local dialect if the person's entire world, thought, and imagination are limited and circumscribed within this national, local idiolect. If the limits of the thinkable and imaginable, the world as we know it, is our language, then a larger framework unquestionably gives one more freedom than a circumscribed and limited framework in the borders of a nation and sometimes the subculture within the very nation (cities and towns have their own colloquial dialects than what is presumed to be the country's main dialect). Willcocks's was a linguistically corrosive proposition, needless to mention estranging and separatist on the national and regional levels and to say nothing of the inevitable break with the linguistic subject's past due to the imminent inability to access the language. It may also be argued that they gradually would lose access to other Arab nations' writing and speech. Language, as Timothy Mitchell observes, was one of the most radical and momentous strategies of the colonizers to restructure Egyptian culture.[74] Colonialism's exploitive strategies to reduce its subjects' linguistic beings, to limit their abilities to articulate the world, to imagine and conceptualize, to think creatively in their language and achieve their maximum potential as linguistic beings, are well known and documented throughout history. There is no need to reiterate them here. The naive assumption that digging up the past is unfruitful since with decolonization and independence the previously colonized countries have rid themselves of colonialism is simply inaccurate. Some of the fruits of these cultural and linguistic policies are still flowering and blooming as have been previously highlighted. As Ngũgĩ wa Thiong'o reminds us in *Decolonising the Mind*, language becomes "a way of life." He argues that it was one of the most important colonial tools in holding the "soul prisoner," which comprised mental and emotional subjugation, compared to bullets, which is the concern of physical subjugation. The postcolonial subject, Ngũgĩ wa Thiong'o intimates, cannot be truly decolonized without decolonizing education and dismantling the values the colonizer made primary for or imposed on its subjects.[75]

DISSONANCE AND THE FAILED READER

Al-Shidyāq relates many anecdotes on the consequences of errors of reading and writing (*taṣḥīf*). He says that Sulaymān b. ʿAbd al-Malik wrote to Prince Ibn Ḥazm to count (*iḥṣī*) the *mukhannathīn* (effeminate men, according to the premodern use of the term), as his scribe had committed an error in writing the *ḥā*ʾ as *khā*ʾ (with a dot over the letter); it thus became the imperative verb castrate (*ikhṣī*), and so the prince called in the people in question and castrated them, the anecdote maintains.[76] Al-Shidyāq seems to construct the narrative around these extreme consequences of language errors, as dark and incredible as they may seem; the anecdote is also adamant on highlighting the cascading effects of poor language or the loss of language. It no longer affects the person in question but it may extend to others, and hence society. The change from the official census to "count" to become the mutilating "castrate" reflects the aforementioned Shidyāqian poetics of errors as physical mutilations, disease, as well as material defects.

Al-Shidyāq was diagnosing the failure of reading not only in his own work but also the failure to modernize from within. He diagnosed the failed reader who would not be able to read his book or would read his book as a "failed novel" and the failed reader qua narrator as "Masher." Despite giving the reader everything inside this book qua archive, there will be failure. It is generally accepted that the author has one chance to guide readers through their book, often done in prefaces, exordiums, or other parts of the book, where the author addresses the reader. Sometimes the exordium is a general guide and sometimes it acts as a textual space to effect a preemptive defense against probable critical attacks. These are all concerns that point to questions of authority over interpretation. Suspecting the reader is surprisingly not a modern or postmodern posture. Al-Jāḥiẓ (d. 255 AH/868 CE) advises us, and anyone who is about to write a book, to treat all potential readers as adversaries and as if they know everything. In other words, he is telling us that our readers are specialists and have plenty of time on their hands for the author and the book (*wa-yanbaghī li-man katab kitāban allā yaktubahu illā ʿalā anna al-nās kullahum lahu aʿdāʾ wa-kullahum ʿālim bi-l-umūr wa-kullahum mutafarrigh lahu*).[77] Al-Shidyāq is no stranger to this advice or to al-Jāḥiẓ, but he opts for a different approach in his exordium, the one chance he has with the reader. He writes a poem as an introduction (*fātiḥat al-kitāb*):

> This book of mine to the sophisticate (*ẓarīf*) will be sophisticated (*ẓarīfan*)
> And smooth-tongued, while to the foolish (*sakhīf*) it will be foolish (*sakhīfan*).
> I have set down in it words and lexical items to bejewel it
> And filled it with dots that shine and letters.[78]

There are two conflicting readings for al-Shidyāq here as outlined in his exordium or what he referred to in his proem as two possible categories of his readers: the intelligent, refined, adabized reader (*ẓarīf*) and the foolish reader (*sakhīf*). The *ẓarīf* vs. *sakhīf* trope is an established category in adab; both designations loosely relate to intelligent and foolish.[79]

Al-Shidyāq does not oppressively depict to us that there is a correct reading and that is why Masher is a failed reader because he does not conform to it. Rather, the failed reader before us is evidently capable of reading and he does read but is incapable of comprehending and providing plausible meanings or critically engaging with what he reads, let alone engaging with his interlocutors meaningfully; he confuses everything he reads. The process of understanding, al-Shidyāq suggests, is not an individual one; it is dependent on realities that are beyond the individual.[80] In other words, understanding, or to become a non-failed reader, depends on the changed cultural and linguistic realities that al-Shidyāq alluded to throughout his work, which precluded understanding as it becomes unsupported by the institutions that would lend this capability to the individual, Masher, son of Pulverizer. We recognize Masher as a failed reader because al-Shidyāq created a distance of error between him and al-Fāriyāq and ultimately us. Al-Fāriyāq provides the awaited answer, most of the time, for Masher's reading and understanding dilemmas. As readers, we are regarding Masher's narrative with caution, we read critically and we also recognize the errors he makes. In this respect, al-Shidyāq created a space that allowed this realization. I should like to argue that this is not a moral distance that should give us any right to judge Masher morally; rather, it is a space of misunderstanding/understanding motivated by healthy questioning and critique that al-Shidyāq proposes as necessary. Al-Fāriyāq is positioned as the well-tempered reader. Masher's reading problem is not represented as essential, that is, he is *essentially* a failed reader but rather as a product of what al-Shidyāq diagnoses in *Leg over Leg* as the "loss of Arabic" hence access to the reservoir of Arabic intellectual thought.

However, if distance can be a condition of understanding, or as suggested in the twelfth century as the Ghazālian *dihlīz* (liminality) as the in-between state required for understanding; it prompts us to ask questions in this critical space (while also being hospitable in an adabized way), as al-Shidyāq intimates. Masher is a guest in the house of *maqāmāt*, while al-Fāriyāq and other characters are to be understood as nineteenth-century figures traversing a premodern linguistic and aesthetic proverbial architecture. Masher could not make use of this liminal state because he is unable to decipher anything in the house of *maqāmāt*, or the thirteenth enclave, without help; he failed linguistically and intellectually. In this respect, it is safe to conclude that he can neither understand nor be understood as a linguistic being. Does this affect Masher's ways of being—his murū'a? Masher to al-Shidyāq, and perhaps also al-Fāriyāq, does not exist; his disoriented identity, alluded to by the intentional misnaming, confirms that he not only failed as a reader, but he has failed as a linguistic being and ultimately as a human being along with the other failed readers encountered in the aforementioned *maqāmāt*.

The lack of successful participation of Masher in the world, or in particular the world of language around him, communicates also the mental being corresponding to it. As Walter Benjamin tells us, "The linguistic being of things is their language; this proposition, applied to man, means: the linguistic being of man is his language. Which signifies: man communicates his own mental being in his language."[81] The inability of Masher to communicate his linguistic being and ultimately his mental being in his language lends purchase to al-Shidyāq's placement of Masher's character that may be perceived as contemporaneous to al-Fāriyāq inside the premodern genre of *maqāma*. In other words, al-Shidyāq housed the characters inside a different aesthetic temporality in these inserted *maqāmāt*. The temporal distancing enforced on the characters played with a number of claims: although the literary and linguistic horizon of the *maqāma* is the present, the characters including Masher are unable to understand either themselves or what is said. Their capacity to understand requires an encounter of several horizons that they are not practicing, nor do these horizons cross their minds. They are unable to travel to the past, linguistically. This then makes al-Shidyāq's subtitle about the *'ujm al-'arab*/*'ajam al-'arab* logical and more understandable.

The fictitious jumbled titles, which may very well allude to the real title if known, by the adabized reader, point to a salient argument in al-Shidyāq's arc: the relationship between language and ontology. The constructed reality of the failed reader comprises masterpieces of the Arabic literary tradition and towering figures that correspond to *a* reality; however, this reality becomes distorted because of a distortion in language on his part. Al-Shidyāq is playing a double game. The loss of language not only would indicate a loss of access to these books, literally (thus it would not be possible to understand these books), but also it would lead to a loss of an ontological reality about these books; they cease to exist. In other words, the failed reader, al-Hāris, the Masher, constructed an alternate reality, or rather, according to al-Shidyāq, crushed the ontological veracity of these texts as he presented them, whether based on his own failed readings or through secondary failed readings because he does not have skilled access to the primary source.

According to premodern scholars, reality and truth (*al-ḥaqīqa*) are divided into three categories (*aqsām*): linguistic (*lughawiyya*), legal (*shar'iyya*), and customary or normative (*'urfiyya*).[82] The legal contains words that should be understood in the legal context. Customary and normative truths and reality contain words that have become terms (*iṣṭilāḥ*) that every group of practitioners in a discipline use among themselves and therefore correspond to a meaning and reality for them.[83] Linguistic truths in themselves are divided into conceptual and metaphorical. Premodern Arab linguists similarly theorized about the relationship between language and truth where conceptual (*'aqliyyan*) truth and metaphor are concerned and where attribution (*isnād*) of actors (*fā'il*) and objects (*maf'ūl*) are concerned. In his expounding of linguist and rhetorician al-Sakkākī's *Miftāḥ al-'ulūm* (d. 626 AH/1229 CE), al-Subkī (d. 773 AH/1371 CE) explains to us in an aptly titled volume celebrating the completion of this task, *'Arūs al-afrāḥ fī sharḥ talkhīṣ al-Miftāḥ*, that truth (*al-ḥaqīqa*) would be the true attribution of the action or its meaning to what it belongs to on the speaker's part in appearance (*fī al-ẓāhir*). The phrase "in appearance," al-Sakkākī's addition, divides into four cases: (a) what conforms with reality (*wāqi'*) and the belief of the speaker (*i'tiqāduhu*); (b) what conforms with reality without believing in it; (c) what conforms with the speaker's belief but not reality; (d) what conforms neither with reality nor with the speaker's belief.[84] Masher's conflation of *real* books with made-up books and what he believes may be their (nonexistent) content therefore constructed this alternate false reality while simultaneously erasing the objective truth of the original books. In the second *maqāma* in *Leg over Leg*, "A *Maqāma* to Make You Sit," al-Hāris finds himself among "a Christian, the other a *Jew*, the next a man with no ideas of his own, who to neither belief nor unbelief will *hew*."[85] They were all debating marriage and divorce, heatedly. With views ranging from divorce being a grave sin, to the possibility of adultery when both parties are denied divorce. The *maqāma*, in the manner of its classical predecessors, especially al-Ḥarīrī, presents the issue from all perspectives. Al-Shidyāq's predecessors engaged in the act of praising and vilifying as a measure of eloquence (e.g., see *al-maqāma al-bikriyya*, for praising and vilifying virgin wives); al-Shidyāq is equally engaged with the topic to present it from all sides.[86] The narrator, al-Hāris, after listening to everyone's views, is asked about his own. He avoided giving an opinion or rather did not have one: "Verily, I replied, 'it is a very great *woe*, a dilemma fit to make tears *flow*. . . . Let there be no misapprehension, knowing each celestial sphere and every *star*, diving where lie Earth's metals and wonders *bizarre*, or comprehending its secrets and things *exotic*, would be easier by far for me than giving a yes or no on such *a topic*.'"[87] When al-Hāris sees al-Fāriyāq approaching, he asks him to weigh in with his opinion on the topic of matrimony. Al-Fāriyāq reiterates that if divorce is permitted, it can be abused by men, but women should not be deprived of this right should they wish. And if all else fails, then a moderate solution is to obtain a divorce and separate. The company including al-Hāris as well as a Muslim man, initially encountered earlier, all laughed according to al-Hāris at al-Fāriyāq's opinion, which he reports that they have "not found in the books in any shape, form, or *way*."[88] However, al-Fāriyāq's opinion, to the discernible reader, can be traced in the Qur'an (Q.2:231, "When you divorce women and they have reached their set time, then either keep or release them in a fair manner. Do not hold on to them with intent to harm them and commit aggression: anyone who does this wrongs himself. Do not make a mockery of God's revelations; remember the favour He blessed you with, and the Scripture and wisdom He sent to teach you. Be mindful of God and know that He has full knowledge of everything").

Al-Hāris's narrative depicts two failures: the initial failure to critique or synthesize anything from the discussion and give an opinion or weigh in meaningfully, and the failure to recognize al-Fāriyāq's reasoned opinion as one that is familiar. To say that it is not found in any book clearly shows a major defect in understanding and error in judgment. There is an indication here of the absence of will to resolve (*ʿazm*). He does not have the knowledge presumed in a narrator; the *ḥaddasa* (to speculate/seek information) continually actualizes the action verb related to his adventures but even the seeking of information is passive—he waits for people to tell him—rather than active. In his narrative, al-Hāris painted his company with the same brush as himself and reported that they all laughed for the reason he reported to us; perhaps they each laughed for a different reason than him or perhaps they did not? Perhaps it is al-Hāris who failed to recognize the allusion?

Al-Hāris exhibits a different kind of failure in the third *maqāma*, "A *Maqāma* to Make You Stand," when he posits the conceits of the *maqāma* as his quizzical stance toward women. Again, in manner of classical *maqāmāt* of mentioning both the negative and positive sides of all issues, after some reflection on women, al-Hāris is still undecided. He goes to the beach where poets meet to discuss all things. He listens to them and still cannot manage to have what he calls the "final word" on the subject. "I still may come across one from who the final word on this matter I can *prise*, thus sparing myself further inquiry and *surmise*, for it seems to me that the speakers were like two horses in a *race*, each rider jockeying with knowledge and rhetoric for *place*. Each, though, I think, spoke according to what his mood *suggested* and not—as should those who report and relate—by ensuring that the truth was fully *tested*."[89] Al-Hāris here admits that he wants to spare himself further inquiry and surmise. Though he seems to be cognizant of the two poets' methods, he is unable to put in the work to critique them equally to come to a conclusion of his own. Critique and reflection (*baṣar*) with resolve/will (*ʿazm*) is one of the benefits of adab as Ibn al-Muqaffaʿ maintains; it is also a proof of the sound mind to choose things "critically after reflection" (*baṣar*) and execute critique with resolve/will (*ʿazm*), he adds.[90] Al-Hāris tells us that he exhibits some understanding but we intuit, from what he said, that he has no resolve to pursue further inquiry and critique; the intellectually dependent al-Hāris waits for al-Fāriyāq to tell him what to think about women to act accordingly. The failure exhibited here is a failure of thinking rather than reading critically, perhaps a logical consequence of the initial failure, which we witnessed in the previous two *maqāmāt*. In the final *maqāma*, "A *Maqāma* to Make You Walk," the topic continues from women in general to marriage in particular. Al-Hāris listens to two parties who weigh in with the pros and cons of marriage. As usual, he cannot decide. "The two schools being thus equally balanced, the two claims in *contention*, I said to myself, 'If only the Fāriyāq were with us today so that to this thorny question he might turn his *attention*.'"[91] Al-Fāriyāq weighs in with a poem that al-Hāris deems a fatwa on women's affairs, "What a paragon! How much insight into women's affairs he *shows*, in verse as much as in *prose*! And how greatly we need from him, concerning these creatures, a *fatwah*, be it delivered in person or *in absentia*!"[92] Al-Shidyāq introduces a *ḥāshiya* (commentary/gloss) at the end of this *maqāma* explaining that because al-Hāris was fond of al-Fāriyāq, he did not take him to task over his poetry, which was awkwardly composed. Al-Shidyāq, posing as commentator, tells us that he does not want to deceive the reader since they developed a friendship from the beginning of the book. The commentary here serves to highlight al-Shidyāq's game as well. Al-Hāris cannot differentiate between awkward poetry or good poetry or make up his mind. His commentary on the poetry in this *maqāma*, and his views elsewhere, are meant to raise suspicion. Should the reader identify with al-Hāris and trust him intellectually, the reader would thereby become equally a failed one, without knowing. Al-Shidyāq's gloss therefore is aimed at urging the reader to read critically and have the resolve to critique, disagree, and become intellectually independent.

BEGINNINGS AND ENDINGS

What is striking in the reception of al-Shidyāq's work is not only how it is often compared to the conventional form of the novel, or if the *maqāma* fits the definition of short story, or if the outdated genre—to some—has a place in this otherwise modern "novel," but ultimately how it is thought of as if it has no past. In other words, some of its reception during the *nahḍa*, and beyond, focuses on the work as if the *maqāma* does not belong to the present because of its past and therefore has no future in either the worlds of the novel or short stories, despite the fact that the form of novel as such is able to contain all genres, even nonverbal and nontextual (pictorial, music sheets, puzzles, riddles, reports, maps, etc.). It is instructive to question why al-Shidyāq's work needs to be framed as a beginning rather than a continuation, a culmination, an innovation, and/or a dialogue with adab. If it is framed as a most desired beginning, or as a desperate need to draw a beginning line, then there must be a desired *ending* line simultaneously drawn? The desire to break free with the past or with tradition may very well be described as nihilistic. There has been what may be best described as a race for the coveted title of the first Arabic novel since 1999, when Bouthaina Shaaban considered Zaynab Fawwāz's *Ḥusn al-ʿawāqib* (Benevolent Consequences) (1899)[93] as the first Arabic novel because it preceded Muḥammad Ḥussein Heikal's *Zaynab* (1914). A year later in Egypt, Jābir ʿAṣfūr republished *Ghābat al-ḥaqq* (The Forest of Truth) (1865) by Francis Marrash with "The First Arabic Novel" on the cover.[94] Then in 2004, Ḥilmī al-Namnam republished the aforementioned *Ḥusn al-ʿawāqib*, still with "The First Arabic Novel" on the cover, and in 2007 a second edition of *Wayy, idhan lastu bi-ifranjī* (Alas, Then I Am Not a Foreigner) (1859) by Khalīl Khūrī, also with "The First Arabic Novel" on the cover.[95] The question then is, How would competing for the title of the first Arabic novel benefit the writing/rewriting of Arabic literary history? Would it inform subsequent studies on Arabic novels? Might the race for "the first Arabic novel" be a teleological one rather than a literary one—one that is eager to measure the first Arabic novel not in literary but "progressive" parameters, where the earlier the date means the earlier this *beginning* is claimed and therefore the earlier the measure of "progress" starts from the measuring point of "now"? The prioritization of this interest is one that is arguably manufactured by what the colonial climate advocated, since the "colonial managers removed or downplayed specific indigenous genres of authority and political decision-making in vernacular languages."[96] This need not often be violent or direct—although there is precedence for it—but can be sinuous. The colonial ecology, through power dynamics, often created different "orders of visibility," which "are constructed by conceptual, methodological, and analytical lenses."[97] It can be argued that this order of visibility is shaped by and therefore shapes "absences in theory, knowledge, and representation and emergences in social and semiotic practices."[98] The hierarchies of genres observed relates to this concealed desire to be not only visible but a participant in this "new literary order" that undoubtedly becomes standardized and taken for granted in practices and ways of seeing and being in the world. These strategic practices inspired by the new literary order will fiercely defend themselves, through their very methods, and seemingly innocuous standards, as forms of gatekeeping, to preserve themselves. The new methods and standards of modern Arabic literature, which inspired the aforementioned contestations of "the first Arabic novel," are participating in this new order, thinking they are catching up with these standards, but in fact they are acquiescing to a grander narrative with standards set before the participation of the Arabic novel in this new order of visibility. Thus, contesting the order of visibility of modern Arabic literature through the question "when was the first Arabic novel" or "whether al-Shidyāq is the first great Arabic novel" becomes meaningful if regarded through questioning this new order of visibility and hierarchical genres.

That said, was al-Shidyāq unaware of the novel form or incapable, aesthetically, stylistically, linguistically, or structurally, of framing and presenting his work as a novel in the nineteenth-century definition and conception of a novel? In this genre-defying oeuvre, a gallimaufry of genres all at once, al-Shidyāq defines what an authored book is in the proem. In his definition of *muṣannaf*, he is aware of his mixing of genres and queries; he questions how a book can be called a book (*muṣannaf*) if it does not contain multiple types of discourse or genres (*inna al-muṣannaf lā yakūn muṣannafan / illā juʿila al-kalām ṣunūfan*).[99] In this respect, he is legitimizing and privileging not the linear novel form but the nonlinear, multidisciplinary works of adab. As Nadia al-Bagdadi rightly asserts, al-Shidyāq's work is its own genre or genre-breaking work.[100] Al-Shidyāq masks almost the entire Arabic lexicon in the narrative, sometimes casually and sometimes forcefully in entry-like insertions in his autobiographical-travel-lexical-*maqāmāt*-inspired narrative masquerading as what has been described by some scholars as the first Arabic novel. But al-Shidyāq was no stranger to the novel form or European literature in general, attested in his many allusions and direct and indirect invocations of Cervantes, Rabelais, Byron, or Swift, to mention a few. That said, his project was more about preserving and repossessing what he represents as the richness of the Arabic language, which in turn would enable everyone to appreciate the classical Arabic texts he repeatedly invokes in his work and also build on this rich reservoir, rather than viewing the *nahḍa* as either a redux or a break with the past. Al-Shidyāq, a Socratic gadfly, wanted it to be a continuum with innovative tools in a similar manner to what he did. Al-Shidyāq neither shunned European literature nor did he embrace it at the expense of Arabic literature; the latter an attitude he likens to "contamination," "disease," and "infection" prefiguring postcolonial theory metaphors.

Al-Shidyāq tells us that those in power are inclined to have the language, and by extension the entire Arabic tradition, remade in the image of the hegemonic cultures.[101] The Arabic language and its literary constituents are then, as al-Shidyāq portrays the picture to us at the time, represented as incompatible with commerce and administration. It thus becomes not only an impediment but an inimical threat to progress and the symbols of modernity. Al-Shidyāq is thus questioning and highlighting to us the assumption that Arabic in the form he presents (not the simplified form of translated novels of the time) is inadequate to the perceived signs of "progress" and "modernity." By adopting this position, he immediately posits himself as a critic of these views, which were undoubtedly popular. This explains to us, as Raḍwā ʿĀshūr maintains, the deliberate obscuring of his work and his lack of much-deserved popularity. Those who write like al-Shidyāq, his literary ancestors, are sometimes seen as the adversaries of literary modernization or as inept, as the aforementioned Najm and Rushdi maintained. The privileging of the novel that al-Shidyāq criticizes thus decides the fate of his work and the literary ancestors he invoked in this tome. Al-Shidyāq's preface decidedly structures the horizon of his book by taking this stance. It thus remains quite unclear why subsequent aforementioned reception insisted on reading it as a "failed, or mediocre novel disguised as an autobiography disguised as travelogue" and recently as a first Arabic novel. In both cases, there is an insistence on denying the horizon of the book, which the author through his agential interest charted.

As Tarek El-Ariss observes, al-Shidyāq was engaged with the question of the production of knowledge and aware of the gradual epistemicide that hegemonic powers were practicing through the intertwinement of the powers of language and translation and the unidirectional flow of knowledge. Al-Shidyāq criticized British and French Arabists. They were the object of his critique in *Leg over Leg* for the weak knowledge of Arabic and blatant errors in their production of knowledge about the region at large and Arabic. Al-Shidyāq also appeared skeptical about their errors (whether they were really a result of poor Arabic or deliberate). Polemics and satire are of course deeply rooted in the Arab-Islamic tradition. Al-Shidyāq therefore was engaged in what El-Ariss called *kashf* and also *faḍḥ* or "affective critique."[102] Unlike some of the intellectually docile literati of the *nahḍa* and those who came after them, consuming and then patching, through recycling, knowledge produced by the very Orientalists al-Shidyāq critiqued or their sycophant disciples, al-Shidyāq was involved in a different project that "knocks over, makes a scene, destroys, and breaks down the casual fantasy of the production of knowledge . . . that [is] tied to flawed epistemological models of Orientalist knowledge."[103] That said, must we ask the uncomfortable question of whether al-Shidyāq's recent surge in popularity, and the changed discourse of critics, owes itself to his farsighted critique that portended postcolonial/decolonial and feminist schools, employing techniques such as reversing the gaze, writing back to the center/empire, and indigenous and alternative modernities, to mention a few?

The short-sighted criticism against al-Shidyāq because of his language that never broke away with the past, during the *nahḍa* and after as I have shown above, regurgitates the same critique of the *maqāmāt* at the hands of some *nahḍa* literati who championed the novel form, and its language, against what they perceived as antiquated genres that host an antiquated form of the Arabic language.[104] The contempt for adab in some literary circles legitimized itself from the perspective that it does not represent the times. To be suitable for the "time," the time of colonial modernity, the work of art, according to these conceptions, must be in the "now." The present moment is the only imaginable moment or horizon in what I call *chrono-narcissism*.[105] Chrono-narcissism considers the only valid human experience as that of *this* time. Chrono-narcissism is unconcerned therefore with the events and people of the past; they are temporal others. In focusing only on the present, the chrono-narcissistic reader is unable to transcend the present moment as one that might not be enough for comprehension or appreciation; the present thus becomes the only horizon for understanding. The work of art becomes the legible experience of the author; it is not a work of imagination nor is there room for lateral readings or what Ibn al-Muqaffaʿ mentioned before as "discourse." Interpretation is conscripted in the present moment and empirical experience, thus literal.

There are two competing traditions of readings presented in the narrative of *Leg over Leg*: one that creates both a continuum with the classical Arabic tradition (adab) and develops it, as is evident in this work; and another that breaks with this tradition of reading in favor of other modes of reading of simplified Arabic and European literature. Al-Shidyāq criticizes the latter but recognizes that he is among the very few in this resistance who truly see it as a loss rather than as an entrance to a certain modernity, as opposed to developing his own modernity that he repeatedly speaks of. Al-Shidyāq's *Leg over Leg* then represents what Caren Kaplan defines as "outlaw genre" in its resistance to what has become culturally available scripts and forms;[106] al-Shidyāq is aware of the loss of language and hence the supportive genres and forms that come with it. ʿĀshūr questions and blames those whom she calls the "aficionados for modernity's" (*al-mughramūn bi-l-ḥadātha*) disregard for al-Shidyāq's project with its astounding value of his experimental accomplishment as he tosses all ready-made forms out of the window and creates a text that defies any categorization (*taṣnīf*) in anteriority or posterity.[107] Indeed, ʿĀshūr classifies scholarly interest in *Leg over Leg* as either one that is interested in reading it as *only* an autobiography, or *only* a text that mimics the European novel but, alas, cannot untie its shackles to premodern adab and it thus fails miserably on both accounts, or a text that cannot be classified altogether and thus cannot be categorized in a genre that belongs to modern literature.[108] Recent and ongoing scholarship, however, is paying due and timely attention to al-Shidyāq's project for what it is.[109]

That said, it is instructive to think of these questions of *beginnings* and *endings* in concert with conceptions of the past. Was there a new developing conception of the past, at least where the literary past is concerned, that effected this temporal fork in conceptualizing al-Shidyāq's work? It is very useful to remind ourselves that the conception of *turāth* as literary heritage as such did not exist prior to the late nineteenth century. Prior meaning of the word existed in the capacity of a financial or monetary inheritance from one's family.[110] The concept is "a product of twentieth-century modernity."[111] Thus, speaking of the *maqāmāt* in al-Shidyāq's case as a posture and a "form" belonging to the past, despite his innovative techniques, tells us more than the attempt to break with the literary past, but that the mental landscape itself viewed the past as "entirely other" in its temporal and methodological difference. Al-Shidyāq's philological games, such as in the quadrupled thirteenth chapter of *maqāmāt*, highlight the hermeneutical interests of understanding and interpretation but also misunderstanding. Like his premodern textual ancestors and participants in the adab sphere, the process of understanding itself often relied on history and a tradition of reading. Understanding, Gadamer argues, is always an "effect" of history. On the other hand, hermeneutical consciousness is that mode of being that is cognizant of its own historical "being effected"—it is "historically effected consciousness" (*wirkungsgeschichtliches Bewußtsein*).

Coda

The Sustainability of *Adab*

In 1935, Taha Hussein authored *Adīb* (Litterateur), a novella. He claims it was based on real-life characters (including a friend of Hussein's) and the letters they exchanged, portraying a friendship between two men—one an Azharite young student and the other a non-Azharite—who are having conversations about literature. Hussein depicts the intellectual inferiority of the Azharite student through the constant mocking of this elder friend about the Arabic conceptions of the literary. The friend mocks the student for paying attention in class and hanging on to every word of the professors' lectures. He does not think that knowledge and education could be realized in Egypt or Egyptian universities; they reside elsewhere: in Europe. The friend then questions the young Azharite about his conception of the "literary," mockingly asking what does he know of the literary, "simile, metaphor, figurative language, and metonymy (*al-tashbīh wa-l-isti*ʿ*āra wa-l-majāz wa-l-kināya*) that they teach you in al-Azhar?"[1]

وحدثني أفهمت شيئًا من حنين القدماء على وجهه حين قرأت ما قرأت من شعر امرئ القيس، وغير امرئ القيس من هؤلاء الذين كانوا يحسنون الذكرى ويجيدون تصوير الوفاء؟ إنما هي عندك ألفاظ تقع في أذنيك كما يقع غيرها من ألفاظ، تفهم الظاهر من معانيها، فإن أعجزك الفهم سألت كتابًا من كتب اللغة فلا ينبئك إلا بظاهرٍ من معانيها، لا تكاد هذه الألفاظ تتجاوز أذنيك إلى عقلك فضلاً عن أن تتجاوزها إلى قلبك وإلى ضميرك فتثير فيهما عاطفة أو هوى أو ميلاً، وتدعوك إلى أن تقدر الحياة كما ينبغي أن تقدر الحياة؛ صدقني إنكم لا تدرسون الشعر ولا تدرسون الأدب، وإنما تدرسون ألفاظاً ومعاني وصوراً ليست من الشعر ولا من الأدب في شيء

And he told me, "Did you understand anything from the nostalgia of the ancients as it was when you read what you read of the poetry of Imruʾ al-Qays, and others, which perfected the act of remembrance and depicting loyalty? It is but words that fall on your ears as other words do; you only understand the surface meaning. And if you fail to understand, you consult one of the books of language and philology, which would [again] only tell you the surface meaning. These words hardly cross from your ears to

> your mind, let alone cross to your heart and conscience, stirring an emotion, a feeling, or an inclination, inviting you to appreciate life as it should be appreciated. Believe me, you do not study poetry, nor do you study adab [literature]; you only study words, meanings, and images that have nothing to do with poetry or adab."[2]

The young Azharite student is depicted as in agreement with and already highly influenced by the views of the new *adīb*, the litterateur as fashioned by Hussein. Hussein tells us that this is a real story based on real people. It may certainly be the case; the student who travels to Europe to study and instead fails in his studies and enjoys the anonymity of being a stranger in a strange city, abandoning himself in what is described in the novel as the life of debauchery (*mujūn*) and exploring and stretching the definitions of pleasure, is hardly original.[3] The veracity of the biographical elements in the novel, or lack thereof, does not undermine the redefining and reshaping of the conception of adab, especially as the character of the Azharite student, who could be understood as younger Hussein himself, seems to be in accord with his friend. Accusations that adab or the understanding of literature as adab by the ancients seem flawed abound in the novel.[4] The friend tells us that recalling his village and the old ways is unpleasant for him. Remembering the *kuttāb*, the palm trees, the water canals, the railroad, all these material forms of life related to his life before going to the city and learning the new definition of literature is bothersome because it "somehow extracts him from what this enjoyable life has to offer" (*yukhrijunī min hādhihi al-ḥayāt al-ladhīdha*).[5] The friend acknowledges that the above became *ṭalal* (ancient or bygone ruins)[6] and that he questions the value (*qīma*) of the *kuttāb* and the palm trees since, as he says, no old book ever mentioned *this* particular *kuttāb* or *these* palm trees and no poet ever wrote poetry for them.[7] A mixture of chrono-narcissism and affected sentimentalism are what Hussein is teaching us to be the foundation of "literary reading" here but also in the confines of one's subjectivity and the denying of not just temporal others but also a sense of exteriority.

Although in the novel it is the Azharite student who is accused of being a "failed reader" because he studies premodern literature and adab and does not know what the ruins really feel like, the friend himself becomes a failed reader. He acknowledges the site of palm trees and other material vestiges of the village as sites of ruin but fails to appreciate or connect the remembrance of the sites to the villages where he had memories as part of the famous trope of bygone ruins (*aṭlāl*). He cannot connect with the ancient books, as they are now wholly *other*; if the book offers an experience that is not about *his kuttāb* or *his* palm trees, he cannot relate. He observes that one may relate poetry on ruins as much as they want but it is the experience of ruins that truly makes it relatable for people like him and his friend, the Azharite, as he addresses him in the letter.[8] The friend here contradicts himself; on the one hand, insisting on personally experiencing the ruins, but also maintaining that they are unrelatable negates not only what Ibn Sīnā (Avicenna) taught us about the poetics of virtual experience of the literary but obstructs "textual empathy." What Hussein is ventriloquizing through the character of the friend is the denial of the disclosive power of the poem and its world. His mockery of the friend in fact is a mockery of the truth, experience, and reality of the very poem; it is a denial of the world that gave the poem its truth and voice. The friend therefore ridicules the poem phenomenologically, to privilege his own subjective voice or truth over the truth of the poem. In this respect, the friend not only denies any act of hospitality toward the world of the poem, he cannot imagine it and he cannot imagine another being, world, or time other than himself. What the friend achieves is a break in the flow of meaning. According to the friend's method, it would be no longer possible to ascertain a meaning or enjoy an empathic continuity of meaning of the ruins with the poem. The friend does not want to "share" a meaning with the poem, nor does he want to compare his feelings to those of ancient poets—his attempt at erasing the meaning of the poem erases its memory accordingly. A continuity of meaning, of relevance, would involve remembering, but the friend erases the memory of the poem's ruins. It is befitting to ask about the way literature imagines the human, whether the imagined human of the text or the imagined human as reader. In other words, the friend's disconnectedness from the poem's truth disconnects the reader emotionally and intellectually as it encourages disconnection from other humans and truths in favor of himself. Is it possible to say that remembering teaches us to be human? Connecting to other times and people instead of being prisoners of time and subjectivity?

In his novel *One Hundred Years of Solitude*, Gabriel García Márquez depicts the loss of memory through the insomnia plague that strikes the fictitious town of Macondo. The first and most devastating aspect of this memory loss was the loss of "the name and notion of things." Aureliano Buendía was the first to notice this troubling symptom:

> One day he was looking for the small anvil that he used for laminating metals and he could not remember its name. His father told him: "Stake." Aureliano wrote the name on a piece of paper that he pasted to the small anvil: *stake*. In that way he was sure of not forgetting it in the future. It did not occur to him that this was the first manifestation of a loss of memory, because the object had a difficult name to remember. But a few days later he discovered that he had trouble remembering almost every object in the laboratory. Then he marked them with their respective names so that all he had to do was read the inscription in order to identify them. When his father told him about his alarm at having forgotten even the most impressive happenings of his childhood, Aureliano explained his method to him and José Arcadio Buendía put it into practice all through the house and later on imposed it on the whole village. With an inked brush he marked everything with its name: *table, chair, clock, door, wall, bed, pan*. He went to the corral and marked the animals and plants: *cow, goat, pig, hen, cassava, caladium, banana*. Little by little, studying the infinite possibilities of a loss of memory, he realized that the day might come when things would be recognized by their inscriptions but that no one would remember their use.[9]

The semantic dementia experienced by the inhabitants of Macondo is characterized in the field of neurology by a breakdown of conceptual knowledge (semantic memory) in the context of relatively preserved day-to-day (episodic) memory.[10] In the field of literary studies, the metaphor serves to highlight the semantic dementia experienced by the replacement of one semantic memory over another, one epistemic reservoir over the other. Al-Shidyāq's *Leg over Leg* did exactly what the father did in the quote above. He put a label, and more, on everything cognizant such that, like the father, the day would come when no one would remember their use, like Masher, son of Pulverizer.

Hussein diminishes and undermines a salient, if not the most significant, feature of adab, as Hans-Georg Gadamer would say, the hermeneutic encounter with *that* which is wholly other (text, person, temporal distance, or horizon): the privileging of the apodictic and apophantic aspects of language, while simultaneously undermining its aesthetic, figurative, or conjectural character (the meaning of ruins or its multiple meanings for multiple people). Hussein, unsurprisingly, wishes to treat literature as if it were a declarative, apophantic language. The legitimization of literature to him can only occur through a language bordering on the scientific in its professed truth or knowledge (i.e., it is true because the experiences happened to his friend, or because that is how he felt, or it is true because a will to treat it as declarative and hence believed, mistakenly, to be as a source of possible "positivist knowledge"), bordering on John Locke's reduction of metaphors and ideas to archetypes. And therefore, to Hussein, for instance, Abū Nuwās's poetry is reduced to archetypal Abbasid *mujūn*; not bearing in mind that the Abbasids were many things and there were poets other than Abū Nuwās. Hussein claims that Abbasid poets, namely, Abū Nuwās, is indicative of the age; an age of "skepticism and *mujūn*" because Muslims possessed, according to Hussein, two things at the time that would constitute a threat to the life of naivete and certitude (*ḥayāt al-sadhāja wa-l-qanāʿa*): one is reason (*ʿaql*) and the other is civilization (*al-ḥaḍāra*).[11] It is remarkable that Hussein paints the ethics of an entire age or period with the same brush he is criticizing: naivete and certitude.

Hussein published his *ḥadīth al-arbaʿāʾ* article in the journal *al-Siyāsa*, which was later collated into a book. This was the periodical site for his literary battles, as they are called. One critic of his methodology is Rafīq al-ʿAẓm, who faulted him for judging an entire period, the second/eighth century, as an age of *mujūn* and skepticism. Hussein's reply to this criticism did not address the methodological critique but instead tried to fault al-ʿAẓm's argument by creating a straw man. He maintained that one should employ skepticism and rationality when engaging in criticism (is this not what al-ʿAẓm did?) and then, insisting on his claims, Hussein indirectly depicted al-ʿAẓm's argument as one that wishes to show Arab-Islamic history with a certain aura of majesty and sacredness (*al-jalāl wa-l-taqdīs*).[12] Al-ʿAẓm is not the only critic of this ideological empiricism advanced by Hussein, an intellectual heir of Locke's literal and fanatic readers. Egyptian poet al-Māzinī faults Hussein for the same methodology. In his book *Qabḍ al-rīḥ* (A Handful of Wind), he maintains that Hussein did not cease cherry-picking a certain corpus of Abbasid poets to paint an image that he claims is one of the age, while categorically denying the existence of other poets and scholars who also belonged to this period. Al-Māzinī intimates that no age, historically speaking, has one side, as Hussein would have us believe, and that no age in history, ancient or modern, was devoid of *mujūn* or skepticism.[13] In one of probably the wittiest articles by al-Māzinī, the latter gives Hussein a taste of his own medicine by writing in jest under the comic section (*fukāhāt*), hypothetically arguing what if a researcher were to investigate the veracity of the existence of someone named Taha Hussein who lived during our time, using Hussein's own so-called method of skepticism. Al-Māzinī is propelled by the latter's denial of the existence of the poet Majnūn Laylā. Invoking Hussein's changing and changed intellectual positions, persona and sartorial way and appearance throughout his life, and the different vocations and offices between university professorship and journalism, al-Māzinī concludes that Hussein would invite not only diverse but contradictory anecdotes that would fail to confirm the veracity of his own existence.[14]

Hussein's methodology did not seek meaning as such, but it rejected all meaning. It is unable to go beyond its own skepticism. In this respect, it ends with and promotes nihilism. Hussein would have us believe that not only has he overcome what Gadamer calls our "thrownness," which is one's own tradition, historicity, vantage point, literally what one finds oneself in, but that he rejects it; indeed, "believing that we are above tradition results in a distorted image of ourselves."[15] The nihilistic method Hussein promotes cannot be but a result of distortion or disillusion. The scientific, almost industrial, technique can be visible too in the diction of the protagonist even as he abandons himself to *mujūn*, a purely sensory set of experiences approached mechanistically. "But now to wantonness, to insane wantonness which knows neither moderation, nor respite, nor reflection. To pleasure, till mind and body are weakened together, till I am forcefully obliged to rest . . . then to work."[16] As King Lear says in the eponymous tragedy by Shakespeare, "Is man no more than this?"[17] Although Hussein would like to have us convinced that the novel belongs to a friend, it is littered with Hussein's Cartesian diction and images. Skepticism was not the only idea Hussein was happy advancing, but one takes note in the aforementioned quote on *mujūn* in the novel of the clangs of mechanistic materialism. Materialism, which gained momentum in the seventeenth century, posits that everything is composed of matter or physical substance, which occupies space either partially or entirely. In this view, all elements of the world "interact by one body pushing another body, making the whole world a clockwork mechanism in which all explanation is based on action by contact and push."[18] Descartes proposed a model of the mind that also regarded the mind to function like a machine, responsible for operating the body-machine, through the pineal gland in the brain.[19] While Hussein celebrates this mechanistic materialism as "excellent literature,"[20] not in the way adab critiques and debates ideas such as "mechanistic materialism," its shortcomings and/or usefulness, but as seeing, according to Hussein, that this expression of what he regards as "emotions and desire" (when no emotions or desires were present, rather mechanistic *mujūn*) is true excellent literature. Another "excellent literature" of mechanical materialism is Fyodor Dostoevsky's *Crime and Punishment*. The novel engaged in a scathing critique of budding materialist and communist ideas and the mechanistic view of the human. Of interest to our discussion is the diction of mechanical motion where Raskolnikov kills Alyona the pawnbroker to test his theory of the extraordinary man. The separation between Raskolnikov's mind and body and the mechanical execution of murder without thought attest to *Crime and Punishment*'s famous critique of materialist thought: "He could not waste even one more moment. He took the axe all the way out, swung it with both hands, scarcely aware of himself, and almost without effort, almost mechanically, brought the butt-end down on her head. His own strength seemed to have no part in it. But the moment he brought the axe down, strength was born in him."[21] Raskolnikov's failure to truly believe in and follow through with mechanistic materialism as well as theories of the extraordinary man, as the novel progresses, is Dostoevsky's critique of their proffered conceptions of the "human."

Even if we are meant to understand the *mujūn* and descent into insanity as part and parcel of miasmic cultural residue from the fin de siècle, pre–World War I culture, the language of machines and modernity is visible. The protagonist would like to treat this wantonness nonstop, like a machine, and only cease if this machine stopped working. It appears then that the discourse on "sentiments and emotions" that he pontificated about does not feature in this equation. The argument advanced by Hussein here, ventriloquized through the friend, established what I call chrononarcissism, the obliviousness of temporal otherness manifest in temporal distance. In this way, historical unconsciousness denies other people's similar experiences in the past as authentic and relatable but demands confirmation of personal experiences (seduced by the force of the immediate and the present) as the only relevant and experienceable ones. Hussein's views are similar to Descartes's discussion of the passions in *Meditations on First Philosophy* (1641), which "concentrates on our disposition to experience sense qualia, which normally mark qualities and differences between qualities of external things in relation to us."[22]

As the novel's new definition of adab suggests, Imru' al-Qays and the poets after him, whose poetry spoke of memory, loss, and grief over the ruins, are irrelevant and inexperienceable to the subjective and nihilist reader. The nihilist is negatively destructive. They, as a reader, belong to a teleological time or progress that imagines itself infinitely better than that of Imru' al-Qays, for instance. Therefore any emotion that was experienced and expressed in the past cannot possibly encompass the conception of a world that does not match the failed reader's, in the latter's understanding. This is all covered under the guise of the impossibility of accessing that emotion as they did in the past. There is no reliance of a past meaning and subsequently no memory or conception of cumulative knowledge and the "continuity of self-understanding."[23] The "continuity of self-understanding in the phenomenon of art imposes an ineluctable task on existence, namely to achieve that continuity of self-understanding which alone can support human existence, despite the demands of the absorbing presence of the momentary aesthetic impression."[24] In the failed reader's mind, living in perpetual chrono-narcissism, they grieve more and their grief is more sincere, they love harder and better; their literal and metaphorical "ruins" are darker, more beautifully damaged and broken than that of poets of ancient times. As a historical narcissist, this reader refuses to believe that the past, dialectically opposed to progress in their understanding, could offer anything and thus in a way, a figure, text, or horizon from the past, which is regarded as temporally inferior, may hold an intellectual, emotional, or moral advantage over them. It is quite the opposite; the past is there to aggrandize the (false) understanding of this reader of their present reading as superior by devaluing and discarding this very past. In the novel, by asking what ancient book spoke about these two particular palm trees, the ancient book ceased speaking to the protagonists/reader through other people's experiences; it needs to address only the reader's own experiences. Or in the friend's understanding of "literature," one needs to have and write about one's real empirical experience; this is *literature* to the friend, and Hussein. It is difficult to speak of a horizon for the nihilist reader, or a vantage point in their hermeneutic encounters with texts or people; it is as if they do not possess a horizon: "Any practice that does not recognize how it is enabled by the conceptual perimeters of its historical and cultural inheritance or, indeed, which tries to break with that inheritance, is nihilistic."[25] There are several types of losses that come with this reading: (a) the loss of the speculative aspect of language; (b) the loss of adab as hospitality and textual and human empathy; (c) the loss of discourse and appropriate method and critique with these texts; and eventually (d) the loss of the imagination. The language of the poem, and by extension all language, henceforth, need only point to the immediate, present, and personal. Not only does this delimit the imagination but it delimits the disclosive power of language. Language, then, in this case points to the world of the reader *only*; it need not point to anyone or anywhere else, nor is it necessary. It thus stands to reason that this reader, when faced with the unfamiliar, that should not be in their immediate and present, would ultimately reject it, perhaps even violently. Trained in accepting only what is representational empirically, the reader cannot imagine that there are propositional languages and hence worlds and others beyond them. In the novel *Adīb*, the friend advances this argument in his letters as he writes to the young student about his experiences in Europe when he crosses the sea and befriends a young French woman; it is only then, he claims, that he metamorphoses from being a donkey, in his words, to becoming a human. "I was a donkey before crossing the sea; and so this young woman (re)turned me into a human being" (*annī kuntu ḥimāran qabla an aʿbur al-baḥr fa-radatnī hādhihi al-fatāh insānan*).[26] As Hussein is redefining literature, adab, and reading in the novel, he is by extension also redefining the human. The relationship between the young Azharite and the older man does not seem palatable as a friendship, with all the toxic patronizing of the elder friend. In light of our discussion, it is perhaps best viewed as an "aspirational relationship," by which I mean a relationship where one entity aspires to be more like the other party. And as we see in the novel, this does not become incumbent on the young Azharite solely, but also through the constant pushing of the elder friend. This is what Egypt, Arabic literature, aspires to be, should be, in the future. In his book *Mustaqbal al-thaqāfa fī miṣr*, Hussein indeed advocates to espouse the values of Western culture and civilization, with all its positive and negative aspects. The most generous reading would view this as an optimistic faith in Western modernity and its ideal of progress; a less generous reading would view this as a (de)formed product of Western education. It is unclear what Hussein is proposing if an accepted definition of Arab modernity would be an attempt to combine two pasts: Arab and Western.[27] But Hussein did not consider the former in his conception of progress to begin with; he considered an ancient Egyptian civilization that belonged to Western civilization via the Mediterranean basin—these are the underpinnings of his ideas.

With a new definition of literature comes a new definition of the human and the ways of being human as the doyen of Arabic literature whose influence on literature and the literary extended beyond the national to the regional. Inviting the young student to come to Paris in his novella to experience life and the literary scene, the friend urges him such that he "sees, hears, feels, things that have no relationship between them and what you read in the poetry of Zuhayr."[28] Hussein's novel progresses and we understand that the friend succumbs to madness and cannot abandon the debauched life of all types of excesses, which is insinuated as a cause of this madness. The novel ends with the young Azharite receiving a suitcase full of the friend's belongings, including his literary writings, delivered by his ex-girlfriend. Hussein tells us that this suitcase has remained with him between thirteen and nineteen years (*biḍʿat ʿashr ʿāman*). He maintains that it "contains excellent literature, truly melancholic, overt, with no match in our language in any of our modern literati" (*adab rāʾiʿ ḥazīn ṣarīḥ, lā ʿahd li-lughatinā bi-mithlihi fī mā yaktub udabāʾuhā al-muḥdathūn*).[29] Hussein tells us that he almost published this novel in a preface of sorts for his friend's writing and ends with a question of whether the circumstances surrounding the literary life in Egypt would allow the publishing of this text. The question is, as is the entire novel, an attempt at redefining and confirming the conception and idea of literature and reading; the focus on the authenticity of experience (to see, hear, feel, touch) as the ultimate measure of literary and human excellence. Hussein never once mentions "think" or "understand" as one of the essential ways of being human or literary. The friend loses his mind, literally (he experiences paranoia and delusions) and metaphorically (he abandons reason from the start): the intellect, an essential part of adab and its pleasures, and of the ways of being human, is dropped out of this new equation of adab and being a literatus and a human being. The new *adīb* loses his mind to surrender to his definition of life, as he understands it, to take over him and that is the only way of being human and a litterateur. The emotional hijacking of the intellect encouraged by Hussein as part of the new definition of literature and reading promoted the atrophying of both reason and meaning. Hussein encourages and privileges the Nietzschean Dionysian (destructive and primal forces of life), but unlike Nietzsche, Hussein abandons the Apollonian (restraint, reason, light, etc.) completely, which Nietzsche views as a necessary balance; both forces are required and essential.[30] Hussein's promotion of the dark, chthonic, and chaotic aspects of the Dionysian and presenting them as progress and literature not only usurped what the Arabic tradition and *turāth* defined as adab but simultaneously emptied adab of its meaning and declared it foolish and unhuman in his presentation of the Dionysian as Apollonian, the Dionysian as the "literary" and the Apollonian as cold and nonliterary—an extremist, fanatical misreading and appropriation of Nietzsche's ideas that obliterated the Apollonian as a cure to possible Dionysian crises. The result is perpetual crisis as we see in *Adīb*.

The focus and stress on emotions as the most salient criteria of making, producing, and appreciating, and receiving a literary text not only insinuated that its premodern literary ancestors are linguistic and philological automata but that they were made into intellectual and emotional *others*. They are depicted as linguistic robots who felt nothing and that premodern authors and their readers are necessarily separate, by virtue of their distant temporality, in their emotional makeup; that is, they did not know the meaning of emotional joy, pain, love, and so on, but only their philological ranges. As some of these prejudices are beginning to be shed now in contemporary scholarship, the premodern texts expressed emotions but also gradations of emotions and nuances of mental and emotional states that would probably startle the most adept of modern readers who are oscillating intellectually and emotionally in a much narrower range linguistically and, by extension, intellectually and emotionally, as al-Shidyāq tells us. Hussein, a sanctified figure in Arabic literary studies, but also a product of colonial modernity, consecrated ways of talking about Arabic literature for generations that still plague the ways texts are received. For instance, he talks about Abbasids, in their entirety, especially Abū Nuwās, in terms of decadence with relevance to wine poetry (*khamriyyāt*), an established genre in Arabic poetry. Hussein here did a number of things: he read Abbasid creative and explorative literary activities as only "expressions of emotional and mental states," expressions of opulence and *mujūn* (though we have no means of verifying that all *mujūn* poetry, conclusively, expresses real-life events of the author, period, and the entire institution called Abbasid adab).

Simultaneously, after creating this reality, he turned his audience into voyeurs and stalkers rather than critics and readers of literature. He invited them to look into literary expressions as expressions of private life, and, in this respect, he turned them from literary critics to moral judges. As part of the ontological reality of the institutions of understandings, he enabled them to turn into naive readers who cannot see beyond the apodictic function of language that expresses the *only* possible world of said texts. The voyeur, who peers into what is perceived as private life, ends up, compulsorily, morally judging the work qua private life (an irrational enterprise to begin with) but rarely aesthetically. The naive reader, infantilized through their cultivated reactions, abandons extended or poetic meanings and instead will opt, like growing children who are still developing from the literalness stage of concrete thinking and experiencing the world to the more advanced types of thinking (analytical, creative, critical, divergent, or abstract), to oscillate between the limited receptions of "morally acceptable" or "morally reprehensible" (accept/refuse); these become the only conceptual coordinates of how the world could be perceived. It is opportune to mention here that this is a departure from adab to literature in the literary sense but also a departure from adab as civility through a failure of understanding and reading and social *poiēsis*. Compare the premodern critic and reader in similar situations where al-Tawḥīdī met poet Ibn al-Ḥajjāj known for his *sukhf* genre and obscene poetry. In fact, he was revered and praised both by the people in the marketplace where he worked as *muḥtasib* and also by the literati and *ʿulamāʾ* of his age.[31] In *al-Imtāʿ wa-l-muʾānasa*, litterateur al-Tawḥīdī recalls his first encounter with Ibn al-Ḥajjāj, telling him: "By God I am amazed by you. . . . You are indeed one of the miracles of God's creatures and the marvels of his worshippers. By God none will believe that you are the very same man who composed your dīwān and that it is yours with all this contradiction which exists between your poetry and the seriousness of your person."[32] In other words, al-Tawḥīdī's exclamatory relating of the meeting between him and Ibn al-Ḥajjāj, like his contemporaries and future readers, acknowledges the existence of a poetic persona of Ibn al-Ḥajjāj and never conflates the two. Al-Tawḥīdī is surprised but acknowledges the poetic persona. The well-tempered reader, like al-Tawḥīdī here, acknowledges that he is reading adab, a creative expression. The reader is not invited to be a voyeur into the private life of Ibn al-Ḥajjāj or to judge him.

The type of reader cultivated in this institution and its grammar of reading advanced by Hussein need not be critical or have resolve; these are tools that have been dulled by the blunt instrument of the forsaking of adab to literature through the teachings of the likes of Hussein, his disciples, and colonial modernity. Unfortunately, this reader is stuck in concrete thinking. The consequences are a threefold irrationality of enabling and allowing the possibility of judgment of (fictional) private lives of people through practicing this type of reading, empowering literalness, and abating literariness. It is an enablement of both chrono-narcissism and certainty-narcissism. The latter is indeed a certainty born out of narcissism that defies what al-Ghazālī taught and practiced as "learned ignorance," to practice skepticism or the *docta ignorantia* developed later by Nicholas of Cusa in the fifteenth century; a belief that certainty through scholastic ratio is unattainable, especially that which is related to the quiddity of the divine. It is apt to ask, What happens when we assign an emotion or a moral judgment/character to a particular historical period? What ethical and political implications do views like this have? The least of problems and most relevant within academe that enables this line of methodology and thinking is research that would be interested in *ways of confirming* the learned certainty instead of being interested in the *technē* or *grammar* of research. To clarify, the difference between these two attitudes would be the difference between al-Shidyāq's canonical reading of adab as he incorporated them not only as "texts" but as *technē*, and praxis; he kept them alive while creating a new text. Hussein's *Adīb*, on the other hand, archived the past. He actively engaged in what Aleida Assmann calls "passive forgetting."[33] He devalued the work and therefore neglected, abandoned, and left it behind, thus condemning it to forgetfulness. Tarek El-Ariss is correct in declaring al-Shidyāq as the continuity bridge between premodern adab and modernity. This argument by El-Ariss comes in concert with al-Musawi's insight that the *nahḍa* and by extension modernists broke with premodern adab. Al-Shidyāq may be an anomaly, one of a few, and as the preface tells us, he does not expect popularity; al-Shidyāq is only experiencing popularity now, for he was not appreciated during his time. What happened, therefore, is the delegitimization of adab through several proxies. Not only that, but there is a shrinkage of the habitus of language and the available usages, meanings that were handed down from adab and its language through the simplification of language in the name of progress, as al-Shidyāq repeatedly told us in *Leg over Leg*. Arabic literature and language of several componential meanings for adab created a crisis of "literalism" and "presentism." There is a mixture of two paradoxes in this new understanding of literature that carried forward, as expressed by the critics of al-Shidyāq and beyond, even by Hussein, the doyen of Arabic literature. The paradox is of combining both conceptions of Romanticism and empiricism. The former rose against the intellectual tyranny of empiricism in Europe and its refusal of metaphor and insistence on describing things as they are or reduced to an idea, an archetype. The view that the work of art, as an expression of the innermost feelings of the individual, and their depiction of their surroundings, takes on the sentimental posture of the Romantics with the empirical realism of Enlightenment. What is proposed is not only catastrophic watering of language but the committing of literary language to reality, and thus to presentism and literalism. The elimination of a crisis of understanding is easier through literalism and simplification. The prerogative that the novelists' narrators and protagonists are expressing their "innermost" emotions and therefore the fiction before us as "real" would not be only easier for the failed reader but it is supported by the empirical posture and borrowed theories. This is not only a dumbing down of the reader but a relegation of literature at large and adab to only a "dear diary" function.

IN SEARCH OF TRADITIONS FORGOTTEN: ADAB, THE LOST TRADITION

"A tradition," Talal Asad explains, "consists essentially of discourses that seek to instruct practitioners regarding the correct form and purpose of a given practice that, precisely because it is established, has a history. These discourses relate conceptually to a past (when the practice was instituted, and from which the knowledge of its point and proper performance has been transmitted) and a future (how the point of that practice can best be secured in the short or long term, or why it should be modified or abandoned), through a present (how it is linked to other practices, institutions, and social conditions)."[34]

This attitude to tradition (what we may call premodern literary works or *turāth*) is reflected in two different approaches to literary criticism: "One adopts the strategy of the canon, investing the text with existential meaning and framing it with an aura; the other adopts the strategy of the archive, aiming at destroying the aura."[35] The attitude of some of these modernist approaches therefore relegated these works to an archive, with a dusty aura buried deep in a past that required the necessity of many a footnote for subsequent readers who are separated temporally by centuries and aesthetically by a forced detachment from the literary style and cultural taste. Might we ask, for example, why is the work of al-Hamadhānī a working cultural memory, a discursive tradition, for al-Ḥarīrī as obvious from the latter's words and as should be in our study of adab but not a working cultural memory in some modern literary treatments? The social value of the work of art, Walter Benjamin maintains, changes as societies change their value systems, which accounts for the changes in artistic style and in the cultural taste of the public.[36] There was no rupture in the history of Islam other than that of colonial modernity. In the epilogue to his magnum opus *The Venture of Islam*, Marshall Hodgson notes that modern Western societies managed to maintain a more coherent continuity than Muslim societies.

> There has been a direct continuity from the oxcart to the horse-drawn wagon to the rapid stagecoach to the railroad to the automobile to the airplane; each shift was relatively moderate, and the tradition was never broken. Similarly, from the Scholastics to Descartes to Hume to Kant to Hegel to Husserl to the Existentialists, the philosophical dialogue has been continuous. By and large, the old books continue to be read, and some of the same terms continue to be used, even if in transformed contexts. It has seemed feasible to integrate modern technicalistic elements with the various elements of older heritage. At the very least, the specialists are working, each in their own specialty, within the full flow of their own special traditions, and the dialogue among themselves is direct and continuous. In other lands, the specialists

> are too often attempting to keep up with a tradition which they do not fully share, in which they are excluded by a relative backwardness from up-to-date and creative participation in the ongoing dialogue.[37]

Cultural memory, Assmann says, creates a framework for communication across the abyss of time.[38] The function of the "canon" and "foundation texts" therein is the preservation of "active working memory of a society that defines and supports the cultural identity of a group."[39] The canonical treatment therefore helps to keep the texts alive and to protect them from acts of "passive forgetting." The passive form of cultural forgetting is related to unintentional acts such as losing, hiding, dispersing, neglecting, abandoning, or leaving something behind. In these cases the objects or ancillary literary texts necessary for contextualizing and appreciating the work in question are not materially destroyed; they fall out of the frames of attention, valuation, and use.[40] Indeed, no premodern lexicon mentions the word *turāth* in the capacity it is used today, in literary and cultural milieus, to refer to heritage, or literary heritage in this specific context. Even Buṭrus al-Bustānī's 1870 lexicon defines this word in concert with premodern lexicons as a financial inheritance. It is a modern invention that contributed to the passive forgetting of a discursive tradition, of adab. One of the most pressing questions I faced writing this book is finding an explanation to the adopting of *turāth* to mean "literary heritage" or "heritage" at large in the modern period. Perhaps locating the exact moment when and how this adoption took place might not advance this discussion. Rather, asking what epistemic ramifications did this adoption accrue might be more beneficial. The premodern use of the word *āthār* meant something close to a discursive discourse, a trace, a tradition to follow where one looks to be acquainted with and build on. In the context of scholarship and books:[41]

> سَأَلْتُ أَحْمَدَ بْنَ حَنْبَلٍ، قُلْتُ، مَا تَرَى لِي مِنَ الْكُتُبِ أَنْ أَنْظُرَ فِيهِ لِتَفْتَحَ لِي الْآثَارَ: رَأْيُ مَالِكٍ، أَوِ الثَّوْرِيِّ، أَوِ الْأَوْزَاعِيِّ؟ [. . .] وَقَالَ: عَلَيْكَ بِالشَّافِعِيِّ، فَإِنَّهُ أَكْثَرُهُمْ صَوَابًا، أَوْ أَتْبَعُهُمْ لِلْآثَارِ
>
> I asked Aḥmad b. Ḥanbal, saying, "Which books do you recommend I read to understand the tradition (study them where they unfold traces [scholarly discourse vestiges] (*āthār*)): The reasoned opinions of Mālik, al-Thawrī, or al-Awzāʿī?" [. . .] "You should follow al-Shāfiʿī, for he is the most accurate or the one who closely adheres to and is knowledgeable of the tradition."

Ibn Ḥanbal (d. 241 AH/855 CE) and his interlocutor are using a term that is already in currency to mean a tradition of books, a canon, or foundational texts necessary for the production of knowledge. Similarly, Ibn Jarīr al-Ṭabarī's (d. 310 AH/923 CE) book *Tahdhīb al-āthār* refers to a collection of accurate sayings attributed to the companions of the Prophet. While it is not inaccurate to surmise that the term was more popular in ḥadīth studies and related fields, it was also used outside it. Scholar al-Bīrūnī's (d. after 442 AH/1050 CE) book *al-Āthār al-bāqiya ʿan al-qurūn al-khāliya* (Remaining Traces of Bygone Times) uses the term in his title to encapsulate the subject matter of his book: the history of nations, and mostly how people across different nations and civilizations measured and indicated time and had different conceptions of time. In his exordium, al-Bīrūnī says that it is not possible to access this information of the past except through books that were left to us to study, and therefore this act itself is *taqlīd*. However, it is through reasoning, al-Bīrūnī maintains, that one must approach this information after overcoming what he calls the common diseases of the self that are found in most people that would impair scholarship or truth-seeking (*al-ḥaqq*): fanaticism/intolerance, biased allegiance, following the vagaries of one's opinions, one-upmanship, and the like (*al-taʿaṣṣub, al-taẓāfur, ittibāʿ al-hawā, al-taghallub bi-l-riʾāsa, wa-ashbāh dhālik*).[42] Of immense interest is al-Bīrūnī's use of *turāth* as well in the exordium to refer to an honor for posterity (*turāthan fī al-aʿqāb*) in relevance to what he describes as his pride in the achievement of this hard work in service of and under patronage of the addressed prince in the exordium.[43] It may appear that *athar/āthār* was also available to al-Bīrūnī in this context; however, it can be safely argued that *āthār* in the aforementioned context of scholarship and books is a kind of interactive knowledge, it is dynamic. In the aforementioned cases of books, anecdotes, and scholarship, it is a continuum where there is a positive/negative interaction; there is critique, reasoning, building on it, and continuation. It is alive. Al-Bīrūnī's use of *turāth* to refer to a sense of honor and glory in this work after his passing points back to him. It is also used in a nonobliging meaning to the reader; the focus is the recipient of this glory. Our knowledge of the *Iliad*'s warrior-heroes like Achilles's, Partoclus's, or Hector's immortal fame and glory (*kleos*, κλέος), in the Trojan War, falls on them, not us; it is their legacy, an inheritance. *Turāth*, observed or not, is actualized through the death of the entity leaving a legacy, as al-Bīrūnī's use indicated. *Āthār*, however, is indicative of *traces* to be followed through; it is a dynamic path left—entities that choose to walk on this path are doing so willingly. *Āthār* therefore presupposes an interactive continuity. Premodern scholars also referred to this sense of interaction and obliging relation through the term "foundational or source/major books" (*ummahāt al-kutub*, lit. the mothers of all books). Ibn Khaldūn uses the expression to refer to the most important *musnad* books as the foundational books in ḥadīth (*wa-hādhihi hiya al-masānīd al-mashhūra fī al-milla wa-hiya ummahāt kutub al-ḥadīth fī al-sunna*).[44] This is also reminiscent of the conception of *tawlīd* (filiation) or filiative relations between works where the newer work relies on the parent/source work for generating new meaning or new knowledge.[45]

There are two conclusions that may be inferred from this: premodern scholarship did not see past works as temporally severed from the lived present moment; it lived in a continuum of cumulative knowledge where the past helped frame the knowledge produced in the present with the belief that it will possibly continue into the future. Despite a cognizance of these temporalities of past, present, future, the memory of the past was lived in what St. Augustine (354–430 CE) described as the experience of time as *distentio animi* (distention of the mind), where the mind experiences time as a threefold flow, as a stream, where there is a memory of the past, present discernability, but also anticipation of the future—all can be experienced at once not independently.[46] The genre of *ʿibar* (moral lessons) in adab is a good example of this; it is an attestation to this conception of time as well. The moral lesson points to a demand on the reader's part where the past, present, and an expected future are experienced all at once; the moral lesson is not irrelevant nor is there a severance with its distant context and characters. The second conclusion is that Arab-Islamic premodern conception of the past as such was different than the modern conception of the past that viewed *turāth* as an apt descriptor of its *āthār*, and by extension this points to a changed conception of the present and ultimately the future.

Did a modern conception of history change the way individuals think about the past, hence the present and future? The very idea of progress that appeared in the seventeenth century in Europe ruled over intellectual thought in posterity and by extension was exported outside Europe to the Global South. It is argued that the idea of "future," hence progress, did not take shape until the eighteenth century with the appearance of philosophy of history in Germany by Kant (1724–1804), Herder (1744–1803), and Hegel (1770–1831). In 1784, Kant proposed an understanding of the philosophy of history where progress can be defined as "regular progression among freely willed actions. In the same way, we may hope that what strikes us in the actions of individuals as confused and fortuitous may be recognised, in the history of the entire species, as a steadily advancing but slow development of man's original capacities."[47] Kant here does not view progress related to individuals, but to the entire human species, where the stage of history actualizes and realizes these developments gradually. Herder, Kant's contemporary, seemed to disagree with this conception of progress, as he saw progress as more individualistic. He regards Kant's "species" as entirely meaningless since the human species is made of "individuals," therefore it is the individual who matters.[48] Herder then adds, "Our philosophy of history shall not wander in this path of the averroean system, according to which the whole human species possesses but one mind; and that indeed of a very low order, distributed to individuals only piecemeal."[49] Herder challenged Kant's assertion that the purpose of history was to educate humanity as a whole, which he reads as an influence of Averroes (Ibn Rushd), rather than focusing on individual experiences.[50] But in Ibn Rushd's discussion of the virtuous city, he goes against Plato's view that it is impossible for people to appoint the philosopher-king, which Ibn Rushd views as pessimistic. Ibn Rushd believes that people can be educated in a way where this would be actualized without going against laws known to people, and then he concludes such as "in our time and our beliefs" (*kamā huwa al-ḥāl fī zamāninā hādhā wa-fī millatinā hādhihi*).[51] Ibn Rushd contends that the time-place he was living in, the twelfth century, because of a certain type of education that individuals have, can be called a virtuous city compliant with religion and human values. Perhaps he was also hopeful. Philosopher Muhammad Abed al-Jabri (1935–2010) reads Ibn

Rushd as closer to Kant and Herder and therefore questions their turn against him. Al-Jabri explains this epistemic severance with the "Averroean path" as a way to establish a philosophy of history by avoiding looking at the past as a deciding factor for the future, considering that Ibn Rushd's "metaphysics," in Herder's understanding, represents a past, and Herder's and Kant's philosophy of history, qua progress, is the future. To further elaborate, the view that the past could offer "a truth" or "truth" makes the future an extension of the past, and any progress therein is but a further explication, a realization, or at best a development for what was already achieved. The Kantian view saw that "truth as a future goal" belongs, naturally, in the future not the past in a teleological view of history; this is the meaning of progress in the philosophy of history for Kant.[52] It is not difficult to see the extension of these views later in Western philosophy, such as with Hegel or Nietzsche, especially the latter, who distinctly advocated for a break with the past through "the capacity to live *unhistorically*."[53] Nietzsche uses animals as an example to illustrate this idea of the ability of unhistorical living and the ability to forget and constantly live in the present, since it is in animals' nature, according to him, to forget. Nietzsche relates, "Whoever cannot settle on the threshold of the moment forgetful of the whole past . . . will never know what happiness is."[54] Nietzsche stresses also that it is only through the unhistorical that people can truly *act* because they are unburdened by the weight of history. The unhistorical man "is unjust to what lies behind him and knows only one right, the right of that which is to become."[55] According to Nietzsche, rejecting the influence to advance into the future is necessary because only the unhistorical man is a "man of action."[56] Only the unhistorical man is "without conscience, so he is also without knowledge."[57]

Were the shapers of culture and institution builders in the Arab world, such as Taha Hussein, for instance, espousing changed definitions of the past, hence the future? Was *turāth*, as opposed to *āthār*, a descriptor indicating a continuity, an unhistorical inheritance, or perhaps ahistorical, relieving the burden of knowledge and influence of the past because the future promises a teleological truth that is not to be found in this past? Hussein is not a stranger to Nietzsche or theories of progress. In a French article on poet al-Mutanabbī in the Francophone magazine *Valeurs* operating in Alexandria, Egypt, Hussein argues that al-Mutanabbī's poetry is philosophically charged with pessimism, like al-Maʿarrī's, and he faults critics, like al-ʿAqqād (1889–1964), for comparing al-Mutanabbī to Nietzsche's Übermensch.[58] It would not be inaccurate to say that Taha Hussein and his disciples espoused what could be understood as the break from the past, because the universal history of progress that Hussein wishes to participate in would not feature that particular past in it. Hussein, writing in the 1940s, advises intellectuals, students, and readers in general "to follow the path of the Europeans and take their route, to be their equals, and to be their partners in civilization, in its good and bad, its sweet and bitter, what is liked and what is disliked, what is praised and what is criticized."[59] Admittedly, it is related that he changed his views throughout his life and had various contributions in education, but it must be noted that the epistemic frameworks that shaped these institutions of learning in modernity owe themselves to the cohort of the intellectual adherents of the structural devaluation of adab.

Hussein and his cohorts are intellectual adherents of a system that is designed to structurally defeat the past because it will remain incompatible with the telos of the "truth" in the future, unless proving that the past, on its own terms, includes a truth for the future. By espousing these Western epistemic frameworks of progress, the past, and history, it is inevitable that a representation of a non-Western past does not, must not, include a "truth" that could be indicative of a conception of progress for the future or it will replace that very idea of progress and the epistemic system it espouses. Hussein's paradoxical engagement with the past, whether through *mujūn*, al-Maʿarrī's philosophy of pessimism, or other topics and figures from the past, is an engagement that aims to run the Kantian progress race but never reaching the finishing line or even critiquing it—despite the fact that he urges us to be "critical and skeptical." Hussein's suggestions that this literature and these literati were experimenting with and holding the same ideas seen in Western philosophy and therefore they were already on track and prefiguring the already prediscovered and prepackaged conceptions and philosophies is a hollow point (al-Mutanabbī as Übermensch, or the pessimism of al-Maʿarrī, or Abbasid *mujūn*). While comparing literatures is hardly the problem, the aforementioned readings are unhistorical; they look for validation of their progress march. To add, these types of unhistorical readings hardly engage with premodern Arabic literature on its own terms to creatively generate knowledge. Is failed reading the only outcome of the unhistorical posture? Nietzsche's unhistorical man is "without conscience." Similarly, when Ibn al-ʿAdīm assessed what he describes as the baseless allegations against al-Maʿarrī, Ibn al-ʿAdīm distinctly describes their perpetrators as "without conscience" and without respect for human sanctity itself (see chapter 5). The failed reader can be easily shaped by the loss of language and access to meaning, through education, hence they become involuntarily unhistorical, or they can choose to become voluntarily unhistorical if it is intellectually profitable. Thomas Bauer's diagnosis of modern times as less tolerant to ambiguity, which thrived in premodern Arab culture, is not inaccurate. However, Bauer's addition that this intolerance, because of Western modernity, is a feature of what he calls "Salafist groups" presumed that it is only through the loss of ambiguity as a cultural feature the modern extremist was born. Extremists and fundamentalists are more than intolerant or failed readers; they are also unhistorical actors. They were relieved of the burden of history. And as the theoretical frameworks of progress and modernity suggest, the unhistorical man, without knowledge, acts without the burden of conscience, without sanctity or justice for anything; they are relieved of knowledge. Does the unhistorical extremist, then, like the Taliban for instance, who ban women's education,[60] among other things, burden themselves with the weight of the history of the lives and travels of ten thousand premodern women ḥadīth scholars, who fill forty-three volumes, who narrated and taught ḥadīth to women and men equally?[61] Does the same, or perhaps another, unhistorical fundamentalist know of the history of critique in Islam concomitant with the sciences of the Qur'an, when a woman critiqued the Prophet's stance on women's rights in divorce prior to and a reason for the revelation of Q.58 (al-Mujādila, "She Who Disputes")? Or maybe the woman who challenged Caliph ʿUmar openly in public on the issue of dowry using the reasoning of Q.4:20? ʿUmar then had to retract his argument and declared that "a woman is right and a man/ʿUmar is wrong," also in public (presumably during a sermon in a setting or gathering where men and women sat together, hence the to-ing and fro-ing).[62] Does the unhistorical extremist know of the numerous women rulers/queens in Muslim Yemen, for instance, whose ruling is described as "economically more prosperous"?[63] What about women soldiers who fought with the Prophet in the early Arab-Islamic military battles and lost their limbs?[64] The examples are too numerous to include in one book in response to both the unhistorical extremism against women in the aforementioned case of the Taliban, or others who share their outlook, but also the simplified understanding of extremism as a problem factored in reading and interpretation, or only that. The absence of historical consciousness, motivated by the championing of the "forgetting" of history, through willful or unintentional forgetting, owing to institutional or cultural policies of education or a multitude of others factors, has effectively altered the experience of the world as known to the unhistorical subject.

The Well-Tempered Reader began with an analogy of a pedagogical tuning system in music that allowed students to move across and express a wide range of tuning, seamlessly but also gradually. Adab's tuning system of human virtues extends beyond the traditional understanding of promoting refinement and moral excellence only. As previously argued, adab is a catalyst in developing the subject's historical consciousness within an ethical framework. This ethical framework points to a sense of a shared order, where it can be safely argued that as adab framed the reading and interpretative practices of individuals, it also framed their social and political practices.[65] It is through this conception of adab that the *nahḍa* figure al-Ṭahṭāwī theorized adab to shape and discuss modern political subjectivities and concepts of freedom, justice, and governance.[66] Al-Ṭahṭāwī's work similarly influenced Muḥammad ʿAbduh (1849–1905), who argued for adab as a political order by conceptualizing it as a holistic framework that integrates individual moral discipline, collective social unity, and political freedom.[67] ʿAbduh's framework argues that people are "pre-political and choose their political order so that the political order becomes a living and self-moving order."[68] As pre-political individuals, they select and establish their own political framework of "rights and duties," further emphasizing the self-constituting nature of adab qua public sphere.[69] The discourse on adab as political freedom for the adabized citizens by al-Ṭahṭāwī and ʿAbduh is indeed plausible. But it must be emphasized, as this book argues, that this political freedom can only be effected through adab's intellectually liberating tools. Therefore, before becoming the adabized citizen, the adabized subject learns the necessary grammar of adab qua engaged citizenship: humanity (murūʾa: hospitality, discourse, critique, will and resolve, method, etc.). The principles of adab guiding the subject's life, where it allowed them to read, critique, but also engage adabfully, with historical consciousness, are the same participatory and agential principles that guide individuals in political engagement.

APPENDIX

التبرّي من معرّة المعرّي

The Exoneration from al-Maʿarri's Humiliation

لله حمدٌ دائمُ الوَلِيّ   ثمّ صلاتُه على النبي
قد نُقِلَ الثقاتُ عَن أبي العَلا   لما أتى للمُرتَضى ودخلا
قال له شخصٌ بِهِ قَد عَثَرا   من ذلِكَ الكلبُ الذي ما أبصَرا
فقال في جوابه قولًا جلِي   مُعَبِّرًا لذلك المجهّلِ
الكلبُ من لَم يَدرِ من أسمائِهِ   سبعينَ موميًا إلى علائِهِ
وقد تَتَبّعتُ دَواوينَ اللُّغَه   لَعَلّني أجمعُ من ذا مَبلَغَه
فجئتُ منها عددًا كثيرًا   وأرتجي فيما بقي تيسيرا
وقد نظمتُ ذاك في هذا الرجز   ليستفيدَها الذي عنها عجز
فسمّهِ هُدِيتَ بالتبرّي   يا صاحِ من معرّةِ المعرّي
من ذلكَ الباقِعُ ثم الوازِعُ   والكلبُ والأبقَعُ ثم الزارعُ
والخيطَلُ السحامُ ثم الأسدُ   والعُربُج العجوزُ ثم الأعقدُ
والأعنقُ الدرباسُ والعَمَلّسُ   والقُطرُبُ الفُرنيُّ ثم الفَلحَسُ
والثَّغِم الطَّلَقُ مع العواءِ   بالمدّ والقَصرِ على استواء
وعُدَّ من أسمائِهِ البصيرُ   وفيهِ لغزٌ قالَه خبيرُ
والعربُ قد سمّوهُ قدمًا في النفيرِ   داعي الضمير ثم هانىء الضمير
وهكذا سموه داعي الكَرَمِ   مشيدَ الذكرِ متمّمَ النعَمِ
ومُثَمّمٌ وكالبٌ وهبلَعُ   ومُنذِرٌ وهجرَع وهَجرَعُ
ثم كُسَيبٌ علَم المذكّرِ   منه من الهمزةِ واللام عَرِي
والقَلَطِيُّ والسلوقِيُّ نِسبَه   كذلك الصينيُّ بذاك أشبَه
والمُستَطيرُ هائجُ الكلابِ   كذا رواهُ صاحبُ العُبابِ
والدرصُ والجروُ مثلّثُ الفا   لوَلَدِ الكلبِ أسامٍ تُلفى
والسمع فيما قاله الصوليُ   وهو أبُو خالدٍ المكنِيُّ
ونقَلوا الزُّهدون للكلابِ   وكلبةٌ يُقالُ لها كَسابِ
مثلُ قطامِ علمًا مَبنِيًّا   وكسبةٌ كذاك نقلًا رُوِيا
وخُذ لها العولَقَ والمُعاوِيَة   ولَعوة وكُن لذاكَ راوِيه

ولدُ الكلبِ من الذيبَة سمّ   عُسبورةً وإن تُزِل حالَم تُلَم
وألحَقوا بذلِكَ الخَيهَفعى   وأن تُمَدَّ فهو جاءَ سمعا
وولدُ الكلبِ من ذيبٍ سُمي   أو ثعلبٍ فيما رَوَوا بالديسَمِ
ثمَّ كلابُ الماءِ بالهراكِلَه   تُدعى وقِس فردًا على ما شاكَلَه

كذاكَ كلبُ الماءِ يَدعى القُندُسا   فيما له ابنُ دحيةٍ قَدِ ائتَسى
وكلبةُ الماءِ هيَ القضاعَه   جميعُ ذاك أثبتوا سَماعَه
وعدّدوا من جنسهِ ابنَ آوى   ومَن سُماه دألٌ قد ساوى
ودُئِلٌ ودُؤلٌ والذُّألان   وافتَح وضُمَّ معجَمًا للذُّألان
كذلك العِلوضُ ثم النوفَلُ   واللعوَضُ السرحوب فيما نَقَلوا
والوَعُّ والعلوشُ ثم الوَعوَعُ   والشغبَرَ الوأواءُ فيما يُسمَعُ
هذا الذي من كُتُبٍ جمعتهُ   وما بدا من بعدِ ذا ألحَقتهُ
والحمدُ للهِ هنا تمامُ   ثمَّ على نبيّهِ السلامُ

All abiding praise to God, the Protecting Friend
Then His salutations upon the Prophet send

The trustworthy scholars have transmitted from Abū al-ʿAlā
Upon his approach to the abode of al-Murtaḍā

That a man rebuked him, whom he'd stumbled over,
"Who is this blind dog—not sober?"

He replied with wisdom, clear in exposition
Enlightening the ignorant with precision:

A dog is a creature whose names exceed knowing
Seventy appellations, to its significance showing

In the vast oceans of our blessed language I dove
Seeking to gather these names, a treasure trove

I thus amassed numerous findings indeed
While in what remains, I seek divine ease to proceed

In *rajaz* meter I've composed this beneficial verse
That those seeking knowledge might easily rehearse

So name it, may God guide you, my companion,
"The Exoneration from al-Maʿarrī's Humiliation"

Among those names are al-Bāqiʿ and al-Wāziʿ
al-Kalb, al-Abqaʿ, followed by al-Zāriʿ

al-Khayṭal, al-Suḥām, then al-Asad in succession
al-ʿUrbuj, al-ʿAjūz, al-Aʿqad in progression

al-Aʿnaq, al-Dirbās, then al-ʿAmallas with grace
al-Quṭrub, al-Furnī, al-Falḥas takes its place

al-Thaghim, al-Ṭalq, with al-ʿAwāʾ too
Both long and short forms are held true

Among its names count al-Baṣīr with care
A hidden wisdom that the learned declare

The Arabs of old named it in times of need
Dāʿī al-Ḍamīr, then Hāniʾ al-Ḍamīr indeed

Thus they bestowed the title Dāʿī al-Karam
Elevating its mention in the realm of *niʿam*

Thamtham, Kālib, and Hablaʿ are known
Mundhir, Hijraʿ, and Hajraʿ are shown

Then Kusayb, masculine in form divine
Free of *hamza* and *lām* in design

al-Qalaṭī, al-Salūqī in relation stand
Like al-Ṣīnī, following this scholarly strand

al-Mustaṭīr, arouser of the canine breed
As the author of *al-ʿUbāb* has decreed

al-Dirṣ and al-Jarw with triple voweling blessed
For the young of dogs, as has been expressed

al-Samʿ as narrated by the wise al-Ṣūlī
Abū Khālid, his epithet, known surely

They transmitted al-Ruhdūn in erudite tone
And Kasāb for the female, in sources shown

Like Qaṭām, a proper noun well preserved
And Kasba, through transmission observed

Take al-ʿAwlaq and al-Muʿāwiya as well
And of Laʿwa in transmission tell

The offspring of dog and she-wolf they name
ʿUsbūra, in which fear no blame

To this they add al-Khayhafʿā in knowledge true
Its extended form also transmitted through

The pup of a wolf-dog union they decree
Or fox-dog, as al-Daysam, all agree

Sea dogs as Harākila are known in lore
Compare the singular as they did before

The seal al-Qundus they also name
For Ibn Diḥya's work did thus claim

al-Quḍāʿa for the sea-bitch they write
All confirmed by transmission's light

Ibn Āwā among its kinds they count
And Duʾal equals this amount

Duʾil, Duʾul—but al-Dhuʾalān preface
With *fatḥa, ḍamma,* and dot in place

al-ʿIlwaḍ and al-Nawfal likewise appear
al-Laʿwaḍ and al-Sarḥūb in the rear

al-Waʿʿ, al-ʿIllūsh, then al-Waʿwaʿ clear
al-Shaghbar, al-Waʾwāʾ as sages hear

This list from authentic books I've drawn
And appended whatever has later dawned

All praise to God as completion nears
And upon His Prophet peace appears

NOTES

INTRODUCTION: THE SUBJECT OF *ADAB*

1. For more on the self in Islam, see Faruque, *Sculpting the Self*, 37; cf. Foucault, "The Subject and Power."

2. Foucault, "The Subject and Power," 781.

3. Williams, *Keywords*. Williams's book is a dictionary of certain key cultural and civilizational word-concepts in English, e.g., "Aesthetics" and "Democracy." Williams traces when the word first appeared, how it was and is used, and its diachronic change and use culturally, thereby tracing the social and intellectual innovations that are carried with these changes. Similar efforts can be found in Arabic studies in the genre of civilizational and/or cultural lexicons (*maʿājim alfāẓ al-ḥaḍāra*). These lexicons are either concerned with one period, e.g., Abbasid cultural keywords, or civilizational concepts and cultural keywords in the works of one author or in a certain genre like poetry. These are all commendable efforts and very much enriching to Arabic studies and can be the nucleus to the gargantuan task of the diachronic approach where a keyword can be traced from pre-Islam to the present day, and the tracing of when a keyword appeared in Arabic culture or changed use; this remains desideratum.

4. For more on adab in other languages of the Islamicate, see Kia, *Persianate Selves*; Kia, "Lingering with *Adab*."

5. Kilpatrick, "Adab," 1:54.

6. al-Anṣārī, *al-Nawādir fī al-lugha*, 309.

7. Ḍaif, *al-ʿAṣr al-jāhilī*, 7.

8. This is a ḥadīth found in the collection of al-Dārimī (d. 255 AH/869 CE), *Musnad al-Dārimī*, vol. 4 ("On the Excellence of the Qur'an"), ḥadīth no. 3358.

9. al-Fayyūmī, *Fatḥ al-qarīb*, 11:13. Al-Fayyūmī had a Sufi explanation for this as the link between acts and thoughts.

10. al-Aṣmaʿī, *al-Aṣmaʿiyyāt*, 56.

11. Ḍaif, *al-ʿAṣr al-jāhilī*, 9.

12. Toorawa, *Ibn Abī Ṭāhir Ṭayfūr*, 2.

13. al-Kātib, "Risālat ʿAbd al-Ḥamīd ilā al-kuttāb"; see also Ibn Qutayba, *Adab al-kātib*; Gully, *The Culture of Letter-Writing*.

14. Ḍaif, *al-ʿAṣr al-jāhilī*, 9.

15. Ibn Qutayba, *Adab al-kātib*, 5–20.

16. al-Khafājī, *Ḥāshiyat al-Shihāb*, 1:14.

17. Heinrichs, "Classification of the Sciences," 120.

18. Heinrichs, "Classification of the Sciences," 139.

19. Heinrichs, "Classification of the Sciences," 139; Makdisi, *Rise of Humanism*, 53ff.

20. Ḍaif, *al-ʿAṣr al-jāhilī*, 7.

21. Brockelmann, "Die Aufgabe der Literaturgeschichte."

22. Brockelmann, "Die Aufgabe der Literaturgeschichte."

23. Brockelmann, "Die Aufgabe der Literaturgeschichte."

24. Michel Foucault asserts that disciplines were born as a result of the mechanism of the penal system's desire for control in France in particular. The need to categorize, classify, and put into hierarchies observed in these social systems was transferred into the fields of the production of knowledge. See Foucault, *Discipline and Punish*.

25. Zaydān, *Tārīkh ādāb al-lugha al-ʿarabiyya*, 13.

26. Zaydān, *Tarīkh ādāb al-lugha al-ʿarabiyya*, 13.

27. Zaydān wrote about this in over twenty-six issues of *al-Hilāl* magazine from January 1894 to January 1895.

28. Jurjī Zaydān, "Tārīkh ādāb al-lugha al-ʿarabiyya," *al-Hilāl*, January 1894, no. 9, 260–61.

29. Amidu Sanni advances "filiation" for these generative relations as "borrowing from others' productions into one's own work, especially in the literary practice, [which] is characterized as filiation." It situates these borrowings in a familial relationship and offers us a chance to think differently about these relationships as opposed to intertextuality. See Sanni, "Filiation," 13.

30. Ledbetter, *Bach's Well-Tempered Clavier*, 36.

31. Homer, *The Odyssey*, 136 (book 3, lines 21–25).

32. O'Donnell, "The *Odyssey*'s Millennia-Old Model of Mentorship."

1. *ADAB* AND/AS *MURŪʾA*

1. Pierre Bourdieu's conception of the habitus was critiqued for its mechanical focus on social norms without reflection on agency or ethics. Aristotle's engagement and formulation of the habitus were motivated by ethical and pedagogical concerns and were more flexible than Bourdieu's conceptions. I learn from Saba Mahmood's critique of certain conceptions of habitus, especially Bourdieu's, and her engagement with previous theorization and reformulations. See Mahmood, *Politics of Piety*, 135ff.

2. Lapidus, "Knowledge, Virtue, and Action," 54.

3. Ibn Khaldūn, *The Muqaddimah*, 346, quoted in Mahmood, *Politics of Piety*, 137.

4. Nederman, "Nature, Ethics, and the Doctrine of 'Habitus,'" 96, quoted in Mahmood, *Politics of Piety*, 137.

5. Fakhry, *History of Islamic Philosophy*, 145.
6. Lapidus, "Knowledge, Virtue, and Action," 55–56.
7. Ibn Qutayba, *ʿUyūn al-akhbār*, 1:411.
8. Ibn Qutayba, *ʿUyūn al-akhbār*, 1:412.
9. Ibn Manẓūr, *Lisān al-ʿarab*, 1:154.
10. al-Fīrūzābādī, *al-Qāmūs al-muḥīṭ*, 52; al-Jawharī, *al-Ṣiḥāḥ*, 1:72.
11. al-Fīrūzābādī, *al-Qāmūs al-muḥīṭ*, 52.
12. al-Jawharī, *al-Ṣiḥāḥ*, 1:72.
13. al-Sharīf al-Jurjānī, *Kitāb al-taʿrīfāt*, 176.
14. al-Zamakhsharī, *Asās al-balāgha*, 2:201.
15. al-Lakhmī, *al-Adab wa-l-murūʾa*.
16. Not much is available on al-Lakhmī's biography; see al-Zarkalī, *al-Aʿlām*, 3:190; Ibn ʿAsākir, *Tahdhīb tārīkh Dimashq*, 6:369; al-Ṣafadī, *al-Wāfī*, 16:147–48.
17. al-Dhahabī, *Tārīkh al-Islām*, 47:163.
18. al-Fāsī, *al-ʿIqd al-thamīn*, 6:381.
19. al-Lakhmī, *al-Adab wa-l-murūʾa*, 12.
20. al-Lakhmī, *al-Adab wa-l-murūʾa*, 12.
21. al-Lakhmī, *al-Adab wa-l-murūʾa*, 12.
22. al-Lakhmī, *al-Adab wa-l-murūʾa*, 13.
23. al-Lakhmī, *al-Adab wa-l-murūʾa*, 13–14.
24. al-Lakhmī, *al-Adab wa-l-murūʾa*, 14–15.
25. al-Lakhmī, *al-Adab wa-l-murūʾa*, 15.
26. al-Lakhmī, *al-Adab wa-l-murūʾa*, 15–16.
27. al-Lakhmī, *al-Adab wa-l-murūʾa*, 15–16.
28. al-Lakhmī, *al-Adab wa-l-murūʾa*, 16–17.
29. al-Lakhmī, *al-Adab wa-l-murūʾa*, 17–18.
30. al-Lakhmī, *al-Adab wa-l-murūʾa*, 18–19.
31. All Qur'anic translations are taken from Abdel Haleem, *The Qur'an*.
32. Ibn al-Marzubān, *al-Murūʾa*, 97.
33. Ibn al-Marzubān, *al-Murūʾa*, 27.
34. Ibn al-Marzubān, *al-Murūʾa*, 115.
35. al-Lakhmī, *al-Adab wa-l-murūʾa*, 19.
36. al-Lakhmī, *al-Adab wa-l-murūʾa*, 19–20.
37. Sadan, *al-Adab al-ʿarabī*, 68–69.
38. al-Washshāʾ, *al-Muwashshā*, 37.
39. al-Washshāʾ, *al-Ẓarf wa-l-ẓurafāʾ* (1907), 32. Al-Washshāʾ also speaks about appearance-related attributes as part of the definition, such as cleanliness, neat and stylish clothes, and use of perfumes.
40. See "Ẓarīf" in *EI2*, htttp://doi.org/10.1163/1573=3912_islam_SIM_8125.
41. al-Washshāʾ, *al-Ẓarf wa-l-ẓurafāʾ* (1953), 1.
42. al-Lakhmī, *al-Adab wa-l-murūʾa*, 14–15.
43. al-Lakhmī, *al-Adab wa-l-murūʾa*, 21.
44. al-Lakhmī, *al-Adab wa-l-murūʾa*, 21.
45. James E. Montgomery reads al-Washshāʾ's ethics as a culmination of what he calls "Aristotelian ethics," as noted in Miskawayh's *Tahdhīb al-akhlāq*. *EI2*, under "ẓarīf." It would

be more useful and productive to read these developments diachronically in their context rather than force the "Aristotelian ethics" on al-Washshāʾ.

46. Ibn al-Muqaffaʿ, *al-Adab al-ṣaghīr wa-l-Adab al-kabīr*, 12.
47. Ibn al-Muqaffaʿ, *al-Adab al-ṣaghīr wa-l-Adab al-kabīr*, 11.
48. Ibn Ḥibbān, *Rawḍat al-ʿuqalāʾ*, 229–32.
49. Ibn Ḥibbān, *Rawḍat al-ʿuqalāʾ*, 220.
50. Ibn Ḥibbān, *Rawḍat al-ʿuqalāʾ*, 220.
51. Ibn ʿAbd Rabbih, *al-ʿIqd al-farīd*, 2:76.
52. Ibn ʿAbd Rabbih, *al-ʿIqd al-farīd*, 2:148.
53. Ibn ʿAbd Rabbih, *al-ʿIqd al-farīd*, 2:150.
54. Ibn ʿAbd Rabbih, *al-ʿIqd al-farīd*, 2:150–51.
55. Ibn Qutayba, *ʿUyūn al-akhbār*, 1:413.
56. Ibn Qutayba, *ʿUyūn al-akhbār*, 1:413.
57. Ibn Ḥibbān, *Rawḍat al-ʿuqalāʾ*, 223.
58. Jarīr b. ʿAṭiyya, *Dīwān Jarīr*, 2:887.
59. Ibn ʿAbd Rabbih, *al-ʿIqd al-farīd*, 2:76.
60. For more on the tools of anti-adab and humor, see Bin Tyeer, *The Qur'an and Aesthetics*.
61. Miskawayh, *Tahdhīb al-akhlāq*, 79.
62. Miskawayh, *Tahdhīb al-akhlāq*, 80–81.
63. al-Ṭahṭāwī, *Manāhij al-albāb*, 34.
64. al-Ṭahṭāwī, *Manāhij al-albāb*, 34.
65. Chittick, *Sufi Doctrine*, 56.
66. al-Ṭahṭāwī, *Manāhij al-albāb*, 34.
67. al-Ṭahṭāwī, *Manāhij al-albāb*, 34.
68. al-Washshāʾ, *al-Muwashshā*, 38.
69. al-Ṭahṭāwī, *Manāhij al-albāb*, 35.
70. al-Ṭahṭāwī, *Manāhij al-albāb*, 30.
71. Amīn, *Fayḍ al-khāṭir*, 2:215–19.
72. Faruque, *Sculpting the Self*, 199.
73. Allan, "How *Adab* Became Literary"; Bin Tyeer, *The Qur'an and Aesthetics*, 1–41; El Shakry, *The Literary Qur'an*; Kia, "Lingering with *Adab*."
74. Ibn al-Marzubān, *al-Murūʾa*, 53.
75. Blankinship, *The End of the Jihad State*.
76. Ḥussein, "al-Murūʾa wa-maẓāhiruhā al-ṣādiqa," 8:16.
77. al-Ṭahṭāwī, *Manāhij al-albāb*, 30–31.
78. al-Ṭahṭāwī, *Manāhij al-albāb*, 31.
79. al-Washshāʾ, *al-Muwashshā*, 38.

2. *ADAB* AS HOSPITALITY

1. Emile Habibi, quoted in ʿAṭṭiya, "Muḥāwalāt ʿalā ṭarīq taʾṣīl al-riwāya al-ʿarabiyya," 139. Habibi's novels engage actively with adab genres such as the *maqāma*, anecdotes, as well as techniques like the famous Jāḥiẓian *jidd wa-hazl* in his works *Sudāsiyyat al-ayyām al-sitta* (The Sextet of the Six Days) and *al-Waqāʾiʿ al-gharība fī ikhtifāʾ Saʿīd Abī al-Naḥs al-Mutashāʾil* (The Secret Life of Saʿīd, the Ill-Fated Pessoptimist).

2. Ibn al-Muqaffaʿ, *al-Adab al-ṣaghīr wa-l-Adab al-kabīr*, 5.

3. Ibn al-Muqaffaʿ, *al-Adab al-ṣaghīr wa-l-Adab al-kabīr*, 6, 98.

4. See al-Baghdādī, *Khizānat al-adab*, 7:177. Al-Baghdādī relates the accusations of heresy but ends with the story of how those in power felt threatened by him because of what he wrote in a matter of dispute between Caliph al-Manṣūr and his uncle rendering the caliph's power void should he betray his uncle; the caliph was offended and ordered Sufyān the governor to see to Ibn al-Muqaffaʿ's death. It is also related that Ibn al-Muqaffaʿ may have had a sharp tongue; it is reported that he insulted Sufyān b. Muʿāwiya's mother, calling her *mughtalima* (lecherous/a whore) and saying that the men of Iraq were not enough for her, so she had to go find more men in Syria. See al-Jahshiyārī, *al-Wuzarāʾ wa-l-kuttāb*, 104–10.

5. Cooperson, "Ibn al-Muqaffaʿ," 346.

6. Kilito, *Min shurfat Ibn Rushd*, 11.

7. Kilito, *Min shurfat Ibn Rushd*, 9, 11.

8. For more on the issue of Ibn al-Muqaffaʿ's preface(s), especially in relation to illustrated manuscripts of *Kalīla wa-Dimna*, see Keegan, "Before and after *Kalīla wa-Dimna*."

9. Kilito, *Min shurfat Ibn Rushd*, 11.

10. Kilito, *Min shurfat Ibn Rushd*, 11.

11. Ḥājjī Khalīfa, *Kashf al-ẓunūn*, 2:1508.

12. Ricoeur, *Sur la traduction*, 20 (my translation).

13. Ricoeur, "Quel éthos nouveau pour l'Europe?," 109 (my translation); cf. Wilhelm, "Pour une herméneutique du traduire."

14. Lambertini, "Mirrors for Princes," 792.

15. Perret and Péquignot, *A Critical Companion*, 3–4.

16. Lambton, *State and Government*, 51.

17. Geary et al., "Courtly Cultures," 191.

18. The most famous in Arabic literary history would be Sir Richard Burton, who was generally acknowledged to have been an agent for the East India Company and is known for his renditions of the *Thousand and One Nights* as well as the *Kama Sutra*. Another is C. K. Scott Moncrieff, the English translator of Marcel Proust's *Remembrance of Things Past*; he used the profession of translation as a cover to gather intelligence for Britain in Mussolini's Italy in the 1920s. See Polizzotti, *Sympathy for the Traitor*, 33.

19. Polizzotti, *Sympathy for the Traitor*, 34.

20. Quoted in Adamson, *al-Kindī*, 23.

21. Quoted in Adamson, *al-Kindī*, 23.

22. For more on Burzūyah, see de Blois, *Burzōy's Voyage to India*.

23. Farrūkh, *Tārīkh al-adab al-ʿarabī*, 2:54–55.

24. Dabashi, "It Was in China," 944.

25. Alphonso-Karakala, "Facets of Panchatantra," 75.

26. For more on frank speech in *Kalīla wa-Dimna*, see London, "Lessons in Frank Speech"; London, "How to Do Things with Fables."

27. London, "How to Do Things with Fables," 211–12.

28. Steiner, "The Uncommon Reader."

29. Bonebakker, "Early Arabic Literature," 409–10. For more, see Patrizi, "Metaphor of the Divine Banquet."

30. Said, *Orientalism*, xix.

31. al-Yamanī, *Muḍāhāt amthāl.*
32. I consult and rely on the Fishbein and Montgomery edition and translation by NYU Abu Dhabi. I also consulted Cheikho's and ʿAzzām and Hussein's editions.
33. Quoted in Genette, *Paratexts*, 196.
34. Genette, *Paratexts*, 1.
35. Arḥīla, *Hājis al-ibdāʿ*, 129.
36. Arḥīla, *Hājis al-ibdāʿ*, 129.
37. ʿAlī b. Khalaf, *Mawādd al-bayān*, 83–86.
38. al-Ḥamawī, *Muʿjam al-udabāʾ*, 6:2454.
39. al-Nawawī, *al-Majmūʿ*, 1:77.
40. Douaihy, "al-Muthaqqaf wa-l-sulṭān wa-l-ḥikāya," 59.
41. al-Ṭībī, *Futūḥ al-ghayb fī al-kashf ʿan qināʿ al-rayb*, 2:226.
42. al-Ṭībī, *Futūḥ al-ghayb fī al-kashf ʿan qināʿ al-rayb*, 2:226.
43. Ibn al-Muqaffaʿ, *Kalīla wa-Dimna*, 19 (section 2.1).
44. See also Beatrice Gründler's discussion on the allegorical nature of the text, "*Kalīla wa-Dimna*: A Unique Work of World Literature." For more on the allegorical nature of the text, see Marroum, "*Kalila wa Dimna*."
45. Cf. Mohamad, "Muqaddimat Ibn al-Muqaffaʿ."
46. See my discussion (Bin Tyeer, *The Qur'an and Aesthetics*, 201) on the *maqāmāt* of both al-Ḥarīrī and al-Hamadhānī, where al-Ḥarīrī discusses different types of negative readers as part of negative reception in his preface; he does this to anticipate critique and thwart it. See also al-Maʿarrī's typology of negative readers in chapter 4 of this book.
47. Ibn al-Muqaffaʿ, *al-Adab al-ṣaghīr wa-l-Adab al-kabīr*, 11.
48. al-Farāhīdī, *Kitāb al-ʿayn*, 7:117.
49. al-Farāhīdī, *Kitāb al-ʿayn*, 7:117.
50. Ibn Fāris, *Maqāyīs al-lugha*, 1:254; al-Fīrūzābādī, *al-Qāmūs al-muḥīṭ*, 351.
51. al-Farāhīdī, *Kitāb al-ʿayn*, 7:117; Ibn Fāris, *Maqāyīs al-lugha*, 1:254.
52. al-Ṣaghānī, *al-Takmila*, 2:421.
53. Ibn Manẓūr, *Lisān al-ʿarab*, 4:65.
54. al-Fīrūzābādī, *al-Qāmūs al-muḥīṭ*, 351.
55. al-Fīrūzābādī, *al-Qāmūs al-muḥīṭ*, 351.
56. al-Zamakhsharī, *Asās al-balāgha*, 1:62.
57. al-Fīrūzābādī, *al-Qāmūs al-muḥīṭ*, 351.
58. al-Zabīdī, *Tāj al-ʿarūs*, 10:207.
59. al-Qasṭallānī, *Sharḥ*, 4:49.
60. Makdisi, *Rise of Humanism*, 30.
61. Makdisi, *Rise of Humanism*, 30.
62. Ibn al-Muqaffaʿ, *al-Adab al-ṣaghīr wa-l-Adab al-kabīr*, 12 (emphasis mine).
63. Ibn al-Muqaffaʿ, *al-Adab al-ṣaghīr wa-l-Adab al-kabīr*, 64.
64. ʿAntarah ibn Shaddād, *War Songs*, 4, 189.
65. Ibn al-Muqaffaʿ, *al-Adab al-ṣaghīr wa-l-Adab al-kabīr*, 27.
66. Ibn Sīnā, *al-Shifāʾ*, 54.
67. Ibn Sīnā, *al-Shifāʾ*, 54.
68. Ibn Sinā, *al-Shifāʾ*, 54.
69. Ibn Sīnā, *al-Shifāʾ*, 54.

70. See Keegan, "Commentarial Acts," chap. 4. I support Keegan's overall reading, but I understand Ibn Sīnā's term more expansively.

71. Ibn Sīnā, *al-Hidāya*, 3:393 (my translation). I thank Elaine van Dalen for weighing in on Ibn Sīnā's *ra'y* in this passage.

72. El-Tobgui, *Ibn Taymiyya on Reason and Revelation*, 338.

73. McGinnis and Reisman, *Classical Arabic Philosophy*, concept, 152; judgment, 224; theorem, 9.

74. Ibn al-Muqaffa', *al-Adab al-ṣaghīr wa-l-Adab al-kabīr*, 12.

75. al-Rāzī, *Mafātīḥ al-ghayb*, 19:89–91.

76. al-Rāzī, *Mafātīḥ al-ghayb*, 19:91–93.

77. Ford, *Origins of Criticism*, 216.

78. Quoted in Ford, *Origins of Criticism*, 85.

79. Quoted in Ford, *Origins of Criticism*, 86. See *Protagoras* 347c–348a, esp. 347c; *Hippias Minor* 365c–d. The problem of allegoresis applies to philosophical texts also; see Gorgias in *Meno* 70c–d.

80. Ford, *Origins of Criticism*, 86.

81. Quoted in Ford, *Origins of Criticism*, 86.

82. See Clark, *Plotinus*; Sperl and Dedes, *Faces of the Infinite*.

83. Zargar, *Polished Mirror*, 239.

84. Ford, *Origins of Criticism*, 87.

85. Bauer, *A Culture of Ambiguity*, 278.

86. An ideal type is a theoretical construct that attempts to encapsulate the essential characteristics of a social phenomenon in a coherent and often exaggerated manner. Developed by Weber, these constructs serve to clarify the complex and varied nature of social life by offering an analytically clear and logically consistent framework for analysis. For more on this, see Weber, "Objectivity in Social Science and Social Policy," as cited in Sung Ho Kim, "Max Weber," *Stanford Encyclopedia of Philosophy* (Winter 2024 Edition), https://plato.stanford.edu/archives/win2024/entries/weber/.

87. Q.49:13, "People, We created you all from a single man and a single woman, and made you into races and tribes so that you should get to know one another."

88. Asad, "The Idea of an Anthropology of Islam," 14.

89. Asad, "The Idea of an Anthropology of Islam," 15.

90. Jansen, "'Postsecularism, Piety and Fanaticism," quoted in Enayet, *Islam and Secularism*, 42.

91. al-Zamakhsharī, *al-Kashshāf*, 3:455.

92. al-Zamakhsharī, *al-Kashshāf*, 3:455.

93. al-Zamakhsharī, *al-Kashshāf*, 3:455.

94. al-Ṭabarī, *Jāmi' al-bayān*, 20:39–40.

95. al-Tha'labī, *al-Kashf wa-l-bayān*, 21:52. Similar to this definition is al-Baghawī's. See al-Baghawī, *Ma'ālim al-tanzīl*, 3:557.

96. al-Jurjānī, *Darj al-durar*, 2:365.

97. al-Jurjānī, *Darj al-durar*, 3:1261.

98. al-Suyūṭī, *Tafsīr al-Jalālayn*, 526.

99. al-Suyūṭī, *Tafsīr al-Jalālayn*, 464.

100. Ibn Kathīr, *Tafsīr*, 6:280; al-Baghawī, *Ma'ālim al-tanzīl*, 3:415.

101. al-Nīsāpūrī, *Gharā'ib al-Qur'ān*, 5:194.

102. al-Ghazālī, *Ma'ārij al-quds fī madārij ma'rifat al-nafs*, 141–43.

3. *ADAB* AS DISCOURSE

1. Gadamer advanced the idea of "historically effected consciousness" (*wirkungsgeschichtliches Bewußtsein*), which acknowledges that all understanding is influenced by the historical contexts in which it takes place. Gadamer emphasizes that understanding and interpretation always take place within a specific "horizon" (*Horizont*) shaped by our historical context and the circumstances in which we find ourselves. See Gadamer, *Truth and Method*.

2. Zīdān, *Ḥayy b. Yaqẓān*, 113–23.

3. Zīdān, *Ḥayy b. Yaqẓān*, 113–23.

4. Idris, "Ibn Ṭufayl's Critique of Politics," 68. The two stories are that of *Ḥayy b. Yaqẓān*, on the one hand, and *Absāl and Salāmān*, on the other.

5. Gutas, "Ibn Ṭufayl on Ibn Sīnā."

6. Gutas, "Ibn Ṭufayl on Ibn Sīnā," 229, 234; Bürgel, "Ibn Ṭufayl"; Idris, "Ibn Ṭufayl's Critique of Politics," 69.

7. For more on the discussion of the two birth origins, see Adamson, "A False Start?"; Fradkin, "Political Thought of Ibn Tufayl"; Malti-Douglas, "*Ḥayy ibn Yaqẓān* as Male Utopia."

8. Quoted in Conrad, "Through the Thin Veil," 261. For more on this, see Adamson, "A False Start?"

9. Ibn Ṭufayl was also a physician and it could be inferred that he was indeed in favor of dissection. For more on dissection in premodern Islam, see Savage-Smith, "Attitudes toward Dissection."

10. McGinnis, "Scientific Methodologies," 307; see also McGinnis, "Avicenna's Naturalized Epistemology."

11. McGinnis, "Scientific Methodologies," 307.

12. McGinnis, "Scientific Methodologies," 307.

13. Elshakry and Idris, "Ibn Tufayl."

14. Idris, "Ibn Ṭufayl's Critique of Politics," 73.

15. al-Rāzī, *Mafātīḥ al-ghayb*, 13:49–50.

16. Zīdān, *Ḥayy b. Yaqẓān*, 91.

17. Zīdān, *Ḥayy b. Yaqẓān*, 205.

18. Hämeen-Anttila, "Suhrawardī's Western Exile," 107.

19. Zīdān, *Ḥayy b. Yaqẓān*, 95–107.

20. Zīdān, *Ḥayy b. Yaqẓān*, 130–31.

21. Zīdān, *Ḥayy b. Yaqẓān*, 132.

22. Zīdān, *Ḥayy b. Yaqẓān*, 132.

23. Attar, *Vital Roots of European Enlightenment*, 90. Attar takes up many of the preceding questions posed in the quotation and offers her own answers and conceptions of these issues. Attar reads the novella within the binaries of secular/religious orthodoxy, where the inhabitants of the island represent religion and religious practice, while Ḥayy represents enlightened thought, defined in the book as one who does not need religion at all. While

Attar offers many insights in her study on Ibn Ṭufayl's novella, it seems at times that a reading of *Ḥayy b. Yaqẓān* as a secular treatise against religion altogether, and not some thought practices that seem to be Ḥayy's critique, is a retroactive one through both an anachronistic lens and methodology. Attar maintains, "Ibn Ṭufayl did not have to flee his country after he wrote his book *Ḥayy Ibn Yaqẓān* in the twelfth century. No one accused him of atheism" (*Vital Roots of European Enlightenment*, 89). Attar is comparing Ibn Ṭufayl's *Ḥayy b. Yaqẓān* to Jean-Jacques Rousseau (1712–78), who had to flee after writing *Émile*. Yet the insistence on reading and representing Ḥayy as almost an anomaly in Arab-Islamic thought through his epistle that advocates for a definition of reason prescribed by European Enlightenment and independent thought may invite such readings. It would have been more useful if Attar used a framework from Arab-Islamic thought.

24. Ahmed, "Islam's Invented Golden Age." For a more expanded discussion of these issues, see Ahmed, "Systematic Growth"; Ahmed, "The *Sullam al-ʿUlūm* of Muḥibballāh al-Bihārī"; Ahmed, "Post-Classical Philosophical Commentaries/Glosses." For more on al-Ghazālī, see Griffel, *Al-Ghazali's Philosophical Theology*; Griffel, "Al-Ghazālī's (d. 1111) *Incoherence of the Philosophers*."

25. González-Ferrín, "The Disobedient Philosopher," 31.

26. Turābī, *Falsafat Ibn Ṭufayl*, 76.

27. Zīdān, *Ḥayy b. Yaqẓān*, 132.

28. Franz Rosenthal maintains that when Ibn Sīnā was asked to author *al-Shifāʾ* he could not mention the sources he referenced as per the scholarly method due to the magnitude of the task. Some of the sources therefore may include others than Aristotle. See Rosenthal, "Critical Approach," 41.

29. Zīdān, *Ḥayy b. Yaqẓān*, 132–33.

30. al-Ghazālī, *al-Qisṭās al-mustaqīm*, 62–69.

31. Zīdān, *Ḥayy b. Yaqẓān*, 133. This is Ibn Ṭufayl's paraphrase of al-Ghazālī. Al-Ghazālī mentions a variation of this quote in his *Mīzān al-ʿamal*, which Ibn Ṭufayl cites as well (*fa-lā khalāṣ illā fī al-istiqlāl . . . al-shukūk hiya al-muwaṣṣila ilā al-ḥaqq fa-man lam yashukk lam yanẓur wa-man lam yanẓur lam yubṣir wa-man lam yubṣir baqiya fī al-ʿamā wa-l-ḍalāl*); see al-Ghazālī, *Mīzān al-ʿamal*, 137. Several scholars have investigated the place of doubt and skepticism in Islamic theology and epistemology based on al-Ghazālī's work. Some of these studies engage in a comparative investigation of al-Ghazālī's thought with René Descartes's "Cartesian doubt." See Iqbal, *Reconstruction of Religious Thought in Islam*, 102; Sheikh, "Al-Ghazzali: Metaphysics"; Najm, "Place and Function of Doubt"; Watt, *Faith and Practice of al-Ghazali*, 12. Al-Ghazālī features as the only chapter representative of classical Islamic thought on skepticism in Heck, "Skepticism in Classical Islam."

32. Gutas, "Empiricism of Avicenna."

33. Mousavian, "Is Avicenna an Empiricist?," 459.

34. Mousavian, "Is Avicenna an Empiricist?," 444, 459–62; see also Marmura, "Some Aspects of Avicenna's Theory," 303; Marmura, "Avicenna's Proof from Contingency," 343.

35. Mousavian, "Is Avicenna an Empiricist?," 450.

36. Zīdān, *Ḥayy b. Yaqẓān*, 144–45.

37. Barolini, "*Paradiso* 33: Invisible Ink."

38. Signori, "Fleeting Flash."

39. Zīdān, *Ḥayy b. Yaqẓān*, 133.

40. Zīdān, *Ḥayy b. Yaqẓān*, 134.
41. Zīdān, *Ḥayy b. Yaqẓān*, 135.
42. Makdisi, *Rise of Humanism*, 13.
43. Zīdān, *Ḥayy b. Yaqẓān*, 135.
44. Zīdān, *Ḥayy b. Yaqẓān*, 135.
45. Ibn Ṭufayl, *Ibn Tufayl's Hayy Ibn Yaqzān: A Philosophical Tale*, 98–99.
46. Moosa, *al-Ghazālī and the Poetics of Imagination*, 109.
47. al-Ghazālī, *al-Munqidh min al-ḍalāl*, 178–79.
48. Moosa, *al-Ghazālī and the Poetics of Imagination*, 109.
49. For more on this debate, see Adamson and Key, "Philosophy of Language."
50. Avicenna (2007a: 22–23), quoted in Adamson and Key, "Philosophy of Language," 90.
51. Zīdān, *Ḥayy b. Yaqẓān*, 196.
52. Ibn Ṭufayl, *Ibn Tufayl's Hayy Ibn Yaqzān: A Philosophical Tale*, 60.
53. Adamson and Key, "Philosophy of Language," 93.
54. Zīdān, *Ḥayy b. Yaqẓān*, 196.
55. Zīdān, *Ḥayy b. Yaqẓān*, 199. Zīdān gives the verse reference as Q.6:44, which is incorrect. It is in fact Q.25:44.
56. Zīdān, *Ḥayy b. Yaqẓān*, 200; Ibn Ṭufayl, *Ibn Tufayl's Hayy Ibn Yaqzān: A Philosophical Tale*, 58.
57. For more on *fiṭra*, see Mohamed, *Fitrah*.
58. Zīdān, *Ḥayy b. Yaqẓān*, 200; Ibn Ṭufayl and Ibn Rushd, *Two Andalusian Philosophers*, 58.
59. Zīdān, *Ḥayy b. Yaqẓān*, 202 (my translation).
60. Moosa, *al-Ghazālī and the Poetics of Imagination*, 109.
61. Selim, "Manṣūr al-Ḥallāj," 26.
62. Moosa, *al-Ghazālī and the Poetics of Imagination*, 48–49.
63. Moosa, *al-Ghazālī and the Poetics of Imagination*, 48–49.
64. Paul Heck discusses this and compares al-Ghazālī's method as a pedagogue to Cusanus (*docta ignorantia*): "Learned ignorance claims that we cannot know the quiddity of things by scholastic *ratio*, chiefly the quiddity of God." Heck, "Teaching Ignorance," 1:229. See also Heck, "*Adab* in the Thought of Ghazālī."
65. The text has a rich history of translation into European languages from the fifteenth century onward. A look at the translation of the book in Europe would also attest to these circulation activities. It was translated into Italian in the second half of the fifteenth century by Pico della Mirandolo, who was a significant figure of the Italian Renaissance; the translation was based on the Hebrew version. A Dutch translation of *Ḥayy b. Yaqẓān*, based on Edward Pococke's Latin translation with the name of the translator withheld, appeared in Amsterdam in 1672. Another Dutch version appeared in 1701 and a second edition was reprinted in Utrecht in 1722. In 1726, in Frankfurt, a German translation appeared by Georg Pritius. See Attar, *Vital Roots of European Enlightenment*, xvii, 20. For other languages such as the Hebrew translation of the text, see Ben-Zaken, *Reading Ḥayy Ibn-Yaqẓān*. Perhaps future studies can also shed light on the translation of *Ḥayy* into Islamicate languages, if any, such as Persian, Ottoman, or Urdu, among other languages and different routes of circulation and reception beyond Europe.
66. *Philosophus autodidactus*.

67. See Ferlier and Gallien, "'Enthusiastick' Uses of the Oriental Tale," 94; Elmarsafy, "Philosophy Self-Taught," 139.

68. Elmarsafy, "Philosophy Self-Taught," 140.

69. In about thirty years, three English translations of the novella appeared in England, each with a different motivation and interest, ranging from theological commerce and vindicating the dismissal of the Church, to the purely scholarly. It appears that the short period of time between these translations can be explained by the theological controversies that each translation generated. "These publications were part of a theological controversy opposing dissenting movements to the Anglican Church and also reflected the growing enthusiasm for oriental imagery." In 1674, Scottish Quaker George Keith saw in the text a "theological illustration of the 'Inner Light,' the 'Immediate Revelation,' which was at the core of his Quaker doctrine." In 1686, George Ashwell titled his translation *An Indian Prince*, with a much-simplified narrative that erased many of the Islamic and Qur'anic references within. Ashwell also included a theological pamphlet addendum to his translation titled "The Book of Nature," advocating a "contemplative religion inspired by Nature that inscribed Ibn Tufayl's discourse in early modern debates on 'natural religion.'" Ferlier and Gallien, "'Enthusiastick' Uses of the Oriental Tale," 109–10.

70. Elmarsafy, "Philosophy Self-Taught," 140–41.

71. Elmarsafy, "Philosophy Self-Taught," 140–41.

72. Holt, *History of the Near East*, 14.

73. Holt, *History of the Near East*, 14.

74. Ockley, *Improvement of Human Reason*, preface (unpaginated).

75. Ockley, *Improvement of Human Reason*, 168.

76. Ockley, *Improvement of Human Reason*, 167.

77. Ockley, *Improvement of Human Reason*, 168.

78. Khan, *Who Is a Muslim?*, 26–27; for more on the "Mahometan" as a concept, see 21–52.

79. See Gadamer, *Truth and Method*.

80. al-Musawi, "The 'Islamic' *Arabian Nights*."

81. Locke, *An Essay Concerning Human Understanding*, bk. 2, chap. 11, 2.

82. Stephen, *English Literature and Society*, 47, quoted in Clark, "'The Whole Internal World His Own,'" 243.

83. Annotation to *The Works of Sir Joshua Reynolds, Knight*, Discourse VIII E660, quoted in Clark, "'The Whole Internal World His Own,'" 241.

84. Locke, *An Essay Concerning Human Understanding*, bk. 2, chap. 31, 1.

85. Foucault, *Order of Things*, 320, 331, quoted in Webb, *Foucault's Archaeology*, 8.

86. Foucault, *Order of Things*, 320, 331, quoted in Webb, *Foucault's Archaeology*, 8.

87. Locke, *An Essay Concerning Human Understanding*, bk. 3, chap. 10, 34.

88. Clark, "'The Whole Internal World His Own,'" 243.

89. Locke, *An Essay Concerning Human Understanding*, bk. 3, chap. 11, 16. See also Clark, "'The Whole Internal World His Own,'" 243.

90. William Blake, "Jerusalem," pl. 15: 14–16, E 159. See also Waterland, *Advice to a Young Student*, 23.

91. Stephen, *English Literature and Society*, 47.

92. Aravamudan, "East-West Fiction," 198.

93. Aravamudan, "East-West Fiction," 200; for more on Islamicate world literature, see Bin Tyeer and Gallien, *Islam and New Directions in World Literature*.

94. For more on intellectual captivity, see Bar-Itzhak, "Intellectual Captivity."

95. This was a short-lived London periodical that appeared for a few months in 1713, to which Pope was a frequent contributor. His essay condemning the abuse of animals was published in issue no. 61.

96. His real name is Antoine Jacob, and he was in a rivalry with Molière (1622–73). Monsieur Fleury wrote *The Reasoning Beasts*, a farce that satirizes his contemporaneous society using animals, which is why Pope is using his work in this letter.

97. Alexander Pope, "Against Barbarity to Animals," *The Guardian*, no. 61, May 21, 1713. This letter also appears in *The Polite Preceptor*.

98. Longxi, "Reception Theory," 312.

99. Gadamer, *Truth and Method*, 290.

100. Pope, "Against Barbarity" (emphasis mine).

101. Elshakry and Idris, "Ibn Tufayl."

102. Sedgwick, *Western Sufism*, 97; for the reference, see Warburton, *Works of Alexander Pope*, 8:166.

103. Subrahmanyam, *Empires between Islam and Christianity*, 342–43.

4. *ADAB* AS CRITIQUE

1. With the exception of Blankinship and Pizzone, "Self-Commentary as Defensive Strategy," which discusses the text's materiality and glosses, and brief aspects and examples of language polysemy, there are no studies to date on this work.

2. al-Maʿarrī, *Zajr al-nābiḥ*, 13.

3. al-Maʿarrī, *Zajr al-nābiḥ*, 82.

4. al-Maʿarrī, *Zajr al-nābiḥ*, 82.

5. al-Maʿarrī, *Zajr al-nābiḥ*, 59.

6. al-Maʿarrī, *al-Luzūmiyyāt*, 1:196.

7. al-Maʿarrī, *Zajr al-nābiḥ*, 75.

8. al-Maʿarrī, *Zajr al-nābiḥ*, 113.

9. Ibn al-Jawzī, *al-Muntaẓim*, 16:24.

10. I owe this idea of being students by generations removed and its relationship to the sense of tradition to my doctoral supervisor, Stefan Sperl. Sperl suggested to me the beautifully transcendental idea that we are connected to teachers we have never met through tradition.

11. al-Garradi, "Image of al-Maʿarrī," 98–99.

12. Ibn al-Jawzī, *al-Muntaẓim*. After Ibn al-Jawzī, this maxim was repeated by al-Dhahabī, *Tārīkh al-Islām*, 27:401. The first to accuse al-Tawḥīdī of *zandaqa* was Ibn Fāris. It should be noted that Yāqūt al-Ḥamawī is not in accord with these opinions; he mentions that there were some rumors about his faith but he confirms al-Tawḥīdī's Sufism in manners and appearance, his asceticism and faith; similarly, Ibn Ḥajar al-ʿAsqalānī relates on the authority of Ibn al-Najjār that al-Tawḥīdī was a man of good faith, a poet and philologist of many commendable works. al-Ḥamawī, *Irshād al-arīb*, 5:1923–46; al-ʿAsqalānī, *Lisān*

al-mīzān, 7:39. For more on this, especially where al-Maʿarrī is concerned, see al-Garradi, "Image of al-Maʿarrī." The author examines the various allegations against al-Maʿarrī and traces the reception of this image in premodern and modern literary criticism and shows convincingly that none of them are substantial but are, as al-Maʿarrī himself stated, baseless and fabricated.

13. Ibn al-ʿAdīm, *Bughyat al-ṭalab*, 2:889.
14. al-ʿAqqād, "Tabārak razzāq al-barriyya."
15. Ibn al-ʿAdīm, *Bughyat al-ṭalab*, 2:889.
16. Ibn Kathīr, *al-Bidāya wa-l-nihāya*, 15:748.
17. Ibn al-Jawzī, *Nawāsikh al-Qurʾān*, 59; al-Ḥanbalī, *Dhayl*, 2:487.
18. Ibn al-Jawzī, *Nawāsikh al-Qurʾān*, 60; al-Ḥanbalī, *Dhayl*, 2:487.
19. al-Ḥanbalī, *Dhayl*, 2:487.
20. al-Anbārī, *Nuzhat al-alibbāʾ*, 262; al-Ṣafadī, *al-Wāfī*, 17:103.
21. al-Zarkalī, *al-Aʿlām*, 4:90; al-Suyūṭī, *Bughyat al-wuʿāt*, 2:43.
22. al-Ḥamawī, *Irshād al-arīb*, 4:1527.
23. al-Ṣafadī, *al-Wāfī*, 17:103.
24. al-Anbārī, *Nuzhat al-alibbāʾ*, 262; al-Ṣafadī, *al-Wāfī*, 17:103; al-Zarkalī, *al-Aʿlām*, 4:90.
25. ʿAbd al-Raḥmān, *Abū al-ʿAlāʾ al-Maʿarrī*, 49, 93–94.
26. Al-Aṣmaʿī seems to be the first to author under this genre in his *Kitāb khalq al-insān*; others followed suit, such as Abū Isḥāq al-Zajjāj (d. 311 AH/922 CE) and al-Khaṭīb al-Iskāfī (d. 420 AH/1029 CE), with the same book title.
27. Ibn al-Jawzī, *al-Mudhish*, 213–14.
28. I searched for this manuscript in all known catalogues, to no avail.
29. Ibn Manẓūr, *Lisān al-ʿarab*, 9:332.
30. Ibn Khaldūn, *The Muqaddimah*, 35.
31. Ibn al-ʿAdīm, *al-Inṣāf*, 58–59. See also al-Jundī, *al-Jāmiʿ fī akhbār Abī al-ʿAlāʾ al-Maʿarrī*, 2:781.
32. al-Badīʿī, *Awj al-taḥarrī*, 66.
33. Rosenthal, *Knowledge Triumphant*, 77.
34. Ibn Ḥazm, *al-Iḥkām*, bk. I, 30, quoted in Rosenthal, *Knowledge Triumphant*, 55.
35. al-Ibshīhī, *al-Mustaṭraf*, bk. I, 23 (Bulāq, 1851), quoted in Rosenthal, *Knowledge Triumphant*, 56.
36. al-Tahānawī, 1646, bk. II, 4ff., quoted in Rosenthal, *Knowledge Triumphant*, 64.
37. DeNicola, *Understanding Ignorance*, 25.
38. al-ʿUmarī, *Masālik al-abṣār*, 15:432–33; cf. Ibn al-ʿAdīm, *al-Inṣāf*, 57.
39. Ibn al-ʿAdīm, *al-Inṣāf*, 106.
40. al-ʿUmarī, *Masālik al-abṣār*, 15:433.
41. al-ʿUmarī, *Masālik al-abṣār*, 15:433.
42. See a summary of this linguistic relationship in the section on plagues (*bāb mā yudhkar fī al-ṭāʿūn*) in al-ʿAynī, *ʿUmdat al-qārī*, 21:256.
43. For more on al-Badīʿī, see *EI3*, Geert Jan van Gelder, under "al-Badīʿī, Yūsuf."
44. For more on this, see al-ʿAmīdī, *al-Ibāna*.
45. al-Zarkalī, *al-Aʿlām*, 8:121, under "al-Buḥturī."
46. Ibn al-Athīr, *al-Mathal al-sāʾir*, 3:226, under "al-sariqāt al-shiʿriyya."

47. al-Badīʿī, *Awj al-taḥarrī*, 40–41.
48. Ibn al-ʿAdīm, *al-Inṣāf*, 57.
49. al-Yamānī, *al-ʿAwāṣim*, 1:75.
50. al-Maqrīzī, *al-Muqqafā al-kabīr*, 6:173; al-Suyūṭī, *Bughyat al-wuʿāt*, 1:185.
51. I could not locate this reference.
52. Ahmed, *What Is Islam?*, 303.
53. Ibn ʿAbd al-Barr's (d. 463 AH/1071 CE) *Kitāb al-inṣāf* is the earliest example; Ibn al-Sīd al-Baṭalyawsī (d. 521 AH/1127 CE) writes on jurisprudence in *al-Inṣāf fī al-tanbīh ʿalā al-asbāb al-latī awjabat al-ikhtilāf bayna al-muslimīn*; Abū al-Barakāt al-Anbārī on Arabic grammar (d. 577 AH/1181 CE) in *al-Inṣāf fī masāʾil al-khilāf bayna al-naḥawiyyīn al-Baṣriyyīn wa-l-Kūfiyyīn*; Sibṭ Ibn al-Jawzī (d. 654 AH/1256 CE) on jurisprudence in *Īthār al-inṣāf fī āthār al-khilāf*; al-Mardāwī (d. 885 AH/1480 CE) on Ḥanbalī jurisprudence in *al-Inṣāf fī maʿrifat al-rājiḥ min al-khilāf*; Shāh Walī Allāh al-Dihlawī (d. 1176 AH/1762–63 CE) on jurisprudence in *al-Inṣāf fī bayān asbāb al-ikhtilāf*; al-Ṣanʿānī (d. 1182 AH/1768 CE) on Sufism in *al-Inṣāf fī ḥaqīqat al-awliyāʾ wa-mā lahum min al-karāmāt wa-l-alṭāf*; Abū al-Ḥasanāt al-Lucknawī (d. 1886) on jurisprudence in *al-Inṣāf fī ḥukm al-iʿtikāf*. One notices here that there is a continuum in the use of the critical category of *inṣāf* in authorship within the Arab-Islamic sciences at large, whether it be Arabic grammar, jurisprudence, or otherwise; a discursive tradition of *inṣāf*.
54. Ibn ʿAbd al-Barr, *al-Inṣāf*.
55. Ibn ʿAbd al-Barr, *Jāmiʿ bayān al-ʿilm*, 1:530.
56. Ibn Ḥibbān, *al-Majrūḥīn*, 2:15.
57. al-Dhahabī, *Tārīkh al-Islām* (2003), 7:309.
58. For more on murūʾa, see al-Lakhmī, *al-Adab wa-l-murūʾa*.
59. al-Lakhmī, *al-Adab wa-l-murūʾa*, 18–19; Ibn al-Marzubān, *al-Murūʾa*, 27.
60. Ibn al-Marzubān, *al-Murūʾa*, 27.
61. Fricker, *Epistemic Injustice*, 104.
62. Fricker, *Epistemic Injustice*, 104.
63. Zheng, "Moral Criticism."
64. Fricker, *Epistemic Injustice*, 107.
65. Ibn al-ʿAdīm, *al-Inṣāf*, 97.
66. Ibn al-ʿAdīm, *al-Inṣāf*, 100.
67. Ibn al-ʿAdīm, *al-Inṣāf*, 116–17.
68. MacIntyre, quoted in Fricker, *Epistemic Injustice*, 82.
69. Al-Qarṭājannī speaks about this throughout, but see al-Qarṭājannī, *Minhāj al-bulaghāʾ*, 221.
70. Sperl, *Mannerism in Arabic Poetry*, 180.
71. Stetkevych, *Cooing of the Dove*, 251–89.
72. See Sperl, *Mannerism in Arabic Poetry*.

5. *ADAB* AS METHOD

1. See Ibn al-Marzubān, *Faḍl al-kilāb*.
2. Moral qualities that are worthy of criticism do not occupy the same space as those of praise, but Ibn Ṭabāṭabā gives them space nonetheless; for example, stinginess, cowardice, impetuousness, ignorance and lack of reason, treachery, conceitedness, failure, depravity,

ingratitude (especially to one's parents), treason, tightness, lack of dignity, lying, inability to control one's fear and being easily scared, ill-mannered, bad winning/inconsiderate victories, cutting off family ties, gossip, disagreements, baseness, obliviousness, envy, crossing the line, pride, frowning/negativity, carelessness, ugliness, unattractiveness and small build, transgressing (the lawful)/lawlessness, weakness, defenselessness, and powerlessness. Among the characteristics worthy of criticism hence *hijā'* is the very general *isā'a* (to wrong or infringe upon s.o.). This is a wide spectrum that could range from a sly backhanded microaggression, an inappropriate look or glance toward someone, to direct verbal and physical assault. See Ibn Ṭabāṭabā, *'Iyār al-shi'r*, 18.

3. Rowson, "An Alexandrian Age."

4. Rowson, "An Alexandrian Age," 110.

5. Rowson, "An Alexandrian Age," 110.

6. al-Musawi, *Medieval Islamic Republic of Letters*, 123–24.

7. Rowson, "An Alexandrian Age," 110.

8. Thomas Bauer makes this distinction between early literature of the Abbasid period, where the boundaries between high and popular were insurmountable, and the blurry boundaries in the Mamluk period. Literary works of the Abbasid period, especially courtly literature, were *representational*, whereas Mamluk literary works were more *participatory* as they involved various classes of people and functioned also as a means of communication. The aesthetics and social function of literature shifted. See Bauer, "Toward an Aesthetics of Mamluk Literature."

9. Bauer, "Means of Communication."

10. See Carter, "Use of Verse."

11. See al-Musawi, *Medieval Islamic Republic of Letters*, 200–201.

12. Bauer, "Mamluk Literature: Misunderstandings and New Approaches," 114.

13. Bauer, "Mamluk Literature: Misunderstandings and New Approaches," 114.

14. al-Anbārī, *Nuzhat al-alibbā'*, 285.

15. al-Ḥamawī, *Irshād al-arīb*, 1:302.

16. al-Ṣafadī, *Nakt al-himyān*, 79. He mentions the incident also in his *al-Wāfī*, 7:64.

17. al-Damīrī, *Ḥayāt al-ḥayawān*, 2:387.

18. Ḥājjī Khalīfa, *Kashf al-ẓunūn*, 1:337.

19. al-'Abbāsī, *Ma'āhid al-tanṣīṣ*, 1:137.

20. al-Labābīdī, *al-Laṭā'if*, 13.

21. al-Labābīdī, *al-Laṭā'if*, 13.

22. al-Labābīdī, *al-Laṭā'if*, 13.

23. al-Sam'ānī, *al-Ansāb*, 5:213–14.

24. For more on refinement, being well dressed, and using perfumes as part of adab, etc., see al-Washshā', *al-Muwashshā*.

25. For more on this *maqāma*, see Bin Tyeer, "Literary Geography," 74–75.

26. For more on the dynamics of space and its configuration in the law and the city vs. wilderness as the "border of the law" in this *maqāma* and others, see Bin Tyeer, "Literary Geography."

27. For more on adab, see Makdisi, *Rise of Humanism*, 93; Bonebakker, "*Adab* and the Concept of *Belles-Lettres*"; Heinrichs, "Classification of the Sciences," 119–20; Holmberg, "*Adab* and Arabic Literature"; al-Musawi, *Medieval Islamic Republic of Letters*; Bin Tyeer, *The Qur'an and Aesthetics*, 7–18.

28. Carter, "Language Control," 71.
29. Carter, "Language Control," 72.
30. Makdisi, *Rise of Humanism*, 93.
31. Carter, "Language Control," 68.
32. Suzanne Stetkevych discusses al-Maʿarrī's linguistic capital in Pierre Bourdieu's terms. See Stetkevych, *Cooing of the Dove*, 155–56, 189.
33. al-Qarṭājannī, *Minhāj al-bulaghāʾ*, 30.
34. al-Qarṭājannī, *Minhāj al-bulaghāʾ*, 67.
35. al-Musawi, *Medieval Islamic Republic of Letters*, 112.
36. al-Ahdal, *al-Taḥarrī*, 39.
37. al-Musawi, *Medieval Islamic Republic of Letters*, 85.
38. al-Ṣaghānī, *al-Takmila*, 4:217.
39. al-Zabīdī, *Tāj al-ʿarūs*, 20:347.
40. al-Ṣaghānī, *al-Takmila*, 4:252.
41. Ibn Manẓūr, *Lisān al-ʿarab*, 10:16.
42. Ibn Sīdah, *al-Muḥkam*, 5:114; Ibn Manẓūr, *Lisān al-ʿarab*, 11:210.
43. al-Jāḥiẓ, *al-Ḥayawān*, 2:349.
44. al-Labābīdī, *al-Laṭāʾif*, 68.
45. al-Ṭaḥāwī, *Mukhtaṣar ikhtilāf al-ʿulamāʾ*, 2:123.
46. al-Jāḥiẓ, *al-Ḥayawān*, 2:283.
47. al-Jāḥiẓ, *al-Ḥayawān*, 2:317.
48. Ibn Manẓūr, *Lisān al-ʿarab*, 12:82.
49. al-Ahdal, *al-Taḥarrī*, 54.
50. Ibn Sīdah, *al-Mukhaṣṣaṣ*, 2:14. Ibn Sīdah quotes al-Aṣmaʿī on defining *al-ʿajūz* as "the blade." Al-Azharī agrees with this definition. Other lexicons mention *al-ʿajūz* as a part of the grip. Perhaps the blade makes sense since al-ʿUkbarī mentions that al-Mutanabbī refers to the sword as *al-shaykh* (the old man), which he explains as the name of the sword as well as *al-ʿajūz* (the old one); see al-ʿUkbarī, *Sharḥ Dīwān al-Mutanabbī*, 4:42. Also, Ibn Fāris relates this definition almost hesitatingly, since he says that if *al-ʿajūz* is one of the names of the sword, it would be because of its age (age of the blade), or the primordial nature of swords and wars since time immemorial. See Ibn Fāris, *Maqāyīs al-lugha*, 4:234.
51. Al-Zabīdī also explains all the uses of the word *ʿajūz* and among them is "war"; see *Tāj al-ʿarūs*, 15:207.
52. al-Labābīdī, *al-Laṭāʾif*, 220.
53. Ibn Qutayba, *Kitāb al-maʿānī*, 1:226.
54. al-Zabīdī, *Tāj al-ʿarūs*, 26:213.
55. Ibn Sīdah, *al-Mukhaṣṣaṣ*, 2:292; al-Ḥimyarī, *Shams al-ʿulūm*, 7:4796.
56. al-Ṣaghānī, *al-Takmila*, 3:352.
57. al-Azharī, *Tahdhīb al-lugha*, 3:218.
58. al-Zabīdī, *Tāj al-ʿarūs*, 35:501.
59. al-Rāzī, *Mukhtār al-ṣiḥāḥ*, 1:238.
60. al-Jāḥiẓ, *al-Ḥayawān*, 1:168.
61. al-Zabīdī, *Tāj al-ʿarūs*, 31:356.
62. al-Zabīdī, *Tāj al-ʿarūs*, 26:90.
63. al-Rāzī, *Mukhtār al-ṣiḥāḥ*, 1:222.
64. al-Hamadhānī, *Maqāmāt*, 30.

65. al-Hamadhānī, *Maqámát of al-Hamadháni*, 39.

66. Ibn Fāris, *Maqāyīs al-lugha*, 4:178.

67. أرى نار ليلى أو يراني بصيرها (I see the campfire of Laylā or her dog sees me); see Ibn al-Jawzī, *Nuzhat al-aʿyun*, 200; Ibn Fāris, *Maqāyīs al-lugha*, 4:15; al-Zabīdī, *Tāj al-ʿarūs*, 10:210.

68. al-Ḥarīrī, *Maqāmāt*, 286.

69. Ibn Ḥamdūn, *al-Tadhkira*, 2:313; al-Zamakhsharī, *Rabīʿ al-abrār*, 5:383; al-Ibshīhī, *al-Mustaṭraf*, 180; al-Labābīdī, *al-Laṭāʾif*, 14.

70. al-Rāzī, *Mukhtār al-ṣiḥāḥ*, 1:272.

71. al-Zabīdī, *Tāj al-ʿarūs*, 22:382; Ibn Manẓūr, *Lisān al-ʿarab*, 8:367.

72. Ibn Sallām, *Kitāb al-silāḥ*, 29.

73. al-Farāhīdī, *Kitāb al-ʿayn*, 2:275.

74. al-Zabīdī, *Tāj al-ʿarūs*, 4:146.

75. al-Thaʿlabī, *al-Kashf*, 6:163.

76. al-Ṣaghānī is the author of *al-ʿUbāb al-zākhir* referred to in the line. See al-Ṣaghānī, *al-Takmila*, 3:93.

77. Ibn Sīdah, *al-Muḥkam*, 8:287.

78. al-Suyūṭī, *al-Muzhir*, 1:400.

79. Spevack, "Jalāl al-Dīn al-Suyūṭī," 387, 389.

80. al-Thaʿālibī, *Thimār al-qulūb*, 252. I was only able to find this reference to al-Ṣūlī that al-Suyūṭī mentions in al-Thaʿālibī.

81. al-Labābīdī, *al-Laṭāʾif*, 116. *Al-rahdūn* is a bird that walks in circular motion. See al-Damīrī, *Ḥayāt al-ḥayawān*, 1:514.

82. al-Zawzanī, *Sharḥ al-muʿallaqāt*, 191.

83. Sells, *Desert Tracings*, 40.

84. *EI3*, under "Ibn Muljam."

85. al-Azhari, *Tahdhīb al lugha*, 3:218, 168, respectively; see also al-Ahdal, *al-Taḥarrī*, 91.

86. Ibn Sīdah, *al-Muḥkam*, 4:464.

87. Ibn Manẓūr, *Lisān al-ʿarab*, 8:276.

88. Lane, *Arabic-English Lexicon*, under "d-ʾ-l."

89. al-Zabīdī, *Tāj al-ʿarūs*, 19:43.

90. al-Zabīdī, *Tāj al-ʿarūs*, 17:276.

91. al-Zabīdī, *Tāj al-ʿarūs*, 31:19.

92. al-Ṣaghānī, *al-Takmila*, 1:157.

93. al-Zabīdī, *Tāj al-ʿarūs*, 22:347.

94. al-Zabīdī, *Tāj al-ʿarūs*, 19:43.

95. al-Zabīdī, *Tāj al-ʿarūs*, 22:347.

96. al-Zabīdī, *Tāj al-ʿarūs*, 1:477; al-Ahdal, *al-Taḥarrī*, 106.

97. al-Shāfiʿī, *al-Risāla*, 34ff.; al-Suyūṭī, *al-Muzhir*, 1:52–53.

98. al-Shāfiʿī, *al-Risāla*, 34ff.; al-Suyūṭī, *al-Muzhir*, 1:52–53.

99. See the use of the number seventy in Q.9:80, "It makes no difference [Prophet] whether you ask forgiveness for them or not: God will not forgive them even if you ask seventy times, because they reject God and His Messenger. God does not guide those who rebel against Him." Note also the famous Muslim adage attributed to Jaʿfar b. Muḥammad, encouraging the act of assuming the best in people and accepting their shortcomings, "Seek seventy excuses for your fellow brothers."

100. See the use of *ism* in Q.2:31–33, "He taught Adam all the names [of things] . . ."

101. al-Suyūṭī, *al-Muzhir*, 1:52–53.

102. al-Jāḥiẓ, *al-Ḥayawān*, 2:348.

103. See Sam Cumming, "Names," *Stanford Encyclopedia of Philosophy* (Fall 2019 Edition), https://plato.stanford.edu/archives/fall2019/entries/names/.

104. See Muhanna, "Why Was the 14th Century a Century of Arabic Encyclopaedism?"; Muhanna, *EI3*, under "Encyclopaedias, Arabic"; Muhanna, *World in a Book*.

105. al-Musawi, *Medieval Islamic Republic of Letters*, 109.

106. al-Musawi, *Medieval Islamic Republic of Letters*, 121.

107.

قلنا: هذا باطلٌ فإن القياس الشَّرعي إنما جاز إثباتُ الأحكام به بالإجماع المتَّفَق عليه وليس فيما تنازعْنا فيه إجماع وليس المقصودُ من إثبات الاسم اللغوي إثباتَ الحكم فإن القياسَ يجري في الأسامي اللغوية قبل الشَّرع على رأي مُثْبتي القياس في اللغة ولأن المعنى في القياس الشَّرعي مطَّرِد وفي القياس اللغوي غيرُ مطَّرد فإن البَنْج لا يسمى خمرا وإن كان يخامِرُ العقل والدار لا تسَمّى قارُورة وإن كانت الأشياء تستقر فيها والغرابُ لا يسمى أبْلَق وإن اجتمع فيه السوادُ والبياض

فليس القياسُ الشرعي كالقياس اللغوي في المعنى وإن تمسكوا بأنّ القياسَ يجري في المصادر نحو ضرب يضرِب ضربا وأكل يأكل أكلا فلسنا نسلم أن اللغة تثبت بالقياس وإنما تثبتُ نقلا عن العرب

We say: This is invalid, because legal analogy only allows the establishment of rulings by consensus, and there is no consensus in what we disputed about. The purpose of establishing the linguistic name is not to establish the ruling, because analogy applies to linguistic names before the law, according to the opinion of those who establish analogy in language; and because the meaning in legal analogy is consistent, while in linguistic analogy it is not. *Henbane* is not called *wine*, even if it intoxicates the mind; and *the house* is not called *a bottle*, even if things settle therein; and *the crow* is not called *piebald*, even if it is both black and white.

Legal analogy is not like linguistic analogy in meaning, even if they insist that analogy applies to verbal nouns, such as *ḍaraba-yaḍribu-ḍarban* [from the verb "to strike"] and *akala-ya'kulu-aklan* [from the verb "to eat"]. We do not accept that language is established by analogy, but rather it is established by transmission from the Arabs. (al-Suyūṭī, *al-Muzhir*, 1:50.)

108. al-Zarkashī, *al-Baḥr al-muḥīṭ*, 7:55.

109. Ibn Jinnī, *al-Khaṣā'iṣ*, 2:445.

110. al-Ṣāḥibī, *al-Ḥalba fī asmā' al-khayl*, 78.

111. Ibn Jinnī, *al-Khaṣā'iṣ*, 2:445.

112. al-Ma'arrī, *al-Lāmi'*, 21.

113. See 'Abbās, *Tārīkh al-naqd*, 390ff.

114. See Ibn Jinnī, *al-Khaṣā'iṣ*, 2:442–43; see also Jaffal, "al-Muṣṭalaḥ al-lughawī."

115. Nadja Germann, *EI3*, under "Lafẓ and ma'nā."

116. Muhanna, *World in a Book*, 8.

117. Zakī Mubārak mentions this and the dispute among the two men and several other litterateurs in his introduction to al-Qayrawānī, *Zahr al-ādāb*, 1:30.

118. Kilito, *Bi-ḥibr khafī*, 24.

119. al-Musawi, *Medieval Islamic Republic of Letters*, 100.

120. Quoted in al-Musawi, *Medieval Islamic Republic of Letters*, 100.

121. al-Musawi, *Medieval Islamic Republic of Letters*, 100.

122. al-Musawi, *Medieval Islamic Republic of Letters*, 117.

123. Muhanna, *World in a Book*, 26. Muhanna makes this observation about the expansiveness of adab within his discussion of al-Nuwayrī's conception of adab in the latter's encyclopedia as well as literary culture in the twelfth and thirteenth centuries; see *World in a Book*, 71–72.

124. See Rosenthal, *Knowledge Triumphant*. Carter also discusses this in the context of grammarians; see "Language Control," 73.

6. *ADAB* AS RESOLVE AND WILL

1. al-Shidyāq, *al-Sāq ʿalā al-sāq*, 65–67.
2. al-Shidyāq, *al-Sāq ʿalā al-sāq*, 65–67.
3. ʿĪsā, "al-Taʿdīl ʿinda al-Shidyāq."
4. al-Shidyāq, *al-Sāq ʿalā al-sāq*, 77; *Leg over Leg*, 1:23 (1.1.1).
5. al-Shidyāq, *al-Sāq ʿalā al-sāq*, 77; *Leg over Leg*, 1:23 (1.1.1).
6. Nadia al-Bagdadi discusses the disappearance of Arabic erotic writings in the nineteenth century in relationship to colonial modernity. See al-Bagdadi, "Eros and Etiquette."
7. *Leg over Leg*, 1:25 (1.1.4).
8. al-Shidyāq, *al-Sāq ʿalā al-sāq*, 78–79.
9. For more on the discussion of error from the perspective of the productive power of misreadings, see Johnson, "Archive of Errors."
10. Spitzer, "Linguistic Perspectivism."
11. Gerli, *Refiguring Authority*, 62.
12. Gerli, *Refiguring Authority*, 62.
13. al-Shidyaq, *al-Sāq ʿalā al-sāq*, 80.
14. al-Shidyāq, *al-Sāq ʿalā al-sāq*, 80.
15. Art historian Erwin Panofsky was the father of habitus; he defined habitus as it relates to Gothic architecture and Scholastic philosophy. Pierre Bourdieu translated his work and offered his own understanding and development of the term, which he took more into the corporeal and material rather than the intellectual and philological understanding of Panofsky. See Hanks, "Pierre Bourdieu."
16. MacIntyre, *After Virtue*, 222.
17. Johnson, "Archive of Errors," 34.
18. Guth, "Adab as the Art to Make the Right Choice."
19. Named after Irish statesman and philosopher Edmund Burke (1729–97), Burkeanism refers to conservatism that puts its trust in tradition. At its heart, Burkean conservatism does not have faith in the intellect of the average human (people are not as smart as they think) and therefore does not necessarily trust in social changes or in people's intellectual ability to lead that change. This is also why Burke did not support the French Revolution, because in his opinion it led to an incompetent government, which was also despotic. Burkeanism can thus be summarized as the exercise of precaution in the political sphere. This may apply elsewhere, especially with the belief in intellectual hierarchies and that people may be unfit to "think" for themselves.
20. Sacks, *Iterations of Loss*, 78.
21. al-Shidyāq, *al-Jāsūs*, 3.

22. al-Shidyāq, *al-Jāsūs*, 3.
23. al-Shidyāq, *al-Jāsūs*, 3.
24. al-Shidyāq, *al-Jāsūs*, 3.
25. al-Shidyāq, *al-Jāsūs*, 3.
26. al-Shidyāq, *al-Jāsūs*, 3.
27. al-Shidyāq, *al-Jāsūs*, 3.
28. al-Shidyāq, *al-Sāq ʿalā al-sāq*, 85.
29. al-Maʿarrī, *Muʿjiz Aḥmad*, 3:276.
30. al-Shidyāq, *al-Sāq ʿalā al-sāq*, 446.
31. al-Shidyāq, *al-Sāq ʿalā al-sāq*, 446.
32. al-Shidyāq, *al-Sāq ʿalā al-sāq*, 448.
33. *Leg over Leg*, 3:111 (3.10.3).
34. *Leg over Leg*, 3:111 (3.10.3); al-Shidyāq, *al-Sāq ʿalā al-sāq*, 448.
35. Ernst Bloch speaks about how hope must be disappointable "or else it would not be hope." It is inseparable from "specific disappointability [*Enttäuschbarkeit*] of informed and self-informed *docto spes* (educated hope)." See Bloch, "Can Hope Be Disappointed?"
36. al-Shidyāq, *al-Sāq ʿalā al-sāq*, 454.
37. Ibn Sīnā, *al-Qānūn*, 2:311.
38. Ibn Ṭabāṭabā, *ʿIyār al-shiʿr*, 17–18.
39. It is also spelled with a *ḥāʾ*. al-Khafājī, *Sharḥ Durrat al-ghawwāṣ*, 604.
40. Ibn Qutayba, *ʿUyūn al-akhbār*, 2:173.
41. For more on the discussion of *qubḥ* and its aesthetic and moral connotations, see Bin Tyeer, *The Qur'an and Aesthetics*.
42. al-Shidyāq, *al-Sāq ʿalā al-sāq*, 458; *Leg over Leg*, 3:120–21.
43. al-Shidyāq, *al-Sāq ʿalā al-sāq*, 459.
44. Humphrey Davies translates the subtitle as "Days, Months, and Years Spent in Critical Examination of the Arabs and Their Non-Arab Peers." He does not stress the "*ʿujm/ʿajam*" of Arabs. See *Leg over Leg*.
45. I rely on Davies's translation for this couplet and all *Leg over Leg* quotes unless stated otherwise.
46. See Mitchell, "Stage of Modernity," 11; Marx, *Capital*, 1:703.
47. Lipking, "Inventing the Common Reader," 165.
48. Lipking, "Inventing the Common Reader," 163.
49. Boswell, *Life of Johnson*, 1387.
50. Black, *The Falls of Clyde*, 215.
51. Kernan, *Samuel Johnson*, 216.
52. See Said, *Humanism*, 68.
53. Hassan, *Tayeb Salih*, 2–3.
54. Hassan, *Tayeb Salih*, 3.
55. Najm, *al-Qiṣṣa*, 231–32.
56. Najm, *al-Qiṣṣa*, 232.
57. Ghose, *Shakespeare in Jest*, 9–10; see also Baldo and Karremann, *Memory and Affect*, 127.
58. Rushdī, *Fann al-qiṣṣa*, 120.
59. Emile Habibi, quoted in ʿAṭṭiya, "Muḥāwalāt ʿalā ṭarīq taʾṣīl al-riwāya al-ʿarabiyya," 139.

60. Salih, *Season of Migration*, 45.

61. Fanon, *The Wretched of the Earth*, 210–11.

62. "Gamāl al-Ghiṭānī: al-insāniyya kulluhā milkī wa-uwwad an aktub ruwāya mithl 'Moby Dick,'" *al-Ḥayāt*, June 9, 2015, https://langue-arabe.fr/حوار-مع-الكاتب-المصري-جمال-الغيطاني-يلخص-فيه-مشوار-حياته-بعد-أكثر-من-50-كتاباً.

63. Raḍwā ʿĀshūr, Robin Creswell, and David Fieni all describe and argue for the consideration of *Leg over Leg* as the first Arabic novel. See ʿĀshūr, *al-Ḥadātha al-mumkina*; Fieni, *Decadent Orientalisms*; Creswell, "The First Great Arabic Novel."

64. Bakhtin, *Dialogic Imagination*, 269.

65. *Leg over Leg*, 2:111.

66. al-Jāḥiẓ, *al-Bayān*, 1:13–16, 52, 70–80.

67. al-Zabīdī, *Tāj al-ʿarūs*, 15:528.

68. Davies reads these substitutions as a lisp on the narrator's part; see *Leg over Leg*, 2:426.

69. Famous examples of *qalb* in the Qur'an: Q.21:33 (*kullun fī falak*); 74:3 (*wa-rabbaka fa-kabbir*). Al-Ḥarīrī, and many others, used this in his *maqāmāt* as well.

70. Sacks, *Iterations of Loss*, 91.

71. I warmly thank Nancy Charley at the Royal Asiatic Society for providing me with the list of publications of the Society's Oriental Translation Fund since its inception. I could not get hold of the minutes, unfortunately. Email message to author, May 13, 2020.

72. Pargiter, *Centenary Volume of the Royal Asiatic Society*, iv.

73. Willcocks coproduced a colloquial Egyptian translation of the Bible down to the reference of the first edition on the front cover as "al-ṭabʿa al-awwalāniyya" instead of "al-ṭabʿa al-ūlā." See Hanna, "When Jesus Speaks Colloquial Egyptian Arabic."

74. Mitchell, "What Is Educated Spoken Arabic?"; Mitchell, *Colonising Egypt*. See also Stadlbauer, "Language Ideologies."

75. Ngũgĩ wa Thiong'o, *Decolonising the Mind*.

76. al-Shidyāq, *al-Jāsūs*, 5.

77. al-Jāḥiẓ, *al-Ḥayawān*, 1:60.

78. *Leg over Leg*, 1:14.

79. For a discussion on these typologies and their use in narrative, see Bin Tyeer, "The Qur'an and the Aesthetics of *Adab*," 287–89.

80. See Gadamer, *Hermeneutics*, 16.

81. Benjamin, "On Language as Such," 64.

82. al-Subkī, *ʿArūs al-afrāḥ*, 2:128.

83. See, for instance, al-Fanārī, *Fuṣūl al-badāʾiʿ*, 1:85; al-Māturīdī, *Taʾwīlāt*, 1:277; al-Suyūṭī, *al-Itqān*, 4:218.

84. al-Subkī, *ʿArūs al-afrāḥ*, 1:136–37. See also al-Tahānawī, *Kashshāf*, 2:1459ff.

85. *Leg over Leg*, 2:284 (2.13.5).

86. For more on this technique, known as *taḥsīn al-qabīḥ wa-taqbīḥ al-ḥasan*, see van Gelder, "Beautifying the Ugly and Uglifying the Beautiful."

87. *Leg over Leg*, 2:288 (2.13.13).

88. *Leg over Leg*, 2:289 (2.13.13).

89. *Leg over Leg*, 3:154–55 (3.13.16).

90. See chapter 2.

91. *Leg over Leg*, 4:312 (4.13.5).

92. *Leg over Leg*, 4:313 (4.13.9).

93. See Shaaban, *Voices Revealed*, quoted in Radmān, "al-Naqd al-ʿarabī," 170.

94. Jābir ʿAṣfūr, "Hawāmish li-l-kitāba: sibāq ʿalā al-riyāḍa," *al-Ḥayāt*, November 17, 2004.

95. Radmān, "al-Naqd al-ʿarabī," 170.

96. Stroud, "Flaming Bourdieu," 261.

97. Kerfoot and Hyltenstam, "Introduction," 7.

98. Kerfoot and Hyltenstam, "Introduction," 6.

99. al-Shidyāq, *al-Sāq ʿalā al-sāq*, 72. Davies translates this as follows: "The classifier is no classifier / if he doesn't put things into classes." *Leg over Leg*, 1:19. The original Arabic contains no diacritics (*tashkīl*) and therefore the line could be read both ways and still be legible (*muṣannif* or *muṣannaf*) in the same way al-Shidyāq used *ʿajam* or *ʿujm* in the subtitle. Al-Shidyāq's employment of ambiguity (*īhām*) is obvious here. In a personal correspondence with the late Humphrey Davies, I discussed this *īhām* of *muṣannaf* that means or reads book, authored book, or classes (*aṣnāf*, sing. *ṣinf*) as types of books/genres. In this instance, the offered translation read the word as *al-muṣannif* (classifier) not *al-muṣannaf* (book). Al-Shidyāq played on the word to include both his authored book (*muṣannaf*) and the genres it espouses (*ṣunūf*). The context of the poem constituting the proem in this section is a defense of his own book since he authored it. This can only point to "another of al-Shidyāq's endless games" as Davies elegantly put it. Email messages to author, May 29–June 1, 2021.

100. al-Bagdadi, "Cultural Function," 394.

101. For more on this argument in the context of Islam and liberalism, see Massad, *Islam in Liberalism*. See also Ahmad, *Religion as Critique*, for an argument on the evolution of medieval religious conversions of non-Christians in the past to the secularization of this conversion rhetoric after the Enlightenment into the present-day discourse of Enlightenment, reason, civilization, modernism, democracy, etc.

102. El-Ariss, "On Cooks and Crooks," 32.

103. El-Ariss, "On Cooks and Crooks," 32.

104. Kāẓim, *al-Maqāmāt*, 159.

105. For more on this, see Bin Tyeer, "Textual Traces."

106. Caren Kaplan coins this term in the context of her argument that hybrid autobiographical forms are a strategic political move for women, ethnic, and immigrant authors who do not wish to narrate their lives according to culturally available scripts and forms. Kaplan, "Resisting Autobiography." Kamran Rastegar also speaks about how *Leg over Leg*, by "mixing the genres of autobiography and travelogue with digressions into satire and reportage, composed in both prose and poetry, the text meanders around unanswered questions exploring the limits of narratives of subjective transformations." Rastegar, *Literary Modernity*, 103.

107. ʿĀshūr, *al-Ḥadātha al-mumkina*, 13.

108. ʿĀshūr, *al-Ḥadātha al-mumkina*, 68.

109. See, for instance, Sacks, *Iterations of Loss*; El-Ariss, *Trials of Arab Modernity*; al-Bagdadi, "Print."

110. See Ibn Manẓūr, *Lisān al-ʿarab*. Even in 1870, Buṭrus al-Bustānī relates this term in his *Muḥīṭ al-Muḥīṭ* as referring to financial inheritance.

111. Massad, *Desiring Arabs*, 17.

CODA: THE SUSTAINABILITY OF *ADAB*

1. Hussein, *Adīb*, 14.
2. Hussein, *Adīb*, 24.
3. See also Joseph Massad's discussion of *mujūn* as it pertains to this novel in *Desiring Arabs*, 62ff. Michael Allan discusses this novel in the context of what he describes as a new sensibility of "literariness" in the context of "provincialism" and "cosmopolitanism" in colonial Egypt; see Allan, *In the Shadow of World Literature*, 115–30.
4. See, for instance, Hussein, *Adīb*, 41.
5. Hussein, *Adīb*, 41.
6. For more on the *aṭlāl* and in Arabic poetry, see Stetkevych, *The Zephyrs of Najd*.
7. Hussein, *Adīb*, 37.
8. Hussein, *Adīb*, 38.
9. Márquez, *One Hundred Years of Solitude*, 29.
10. Rascovsky et al., "'The Quicksand of Forgetfulness.'"
11. Hussein, *Ḥadīth al-arbiʿāʾ*, 2:475.
12. Taha Hussein, "Kayfa nafham al-tārīkh," *al-Siyāsa*, February 22, 1923.
13. al-Māzinī, *Qabḍ al-rīḥ*, 29–33.
14. Ibrāhīm al-Māzinī, "Ṭahā Ḥussein fī mīzān al-tashkīk," *al-Zahrāʾ*, no. 10, October 1, 1925, 612–17.
15. Holtzen and Hill, "Gadamer's Hermeneutics of Trust," 91.
16. Hussein, *Adīb*, 128.
17. Shakespeare, *King Lear*, 76.
18. Percival, "Descartes' Model of Mind," 1–2.
19. Percival, "Descartes' Model of Mind," 1–2.
20. Hussein, *Adıb*, 95.
21. Dostoevsky, *Crime and Punishment*, 80–81.
22. Schmitter, "17th and 18th Century Theories of Emotions."
23. See Gadamer, *Truth and Method*, 83.
24. See Gadamer, *Truth and Method*, 83–87.
25. Davey, *Unquiet Understanding*, 18.
26. Hussein, *Adīb*, 84.
27. Khoury, *al-Dhākira al-mafqūda*, 30.
28. Hussein, *Adīb*, 95.
29. Hussein, *Adīb*, 108.
30. See Nietzsche's *Birth of Tragedy*. Nietzsche presents a duality between the Greek mythical figures of Dionysus, god of the grape harvest, insanity, ritual madness, and religious ecstasy but also theater and festivals in ancient Greek religion. Euripides's tragedy *The Bacchae* offers an excellent depiction of Dionysus and his cult and the gradual slip into religious, ritual, and sexual ecstasy to the point of losing all reason and destruction of self and others (which culminates in the character of the mother Agave losing reason, and in a moment of ecstasy in her Bacchic ritual decapitates her own son, Pentheus); the loss of reason to sexual ecstasy is reminiscent of the character in Hussein's novel. Apollo is the god of sun, light, and poetry. Known for his rule over intellect, education, medical, and healing powers; he stands in Nietzsche's account as a necessary balance against the chthonic forces of the Dionysian impulses, which, if left unchecked, may lead to ruin.

31. Antoon, *Poetics of the Obscene*, 7–10.
32. Quoted in Antoon, *Poetics of the Obscene*, 8.
33. Assmann, "Canon and Archive."
34. Asad, "Anthropology of Islam," 14.
35. Greenblatt and Gallagher, quoted in Assmann, "Canon and Archive," 100–102.
36. Benjamin, "The Work of Art in the Age of Mechanical Reproduction."
37. Hodgson, *Venture of Islam*, 3:419.
38. Assmann, "Canon and Archive," 97.
39. Assmann, "Canon and Archive," 105–6.
40. Assmann, "Canon and Archive," 97–98.
41. Ibn Manẓūr, *Mukhtaṣar tārīkh Dimashq li-Ibn ʿAsākir*, 21:389.
42. al-Bīrūnī, *al-Āthār al-bāqiya*, 5.
43. al-Bīrūnī, *al-Āthār al-bāqiya*, 4.
44. Ibn Khaldūn, *Tārīkh Ibn Khaldūn*, 1:599.
45. Sanni, "Filiation."
46. Saint Augustine, *Confessions*, 221–45. This is in Book 11, where Augustine discusses the nature of time itself and its relationship to eternity, motion of objects, the soul and mind.
47. Kant, "Idea for a Universal History with a Cosmopolitan Purpose," 41.
48. al-Jabri, "al-Māḍī wa-l-mustaqbal . . . ayyahumā yaḥkum al-ākhar?," part 1.
49. von Herder, *Outlines of a Philosophy of the History of Man*, 226.
50. Rosemann, "Wandering in the Path of the Averroean System," 185.
51. Ibn Rushd, *al-Ḍarūrī fī al-siyāsa*, 138–39; al-Jabri, "al-Māḍī wa-l-mustaqbal . . . ayyahumā yaḥkum al-ākhar?," part 1.
52. al-Jabri, "al-Māḍī wa-l-mustaqbal . . . ayyahumā yaḥkum al-ākhar?," part 1.
53. Nietzsche, *On the Advantage and Disadvantage of History for Life*, 9.
54. Nietzsche, *On the Advantage and Disadvantage of History for Life*, 9.
55. Nietzsche, *On the Advantage and Disadvantage of History for Life*, 12.
56. Nietzsche, *On the Advantage and Disadvantage of History for Life*, 12.
57. Nietzsche, *On the Advantage and Disadvantage of History for Life*, 12.
58. Hussein, "Masīrat al-shāʿir al-kubrā," 91–104 ["La grande aventure d'un poet"].
59. Hussein, *Mustaqbal al-thaqāfa fī Miṣr*, 43.
60. See, for example, Human Rights Watch, "Taliban's Attack on Girls' Education Harming Afghanistan's Future," September 17, 2024; Wilson Center, "Preventing the Next Kabul: Confronting the Houthi's Violent Suppression of Women in Yemen," March 23, 2023; Carnegie Endowment for International Peace, "Gender Segregation at Sanaa University: A Worrying Trend for Yemen," September 25, 2023; NPR, "'The Taliban Took Our Last Hope': College Education Is Banned for Women in Afghanistan," December 20, 2022; Human Rights Watch, "Nigeria: Boko Haram Targeting Schools," March 7, 2012.
61. See Nadwi, *al-Muḥaddithāt: The Women Scholars in Islam*.
62. Ibn Kathīr, *Musnad al-Fārūq*, 2:501.
63. See, for instance, Hambly, *Women in the Medieval Islamic World*; Ḥamza, *Nisāʾ ḥakamna al-Yaman*.
64. See, for instance, al-Dhahabī, *Siyar aʿlām al-nubalāʾ*, 2:278, where he discusses a certain Nusayba b. Kaʿb who lost her arm in battle and was described as a brave warrior, scholar, wife, and mother.

65. McLarney, "Freedom, Justice, and the Power of *Adab*."
66. McLarney, "Freedom, Justice, and the Power of *Adab*."
67. Ryle-Hodges, "Muḥammad ʿAbduh's Notion of Political *Adab*."
68. Ryle-Hodges, "Muḥammad ʿAbduh's Notion of Political *Adab*," 360.
69. Ryle-Hodges, "Muḥammad ʿAbduh's Notion of Political *Adab*," 344.

BIBLIOGRAPHY

ʿAbbās, Iḥsān. *Tārīkh al-naqd al-adabī ʿinda al-ʿarab*. 4th ed. Dār al-Thaqāfa, 1983.

al-ʿAbbāsī, ʿAbd al-Raḥīm. *Maʿāhid al-tanṣīṣ ʿalā shawāhid al-talkhīṣ*. Edited by Muḥammad Muḥyī al-Dīn ʿAbd al-Ḥamīd. 2 vols. ʿĀlam al-Kutub, n.d.

ʿAbd al-Raḥmān, ʿĀʾisha. *Abū al-ʿAlāʾ al-Maʿarrī*. al-Muʾassasa al-Miṣriyya al-ʿĀmma, 1965.

Abdel Haleem, M. A. S., trans. *The Qurʾan*. Revised ed. Oxford University Press, 2010.

Adamson, Peter. "A False Start? The Two Beginnings of Ibn Ṭufayl's *Ḥayy ibn Yaqẓān*." Unpublished paper.

Adamson, Peter. *al-Kindī*. Oxford University Press, 2007.

Adamson, Peter, and Alexander Key. "Philosophy of Language in the Medieval Arabic Tradition." In *Linguistic Content: New Essays on the History of Philosophy of Language*, edited by Margaret Cameron and Robert J. Stainton, 74–99. Oxford University Press, 2015.

al-Ahdal, Muḥammad ʿAbd al-Raḥmān Shamīla. *al-Taḥarrī fī al-tabarrī min maʿarrat al-Maʿarrī*. Dār al-Minhāj, 2011.

Ahmad, Irfan. *Religion as Critique: Islamic Critical Thinking from Mecca to the Marketplace*. University of North Carolina Press, 2017.

Ahmed, Asad Q. "Islam's Invented Golden Age." Open Democracy, October 28, 2013. https://www.opendemocracy.net/en/openindia/islams-invented-golden-age.

Ahmed, Asad Q. "Post-Classical Philosophical Commentaries/Glosses: Innovation in the Margins." *Oriens* 41, no. 3–4 (2013): 317–48.

Ahmed, Asad Q. "The *Sullam al-ʿUlūm* of Muḥibballāh al-Bihārī (d. 1707): A Milestone in Arabo-Islamic Logic." In *The Oxford Handbook of Islamic Philosophy*, edited by Khaled El-Rouayheb and Sabine Schmidtke, 488–508. Oxford University Press, 2016.

Ahmed, Asad Q. "Systematic Growth in Sustained Error: A Case Study in the Dynamism of Post-Classical Islamic Scholasticism." In *The Islamic Scholarly Tradition: Studies in History, Law, and Thought in Honor of Professor Michael Allan Cook*, edited by Asad Q. Ahmed, Michael Bonner, and Behnam Sadeghi, 343–78. Brill, 2011.

Ahmed, Shahab. *What Is Islam? The Importance of Being Islamic*. Princeton University Press, 2016.

ʿAlī b. Khalaf. *Mawādd al-bayān*. Edited by Ḥātim Ṣāliḥ al-Ḍāmin. Dār al-Bashāʾir li-l-Ṭibāʿa wa-l-Nashr wa-l-Tawzīʿ, 2002.

Allan, Michael. "How *Adab* Became Literary: Formalism, Orientalism and the Institutions of World Literature." *Journal of Arabic Literature* 43 (2012): 172–96.

Allan, Michael. *In the Shadow of World Literature: Sites of Reading Colonial Egypt*. Princeton University Press, 2016.

Alphonso-Karakala, John B. "Facets of Panchatantra." *Indian Literature* 18, no. 2 (April–June 1975): 73–91.

al-ʿAmīdī, Abū Saʿīd. *al-Ibāna ʿan sariqāt al-Mutanabbī lafẓan wa-maʿnan*. Edited by Ibrāhīm al-Dusūqī al-Bisāṭī. Dār al-Maʿārif, 1961.

Amīn, Aḥmad. *Fayḍ al-khāṭir*. 8 vols. Muʾassasat Hindāwī li-l-Taʿlīm wa-l-Thaqāfa, 2017.

al-Anbārī, ʿAbd al-Raḥmān b. Muḥammad. *Nuzhat al-alibbāʾ fī ṭabaqāt al-udabāʾ*. Edited by Ibrāhīm al-Sāmirrāʾī. Maktabat al-Manār, 1985.

al-Anṣārī. *al-Nawādir fī al-lugha*. Edited by Muḥammad ʿAbd al-Qādir Aḥmad. Dār al-Shurūq, 1981.

ʿAntarah ibn Shaddād. *War Songs*. Edited by James E. Montgomery. Translated by James E. Montgomery with Richard Sieburth. New York University Press, 2018.

Antoon, Sinan. *The Poetics of the Obscene in Premodern Arabic Poetry: Ibn al-Ḥajjāj and Sukhf*. Palgrave Macmillan, 2014.

al-ʿAqqād, ʿAbbās Maḥmūd. "Tabārak razzāq al-barriyya." *al-Risāla*, no. 591 (1944): 1–4.

Aravamudan, Srinivas. "East-West Fiction as World Literature: The 'Hayy' Problem Reconfigured." *Eighteenth-Century Studies* 47, no. 2 (Winter 2014): 195–231.

Arḥīla, ʿAbbās Aḥmad. *Hājis al-ibdāʿ fī al-turāth*. al-Muʾassasa al-ʿArabiyya li-l-Fikr wa-l-Ibdāʿ, 2017.

Asad, Talal. "The Idea of an Anthropology of Islam." *Qui Parle* 17, no. 2 (Spring/Summer 2009): 1–30.

Asad, Talal. *Formations of the Secular: Christianity, Islam, Modernity*. Stanford University Press, 2003.

ʿĀshūr, Raḍwā. *al-Ḥadātha al-mumkina*. Dār al-Shurūq, 2009.

al-Aṣmaʿī, ʿAbd al-Malik b. Qurayb. *al-Aṣmaʿiyyāt*. Edited by Aḥmad Muḥammad Shākir and ʿAbd al-Salām Muḥammad Hārūn. Dār al-Maʿārif, 1993.

al-ʿAsqalānī, Ibn Ḥajar. *Lisān al-mīzān*. Edited by Dāʾirat al-Maʿārif al-Niẓāmiyya—India. 7 vols. Muʾassasat al-Aʿlamī li-l-Maṭbūʿāt, 1971.

Assmann, Aleida. "Canon and Archive." In *Cultural Memory Studies: An International and Interdisciplinary Handbook*, edited by Astrid Erll and Ansgar Nünning, 97–108. De Gruyter, 2010.

Attar, Samar. *The Vital Roots of European Enlightenment: Ibn Tufayl's Influence on Modern Western Thought*. Lexington Books, 2010.

ʿAṭṭiya, Aḥmad Muḥammad. "Muḥāwalāt ʿalā ṭarīq taʾṣīl al-riwāya al-ʿarabiyya." *Ibdāʿ* (January 1985).

Auerbach, Erich. "Odysseus' Scar." In *Mimesis: The Representation of Reality in Western Literature*, translated by Willard R. Trask, 3–23. Princeton University Press, 1953.

Auerbach, Erich. "Philology and Weltliteratur." Translated by Marie Said and Edward Said. *The Centennial Review* 13, no. 1 (Winter 1969): 1–17.

al-ʿAynī, Badr al-Dīn. *ʿUmdat al-qārī sharḥ Ṣaḥīḥ al-Bukhārī*. 25 vols. Dār Iḥyāʾ al-Turāth al-ʿArabī, n.d.

al-Azharī, Muḥammad b. Aḥmad. *Tahdhīb al-lugha*. Edited by Muḥammad ʿIwaḍ. 8 vols. Dār Iḥyāʾ al-Turāth al-ʿArabī, 2001.

al-Badīʿī, Yūsuf. *Awj al-taḥarrī ʿan ḥaythiyyat Abī al-ʿAlāʾ al-Maʿarrī*. Edited by Ibrāhīm al-Kīlānī. Maṭbaʿat al-Taraqqī, 1944.

al-Bagdadi, Nadia. "The Cultural Function of Fiction: From the Bible to Libertine Literature—Historical Criticism and Social Critique in Ahmad Faris al-Shidyaq." *Arabica* 46 (1999): 375–401.

al-Bagdadi, Nadia. "Eros and Etiquette: Reflections on the Ban of a Central Theme in Nineteenth-Century Arab Writings." In *Sex and Desire in Muslim Cultures: Beyond Norms and Transgression from the Abbasids to the Present Day*, edited by Aymon Kreil, Lucia Sorbera, and Serena Tolino, 113–30. I.B. Tauris, 2021.

al-Bagdadi, Nadia. "Print, Script and Free-Thinking in Arabic Letters of the 19th Century: The Case of al-Shidyāq." *Al-Abhath* 48–49 (2001): 99–122.

al-Baghawī, Ḥusayn b. Masʿūd. *Maʿālim al-tanzīl fī tafsīr al-Qurʾān*. Edited by ʿAbd al-Razzāq al-Mahdī. 5 vols. Dār Iḥyāʾ al-Turāth al-ʿArabī, 1999.

al-Baghdādī, ʿAbd al-Qādir b. ʿUmar. *Khizānat al-adab wa-lubb lubāb lisān al-ʿarab*. Edited by ʿAbd al-Salām Muḥammad Hārūn. 13 vols. Maktabaṭ al-Khānjī, 1997.

Bakhtin, Mikhail M. *The Dialogic Imagination: Four Essays*. Translated by Caryl Emerson and Michael Holquist. University of Texas Press, 1981.

Baldo, Jonathan, and Isabel Karremann, eds. *Memory and Affect in Shakespeare's England*. Cambridge University Press, 2023.

Bar-Itzhak, Chen. "Intellectual Captivity." *Journal of World Literature* 5, no. 1 (2020): 81–96.

Barolini, Teodolinda. "*Paradiso* 33: Invisible Ink." *Baroliniano*, Digital Dante. Columbia University Libraries, 2014. https://digitaldante.columbia.edu/dante/divine-comedy/paradiso/paradiso-33/.

Bauer, Thomas. "Ayna hādhā min al-Mutanabbī! Toward an Aesthetics of Mamluk Literature." *Mamluk Studies Review* 17 (2013): 5–22.

Bauer, Thomas. *A Culture of Ambiguity: An Alternative History of Islam*. Translated by Hinrich Biesterfeldt and Tricia Tunstall. Columbia University Press, 2021.

Bauer, Thomas. "Mamluk Literature as a Means of Communication." In *Ubi sumus? Quo vademus? Mamluk Studies: State of the Art*, edited by Stephan Conermann, 23–56. Vandenhoeck & Ruprecht, 2013.

Bauer, Thomas. "Mamluk Literature: Misunderstandings and New Approaches." *Mamluk Studies Review* 9, no. 2 (2005): 105–32.

Bellino, Francesca. "Developing a Knowledge System Based on Adab: Birds Fluttering from Ibn Qutayba's *Adab al-Kātib* to the *ʿUyūn al-Akhbār*." In *L'Adab, toujours recommencé: "Origins," Transmissions, and Metamorphoses of Adab Literature*, edited by Francesca Bellino, Catherine Mayeur-Jaouen, and Luca Patrizio, 216–55. Brill, 2023.

Benjamin, Walter. *Illuminations: Essays and Reflections*. Edited by Hannah Arendt. Translated by Harry Zohn. Schocken Books, 1968.

Benjamin, Walter. "On Language as Such." In *Selected Writings, Volume 1: 1913–1926*, edited by Marcus Bullock and Michael W. Jennings, 62–74. Harvard University Press, 1996.

Ben-Zaken, Avner. *Reading Ḥayy Ibn-Yaqẓān: A Cross-Cultural History of Autodidactism*. Johns Hopkins University Press, 2011.

Bin Tyeer, Sarah R. "The Literary Geography of Meaning in the *Maqāmāt* of al-Hamadhānī and al-Ḥarīrī." In *The City in Arabic Literature: Classical and Modern Perspectives*, edited by Nizar F. Hermes and Gretchen Head, 63–80. Edinburgh University Press, 2018.

Bin Tyeer, Sarah R. "The Qur'an and the Aesthetics of *Adab*: *Ḥikāyat Abī'l-Qāsim al-Baghdādī* by Abū'l-Muṭahhar al-Azdī (fl. Fifth/Eleventh Century)." In *The Qur'an and Adab: The Shaping of Literary Traditions in Classical Islam*, edited by Nuha Alshaar, 273–312. Oxford University Press in association with the Institute of Ismaili Studies, 2019.

Bin Tyeer, Sarah R. *The Qur'an and the Aesthetics of Premodern Arabic Prose*. Palgrave Macmillan, 2016.

Bin Tyeer, Sarah R. "Textual Traces: Historical Consciousness between Intertextuality and Filiation." [In Arabic.] *al-Markaz: Majallat al-Dirāsāt al ʿArabiyya* 1 (2022): 204–26.

Bin Tyeer, Sarah R., and Claire Gallien, eds. *Islam and New Directions in World Literature*. Edinburgh University Press, 2022.

al-Bīrūnī. *al-Āthār al-bāqiya ʿan al-qurūn al-khāliya*. Maktabat al-Thaqāfa al-Dīniyya, 2008.

Black, John. *The Falls of Clyde, or The Fairies: A Scottish Dramatic Pastoral in Five Acts*. Edinburgh, 1806.

Blankinship, Kevin, and Aglae Pizzone. "Self-Commentary as Defensive Strategy in the Works of John Tzetzes (d. 1180 CE) and Abū al-ʿAlāʾ al-Maʿarrī (d. 1057 CE)." *Philological Encounters* 8 (2022): 1–37.

Blankinship, Khalid Yahya. *The End of the Jihad State: The Reign of Hishām Ibn ʿAbd al-Malik and the Collapse of the Umayyads*. SUNY Press, 1994.

Bloch, Ernst. "Can Hope Be Disappointed?" In *Literary Essays*, translated by Andrew Joron et al., 339–45. Stanford University Press, 1998.

de Blois, François. *Burzōy's Voyage to India and the Origin of the Book of Kalīlah wa Dimnah*. Royal Asiatic Society, 1990.

Bonebakker, S. A. "*Adab* and the Concept of *Belles-Lettres*." In *Abbasid Belles-Lettres*, edited by Julia Ashtiany, T. M. Johnstone, J. D. Latham, and R. B. Serjeant, 16–30. Cambridge University Press, 1990.

Bonebakker, S. A. "Early Arabic Literature and the Term *Adab*." *Jerusalem Studies in Arabic and Islam* 5 (1984): 389–421.

Boswell, James. *Life of Johnson*. Edited by R. W. Chapman. Oxford University Press, 1998.

Brockelmann, Carl. "Die Aufgabe der Literaturgeschichte." In *Geschichte der Arabischen Litteratur*. Brill, 2018. https://doi.org/10.1163/1877-0037_brock_d1e22.

Bürgel, J. C. "Ibn Ṭufayl and His *Ḥayy ibn Yaqẓān*: A Turning Point in Arabic Philosophical Writing." In *The Legacy of Muslim Spain*, edited by Salma Khadra Jayyusi, 830–48. Brill, 1992.

Carter, Michael G. "Language Control as People Control in Medieval Islam: The Aims of the Grammarians in Their Cultural Context." *Al-Abhath* 31 (1983): 65–84.

Carter, Michael G. "The Use of Verse as a Pedagogical Medium, Principally in the Teaching of Grammar." In *Knowledge and Education in Classical Islam: Religious Learning between Continuity and Change*, edited by Sebastian Günther, 2 vols., 1:449–74. Brill, 2020.

Chittick, William C. *The Sufi Doctrine of Rumi*. World Wisdom, 2005.

Clark, S. H. "'The Whole Internal World His Own': Locke and Metaphor Reconsidered." *Journal of the History of Ideas* 59, no. 2 (April 1998): 241–65.

Clark, Stephen R. L. *Plotinus: Myth, Metaphor, and Philosophical Practice*. University of Chicago Press, 2018.

Conrad, Lawrence I. "Through the Thin Veil: On the Question of Communication and the Socialization of Knowledge in *Ḥayy ibn Yaqẓān*." In *The World of Ibn Ṭufayl: Interdisciplinary Perspectives on Ḥayy ibn Yaqẓān*, edited by Lawrence I. Conrad, 238–66. Brill, 1996.

Conrad, Lawrence I., ed. *The World of Ibn Ṭufayl: Interdisciplinary Perspectives on Ḥayy ibn Yaqẓān*. Brill, 1996.

Cooperson, Michael. "Ibn al-Muqaffaʿ." In *Medieval Islamic Encyclopedia*, vol. 1, edited by Joseph W. Meri, 346. Routledge, 2006.

Creswell, Robin. "The First Great Arabic Novel." *New York Review*, October 8, 2015. https://www.nybooks.com/articles/2015/10/08/first-great-arabic-novel/.

Dabashi, Hamid. "It Was in China, Late One Moonless Night." *Social Research* 70, no. 3 (Fall 2003): 935–80.

Ḍaif, Shawqī. *al-ʿAṣr al-jāhilī*. Dār al-Maʿārif, 1960.

al-Damīrī, Muḥammad b. Mūsā. *Ḥayāt al-ḥayawān al-kubrā*. 2 vols. Dār al-Kutub al-ʿIlmiyya, 2003.

al-Dārimī, ʿAbd Allāh b. ʿAbd al-Raḥmān. *Musnad al-Dārimī*. Edited by Ḥusayn Salīm Asad al-Dārānī. 6 vols. Dār al-Mughnī, 2000.

Davey, Nicholas. *Unquiet Understanding: Gadamer's Philosophical Hermeneutics*. SUNY Press, 2006.

DeNicola, Daniel R. *Understanding Ignorance: The Surprising Impact of What We Don't Know*. MIT Press, 2017.

al-Dhahabī, Muḥammad b. Aḥmad. *Siyar aʿlām al-nubalāʾ*. Edited by Shuʿayb al-Arnāʾūṭ et al. 25 vols. Muʾassasat al-Risāla, 1985.

al-Dhahabī, Muḥammad b. Aḥmad. *Tārīkh al-Islām*. Edited by ʿUmar ʿAbd al-Salām al-Tadmurī. 52 vols. Dār al-Kitāb al-ʿArabī, 1993.

al-Dhahabī, Muḥammad b. Aḥmad. *Tārīkh al-Islām*. Edited by Bashshār ʿAwwād Maʿrūf. 17 vols. Dār al-Gharb al-Islāmī, 2003.

Dostoevsky, Fyodor. *Crime and Punishment*. Translated by Richard Pevear and Larissa Volokhonsky. Vintage Books, 1993.

Douaihy, Jabbour. "al-Muthaqqaf wa-l-sulṭān wa-l-ḥikāya." *Majallat al-Ijtihād*, no. 4 (Fall 1989): 53–65.

El-Ariss, Tarek. "On Cooks and Crooks: Aḥmad Fāris al-Shidyāq and the Orientalists in England and France (1840s–1850s)." In *The Muslim Reception of European Orientalism: Reversing the Gaze*, edited by Susannah Heschel and Umar Ryad, 14–38. Routledge, 2019.

El-Ariss, Tarek. *Trials of Arab Modernity: Literary Affects and the New Political*. Fordham University Press, 2013.

Elmarsafy, Ziad Magdy. "Philosophy Self-Taught: Reason, Mysticism and the Uses of Islam in the Early Enlightenment." In *L'Islam visto da Occidente*, edited by Emanuele Colombo, 135–55. Marietti, 2009.

El-Rouayheb, Khaled, and Sabine Schmidtke, eds. *The Oxford Handbook of Islamic Philosophy*. Oxford University Press, 2016.

El Shakry, Hoda. *The Literary Qur'an*. Fordham University Press, 2019.

Elshakry, Marwa, and Murad Idris. "Ibn Tufayl and the Story of the Feral Child of Philosophy." Aeon, March 26, 2019. https://aeon.co/ideas/ibn-tufayl-and-the-story-of-the-feral-child-of-philosophy.

El-Tobgui, Carl Sharif. *Ibn Taymiyya on Reason and Revelation: A Study of Darʾ taʿāruḍ al-ʿaql wa-l-naql*. Brill, 2020.

Enayet, Hadi. *Islam and Secularism in Post-Colonial Thought: A Cartography of Asadian Genealogies*. Palgrave Macmillan, 2017.

Fakhry, Majid. *A History of Islamic Philosophy*. 3rd ed. Columbia University Press, 2004.

al-Fanārī, Muḥammad b. Ḥamza. *Fuṣūl al-badāʾiʿ fī uṣūl al-sharāʾiʿ*. Edited by Muḥammad Ḥasan Ismāʿīl. 2 vols. Dār al-Kutub al-ʿIlmiyya, 2006.

Fanon, Frantz. *The Wretched of the Earth*. Translated by Constance Farrington. Grove Press, 1963.

al-Farāhīdī, al-Khalīl b. Aḥmad. *Kitāb al-ʿayn*. Edited by Mahdī al-Makhzūmī and Ibrāhīm al-Sāmirrāʾī. 8 vols. Dār wa-Maktabat al-Hilāl, n.d.

Farrūkh, ʿUmar. *Tārīkh al-adab al-ʿarabī*. 6 vols. Dār al-ʿIlm li-l-Malāyīn, 1981.

Faruque, Muhammad U. *Sculpting the Self: Islam, Selfhood, and Human Flourishing*. Michigan University Press, 2021.

al-Fāsī, Taqī al-Dīn. *al-ʿIqd al-thamīn fī tārīkh al-balad al-amīn*. 7 vols. Dār al-Kutub al-ʿIlmiyya, 1998.

al-Fayyūmī, Ḥasan b. ʿAlī. *Fatḥ al-qarīb al-mujīb ʿalā al-targhīb wa-l-tarhīb*. Edited by Muḥammad Isḥāq Muḥammad Ibrāhīm. 15 vols. Dār al-Salām, 2018.

Ferlier, Louisiane, and Claire Gallien. "'Enthusiastick' Uses of the Oriental Tale: The English Translations of Ibn Tufayl's *Hayy Ibn Yaqdhan* in the Eighteenth Century." In *Eastern Resonances in Early Modern England: Receptions and Transformations from the Renaissance to the Romantic Period*, edited by Claire Gallien and Ladan Niayesh, 93–114. Palgrave Macmillan, 2019.

Fieni, David. *Decadent Orientalisms: The Decay of Colonial Modernity*. Fordham University Press, 2020.

al-Fīrūzābādī, Muḥammad b. Yaʿqūb. *al-Qāmūs al-muḥīṭ*. Edited by Muḥammad Naʿīm al-ʿIrqsūsī. Muʾassasat al-Risāla li-l-Ṭibāʿa wa-l-Nashr wa-l-Tawzīʿ, 2005.

Ford, Andrew. *The Origins of Criticism: Literary Culture and Poetic Theory in Classical Greece*. Princeton University Press, 2002.

Foucault, Michel. *Discipline and Punish: The Birth of the Prison*. Translated by Alan Sheridan. Vintage Books, 1975.

Foucault, Michel. "The Subject and Power." *Critical Inquiry* 8, no. 4 (1982): 777–95.

Fradkin, Hillel. "The Political Thought of Ibn Tufayl." In *The Political Aspects of Islamic Philosophy: Essays in Honor of Muhsin S. Mahdi*, edited by Charles E. Butterworth, 234–61. Harvard University Press, 1992.

Fricker, Miranda. *Epistemic Injustice: Power and the Ethics of Knowing*. Oxford University Press, 2007.

Gadamer, Hans-Georg. *Hermeneutics, Religion, and Ethics*. Translated by Joel Weinsheimer. Yale University Press, 2008.

Gadamer, Hans-Georg. *Truth and Method* [*Warheit und Methode*]. Translated and edited by Garrett Bowden and John Cumming. Seabury Press, 1975.

al-Garradi, Tahir K. "The Image of al-Maʿarrī as an Infidel among Medieval and Modern Critics." PhD diss., University of Utah, 1987.

Geary, Patrick J., Daud Ali, Paul S. Atkins, et al. "Courtly Cultures: Western Europe, Byzantium, the Islamic World, India, China, and Japan." In *The Cambridge Companion to Global History*. Vol. 5, *Expanding Webs of Exchange and Conflict, 500CE–1500CE*, edited by Benjamin Z. Kedar and Merry E. Wiesner-Hanks, 179–205. Cambridge University Press, 2015. https://doi.org/10.1017/CBO9780511667480.

Genette, Gérard. *Paratexts: Threshold of Interpretation*. Translated by Jane E. Lewin. Cambridge University Press, 1987.

Gerli, E. Michael. *Refiguring Authority: Reading, Writing, and Rewriting in Cervantes*. University Press of Kentucky, 1995.

al-Ghazālī, Abū Ḥāmid. *Ma ʿārij al-quds fī madārij ma ʿrifat al-nafs*. Dār al-Āfāq al-Jadīda, 1975.

al-Ghazālī, Abū Ḥāmid. *Mīzān al-ʿamal*. Dār al-Kitāb al-ʿArabī, n.d.

al-Ghazālī, Abū Ḥāmid. *al-Munqidh min al-ḍalāl*. Edited by ʿAbd al-Ḥalīm Maḥmūd. Dār al-Kutub al-Ḥadītha, 1974.

al-Ghazālī, Abū Ḥāmid. *al-Qisṭās al-mustaqīm*. Edited by Maḥmūd Bījū. al-Maṭbaʿa al-ʿIlmiyya, 1993.

Ghose, Indira. *Shakespeare in Jest*. Routledge, 2021.

González-Ferrín, Emilio. "The Disobedient Philosopher: Subtle Humanistic Insurgence in Ibn Tufayl." In *Disobedient Practices: Textual Multiplicity in Medieval and Golden Age Spain*, edited by Anne Roberts and Belén Bistué, 17–35. Juan de la Cuesta, 2015.

Griffel, Frank. "Al-Ghazālī's (d. 1111) *Incoherence of the Philosophers*." In *The Oxford Handbook of Islamic Philosophy*, edited by Khaled El-Rouayheb and Sabine Schmidtke, 191–209. Oxford University Press, 2016.

Griffel, Frank. *Al-Ghazali's Philosophical Theology*. Oxford University Press, 2009.

Gründler, Beatrice. "*Kalīla wa-Dimna*: A Unique Work of World Literature." Freie Universität Berlin. https://www.geschkult.fu-berlin.de/en/e/kalila-wa-dimna/topics/World-Literature.html.

Gully, Adrian. *The Culture of Letter-Writing in Pre-Modern Islamic Society*. Edinburgh University Press, 2008.

Günther, Sebastian, ed. *Knowledge and Education in Classical Islam: Religious Learning between Continuity and Change*. 2 vols. Brill, 2020.

Gutas, Dimitri. "The Empiricism of Avicenna." *Oriens* 40 (2012): 391–436.

Gutas, Dimitri. "Ibn Ṭufayl on Ibn Sīnā's Eastern Philosophy." *Oriens* 34 (1994): 222–41.

Guth, Stephan. "Adab as the Art to Make the Right Choice between Local Tradition and Euromania: A Comparative Analysis of Khalil al-Khuri's *Way, idhan lastu bi-Ifranī!* (1859) and Aḥmed Midḥat's *Felāṭūn Beğ ile Raḳım Efendī* (1875), or: On the Threshold of Nationalising Middle Eastern Culture." In *Adab and Modernity: A "Civilising Process"? (Sixteenth–Twenty-First Century)*, edited by Catherine Mayeur-Jaouen, 311–45. Brill, 2020.

Ḥājjī Khalīfa. *Kashf al-ẓunūn ʿan asāmī al-kutub wa-l-funūn*. 6 vols. Maktabat al-Muthannā, 1941.

al-Hamadhānī, Badīʿ al-Zamān. *Maqāmāt*. Turath.io. https://app.turath.io/book/28113.

al-Hamadhānī, Badīʿ al-Zamān. *The Maqámát of Badíʿ al-Zamán al-Hamadhání*. Translated by W. J. Prendergast. Luzac & Co., 1915.

al-Ḥamawī, Yāqūt. *Irshād al-arīb ilā ma ʿrifat al-adīb*. Edited by Iḥsān ʿAbbās. 7 vols. Dār al-Gharb al-Islāmī, 1993.

al-Ḥamawī, Yāqūt. *Mu ʿjam al-udabāʾ*. Edited by Iḥsān ʿAbbās. 7 vols. Dār al-Gharb al-Islāmī, 1993.

Hambly, Gavin R. G., ed. *Women in the Medieval Islamic World*. Palgrave Macmillan, 1999.

Hämeen-Anttila, Jaakko. "Suhrawardī's Western Exile as Artistic Prose." *Ishraq* 2 (2011): 105–18.

Ḥamza, ʿIffat Wiṣāl. *Nisāʾ ḥakamna al-Yaman*. Dār Ibn Ḥazm, 1999.

al-Ḥanbalī, Ibn Rajab. *Dhayl ṭabaqāt al-ḥanābila*. 5 vols. al-ʿUbikān, 2003.

Hanks, William F. "Pierre Bourdieu and the Practices of Language." *Annual Review of Anthropology* 34 (2005): 67–83. https://doi.org/10.1146/annurev.anthro.33.070203.143907.

Hanna, Sameh. "When Jesus Speaks Colloquial Egyptian Arabic: An Incarnational Understanding of Translation." In "Translation and Religion: Crafting Regimes of Identity," edited by Hephzibah Israel and Matthias Frenz. Thematic issue, *Religion* 49, no. 3 (2019): 364–87.

al-Ḥarīrī. *Maqāmāt Abī Zayd al-Sarūjī*. Translated by Michael Cooperson. New York University Press, 2020.

Hassan, Waïl S. *Tayeb Salih: Ideology and the Craft of Fiction*. Syracuse University Press, 2003.

Heck, Paul L. "*Adab* in the Thought of Ghazālī (d. 505/1111): In the Service of Mystical Insight." In *Ethics and Spirituality in Islam: Sufi Adab*, edited by Francesco Chiabotti, Eve Feuillebois-Pierunek, Catherine Mayeur-Jaouen, and Luca Patrizi, 298–324. Brill, 2016.

Heck, Paul L. "Skepticism in Classical Islam: The Case of al-Ghazālī." In *Skepticism: From Antiquity to the Present*, edited by Diego Machuca and Baron Reed, 196–208. Bloomsbury, 2018.

Heck, Paul L. "Teaching Ignorance: The Case of al-Ghazālī (d. 505/1111)." In *Knowledge and Education in Classical Islam: Religious Learning between Continuity and Change*, edited by Sebastian Günther, 2 vols., 1:223–43. Brill, 2020.

Heinrichs, Wolfhart. "The Classification of the Sciences and the Consolidation of Philology in Classical Islam." In *Centres of Learning: Learning and Location in Pre-Modern Europe and the Near East*, edited by Jan Willem Drijvers and Alasdair A. MacDonald, 119–39. Brill, 1995.

al-Ḥimyarī, Nashwān b. Saʿīd. *Shams al-ʿulūm wa-dawāʾ kalām al-ʿarab min al-kulūm*. Edited by Ḥusayn b. ʿAbd Allāh al-ʿAmrī, Muṭahhar b. ʿAlī al-Iryānī, and Yūsuf Muḥammad ʿAbd Allāh. 11 vols. Dār al-Fikr, 1999.

Hodgson, Marshall G. S. *The Venture of Islam*. Vol. 3, *The Gunpowder Empires and Modern Times*. University of Chicago Press, 1974.

Holmberg, Bo. "*Adab* and Arabic Literature." In *Literary History: Towards a Global Perspective*. Vol. 1, *Notions of Literature across Times and Cultures*, edited by A. Pettersson and G. Lindberg-Wada, 180–205. De Gruyter, 2006.

Holt, P. M. *Studies in the History of the Near East*. Frank Cass, 1973.

Holtzen, Wm. Curtis, and Matthew Nelson Hill. "Gadamer's Hermeneutics of Trust: Ontological and Reflective." In *In Spirit and in Truth: Philosophical Reflections on Liturgy and Worship*, edited by Wm. Curtis Holtzen and Matthew Nelson Hill, 87–108. Claremont Press, 2016.

Homer. *The Odyssey*. Translated by Emily Wilson. W. W. Norton, 2018.

Ḥussein, Muḥammad al-Khiḍr. "al-Murūʾa wa-maẓāhiruhā al-ṣādiqa." In *Mawsūʿat al-aʿmāl al-kāmila li-l-Imām Muḥammad al-Khiḍr Ḥussein*, edited by ʿAlī al-Riḍā al-Ḥusaynī, 15 vols., 8:8–16. Dār al-Nawādir, 2010.

Hussein, Taha. *Adīb*. Muʾassasat Hindāwī li-l-Taʿlīm wa-l-Thaqāfa, 2017.

Hussein, Taha. *Ḥadīth al-arbiʿāʾ*. 3 vols. Muʾassasat Hindāwī li-l-Taʿlīm wa-l-Thaqāfa, 2012.

Hussein, Taha. "Masīrat al-shāʿir al-kubrā." In *Min al-shāṭiʾ al-ākhar: kitābāt Taha Hussein al-firinsiyya*. Translated by ʿAbd al-Rashīd al-Ṣādiq al-Maḥmūdī. al-Markaz al-Qawmī li-l-Tarjama, 2008. [In French: "La grande aventure d'un poet." *Valeurs* 7 and 8, October 1946 and January 1947.]

Hussein, Taha. *Mustaqbal al-thaqāfa fī Miṣr*. Mu'assasat Hindāwī li-l-Ta'līm wa-l-Thaqāfa, 2017.

Ibn 'Abd al-Barr, Yūsuf b. 'Abd Allāh. *al-Inṣāf fīmā bayna 'ulamā' al-muslimīn fī qirā'at bismilllāh al-raḥmān al-raḥīm fī fātiḥat al-kitāb*. Edited by 'Abd al-Laṭīf b. Muḥammad al-Jīlānī al-Maghribī. Aḍwā' al-Salaf, 1997.

Ibn 'Abd al-Barr, Yūsuf b. 'Abd Allāh. *Jāmi' bayān al-'ilm wa-faḍlihi*. Edited by Abū al-Ashbāl al-Zuhayrī. 2 vols. Dār Ibn al-Jawzī, 1994.

Ibn 'Abd Rabbih, Aḥmad b. Muḥammad. *al-'Iqd al-farīd*. Edited by Mufīd Muḥammad Qumayḥa. 8 vols. Dār al-Kutub al-'Ilmiyya, 1983.

Ibn al-'Adīm, Kamāl al-Dīn. *Bughyat al-ṭalab fī tārīkh Ḥalab*. Edited by Suhayl Zakkār. 12 vols. Dār al-Fikr, 1988.

Ibn al-'Adīm, Kamāl al-Dīn. *al-Inṣāf wa-l-taḥarrī fī daf' al-ẓulm 'an Abī al-'Alā' al-Ma'arrī*. Edited by 'Abd al-'Azīz Harfūsh. Dār al-Jūlān, 2007.

Ibn 'Asākir, 'Alī b. Ḥasan. *Tahdhīb tārīkh Dimashq al-kabīr*. Edited by 'Amr b. Gharāma al-'Umrawī. 80 vols. Dār al-Fikr li-l-Ṭibā'a wa-l-Nashr wa-l-Tawzī', 1995.

Ibn al-Athīr, Ḍiyā' al-Dīn. *al-Mathal al-sā'ir fī adab al-kātib wa-l-shā'ir*. Edited by Aḥmad al-Ḥūfī and Badawī Ṭabāna. 4 vols. Dār Nahḍat Miṣr, n.d.

Ibn Fāris. *Maqāyīs al-lugha*. Edited by 'Abd al-Salām Muḥammad Hārūn. 6 vols. Dār al-Fikr, 1979.

Ibn Ḥamdūn, Muḥammad b. al-Ḥasan. *al-Tadhkira al-ḥamdūniyya*. Edited by Iḥsān 'Abbās. 10 vols. Turath.io. https://app.turath.io/book/10646.

Ibn Ḥibbān, Muḥammad. *al-Majrūḥīn min al-muḥaddithīn wa-l-du'afā' wa-l-matrūkīn*. Edited by Maḥmūd Ibrāhīm Zāyid. 3 vols. Dār al-Wa'y, 1976.

Ibn Ḥibbān, Muḥammad. *Rawḍat al-'uqalā' wa-nuzhat al-fuḍalā'*. Edited by Muḥammad Muḥyī al-Dīn 'Abd al-Ḥamīd et al. Dār al-Kutub al-'Ilmiyya, 1977.

Ibn al-Jawzī. *al-Mudhish*. Edited by Marwān Qabbānī. Dār al-Kutub al-'Ilmiyya, 1985.

Ibn al-Jawzī. *al-Muntaẓim fī tārīkh al-umam wa-l-mulūk*. Edited by Muḥammad 'Abd al-Qādir 'Aṭā' and Muṣṭafā 'Abd al-Qādir 'Aṭā'. 19 vols. Dār al-Kutub al-'Ilmiyya, 1992.

Ibn al-Jawzī. *Nawāsikh al-Qur'ān*. Edited by Muḥammad Ashraf 'Alī al-Milībārī. 'Imādat al-Baḥth al-'Ilmī bi-l-Jāmi'a al-Islāmiyya, 2003.

Ibn al-Jawzī. *Nuzhat al-a'yun al-nawāẓir fī 'ilm al-wujūh wa-l-naẓā'ir*. Turath.io. https://app.turath.io/book/6334.

Ibn Jinnī, Abū al-Fatḥ 'Uthmān. *al-Khaṣā'iṣ*. Edited by Muḥammad 'Alī al-Najjār. 3 vols. Dār al-Hudā li-l-Ṭibā'a wa-l-Nashr, n.d.

Ibn Kathīr. *al-Bidāya wa-l-nihāya*. Edited by 'Abd Allāh b. 'Abd al-Muḥsin al-Turkī. 20 vols. Dār Hajr li-l-Ṭibā'a wa-l-Nashr, 1997.

Ibn Kathīr. *Musnad al-Fārūq*. Edited by Imām b. 'Alī b. Imām. 3 vols. Dār al-Falāḥ, 2009.

Ibn Kathīr. *Tafsīr al-Qur'ān al-'aẓīm*. Edited by Sāmī b. Muḥammad Salāma. 8 vols. Dār Ṭayba li-l-Nashr wa-l-Tawzī', 1999.

Ibn Khaldūn. *The Muqaddimah: An Introduction to History*. Translated by Franz Rosenthal. Pantheon Books, 1958.

Ibn Khaldūn. *Tārīkh Ibn Khaldūn*. Edited by Suhayl Zakkār. 8 vols. Dār al-Fikr, 1981.

Ibn Manẓūr. *Lisān al-'arab*. 15 vols. Dār Ṣādir, 1993.

Ibn Manẓūr. *Mukhtaṣar tārīkh Dimashq li-Ibn 'Asākir*. Edited by Rawḥiyya al-Naḥḥās et al. 29 vols. Dār al-Fikr li-l-Ṭibā'a wa-l-Nashr wa-l-Tawzī', 1984.

Ibn al-Marzubān, Muḥammad b. ʿImrān. *Faḍl al-kilāb ʿalā kathīr mimman labis al-thiyāb*. Edited by Rex Smith and Muḥammad ʿAbd al-Ḥalīm. al-Jamal, 2003.

Ibn al-Marzubān, Muḥammad b. ʿImrān. *al-Murūʾa*. Edited by Muḥammad Khayr Ramaḍān Yūsuf. Dār Ibn Ḥazm, 1999.

Ibn al-Muqaffaʿ. *al-Adab al-ṣaghīr wa-l-Adab al-kabīr*. Dār Ṣādir, n.d.

Ibn al-Muqaffaʿ. *Kalīla wa-Dimna*. Edited by Michael Fishbein. Translated by Michael Fishbein and James E. Montgomery. New York University Press, 2021.

Ibn Qutayba, ʿAbd Allāh b. Muslim. *Adab al-kātib*. Edited by Muḥammad al-Dalī. Muʾassasat al-Risāla, 1982.

Ibn Qutayba, ʿAbd Allāh b. Muslim. *Kitāb al-maʿānī al-kabīr fī abyāt al-maʿānī*. 3 vols. Turath.io. https://app.turath.io/book/25837.

Ibn Qutayba, ʿAbd Allāh b. Muslim. *ʿUyūn al-akhbār*. 4 vols. Dār al-Kutub al-ʿIlmiyya, 1997.

Ibn Rushd. *al-Ḍarūrī fī al-siyāsa*. Translated Aḥmad Shaḥlān. Markaz Dirāsāt al-Wiḥda al-ʿArabiyya, 1998.

Ibn Sallām, Abū ʿUbayd al-Qāsim. *Kitāb al-silāḥ*. Edited by Ḥātim Ṣāliḥ al-Ḍāmin. Muʾassasat al-Risāla li-l-Ṭibāʿa wa-l-Nashr wa-l-Tawzīʿ, 1985.

Ibn Sīdah [Ibn Sayyidihi], Abū al-Ḥasan ʿAlī b. Ismāʿīl. *al-Muḥkam wa-l-muḥīṭ al-aʿẓam*. 10 vols. Turath.io. https://app.turath.io/book/9757.

Ibn Sīdah [Ibn Sayyidihi], Abū al-Ḥasan ʿAlī b. Ismāʿīl. *al-Mukhaṣṣaṣ*. 5 vols. Turath.io. https://app.turath.io/book/3590.

Ibn Sīnā. *al-Hidāya fī al-manṭiq*. Edited by Muḥammad Aḥmad ʿAbd al-Ḥalīm. 3 vols. Dār al-Kutub al-ʿIlmiyya, 1971.

Ibn Sīnā. *al-Qānūn fī al-ṭibb*. Edited by Muḥammad Amīn al-Ḍināwī. 3 vols. Dār al-Kutub al-ʿIlmiyya, 1999.

Ibn Sīnā. *al-Shifāʾ: al-manṭiq, kitāb al-shiʿir*. Edited by ʿAbd al-Raḥmān Badawī. al-Dār al-Maṣriyya li-l-Taʾlīf wa-l-Tarjama, 1966.

Ibn Ṭabāṭabā, Abū al-Ḥasan. *ʿIyār al-shiʿr*. Edited by ʿAbd al-ʿAzīz b. Nāṣir al-Māniʿ. Maktabat al-Khānjī, n.d.

Ibn Ṭufayl. *Ibn Tufayl's Hayy Ibn Yaqzān: A Philosophical Tale*. Translated by Lenn E. Goodman. University of Chicago Press, 2009.

Ibn Tufayl and Ibn Rushd. *Two Andalusian Philosophers*. Translated by Jim Colville. Routledge, 2013.

al-Ibshīhī, Shihāb al-Dīn. *al-Mustaṭraf fī kull fann mustaẓraf*. Edited by Saʿīd Muḥammad al-Laḥḥām. Turath.io. https://app.turath.io/book/23802.

Idris, Murad. "Ibn Ṭufayl's Critique of Politics." *Journal of Islamic Philosophy* 7 (2011): 67–102.

Iqbal, Muhammad. *The Reconstruction of Religious Thought in Islam*. Iqbal Academy, 1989.

ʿĪsā, Ranā. "al-Taʿdīl ʿinda al-Shidyāq: al-siyāsa wa-afkāruhā fī zaman al-istʿimār." al-Jumhūriyya, March 7, 2016. https://aljumhuriya.net/ar/2016/03/07/34672/.

al-Jabri, Muhammad Abed. "al-Māḍī wa-l-mustaqbal . . . ayyahumā yaḥkum al-ākhar?" *Fikr wa-Naqd* 51 (September 2003). https://www.aljabriabed.net/n51_02jab_pass.htm.

Jaffal, Maḥmūd ʿAbd Allāh. "al-Muṣṭalaḥ al-lughawī ʿinda Ibn Jinnī fī *Kitāb al-khaṣāʾiṣ*." *Majallat Majmaʿ al-Lugha al-ʿArabiyya al-Urdunī* 71 (2006): 59–127.

al-Jāḥiẓ, Abū ʿUthmān. *al-Bayān wa-l-tabyīn*. 3 vols. Dār wa-Maktabat al-Hilāl, 2002.

al-Jāḥiẓ, Abū ʿUthmān. *Kitāb al-ḥayawān*. Edited by Muḥammad Bāsil ʿUyūn al-Sūd. 7 vols. Turath.io. https://app.turath.io/book/23775.

al-Jahshiyārī, Muḥammad b. ʿAbdūs. *al-Wuzarāʾ wa-l-kuttāb*. Edited by Muṣṭafā al-Saqqā, Ibrāhīm al-Ibyārī, and ʿAbd al-Ḥafīẓ Shalabī. Muṣṭafā al-Bābī al-Ḥalabī, 1938.

Jansen, Yolande. "Postsecularism, Piety and Fanaticism: Reflections on Jürgen Habermas' and Saba Mahmood's Critiques of Secularism." *Philosophy & Social Criticism* 37, no. 9 (2011): 977–98.

Jarīr b. ʿAṭiyya. *Dīwān Jarīr: bi-sharḥ Muḥammad b. Ḥabīb*. Edited by Nuʿmān Muḥammad Amīn Ṭāhā. 3 vols. Dār al-Maʿārif, 1969.

al-Jawharī, Ismāʿīl b. Ḥammād. *al-Ṣiḥāḥ*. Edited by Aḥmad ʿAbd al-Ghafūr ʿAṭṭār. 6 vols. Dār al-ʿIlm li-l-Malāyīn, 1987.

Johnson, Rebecca Carol. "Archive of Errors: Aḥmad Fāris al-Shidyāq, Literature, and the World." *Middle Eastern Literatures* 20, no. 1 (2017): 31–50.

al-Jundī, Muḥammad Salīm. *al-Jāmiʿ fī akhbār Abī al-ʿAlāʾ al-Maʿarrī wa-āthārihi*. Edited by ʿAbd al-Hādī Hāshim. 3 vols. Maṭbūʿāt al-Majmaʿ al-ʿIlmī al-ʿArabī bi-Dimashq, 1962–64.

al-Jurjānī, ʿAbd al-Qāhir. *Darj al-durar fī tafsīr al-āy wa-l-suwar*. Edited by Ṭalʿat Ṣalāḥ al-Farḥān and Muḥammad Adīb Shakūr Amrīr. 4 vols. Dār al-Fikr, 2009.

Kant, Immanuel. "Idea for a Universal History with a Cosmopolitan Purpose." In *Kant: Political Writings*, edited by H. S. Reiss, translated by H. B. Nisbet, 41–53. Cambridge University Press, 1970.

Kaplan, Caren. "Resisting Autobiography: Out-Law Genres and Transnational Feminist Subjects." In *De/Colonizing the Subject: The Politics of Gender in Women's Autobiography*, edited by Sidonie Smith and Julia Watson, 115–38. University of Minnesota Press, 1992.

al-Kātib, ʿAbd al-Ḥamīd. "Risālat ʿAbd al-Ḥamīd ilā al-kuttāb." In *Rasāʾil al-bulaghāʾ*, edited by Muḥammad Kurd ʿAlī, 127–30. Muʾassasat Hindāwī li-l-Taʿlīm wa-l-Thaqāfa, 2022.

Kāẓim, Nādir. *al-Maqāmāt wa-l-talaqqī: baḥth fī anmāṭ al-talaqqī li-Maqāmāt al-Hamadhānī fī al-naqd al-ʿarabī al-ḥadīth*. al-Muʾassasa al-ʿArabiyya li-l-Dirāsāt wa-l-Nashr, 2003.

Keegan, Matthew L. "Before and after *Kalīla wa-Dimna*: An Introduction to the Special Issue on Animals, *Adab*, and Fictivity." *Journal of Abbasid Studies* 8 (2021): 1–11.

Keegan, Matthew L. "Commentarial Acts and Hermeneutical Drama." PhD diss., New York University, 2017.

Kerfoot, Caroline, and Kenneth Hyltenstam. "Introduction: Entanglement and Orders of Visibility." In *Entangled Discourses: South-North Orders of Visibility*, edited by Caroline Kerfoot and Kenneth Hyltenstam, 1–15. Routledge, 2017.

Kernan, Alvin B. *Samuel Johnson and the Impact of Print*. Princeton University Press, 1989.

al-Khafājī, Shihāb al-Dīn. *Ḥāshiyat al-Shihāb ʿalā tafsīr al-Bayḍāwī* [*ʿInāyat al-qāḍī wa-kifāyat al-rāḍī*]. 8 vols. Dār Ṣādir, n.d.

al-Khafājī, Shihāb al-Dīn. *Sharḥ Durrat al-ghawwāṣ fī awhām al-khawāṣṣ*. Edited by ʿAbd al-Ḥafīẓ Farghalī ʿAlī Quranī. Dār al-Jīl, 1996.

Khan, Maryam Wasif. *Who Is a Muslim? Orientalism and Literary Populisms*. Fordham University Press, 2021.

Khoury, Elias. *al-Dhākira al-mafqūda*. Muʾassasat al-Abḥāth al-ʿArabiyya, 1982.

Kia, Mana. "Lingering with *Adab* before Rushing to Literature." *History of Humanities* 9, no. 1 (Spring 2024): 65–79.

Kia, Mana. *Persianate Selves: Memories of Place and Origin before Nationalism*. Stanford University Press, 2020.

Kilito, Abdelfattah. *Bi-ḥibr khafī*. Dār Tūbqāl, 2018.

Kilito, Abdelfattah. *Min shurfat Ibn Rushd*. [Translated from the French *Du Balcon d'Averroës*.] Dār Tūbqāl, 2009.

Kilpatrick, Hilary. "Adab." In *Encyclopedia of Arabic Literature*, edited by Julie Scott Meisami and Paul Starkey, 2 vols., 1:54–56. Routledge, 1998.

al-Labābīdī, Aḥmad b. Muṣṭafā. *al-Laṭāʾif fī al-lugha: muʿjam asmāʾ al-ashyāʾ*. Dār al-Faḍīla, n.d.

al-Lakhmī, Ṣāliḥ b. Janāḥ. *al-Adab wa-l-murūʾa*. Dār al-Ṣaḥāba li-l-Turāth bi-Ṭanṭā, 1992.

Lambertini, Roberto. "Mirrors for Princes." In *Encyclopedia of Medieval Philosophy*, edited by Henrik Lagerlund, 791–97. Springer, 2011. https://doi.org/10.1007/978-1-4020-9729-4_338.

Lambton, Ann K. S. *State and Government in Medieval Islam*. Routledge, 2013.

Lane, Edward William. *An Arabic-English Lexicon*. London, 1867.

Lapidus, Ira M. "Knowledge, Virtue, and Action: The Classical Muslim Conception of *Adab* and the Nature of Religious Fulfillment in Islam." In *Moral Conduct and Authority: The Place of Adab in South Asian Islam*, edited by Barbara Daly Metcalf, 38–61. University of California Press, 1984.

Ledbetter, David. *Bach's Well-Tempered Clavier: The 48 Preludes and Fugues*. Yale University Press, 2002.

Lipking, Lawrence. "Inventing the Common Reader: Samuel Johnson and the Canon." In *Interpretation and Cultural History*, edited by Joan H. Pittock and Andrew Wear, 153–74. Palgrave Macmillan, 1991.

Locke, John. *An Essay Concerning Human Understanding: In Four Books*. London, n.d.

London, Jennifer. "Lessons in Frank Speech: Re-reading Stories from *Kalila wa Dimna*." *al-ʿUsur al-Wusta* 19, no. 1 (April 2007): 11–13.

London, Jennifer. "How to Do Things with Fables." *History of Political Thought* 29, no. 2 (Summer 2008): 189–212.

Longxi, Zhang. "The Classical and the Limitations of Reception Theory." In *Reading the Past across Space and Time*, edited by Brenda Deen Schildgen and Ralph Hexter, 299–319. Palgrave Macmillan, 2016.

Lorenz, Chris. "It Takes Three to Tango: History between the 'Practical' and the 'Historical' Past." *Storia della Storiografia* 64, no. 1 (2014): 29–46.

al-Maʿarrī, Abū al-ʿAlāʾ. *al-Lāmiʿ al-ʿazīzī*. Edited by Muḥammad Saʿīd al-Mawlawī. Markaz al-Malik Fayṣal li-l-Buḥūth wa-l-Dirāsāt al-Islāmiyya, 2008.

al-Maʿarrī, Abū al-ʿAlāʾ. *al-Luzūmiyyāt*. Edited by Amīn ʿAbd al-ʿAzīz al-Khānjī. 2 vols. Maktabat al-Khānjī, n.d.

al-Maʿarrī, Abū al-ʿAlāʾ. *Muʿjiz Aḥmad* [*Sharḥ Dīwān al-Mutanabbī*]. 4 vols. N.p., n.d.

al-Maʿarrī, Abū al-ʿAlāʾ. *Zajr al-nābiḥ: muqtaṭafāt*. Edited by Amjad Ṭrābulsī. Maṭbūʿāt Majmaʿ al-Lugha al-ʿArabiyya, 1982 [1965].

MacIntyre, Alasdair. *After Virtue: A Study in Moral Theory*. 3rd ed. University of Notre Dame Press, 2007.

Mahmood, Saba. *The Politics of Piety: Islamic Revival and the Feminist Subject*. Princeton University Press, 2005.

Makdisi, George. *The Rise of Colleges: Institutions of Learning in Islam and the West*. Edinburgh University Press, 1991.

Makdisi, George. *The Rise of Humanism in Classical Islam and the Christian West*. Edinburgh University Press, 1990.

Malti-Douglas, Fedwa. "*Ḥayy ibn Yaqẓān* as Male Utopia." In *The World of Ibn Ṭufayl*, edited by Lawrence Conrad, 52–68. Brill, 1996.

The Maqámát of Badí' al-Zamán al-Hamadhání. Translated by W. J. Prendergast. Lucaz, 1915.

al-Maqrīzī, Aḥmad b. ʿAlī. *al-Muqqafā al-kabīr*. Edited by Muḥammad al-Yaʿlāwī. 8 vols. Dār al-Gharb al-Islāmī, 2006.

Marmura, Michael. "Avicenna's Proof from Contingency for God's Existence in the Metaphysics of the *Shifāʾ*." *Medieval Studies* 42 (1980): 337–52.

Marmura, Michael. "Some Aspects of Avicenna's Theory of God's Knowledge of Particulars." *Journal of the American Oriental Society* 82, no. 3 (1962): 299–312.

Márquez, Gabriel García. *One Hundred Years of Solitude*. Translated by Gregory Rabassa. Avon Books, 1970.

Marroum, Marianne. "*Kalila wa Dimna*: Inception, Appropriation, and Transmimesis." *Comparative Literature Studies* 48 (2011): 512–40.

Marx, Karl. *Capital: A Critique of Political Economy*. 3 vols. International Publishers, 1967.

Massad, Joseph A. *Desiring Arabs*. University of Chicago Press, 2007.

Massad, Joseph A. *Islam in Liberalism*. University of Chicago Press, 2015.

al-Māturīdī, Abū Manṣūr. *Taʾwīlāt ahl al-sunna: tafsīr al-Māturīdī*. Edited by Majdī Bāsallūm. 10 vols. Dār al-Kutub al-ʿIlmiyya, 2005.

al-Māzinī, Ibrāhīm ʿAbd al-Qādir. *Qabḍ al-rīḥ*. Muʾassasat Hindāwī li-l-Taʿlīm wa-l-Thaqāfa, 2017.

McGinnis, Jon. "Avicenna's Naturalized Epistemology and Scientific Method." In *The Unity of Science in the Arabic Tradition: Science, Logic, Epistemology and Their Interactions*, edited by Shahid Rahman, Tony Street, and Hassan Tahiri, 129–52. Springer, 2008.

McGinnis, Jon. "Scientific Methodologies in Medieval Islam." *Journal of the History of Philosophy* 41, no. 3 (2003): 307–27.

McGinnis, Jon, and David C. Reisman, eds. and trans. *Classical Arabic Philosophy: An Anthology of Sources*. Hackett Publishing House, 2007.

McLarney, Ellen. "Freedom, Justice, and the Power of *Adab*." *International Journal of Middle East Studies* 48 (2016): 25–46.

Miskawayh, Aḥmad b. Muḥammad. *Tahdhīb al-akhlāq wa-taṭhīr al-aʿrāq*. Edited by Ibn al-Khaṭīb. Maktabat al-Thaqāfa al-Dīniyya, 1998.

Mitchell, Timothy. *Colonising Egypt*. Cambridge University Press, 1991.

Mitchell, Timothy. "The Stage of Modernity." In *Questions of Modernity*, edited by Timothy Mitchell, 1–34. University of Minnesota Press, 2000.

Mitchell, Timothy. "What Is Educated Spoken Arabic?" *International Journal of the Sociology of Language* 61 (1986): 7–32.

Mohamad, Walat. "Muqaddimat Ibn al-Muqaffaʿ li-*Kalīla wa-Dimna*: mustawayāt al-qariʾ." *Edebiyat Fakültesi Dergisi*, no. 32 (2014): 127–42.

Mohamed, Yasien. *Fitrah: The Islamic Concept of Human Nature*. Ta Ha Publishers Ltd., 1996.

Moosa, Ebrahim. *al-Ghazālī and the Poetics of Imagination*. University of North Carolina Press, 2005.

Mousavian, Seyed N. "Is Avicenna an Empiricist?" In *Mathematics, Logic, and Their Philosophies: Essays in Honour of Mohammad Ardeshir*, edited by Mojtaba Mojtahedi, Shahid Rahman, and Mohammad Saleh Zarepour, 443–74. Springer, 2021.

Muhanna, Elias. "Why Was the 14th Century a Century of Arabic Encyclopaedism?" In *Encyclopaedias and Encyclopaedism from Antiquity to the Renaissance*, edited by Jason König and Greg Woolf, 343–56. Cambridge University Press, 2013.

Muhanna, Elias. *The World in a Book: Al-Nuwayri and the Islamic Encyclopedic Tradition*. Princeton University Press, 2018.

al-Musawi, Muhsin J. "The 'Islamic' *Arabian Nights* in World Imaginaries." In *Islam and New Directions in World Literature*, edited by Sarah R. Bin Tyeer and Claire Gallien, 217–52. Edinburgh University Press, 2022.

al-Musawi, Muhsin J. *The Medieval Islamic Republic of Letters: Arabic Knowledge Production*. Notre Dame University Press, 2015.

Nadwi, Akram. *al-Muḥaddithāt: The Women Scholars in Islam*. Interface Publications, 2007.

Najm, Muḥammad Yūsuf. *al-Qiṣṣa fī al-adab al-ʿarabī al-ḥadīth: 1870–1914*. Dār Miṣr li-l-Ṭibāʿa, 1966 [1952].

Najm, Sami M. "The Place and Function of Doubt in the Philosophies of Descartes and al-Ghazzali." *Philosophy East and West* 16, no. 3–4 (1966): 133–41.

al-Nawawī, Yaḥyā b. Sharaf. *al-Majmūʿ: sharḥ al-Muhadhdhab*. 9 vols. Dār al-Fikr, 1996.

Nederman, Cary J. "Nature, Ethics, and the Doctrine of 'Habitus': Aristotelian Moral Psychology in the Twelfth Century." *Traditio* 45 (1990): 87–110.

Ngũgĩ wa Thiong'o. *Decolonising the Mind: The Politics of Language in African Literature*. James Currey, 1986.

Nietzsche, Friedrich. *On the Advantage and Disadvantage of History for Life*. Translated by Peter Preuss. Hackett Publishing Company, Inc., 1980.

al-Nīsāpūrī, Niẓām al-Dīn. *Gharāʾib al-Qurʾān wa-raghāʾib al-furqān*. Edited by Zakariyyā ʿUmayrāt. 6 vols. Dār al-Kutub al-ʿIlmiyya, 1995.

Ockley, Simon. *The Improvement of Human Reason, Exhibited in the Life of Hai Ebn Yokdhan*. London, 1708.

O'Donnell, B. R. J. "The *Odyssey*'s Millennia-Old Model of Mentorship." *The Atlantic*, October 13, 2017. https://www.theatlantic.com/business/archive/2017/10/the-odyssey-mentorship/542676/.

Pargiter, Frederick Eden, ed. *Centenary Volume of the Royal Asiatic Society of Great Britain and Ireland 1823–1923*. Royal Asiatic Society, 1923.

Patrizi, Luca. "The Metaphor of the Divine Banquet." In *Knowledge and Education in Classical Islam: Religious Learning between Continuity and Change*, edited by Sebastian Günther, 2 vols., 2:516–38. Brill, 2020.

Paul, Herman. *Hayden White*. Polity, 2011.

Percival, Ray Scott. "Descartes' Model of Mind." In *The Encyclopedia of Clinical Psychology*, edited by Robin L. Cautin and Scott O. Lilienfeld, 1–8. John Wiley & Sons, 2015.

Perret, Noëlle-Laetitia, and Stéphane Péquignot, eds. *A Critical Companion to the "Mirrors for Princes" Literature*. Brill, 2022.

Philosophus autodidactus, sive Epistola Abi Jaafar Ebn Tophail de Hai Ebn Yokdhan . . . 2nd ed. Oxonii, E Theatro Sheldoniano, 1700 [1671].

The Polite Preceptor or, A Collection of Entertaining and Instructive Essays; Selected from the Best English Writers. London, 1776.

Polizzotti, Mark. *Sympathy for the Traitor: A Translation Manifesto*. MIT Press, 2018.

al-Qarṭājannī, Ḥāzim. *Minhāj al-bulaghāʾ wa-sirāj al-udabāʾ*. Edited by Muḥammad al-Ḥabīb b. al-Khawja. Dār al-Gharb al-Islāmī, 1986.

al-Qasṭallānī, Shihāb al-Dīn. *Sharḥ al-Qasṭallānī* [*Irshād al-sārī li-sharḥ Ṣaḥīḥ al-Bukhārī*]. 10 vols. al-Maktaba al-Amīriyya, 1905.

al-Qayrawānī, Ibrāhīm b. ʿAlī al-Ḥuṣrī. *Zahr al-ādāb wa-thamar al-albāb*. Edited by Zakī Mubārak. 4 vols. Dār al-Jīl, n.d.

Radmān, Rabīʿ Ṭālib Mahdī. "al-Naqd al-ʿarabī wa-ishkāliyyat al-riwāya al-ūlā fī al-adab al-ḥadīth." *Ḥawliyyāt* 16 (2015): 167–80.

Rascovsky, Katya, Matthew E. Growdon, Isela R. Pardo, Scott Grossman, and Bruce L. Miller. "'The Quicksand of Forgetfulness': Semantic Dementia in *One Hundred Years of Solitude*." *Brain* 132, no. 9 (September 2009): 2609–16.

Rastegar, Kamran. *Literary Modernity between the Middle East and Europe: Textual Transactions in Nineteenth-Century Arabic, English, and Persian Literatures*. Routledge, 2007.

al-Rāzī, Fakhr al-Dīn. *Mafātīḥ al-ghayb*. 32 vols. Dār Iḥyāʾ al-Turāth al-ʿArabī, 1999.

al-Rāzī, Zayn al-Dīn ʿAbd al-Qādir al-Ḥanafī. *Mukhtār al-ṣiḥāḥ*. Edited by Yūsuf al-Shaykh Muḥammad. al-Maktaba al-ʿAṣriyya, 1999.

Ricoeur, Paul. "Quel éthos nouveau pour l'Europe?" In *Imaginer l'Europe: le marché intérieur européen, tâche culturelle et économique*, edited by Peter Koslowski, 108–16. Editions du Cerf, 1992.

Ricoeur, Paul. *Sur la traduction*. Bayard, 2004.

Rosemann, Philipp W. "Wandering in the Path of the Averroean System: Is Kant's Doctrine on the 'Bewußtsein überhaupt' Averroistic?" *American Catholic Philosophical Quarterly* 73 (1999): 185–230.

Rosenthal, Franz. "The Critical Approach." In *The Technique and Approach of Muslim Scholarship*, 41–89. Pontificum Institutum Biblicum, 1947.

Rosenthal, Franz. *Knowledge Triumphant: The Concept of Knowledge in Medieval Islam*. Brill, 2007.

Rowson, Everett K. "An Alexandrian Age in Fourteenth-Century Damascus: Twin Commentaries on Two Celebrated Arabic Epistles." *Mamluk Studies Review* 7 (2003): 97–110.

Rushdi, Rashad. *Fann al-qiṣṣa al-qaṣīra*. Maktabat al-Anglo al-Miṣriyya, 1964 [1958].

Ryle-Hodges, William. "Muḥammad ʿAbduh's Notion of Political *Adab*: Ethics as a Virtue of Modern Citizenship in Late 19th Century Khedival Egypt." *Journal of Islamic Studies* 21 (2021): 339–64.

Sacks, Jeffrey. *Iterations of Loss: Mutilation and Aesthetic Form, al-Shidyaq to Darwish*. Fordham University Press, 2015.

Sadan, Joseph. *al-Adab al-ʿarabī al-hāzil wa-nawādir al-thuqalāʾ: al-ʿāhāt wa-l-masāwiʾ al-insāniyya wa-makānatuhā fī al-adab al-rāqī*. Kamel Verlag, 2007.

al-Ṣafadī, Khalīl b. Aybak. *Nakt al-himyān fī nukat al-ʿumyān*. Edited by Muṣṭafā ʿAbd al-Qādir ʿAṭāʾ. Dār al-Kutub al-ʿIlmiyya, 2007.

al-Ṣafadī, Khalīl b. Aybak. *al-Wāfī bi-l-wafayāt*. Edited by Aḥmad al-Arnāʾūṭ and Turkī Muṣṭafā. 29 vols. Dār Iḥyāʾ al-Turāth, 2000.

al-Ṣaghānī, al-Ḥasan b. Muḥammad. *al-Takmila wa-l-dhayl wa-l-ṣila*. Edited by Ibrāhīm Ismāʿīl al-Ibyārī et al. 6 vols. Dār al-Kutub, 1970–79.

al-Ṣāḥibī, al-Tājī. *al-Ḥalba fī asmāʾ al-khayl al-mashhūra fī al-jāhiliyya wa-l-Islām*. https://app.turath.io/book/7050.

Said, Edward. *Humanism and Democratic Criticism*. Columbia University Press, 2004.

Said, Edward. *Orientalism*. Penguin, 2003.

Saint Augustine. *Confessions*. Translated by Henry Chadwick. Oxford University Press, 1991.

al-Sakhāwī, Muḥammad b. ʿAbd al-Raḥmān. *Fatḥ al-mughīth bi-sharḥ Alfiyyat al-ḥadīth*. Edited by ʿAlī Ḥusayn ʿAlī. 4 vols. Maktabat al-Sunna, 2003.

Salih, Tayeb. *Season of Migration to the North*. Translated by Denys Johnson-Davies. New York Review Books, 1969.

al-Samʿānī, ʿAbd al-Karīm b. Muḥammad. *al-Ansāb*. Edited by ʿAbd al-Raḥmān b. Yaḥyā al-Muʿallamī al-Yamānī et al. 5 vols. Majlis Dāʾirat al-Maʿārif al-ʿUthmāniyya, 1962.

Sanni, Amidu. "Filiation: The Arabic Theorist's Prescription for Artistic Excellence." *Quaderni di Studi Arabi* 12 (1994): 3–14.

Savage-Smith, Emily. "Attitudes toward Dissection in Medieval Islam." *Journal of the History of Medicine and Allied Sciences* 50, no. 1 (1995): 67–110.

Schmitter, Amy M. "17th and 18th Century Theories of Emotions." In *Stanford Encyclopedia of Philosophy* (Summer 2021 Edition). https://plato.stanford.edu/entries/emotions-17th18th/.

Sedgwick, Mark. *Western Sufism: From the Abbasids to the New Age*. Oxford University Press, 2017.

Selim, Samah. "Manṣūr al-Ḥallāj and the Poetry of Ecstasy." *Journal of Arabic Literature* 21, no. 1 (1990): 26–42.

Sells, Michael A., trans. *Desert Tracings: Six Classic Arabian Odes*. Wesleyan University Press, 1989.

Shaaban, Bouthaina. *Voices Revealed: Arab Women Novelists, 1898–2000*. Lunne Rienner, 2009.

al-Shāfiʿī, Muḥammad b. Idrīs. *al-Risāla*. Edited by Aḥmad Shākir. Maktabat al-Ḥalabī, 1940.

Shakespeare, William. *King Lear*. Edited by Stephen Orgel. Penguin Classics, 2000.

al-Sharīf al-Jurjānī, ʿAlī b. Muḥammad. *Kitāb al-taʿrīfāt*. Edited by Muḥammad Ṣiddīq al-Minshāwī. Dār al-Faḍīla, n.d.

Sheikh, Saeed. "Al-Ghazzali: Metaphysics." In *A History of Muslim Philosophy*, vol. 1, edited by M. M. Sharif, 587–88. Otto Harrassowitz, 1963.

al-Shidyāq, Aḥmad Fāris. *al-Jāsūs ʿalā al-qāmūs*. Maṭbaʿat al-Jawāʾib, 1881.

al-Shidyāq, Aḥmad Fāris. *Leg over Leg*. Translated by Humphrey Davies. 4 vols. New York University Press, 2015.

al-Shidyāq, Aḥmad Fāris. *al-Sāq ʿalā al-sāq fīmā huwa al-Fāriyāq*. Dār Maktabat al-Ḥayāt, n.d.

Signori, Marco. "The Fleeting Flash of Prophetic Vision from al-Ġazālī to Dante." Dante and Arabic Philosophy, Italian Colloquium, Columbia University, April 13, 2023.

Sperl, Stefan. *Mannerism in Arabic Poetry: A Structural Analysis of Selected Texts (3rd Century A.H./9th Century A.D.–5th Century A.H./11th Century A.D.)*. Cambridge University Press, 1989.

Sperl, Stefan, and Yorgos Dedes, eds. *Faces of the Infinite: Neoplatonism and Poetry at the Confluence of Africa, Asia and Europe*. Oxford University Press, 2022.

Spevack, Aaron. "Jalāl al-Dīn al-Suyūṭī." In *Essays in Arabic Literary Biography II: 1350–1850*, edited by Joseph E. Lowry and Devin J. Stewart, 386–409. Harrassowitz Verlag, 2009.

Spitzer, Leo. "Linguistic Perspectivism in *Don Quijote*." In *Linguistics and Literary History: Essays in Stylistics*, 41–73. Princeton University Press, 1948.

Stadlbauer, Susanne. "Language Ideologies in the Arabic Diglossia of Egypt." *Colorado Research in Linguistics* 22 (2010). https://doi.org/10.25810/tdja-6p88.

Steiner, George. "The Uncommon Reader." In *No Passion Spent: Essays 1978–1995*, 1–19. Yale University Press, 1996.

Stephen, Leslie. *English Literature and Society in the Eighteenth Century*. Gerald Duckworth, 1904.

Stetkevych, Jaroslav. *The Zephyrs of Najd: The Poetics of Nostalgia in the Classical Arabic Nasib*. Chicago University Press, 1993.

Stetkevych, Suzanne. *The Cooing of the Dove and the Cawing of the Crow: Late ʿAbbāsid Poetics in Abū al-ʿAlāʾ al-Maʿarrī's* Saqt al-Zand *and* Luzūm Mā Lā Yalzam. Brill, 2023.

Stroud, Christopher. "Flaming Bourdieu Socioculturally: Alternative Forms of Linguistic Legitimacy in Postcolonial Mozambique." *Multilingua* 21 (2002): 247–73.

al-Subkī, Tāj al-Dīn. *ʿArūs al-afrāḥ fī sharḥ talkhīṣ al-Miftāḥ*. Edited by ʿAbd al-Ḥamīd Hindāwī. 2 vols. al-Maktaba al-ʿAṣriyya li-l-Ṭibāʿa wa-l-Nashr, 2003.

Subrahmanyam, Sanjay. *Empires between Islam and Christianity, 1500–1800*. SUNY Press, 2019.

al-Suyūṭī, Jalāl al-Dīn. *Bughyat al-wuʿāt*. Edited by Muḥammad Abū al-Faḍl Ibrāhīm. 2 vols. al-Maktaba al-ʿAṣriyya, n.d.

al-Suyūṭī, Jalāl al-Dīn. *al-Itqān fī ʿulūm al-Qurʾān*. Edited by Muḥammad Abū al-Faḍl Ibrāhīm. 4 vols. al-Hayʾa al-Miṣriyya al-ʿĀmma li-l-Kitāb, 1974.

al-Suyūṭī, Jalāl al-Dīn. *al-Muzhir fī ʿulūm al-lugha wa-anwāʿihā*. Edited by Fuʾād ʿAlī Manṣūr. 2 vols. Dār al-Kutub al-ʿIlmiyya, 1998.

al-Suyūṭī, Jalāl al-Dīn, and Jalāl al-Dīn al-Maḥallī. *Tafsīr al-Jalālayn*. Dār al-Ḥadīth, n.d.

al-Ṭabarī, Muḥammad b. Jarīr. *Jāmiʿ al-bayān ʿan taʾwīl āy al-Qurʾān*. Edited by Aḥmad Muḥammad Shākir. 24 vols. Muʾassasat al-Risāla, 2000.

al-Tahānawī, Muḥammad b. ʿAlī. *Kashshāf iṣṭilāḥāt al-funūn*. Edited by ʿAlī Daḥrūj. 2 vols. Maktabat Lubnān, 1996.

al-Ṭaḥāwī, Abū Jaʿfar. *Mukhtaṣar ikhtilāf al-ʿulamāʾ*. 5 vols. Turath.io. https://app.turath.io/book/6222.

al-Ṭahṭāwī, Rifāʿa Rāfiʿ. *Manāhij al-albāb al-miṣriyya fī mabāhij al-ādāb al-ʿaṣriyya*. Muʾassasat Hindāwī li-l-Taʿlīm wa-l-Thaqāfa, 2017.

al-Thaʿālibī, ʿAbd al-Malik b. Muḥammad. *Thimār al-qulūb fī al-muḍāf wa-l-mansūb*. Dār al-Maʿārif, n.d.

al-Thaʿlabī, Aḥmad b. Muḥammad. *al-Kashf wa-l-bayān ʿan tafsīr al-Qurʾān*. 33 vols. Dār al-Tafsīr, 2015.

al-Ṭībī. *Futūḥ al-ghayb fī al-kashf ʿan qināʿ al-rayb* [*Ḥāshiyat al-Ṭībī ʿalā al-Kashshāf*]. Edited by Īyād Aḥmad al-Ghawj. 17 vols. Jāʾizat Dubai al-Dawliyya li-l-Qurʾān al-Karīm, 2013.

Toorawa, Shawkat M. *Ibn Abī Ṭāhir Ṭayfūr and Arabic Writerly Culture: A Ninth-Century Bookman in Baghdad*. RoutledgeCurzon, 2005.

Turābī, Muḥammad Abū ʿĀqila. *Falsafat Ibn Ṭufayl wa-manhajuhu fī al-tarbiya*. Dār al-Bayān li-l-Nashr wa-l-Tawzīʿ, 1999.

al-ʿUkbarī, Abū al-Baqāʾ. *Sharḥ Dīwān al-Mutanabbī*. 4 vols. Turath.io. https://app.turath.io/book/6908.

al-ʿUmarī, Ibn Faḍlallāh. *Masālik al-abṣār fī mamālik al-amṣār*. 27 vols. al-Majmaʿ al-Thaqāfī, 2002.

van Gelder, Geert Jan. "Beautifying the Ugly and Uglifying the Beautiful: The Paradox in Classical Arabic Literature." *Journal of Semitic Studies* 48, no. 2 (2003): 321–51.

von Herder, Johann Gottfried. *Outlines of a Philosophy of the History of Man*. Translated by T. Churchill. London, 1800. Reprinted, Bergman, 1966.

Warburton, William, ed. *The Works of Alexander Pope Esq*. 9 vols. London, 1757.
al-Washshāʾ, Muḥammad b. Isḥāq. *al-Muwashshā: al-ẓarf wa-l-ẓurafāʾ*. Dār Ṣādir, 1965.
al-Washshāʾ, Muḥammad b. Isḥāq. *al-Ẓarf wa-l-ẓurafāʾ*. Cairo, 1907.
al-Washshāʾ, Muḥammad b. Isḥāq. *al-Ẓarf wa-l-ẓurafāʾ*. Edited by Kamāl Muṣṭafā. Maktabat al-Khānjī, 1953.
Waterland, Daniel. *Advice to a Young Student: With a Method of Study for the First Four Years*. London, 1730.
Watt, W. Montgomery. *The Faith and Practice of al-Ghazali*. Kazi Publications, 1982.
Webb, David. *Foucault's Archaeology: Science and Transformation*. Edinburgh University Press, 2012.
Weber, Max. "Objectivity in Social Science and Social Policy." In *The Methodology of the Social Sciences*, edited and translated by Edward A. Shils and Henry A. Finch, 50–112. Free Press, 1949 [1904].
White, Hayden. *The Practical Past*. Northwestern University Press, 2014.
Wilhelm, Jane Elisabeth. "Pour une herméneutique du traduire." In *Übersetzung und Hermeneutik/Traducton et Herméneutique*, edited by Larisa Cercel, 91–115. Zeta Books, 2009.
Williams, Raymond. *Keywords: A Vocabulary of Culture and Society*. Oxford University Press, 1975.
The Works of Sir Joshua Reynolds, Knight. Edited by Edmund Malone. 3 vols. London, 1798.
al-Yamanī, Abū ʿAbd Allāh Muḥammad. *Muḍāhāt amthāl kitāb Kalīla wa-Dimna bi-mā ashbahuhā min ashʿār*. Edited by Muḥammad Yūsuf Najm. Dār al-Thaqāfa, 1961.
al-Yamānī, Ibn al-Wazīr. *al-ʿAwāṣim wa-l-qawāṣim fī al-dhabb ʿan sunnat Abī al-Qāsim*. Edited by Shuʿayb al-Arnāʾūṭ. 9 vols. Muʾassasat al-Risāla li-l-Ṭibāʿa wa-l-Nashr wa-l-Tawzīʿ, 1994.
al-Zabīdī, Murtaḍā. *Tāj al-ʿarūs*. 40 vols. Dār al-Hidāya, 1965–94.
al-Zamakhsharī, Maḥmūd b. ʿUmar. *Asās al-balāgha*. Edited by Muḥammad Bāsil ʿUyūn al-Sūd. 2 vols. Dār al-Kutub al-ʿIlmiyya, 1998.
al-Zamakhsharī, Maḥmūd b. ʿUmar. *al-Kashshāf*. 3rd ed. 4 vols. Dār al-Kitāb al-ʿArabī, 1987.
al-Zamakhsharī, Maḥmūd b. ʿUmar. *Rabīʿ al-abrār wa-nuṣūṣ al-akhyār*. Edited by ʿAbd al-Amīr ʿAlī Mahnā. 5 vols. Turath.io. https://app.turath.io/book/10668.
Zargar, Cyrus Ali. *The Polished Mirror: Storytelling and the Pursuit of Virtue in Islamic Philosophy in Sufism*. Oneworld Publications, 2017.
al-Zarkalī, Khayr al-Dīn. *al-Aʿlām*. 8 vols. Dār al-ʿIlm li-l-Malāyīn, 2002.
al-Zarkashī, Muḥammad b. Bahādur. *al-Baḥr al-muḥīṭ fī uṣūl al-fiqh*. 8 vols. Dār al-Kutubī, 1994.
al-Zawzanī, al-Ḥusayn b. Aḥmad. *Sharḥ al-muʿallaqāt al-sabʿ*. Dār Iḥyāʾ al-Turāth al-ʿArabī, 2002.
Zaydān, Jurjī. *Tārīkh ādāb al-lugha al-ʿarabiyya*. Muʾassasat Hindāwī li-l-Taʿlīm wa-l-Thaqāfa, 2013.
Zheng, Robin. "Moral Criticism and Structural Injustice." *Mind* 130, no. 518 (April 2021): 503–35.
Zīdān, Yūsuf. *Ḥayy b. Yaqẓān: al-nuṣūṣ al-arbaʿa wa-mubdiʿūhā*. Dār al-Shurūq, 2008.

INDEX

al-ʿAbbāsī, ʿAbd al-Raḥīm, 106
Abbasid period, 4, 34, 40, 105, 120, 154–55, 159
Abdel Haleem, Muhammad A. S., 55
ʿAbduh, Muḥammad, 168
Abel, 66
Abjad al-ʿulūm (al-Qunūjī), 7
Abraham (Ibrāhīm), 66–67
Absāl (in *Ḥayy b. Yaqẓān*), 14, 61, 73–74, 76–77
Abū Bishr Mattā b. Yūnus, 14, 105
Abū Dāwūd al-Sijistānī, 97–98
Abū Khālid (dog), 114
Abū Nuwās, 124, 154, 159
Abū Rushd, 137
Abū Tammām, 94–96
Achilles (in the *Iliad*), 164
ACLA (American Comparative Literature Association), 1
active intellect (*al-ʿaql al-faʿʿāl*), 65
adab: compared to wealth, 26–27; as cultivating the mind, 51–52; and discourse, 51–55; as essential for a functioning society, 33; establishment as independent discipline, 5; false readings and errorism, 17, 101–2; grammar of, 8; as humanizing reason, 32; Ibn ʿAbd Rabbih's writings on, 27–28; lack of, 29–31; in Mamluk period, 104; modernization of, 31–36; as murūʾa, 12–13; murūʾa as the guiding principle of, 24; nullifiers of, 25–26; offering space to others, 76; and power, 19, 26–29, 120; semantic evolution of term, 2–3; sustainability of, 16–17, 151–62; tools of, gradual disappearing of, 124
Adab al-kātib (Ibn Qutayba), 4, 120–21
adabized readers. *See* readers
al-Adab al-kabīr (Ibn al-Muqaffaʿ), 38, 52
al-Adab al-ṣaghīr (Ibn al-Muqaffaʿ), 38, 48–49
adab sphere: adab becoming praxis, 43; conditions of reading, creation of, 40; enactment of adab, 43; filiative conversations between texts on adab, 9; generative and conceptual creativity, 55; link to intellectual and social virtues, 17; social adabization through, 13; text as interlocutor in, 64
al-Adab wa-l-murūʾa (al-Lakhmī), 20
Adam, 32, 66–67
Adams, Thomas, 78
Adamson, Peter, 66
Adams Professor of Arabic (Cambridge University), 79
Adīb (Hussein), 151–62
al-adīb al-ẓarīf (the refined litterateur), 23
ahl al-dhakāʾ wa-l-baṣīra (people of intelligence and insight), 70
ahl al-jadal (sophists), 70
ahl al-salāma (people of safety), 70
Aḥmad b. Ḥanbal, 163
Ahmed, Asad Q., 69
Ahmed, Shahab, 96
akhlāq (ethics), 40

al-Akhṭal, 111
al-ʿaks al-lafẓī (linguistic reversal), 139
Albertus Magnus (Albert the Great), 72
Alexandrian qualities (Rowson), 104
Alfiyya (Ibn Mālik), 105, 139
Algeria, 34
ʿAlī b. Abī Ṭālib, 23, 114
ʿAlī b. al-Ḥusayn, 60–61
ʿAlī b. Khalaf, 45
ʿAlī b. al-Madīnī, 97
allegories. See *mathal* (figurative language)
alterity and identity paradox, 39
ambiguity, low tolerance of, in Western modernity, 57
American Comparative Literature Association (ACLA), 1
al-Āmidī, Abū al-Qāsim, 137
Amin, Ahmad, 33
ʿāmmiyya (colloquial dialect), 139
al-Anbārī, ʿAbd al-Raḥmān b. Muḥammad, 75, 105
Andalusia, 9, 27, 112
animal cruelty, 83–84
animal fables, 12, 41–42
animals, hierarchy of, 30–31
al-Ansāb (al-Samʿānī), 106
ʿAntarah b. Shaddād, 52
anti-adab, 29–31
antisocial behavior, 21
apodictic and apophantic aspects of language, 154
Apollonian presentations (Nietzsche), 159
Apology (Plato), 122
ʿaql. *See* reason
al-ʿaql al-faʿʿāl (active intellect), 65
al-ʿAqqād, ʿAbbās Maḥmūd, 88
Ārāʾ ahl al-madīna al-fāḍila (al-Fārābī), 69
Arab culture, 4, 167
Arabic language: common solecisms of non-Arabs, 137–38; elevated language in novels, 135; expansiveness of (*ittisāʿ*), 118; foreign influences on, 126–27; *fuṣḥā* and *ʿāmmiyya*, 139; grammatical mistakes, 131; impossibility of absolute mastery of, 115–16; learning, as increasing murūʾa, 28, 75; lexicons in, 110–11; linguistic truths, 143; literary modernity, 126; loss of, in *Leg over leg*, 142; novels in, 145–49; at Oxford and Cambridge, 78; secrets of, 75; al-Shidyāq's defense of, 127–28; strange and rare qualities, 122–23; study of, 5–7; synonyms, mastery of, 106. *See also* language; premodern texts
Arab-Islamic ethics, frameworks of, 18
Arab-Islamic literature: Ibn al-Muqaffaʿ's departure from elitist authorial practices, 47; role of prefaces in, 45–46. *See also* books; poetry
Arab-Persian cultural wars (*shuʿūbiyya*), 29, 38
Aravamudan, Srinivas, 82, 84
archetypes, 81
Argos (dog of Odysseus), 103
Aristotelian induction, 66, 69
Aristotle: declining influence of, 80; on figurative language, 13, 57; on habitus and ethics, 18–19; on happiness, 69; Ibn Sīnā's commentary on, 69–70; induction, 66
ars erotica, 124
art, social value of, 162
articulateness (*al-faṣāḥa*), 24
ʿArūs al-afrāḥ fī sharḥ talkhīṣ al-Miftāḥ (al-Subkī), 143
al-asad (lion), 111
Asad, Talal, 58, 162
asceticism (*zuhd*), 35
ʿAṣfūr, Jābir, 146
al-Ashraf, al-Qāḍī, 94
ʿĀshūr, Raḍwā, 147, 149
al-Aṣmaʿī, ʿAbd al-Malik b. Qurayb, 29, 106
Assmann, Aleida, 161, 163
al-Āthār al-bāqiya ʿan al-qurūn al-khāliya (al-Bīrūnī), 163
āthār, premodern usage of term, 163
atheism, false allegations against al-Maʿarrī, 91–92
Athena (in the *Odyssey*), 11
attire. *See* garments
author-reader relationship, 40, 43
autobiography, 15, 134, 148, 149
Avicenna. *See* Ibn Sīnā
Awj al-taḥarrī ʿan ḥaythiyyat Abī al-ʿAlāʾ al-Maʿarrī (al-Badīʿī), 91–92
al-Awzāʿī, 163
Ayyūb, al-Malik al-Ṣāliḥ, 94
Azar, 67
al-Azhar University, 151
al-ʿAẓm, Rafīq, 154

Bach, Johann Sebastian, 10
al-Badīʿī, Yūsuf, 14, 85, 90–96, 100–101
al-Bagdadi, Nadia, 147
Baghdad, 9, 58–59, 67, 89
Baghdad translation movement, 40
Bakhtin, Mikhail, 136
al-balāgha (eloquence), 24

banquet (*ma'duba*): as original acceptation of adab, 3; and reading hospitality, 43
baṣar (critical reflection): compared with insight (*baṣīra*), 61; Ibn al-Muqaffa''s use of term, 49
al-Bassāmī, 26
Bauer, Thomas, 57, 105, 167
Benjamin, Walter, 142, 162
Bible, the, 83, 139
bigotry (*jahl*), 25
biographies, study of, 4
al-Bīrūnī, 163–64
Black, John, 133
Blake, William, 81–82
blind imitation. See *taqlīd*
blood feuds, 25
Bobby the stray dog (in Levinas), 103
Boccaccio, Giovanni, 135
books: delegitimization and fanatical readings of, 82–83; eighteenth-century readers in Britain, 133; elitist authorial practices, 47; foundational or source (*ummahāt al-kutub*), 164; al-Jāḥiẓ's advice to writers of, 141; knowledge, chapters devoted to, 92; levels of reading, 46–48; loss of access to, through loss of language, 143; misreading and textual disfigurement, 86; prefaces, significance of, 44–46, 140–41; short story format, 135; Taha Hussein's *Adīb*, 151–53; tradition of reading, 58–63. *See also* poetry; premodern texts
Bourdieu, Pierre, 126
Bracciolini, Poggio, 135
Britain: animal abuse in, 83; attempts in Egypt to supplant *fuṣḥā* with *'āmmiyya*, 139; "dandy" in British Romanticism, 24; eighteenth-century reading landscape in, 133; reactions to *Ḥayy b. Yaqẓān* in, 78–84; transformation of reading landscape in, 133; translation of Arabic literary works, 139. *See also* colonialism
British Arabists, 148
British Romanticism, 24
Brockelmann, Carl, 5–7, 9, 34
Bugiale club, 135
al-Buḥturī, 95
Bukhara, 58
al-Burhān (Ibn Sīnā), 66
burial, 66
Burzūyah the physician, 41
al-Bustānī, Buṭrus, 163
Byron, George Gordon, 122
Byzantium, 34
Cain and Abel, 66
caprice and vagaries (*al-hawā*), 21
Carter, Michael G., 107, 108
castration incident, 140
Cato the Elder, 83
Caucasus, 34
Çelebi, Kâtip, 7, 106
celestial bodies, 66, 67, 71
Central Asia, 34
Cervantes, Miguel de, 122
chancery culture, 4
character: diverse typologies in road ḥadīth, 50; habitus as formative of, 19; *Kalīla wa-Dimna*, as concerned with refinement of, 39; tests of, 22; *ẓarf* (refinement), 24–25
Chekhov, Anton, 135
children, education of. *See* education; pedagogy
chivalry, 20
chrono-narcissism, 148–49, 152, 157, 160
cities (*madīna*), 35
Clarissa (Richardson), 133
clavier, 10
clothes. *See* garments
colloquial dialect (*'āmmiyya*), 139–40
colonialism: and alignment with European culture 6, 9, 34; devaluation of language, as strategy under, 139–40; fear of ambiguity after, 57; "greenhouse modernities," 133; *nahḍa* as linked to, 126; precolonial history, devaluation of, 136; as rupture in history of Islam, 162; translated literary works during, 139
committing referent (*iḥāla*), 101
communism, 156
compartmentalization of emotions, 98
conditions of reading, 13, 40–41, 78
conflict resolution, 17
consciousness, historically effected, 150
continuity, in societal change, 162
Convivio (Dante), 72
Cordoba, 27
corruption in society, impact on individual's murū'a, 31–32
cortesia (courtesy), 43
cosmopolitanism: Abbasid, 34; Aravamudan's advocacy for multiple historical cosmopolitanisms, 82; conditions of reading, 41. *See also* modernity; progress
courage, 20, 33–34
courtesy (*cortesia*), 43
Crime and Punishment (Dostoevsky), 156
criminal legal trials, 108

crisis: as essential for realizing murū'a, 35–36; instability of reading, 17; of understanding, 17, 64, 71
critical justice (*inṣāf*), 22–23
critical justice scholarship, 90–92
cross-cultural exchange, in translation, 40
cultural memory, 163. *See also* memory, loss of
customary (*'urfiyya*) truths, 143

Dablishim (Indian king), 41–42, 155
Ḍaif, Shawqī, 4–5, 7–8
Damascus, 60, 94
al-Damīrī, 105
dandy archetype, 24
Dante Alighieri, 71
Dār al-'Ilm, Baghdad, 90
death, 66, 71
Decameron (Boccaccio), 135
Decolonising the Mind (Ngũgĩ), 140
defamiliarization (*al-ighrāb*), 109
deliberate misinterpretation (*ṭa'n*), 94
deliberative thinking (*ra'y*), 53–54
Derrida, Jacques, 44
de Sacy, Silvestre, 139
Descartes, 155–56
desert lore, 116–17
Deuteronomy, book of, 83
al-Dhahabī, Muḥammad b. Aḥmad, 20, 92, 95
Dhāhūl b. Ghāfūl, 129
dialects, 139–40
dictionaries, 127, 133. *See also* lexicons
Dictionary of the English Language (Johnson), 133
Die Kultur der Ambiguität (Bauer), 57
difficulties, overcoming (*istishāl al-ṣa'b*), 33
dihlīzī liminal spaces, 76–77, 142
Dionysian crises (Nietzsche), 159
discourse (*shu'ūb al-ḥadīth* of Ibn al-Muqaffa'), 44, 46, 51–55
disengagement, poetics of, 102
dissonance, 10, 11, 41, 94
distentio animi (St. Augustine), 164–65
Dīwān al-ḥayawān (al-Suyūṭī), 106
docta ignorantia (learned ignorance), 77, 161
Doctrine of the Virtuous City (al-Fārābī), 69
dogs: al-Khawārizmī's retort, 106; al-Ma'arrī's counter-insult, 15, 103–4; names of, across time, 120; ontological limits of, 115–17; philology of, 109–15
Donne, John, 81
Don Quijote (Cervantes), 125
Dostoevsky, Fyodor, 156
dream interpretation, 128–31
Dryden, John, 83

ecology of legitimization, 78–83
education: and adab, 30; as differentiating man from beast, 27; reader typologies, 47–48; al-Ṭahṭāwī's views on progress, 31. *See also* pedagogy
Egypt, 9, 31, 94, 120, 139, 151, 158, 166
El-Ariss, Tarek, 148, 161
elitism, 17, 47
eloquence (*al-balāgha*), 24, 26–27, 46
Elshakry, Marwa, 66
empirical thinking, vs. figurative language, 80
empiricism, 71–72
encyclopedic tradition: Ibn al-Nadīm's *Fihrist*, 6; *Kashf al-ẓunūn* of Kâtip Çelebi 7; lexicons, 109; al-Suyūṭī's *urjūza* as part of, 117. *See also* premodern texts
endogenous hospitality, 38, 43–44
engagement, poetics of, 109
England, reactions to *Ḥayy b. Yaqẓān* in, 78–84. *See also* Britain; colonialism
Enlightenment, 79, 82
envy and narrowness of perspective, 41
error, al-Shidyāq's synonyms of, 124
errorism, 17, 101–2
Essay Concerning Human Understanding, An (Locke), 57, 80
European culture, 134; alignment with, 6, 9; literary modernity, 126; in Taha Hussein's thought, 157–58
Eve, 66–67
examination, scientific method, 66
excellence, critical reflection and resolve, necessity of, 49
excess (*ifrāṭ*), 33
exegesis. See *tafsīr*
Exodus, book of, 103
exogenous hospitality, 38–46
exordiums, significance of, 44–46, 140–41
experiential Sufism (*ahl al-dhawq*), 70
experimentation, 66
extremism, 167

Facetiae, the, 135
"factory of lies" (*maṣna' al-akādhīb*), 135
Fāḍil b. Nāṭiq (Ibn al-Nafīs), 68
Faḍl al-kilāb (Ibn al-Marzubān), 103
Faḍl b. Dalham, 34
fāḥish (indecorous words), interpretation (*ta'wīl*) of, 123–24. *See also* insults

failed reading, 128, 140–45, 152, 157, 167
Fakhry, Majid, 19
false readings and errorism, 17, 101–2
fanatical readings, 83, 159
Fanon, Frantz, 136
al-Fārābī, 45, 68–69
al-Farāhīdī, al-Khalīl b. Aḥmad, 49, 113, 127
al-Farazdaq, 30, 112
al-Fāriyāq (in *Leg over leg*): bad breath, as metaphorical device, 130–31; incompetence of as dream interpreter, 128–30; narrator as information seeker, 138, 141. See also *Leg over Leg*; al-Shidyāq
al-Fāriyāqiyya (in *Leg over leg*), 123, 131–32
Farrūkh, ʿUmar, 41–42
al-faṣāḥa (articulateness), 24, 26, 29
Fawwāz, Zaynab, 146
Fayḍ al-khāṭir (Amin), 33
al-Fayyūmī, Ḥasan b. ʿAlī, 3
figurative language: crisis of understanding and mystical experience, 72–73; Ibn al-Muqaffaʿ's preference for, 54; Neoplatonic use and Judeo-Christian influence, 57; in the Qur'an, 58–60, 75. See also *mathal* (figurative language)
Fihrist (Ibn al-Nadīm), 6
finite monoliths, 99
fiqh, field of, 98–99
First Cause, 66–67
al-Fīrūzābādī, Muḥammad b. Yaʿqūb, 19, 49–50
fiṭra (uncorrupted natural disposition), 74
Fleury, Monsieur, 83
food and semantic origins of term "adab," 3
foolishness (*ḥumq*), 21, 25
foolish readers (*sakhīf*), 141
fore-understanding (*Vorverständnis*), 80
Foucault, Michel, 2
French Arabists, 148
French Romanticism, 24
friendship, traveling together, as means of truly knowing someone, 22
fundamentalism, 167
fuṣḥā Arabic, 139

Gadamer, Hans-Georg, 14, 65, 80, 83, 150, 154–55
garments, and murūʾa, 23, 29, 106
al-Garradi, Tahir, 87
gender: dandyism, 24; and murūʾa, 20–21; *ẓarīf*, gender neutrality of the term, 25
generosity: *makārim al-akhlāq* as the sum of virtues, 35–36; and murūʾa, 20
Genette, Gérard, 44
Germany, 165
Geschichte (Brockelmann), 5
Ghābat al-ḥaqq (Marrash), 146
al-Ghanwī, Sahm b. Ḥanẓala, 3, 64
al-Ghazālī, Abū Ḥāmid: allegory of light, 61; Aristotelian and moral formation, 18; Dante's familiarity with, 71–72; *dihlīzī* liminal space, 76–78, 142; God, linguistic references to as metaphorical, 73, 76; Ibn Ṭufayl's differences with, 70, 72; on the inadequacy of language, 73, 76; intellectual independence, 51; learned ignorance, 161; misreadings of *Mishkāt al-anwār*, 13, 64, 72, 82; al-Nīsāpūrī's references to, 61
al-Ghitani, Gamal, 136–37
al-Ghurba al-gharbiyya (al-Suhrawardī), 67
globalization, 137
God, 75–76, 161; linguistic references as metaphorical, 73, 76
good life, the, 13, 26, 49, 52
governance, 27, 28, 120, 168
grammar of adab, 8–9, 12, 17, 62, 63, 76, 169
grammatical mistakes, 131
grammatical shifts (*iltifāt*), 102
Greek culture, 4
Greek philosophy, 55–58, 68
"greenhouse modernities," 133
Guardian, The, 83
Gutas, Dimitri, 65
Guy de Maupassant, 135

Habibi, Emile, 37, 135
habitus: acquiring, through repetition, 18–19; as "habit of mind," 125; intellectual, as imposed, 76; *malaka* (Ibn Khaldūn), 18–19
ḥadīth al-arbaʿāʾ article (Hussein), 154
ḥadīth studies: critical justice in assessment of narrators, 14; eloquence, 46; ethics and murūʾa, 19, 23, 28; female scholars of, 20, 167–68; grammar, importance of in, 29; *al-jarḥ wa-l-taʿdīl* (science of criticism and praise), 97; lexical analysis of *majbūr*, 50; al-Maʿarrī's engagement with, 100; reason (*ʿaql*), 26; reliability of transmitters (*isnād*), 97–99
ḥads (intuition), 61, 71
Haifa, 37
al-Hamadhānī, Badīʿ al-Zamān, 119, 138, 162
al-Ḥamawī, Yāqūt, 45, 88–89, 95, 99, 106
hanging ode (*muʿallaqa*), 52
happiness, 35, 69, 137, 166
al-ḥaqīqa (reality and truth), 143. *See also* truth
hardship, importance of, 32

al-Ḥarīrī, 105, 107, 112, 138, 162
al-Hāris b. Hithām (in *Leg over leg*), 135, 137
al-Ḥārith b. Hammām (in *maqāmāt* of al-Ḥarīrī), 138
Hārūn al-Rashīd, 20, 106
al-hawā (caprice and vagaries), 21
Ḥayāt al-ḥayawān al-kubrā (al-Damīrī), 105
Ḥayy b. Yaqẓān (Ibn Ṭufayl): absence of language, 72–77; adab as discourse, 13; case study of, 9, 64; empiricism, 71–72; encounter with Absāl, 73–74; Ibn Sīnā's intertext to, 65–66; literary responses to, 67–68; and Miskawayh's hierarchy of animals, 31; purity of self, 62, 64–65; reactions to, in Britain, 78–84; text as interlocutor, 65–71
Healing, The Book of (Ibn Sīnā), 65–66, 70
heart (*qalb*): perception of (*baṣar*), 49; purity of, 61–62
Hector (in the *Iliad*), 164
Heikal, Muḥammad Ḥussein, 146
Heinrichs, Wolfhart, 4–5
Hemingway, Ernest, 135
von Herder, Johann Gottfried, 165
hereafter, the, 50, 54, 69
Heroides (Ovid), 83
hierarchy of animals, 30–31
hijāʾ (invective poetry), 103, 108
ḥikma (wisdom), 39
Ḥimyar, 115
al-Ḥimyarī, Nashwān, 112
Hishām b. ʿAbd al-Malik, 34
historically effected consciousness, 150
Hodgson, Marshall, 162–63
Homer, 11
horizontal reader typologies, 48
horse, in dreams, 128
hospitality: endogenous, 43–44; exogenous, 38–43; Ibn Janāḥ's advice on, 23; linguistic, 39; and murūʾa, 20; reading hospitality, 43; and semantic origins of term "adab," 3; as the sum of virtues (*makārim*) and test of ethical ideals, 36
humanism: abstract theorization of, possible sources for, 18; and conflict resolution, 17; through exercising murūʾa, 13
ḥumq (senselessness/foolishness), 21, 25
Ḥusn al-ʿawāqib (Fawwāz), 146
Ḥussein, Muḥammad al-Khiḍr, 34–35
Hussein, Taha, 33, 151–61, 166–67
hyenas, 111
hygienic practices, 131
hypocrisy, 21
Ibn ʿAbbās, 61
Ibn ʿAbd al-Barr, Yūsuf b. ʿAbd Allāh, 96–97
Ibn ʿAbd Rabbih, Aḥmad b. Muḥammad, 27–28, 32, 38–48, 50–55
Ibn al-ʿAdīm, Kamāl al-Dīn: critical justice scholarship, 90–92; identification of forged lines of poetry, 87–88; *inṣāf* as critical methodology, 92–96; literary defense of al-Maʿarrī, 14, 85, 100–101, 167
Ibn al-ʿAmīd, 119
Ibn al-Athīr, Ḍiyāʾ al-Dīn, 95
Ibn Bājja, 68
Ibn Durayd, 111
Ibn Fāris, 49, 106, 113
Ibn al-Ḥajjāj, 160
Ibn Hammām (in *maqāmāt* of al-Ḥarīrī), 107
Ibn Ḥanbal, Aḥmad, 163
Ibn Ḥazm, 92, 137
Ibn Ḥazm (prince), 140
Ibn Ḥibbān, Muḥammad, 26–27, 29, 32
Ibn Janāḥ: on antisocial behavior, 21; definition of murūʾa, 21; ethical-intellectual foundations of adab and murūʾa, 16, 19–20; on hospitality, 23; nullifiers of adab, 25–26; on preparedness, 22; reason (*ʿaql*), role in moral perfection, 25; on travel, 22
Ibn al-Jawzī, 87–90, 92, 99, 113
Ibn Jinnī, Abū al-Fatḥ ʿUthmān, 118–19
Ibn Kathīr, 60–61, 88–89, 92, 99
Ibn Khaldūn, 18, 90, 164
Ibn al-Khaymī, 96
Ibn Mālik, 105, 139
Ibn Manẓūr, 19, 49, 90, 111–12
Ibn al-Marzubān, Muḥammad b. ʿImrān, 12, 22–23, 26, 34, 103
Ibn al-Muljam, 114
Ibn al-Muqaffaʿ, Abū Muḥammad ʿAbd Allāh: adab and discourse, 51–55; adabized readers, formation of, 62; allowing space for reader discourse, 78; *baṣar* (critical reflection), 49–50; behavioral and textual parts of adab, 23; classification of imagined readers, 47–48; endogenous hospitality, 43–44; exogeneous hospitality, 38–43; exordium to *Kalīla wa-Dimna*, 44; goal of achieving the good life, 25–26, 49, 52, 54; heresy, false charge of, 38; identification of diverse reader types, 47–48; indirect frank speech, use of, 42; *Kalīla wa-Dimna*, 9, 13, 37–43; *mathal* (figurative language), use of, 46–48, 52, 72; *naẓar* and *baṣar*, use of, 51; origins of *Kalīla wa-Dimna*, 41–42; origins of nickname, 37; reading

hospitality, in writings of, 43–44; *shu'ūb al-ḥadīth* (discourse), 44, 46, 52–55; theorization of the polity, role in, 40; works of, 38
Ibn Mu'ṭī, 105
Ibn al-Nadīm, 6
Ibn al-Nafīs, 68
Ibn Nāṣir, 87
Ibn Nubāta, 120
Ibn Qutayba, 'Abd Allāh b. Muslim, 4, 28–29, 120–21, 131
Ibn al-Rawandī, 87–88
Ibn al-Rūmī, 88, 114
Ibn Rushd, 18, 138, 165, 166
Ibn Sīdah (Ibn Sayyidihi), Abū al-Ḥasan 'Alī b. Ismā'īl, 112–13, 127, 130–31
Ibn Sīnā (Avicenna): on bad breath, 130; on the benefit of *amthāl* (allegories), 52–53; empiricism debate, 71–72; *al-Ghurba al-gharbiyya*, 67–69; *ifādat al-ārā'* (conclusions from hypothetical situations), 53–54; influence on Ibn Ṭufayl, 69–70; language as mental content, 14; on logic without vocal form, 73; *ra'y* as reasoned opinion, 53–54; *Risālat Ḥayy b. Yaqẓān*, 65–67; theoretical Sufism (*ahl al-naẓar*), 69–70; virtual experience of the literary, 152
Ibn Ṭabāṭabā, 130
Ibn Ṭufayl: adab as discourse, 13–14, 31; case study of *Ḥayy b. Yaqẓān*, 9; al-Ghazālī, position on, 70; al-Ghazālī's influence on, 71, 77–78; *Ḥayy b. Yaqẓān* as literary interlocutor, 64–71; on inadequacy of language, 72–73; intellectual independence, emphasis on, 51; and Miskawayh's hierarchy of animals, 30–31; on misreading al-Ghazālī, 72, 82; misread works as deliberate injustice (*ẓulm*), 14; position on prophecy and religion, 69; purity of self, 62
Ibrāhīm (Abraham), 66–67
al-Ibshīhī, Shihāb al-Dīn, 92
Idealtypus (ideal type in Weberian thought), 57
identity and alterity paradox, 39
Idris, Murad, 65–66
ifādat al-ārā' (conclusions from hypothetical scenarios), 53–54, 64
al-'iffa (purity/virtue), 24
ifrāṭ (excess), 33
al-ighrāb (defamiliarization), 109
ignorance (*jahl*), 25, 55, 77, 86
iḥāla (committing referent), 101
iḥsān (doing good), 23
Iḥyā' 'ulūm al-dīn (al-Ghazālī), 72
ijtihād, 50, 134
Iliad (Homer), 164
Illuminationist (*ishrāqī*) philosophical tradition, 67
iltifāt (grammatical shifts), 102
imitations (*mu'āraḍāt*), 68
impartiality, 97
imperialism, 137. *See also* colonialism
Imru' al-Qays, 151, 156
independent thinking, 62, 76, 78
India, 7, 41
indirect frank speech technique, 42
induction, Aristotelian, 66
influence, 26–28, 120
inṣāf (intellectual justice): as a critical category of thought, 96–99; critical justice scholarship, 90–92; and critique as *naẓar*, 72; in ḥadīth sciences, 97–99; of Ibn al-'Adīm toward al-Ma'arrī, 14; Ibn Ḥibbān's inclusion of, within murū'a, 26; as an Islamic imperative, 84–87; lack of, and fanaticism, 82–83; neutral investigation of al-Badī'ī, 95–96; as an umbrella virtue, 22–23
al-Inṣāf wa-l-taḥarrī fī daf' al-ẓulm 'an Abī al-'Alā' al-Ma'arrī (Ibn al-'Adīm), 14, 85
insight. See *baṣar*
insults: adabizing, 15, 120; as used to dehumanize, 103–4; dog, counter-insult of al-Ma'arrī, 105–9; *hijā'* (invective poetry), 103, 108
integrity (*al-nazāha/sharaf al-nafs*), 24, 33
intellective reasoning, 14, 71
intellectual authoritarianism: Ibn al-Muqaffa''s resistance to, 47; example of Pharoah, 77
intellectual servility, 50
intelligence and insight, people of (*ahl al-dhakā' wa-l-baṣīra*), 70
introductions, significance of, in literary works, 44–46, 140–41
intuition (*ḥads*), 61, 71
invective poetry (*hijā'*), 103, 108
inversion (*qalb*), 139
al-'Iqd al-farīd (Ibn 'Abd Rabbih), 27–28
Irshād al-arīb ilā ma'rifat al-adīb (Yāqūt al-Ḥamawī), 105
'Īsā b. Hishām (in *maqāmāt* al-Hamadhānī), 138
ishrāqī (Illuminationist) philosophical tradition, 67
Islam: development of ethical meaning of adab, 4; knowledge and learning in, 57; logocentrism in, 108; Neoplatonist presence in some intellectual traditions, 56–57

isnād, in ḥadīth sciences, 97–99. *See also* ḥadīth studies
'Iyār al-shi'r (Ibn Ṭabāṭabā), 130

al-Jabri, Muhammad Abed, 165–66
jackals, 111
al-Jāḥiẓ, Abū 'Uthmān, 20, 25, 111, 116–20, 137; advice of, to writers of books, 141
jahl (ignorance/bigotry), 25, 86, 110
jahl-inducing frameworks, 101–2
al-jarḥ wa-l-ta'dīl (science of criticism and praise), 97. *See also* ḥadīth studies
Jarīr b. 'Aṭiyya, 29–30
al-Jāsūs 'alā al-qāmūs (al-Shidyāq), 126–27
al-Jawālīqī, 4
al-Jawharī, Ismā'īl b. Ḥammād, 113
jesting, 28, 30
jewelry, 28
Johnson, Samuel, 133–34
Jonas, book of, 83
Judeo-Christian thought, 56–57
judgment, compared to wit, 80–81
juristic *qiyās*, 118
al-Jurjānī, 'Abd al-Qāhir, 59–60, 75, 119
al-Jurjānī, al-Sharīf, 20
justice, as prevailing over blood ties, 97–98. See also *inṣāf*

kadhib (lying), as nullifying adab, 25
Kalīla wa-Dimna (Ibn al-Muqaffa'), 9, 12–13, 37–44, 46, 52–53, 62, 78, 83, 130
Kant, Immanuel, 79, 165–66
Kaplan, Caren, 149
Kashf al-ẓunūn (Çelebi), 7
al-Kātib, 'Abd al-Ḥamīd b. Yaḥyā, 38
Keegan, Matthew L., 53
Khadīja bt. Shihāb al-Dīn b. Aḥmad, 20
Khalīfa, Ḥājjī, 39, 106
khamriyyāt (wine poetry), 159
Kharijites (sect), 114
al-Khaṣā'iṣ (Ibn Jinnī), 119
al-Khawāfī, Abū Manṣūr, 89
al-Khawārizmī, Muḥammad b. al-'Abbās, 106, 119
al-khawāṣṣ (the distinctive ones), 70
Khosraw Anūshirvān (Sassanid king), 41
Khūrī, Khalīl, 146
Kilito, Abdelfattah, 38–39, 119
al-Kindī, 40–41, 45
King Amarasakti, 42
King Lear, 155
Kitāb al-'ayn (al-Farāhīdī), 127
Kitāb al-hamza wa-l-radif (al-Ma'arrī), 94
Kitāb al-ḥayawān (al-Jāḥiẓ), 116
Kitāb al-inṣāf (Ibn 'Abd al-Barr), 96–97
Kitāb al-muṭāwil (Ibn al-Khaymī), 96
Kitāb al-muwāzana bayna Abī Tammām wa-l-Buḥturī (al-Āmidī), 137
Kitāb al-sāq 'alā al-sāq. See *Leg over leg*
knowledge: definitions of, among Muslim scholars, 92–93; flawed epistemological models in Orientalism, 148; *inṣāf* and production of, 92–96; Islam's fascination with, 57; language and production of, 123, 148; literary texts, 4–5; and power, 120; tree, metaphor of, 55; veracity of, 91
kuttāb (secretaries), 4

al-Lababīdī, Aḥmad b. Muṣṭafā, 106, 111–12
Labīd, 114
lack (*tafrīṭ*), 33
lafẓ (utterance), 54
al-Lakhmī, Ṣāliḥ b. Janāḥ, 12, 20
Lambertini, Roberto, 39
language: absence of, 72–78; apodictic and apophantic aspects of, 154; and colonialism, 139–40; deficiency in, as malady, 130–32; ethos of translation, 39; grammatical mistakes, 131; and knowledge production of al-Shidyāq, 123; and linguistic being, 142; as marker of civility, 29; phenomenology of, 125; registers of, as medium for insults, 107; simplification of, in name of progress, 139, 161; status of *adīb* through proper use of, 108. *See also* Arabic language
Lapidus, Ira, 18, 19
lathgha (solecism), theorization of, 137–38
Latin translation of *Ḥayy b. Yaqẓān*, 78
Laud (archbishop), 78
Laylā Majnūn, 103, 112, 155
lazy reading, antidote to, 48
leadership: adab as social capital to achieve, 32; knowledge and power relationship, 120; marginalization of Arabic as language of, 127; al-Shidyāq on loss of language and, 128, 130
learned ignorance, 77, 161
Lebanon, 9
legal (*shar'iyya*) truths, 143
legitimization of adab: al-Bassāmī's lines of poetry on, 26; through the character of Absāl, 75; as context of Ibn al-Muqaffa''s translation of *Kalīla wa-Dimna*, 40; ecology of legitimization, 78–83; through pluralistic reading engagement, 44; as sociopolitical

asset, 27; speaking in *mathal*, 48–51; through universal aims, 51–52; use of term, 1
Leg over Leg (al-Shidyāq): as case study 9, 15–16; al-Fāriyāq's incompetence, 128–30; form and ideology, 136; as genre-breaking, 147–50; loss of Arabic, 142; *maqāmāt* inclusion of, 137–40; marriage and divorce debate, 143–44; poetry in exordium to, 141; readiness of al-Shidyāq to defend, 125; resistance and engagement with European literary traditions, 122; satire in, 127–28; semantic memories, 154; unconventional literary form of, 132–37
Leiden, 6
Levinas, Emmanuelle, 103
lexicons, 15, 110–11, 127
light, *mathal* of, in the Qur'an, 59–61
linguistic beings, 16, 42, 72–78, 137, 140, 142
linguistic hospitality, 39
linguistic (*lughawiyya*) truths, 143
linguistic *qiyās*, 118
linguistic reversal (*al-ʿaks al-lafẓī*), 139
lion (*al-asad*), 111
Lisbon, 96
lisping, 137
literalism, danger of, 77
literary criticism of premodern texts, two approaches to, 162
literary modernity in Arab tradition, 126
literary texts, study of, 4–5. *See also* Arabic language; poetry
Locke, John, 57, 71, 80–83, 124, 154
logic, 14, 52
logocentrism, 108
love, 32
lying (*kadhib*), as nullifying adab, 25

Maʿāhid al-tanṣīṣ ʿalā shawāhid al-talkhīṣ (al-ʿAbbāsī), 106
al-Maʿarrī, Abū al-ʿAlāʾ: attacks on, 89–90; counter-insult of, 103–10; critical justice works (*inṣāf*) in defense of, 90–92; forged poetry attributed to, 87–88; good reputation of, among peers, 100; Ibn al-ʿAdīm's defense of, 14, 85, 100–101; pessimism, 166–67; poetry of, 92–96; *sharḥ* (commentary) on al-Mutanabbī's *dīwān*, 118–19; *Zajr al-nābiḥ*, 9, 12, 14–15, 85–87
MacIntyre, Alasdair, 126
maʾduba. *See* banquet
Mahmood, Saba, 18
"Mahometan," Ockley's use of concept of, 79
Majallat al-hidāya al-islāmiyya, 34
majbūr, as antonym to *mubtaṣir*, 50
Majnūn Laylā, 103, 112, 155
Makamat of Rhetorical Anecdotes (de Sacy), 139
makārim al-akhlāq, as the sum of virtues, 35–36
Makdisi, George, 5, 50
malaka (habitus): Fakhry's use of term, 19; use of term in Ibn Khaldūn's work, 18
Mālik, 163
Mamluk period, 104–5, 111, 117, 119–20
Mamur (in *Season of Migration to the North*), 136
maʿnā (meaning), 54
Manāhij al-albāb (al-Ṭahṭāwī), 31
manfaʿa (benefit), in al-Ṭahṭāwī's thought, 31
manliness, 20. *See also* murūʾa
Mansfield, Katherine, 135
al-Manṣūr (Abbasid caliph), 38, 40
al-Maqāma al-shiʿriyya (al-Ḥarīrī), 107, 138
maqāmāt, 137–40. *See also* premodern texts
al-Maqāmāt (al-Hamadhānī), 112, 119, 138
al-Maqrīzī, Aḥmad b. ʿAlī, 96
Márquez, Gabriel García, 153
al-Marrākushī, 66
Marrash, Francis, 146
marriage and divorce debate, 143–44
Masālik al-abṣār fī mamālik al-amṣār (al-ʿUmarī), 93
Masher, son of Pulverizer (in *Leg over leg*), 137–38, 140–43
Maslama b. ʿAbd al-Malik, 29
materialism, 155–56
mathal (figurative language): as conducive to discourse, 54–55; as discourse and reader formation, 62; in Greek and Western philosophy, 55–58; and legitimization of adab, 48–51; levels of reading, 46–48; Plato's views on, 55–56; purpose and elements of, 46; purpose of, in Ibn Sīnā's thought, 52–53; in the Qur'an, 58–59; al-Zamakhsharī on, 58–59
mathematics and morality, 82
Mattā b. Yūnus, 14, 105
mawʿiẓa (moral exhortation), 39
al-Māzinī, Ibrāhīm ʿAbd al-Qādir, 154–55
meaning (*maʿnā*), 54
mechanistic materialism, 155–56
Meditations on First Philosophy (Descartes), 156
memory, loss of, 153–54, 157, 161, 163, 168
MESA (Middle East Studies Association) panels, 1
Metamorphoses (Ovid), 83
metaphor. See *mathal* (figurative language)
metaphysics, 66, 166

method, adab as, 15
Michel de Montaigne, 83
Middle East, 133
Middle East Studies Association (MESA) panels, 1
Miftāḥ al-ʿulūm (al-Sakkākī), 143
Milton, John, 81
mimesis, role in shaping habitus, 18
mirrors for princes genre, 39, 53
Mishkāt al-anwār (al-Ghazālī), 13, 61, 64, 72
Miskawayh, Aḥmad b. Muḥammad, 30–31
mispronunciation, mockery of, 138
Mitchell, Timothy, 140
MLA (Modern Language Association), 1
modernity: and Arabic language, 147; chrono-narcissism and the rejection of adab, 148; and creation of reader types 133; Hussein's views on, 156, 158, 159; institutional shaping of passive reading, 160, 167; low tolerance for "ambiguity," 57; and murūʾa, 31–36; *nahḍa* debates, 126; al-Shidyāq as bridge between premodern adab and, 161; al-Shidyāq's resistance to dominant narratives of, 149. *See also* colonialism; cosmopolitanism; progress
Modern Language Association (MLA), 1
Modern Standard Arabic (MSA), 139
Montgomery, James E., 24
Moosa, Ebrahim, 73, 77
moral exhortation (*mawʿiẓa*), 39
Moralia (Plutarch), 83
morality and mathematics, 82
morals and virtues, 4
Moses, 65, 67, 77
MSA (Modern Standard Arabic), 139
muʿallaqa (hanging ode), 52
muʿāraḍāt (imitations), 68
al-Mubarrad, 24
muftis (jurisconsult), intellectual servility vs. *ijtihād* among, 50
Muhanna, Elias, 117, 120
al-Muḥkam (Ibn Sīdah), 127
mukhaḍram poets, 3
al-Mukhaṣṣaṣ (Ibn Sīdah), 112
Mukhtār al-ṣiḥāḥ (al-Rāzī), 112
Mulḥat al-iʿrāb (al-Ḥarīrī), 105
al-Munqidh min al-ḍalāl (al-Ghazālī), 73
Muqaddimah, The (Ibn Khaldūn), 18–19
al-Murtaḍā, al-Sharīf, 14–15, 103
murūʾa: adab as, 12–13; Arabic language and, 28, 75; crisis, as essential for realizing, 35; development of concept of, 19–20; al-Fīrūzābādī's definition, 19–20; and gender, 20–21; generosity of spirit, 20; as guiding principle of adab, 24; ḥadīth on, 23, 98; as humanizing reason, 32; Ibn ʿAbd Rabbih's work on, 27–28; Ibn Ḥibbān's definition of, 26; Ibn Janāḥ's definition of, 21; Ibn al-Marzubān's work on, 26; and independent thinking, 76; school of, 33–34; Taha Hussein's school of blueprint of, 33–34; al-Ṭahṭāwī's views on, 32; as a way of life, 1–2. *See also* adab
al-Murūʾa wa-l-adab (Ibn Janāḥ), 16
al-Musawi, Muhsin J., 80, 109, 120, 161
Mustafa Saʿeed (in *Season of Migration to the North*), 136
Mustaqbal al-thaqāfa fī miṣr (Hussein), 158
al-Mutanabbī, 32, 70–71, 90, 94, 96, 118–19, 128, 166
mutashābihāt (allegorical verses), 59–60
al-Muzhir fī ʿulūm al-lugha wa-anwāʿihā (al-Suyūṭī), 113, 115, 118
mystical experiences, as ineffable, 73

nahḍa, 6, 82, 126, 134, 145, 147–48, 161
Nahrawān, battle of, 114
Najm, Muhammad Yusuf, 134–36, 148
Najr al-zajr (al-Maʿarrī), 91
Nakt al-himyān fī nukat al-ʿumyān (al-Ṣafadī), 105
al-Namnam, Ḥilmī, 146
Naṣr al-aʿyān ʿalā sharr al-ʿumyān (al-Yamānī), 96
al-Nawawī, Yaḥyā b. Sharaf, 45–46
al-nazāha (integrity), 24
naẓar (critique), 14, 51, 72, 75, 76, 83, 123
al-Naẓẓām, Ibrāhīm, 46
Neoplatonism, 56–57
nēpios (disconnected), 11
neutral investigations, 95–96
Newton, Isaac, 82
Ngũgĩ wa Thiong'o, 140
Nicholas of Cusa, 77, 161
Nietzsche, Friedrich, 34, 159, 166
nihilism, 83, 146, 155–57
al-Nīsāpūrī, Niẓām al-Dīn, 61
Niẓāmiyya library, 94
Niẓāmiyya school, 5
nomocentric frameworks, 1
normative (*ʿurfiyya*) truths, 143
normativity of adab, 2
North Africa, 34
novels, 15, 145–49

obscene poetry, 160
Ockley, Simon, 78–83
Odysseus, 11
Odyssey (Homer), 11
One Hundred Years of Solitude (Márquez), 153
oration, 4
Orientalism, 6–7, 80, 82–83, 125–27, 139, 148
Oriental Translation Fund, 139
Ottoman period, 7, 106, 127, 134
Ovid, 83
Oxford, University of, 78

Pahlavi dynasty, 41–42
Panchatantra fables, 42
Panofsky, Erwin, 126
parables. See *mathal* (figurative language)
Paradiso (Dante), 71
Partoclus (in the *Iliad*), 164
passive forgetting, 161, 163
pedagogy: divine providence in knowledge and learning, 30–31; ethical context in virtue training, 18; of al-Ghazālī, 72; reader typologies, 47–48. *See also* education
people of safety (*ahl al-salāma*), 70
perfume, 28
perseverance, as aspect of murūʾa, 34
Persia, 37
Persian-Arab cultural wars (*shuʿūbiyya*), 29, 38
Persian culture, 4, 29
Phaedrus (Plato), 56
Pharoah, 77
phenomenology of language, 125
philology, 109–15
philosophy and prophecy, 69
Pirandello, Luigi, 135
plagiarism (*sariqa*), 107, 120
plague (*ṭāʿūn*), 94
Plato, 13, 55–57, 165
Plotinus, 56–57
pluralism, in literary reception, 44
Plutarch, 83
Pococke, Edward, 78–79
poetic persona, 124, 160
poetry: Abū Tammām, al-Mutanabbī, and al-Buḥturī, 94–96; of al-Akhṭal, 111, 141; ʿAntarah b. Shaddād's *muʿallaqa*, 52; al-Aṣmaʿī's synonyms, 106; early usage of term "adab," 3; forgeries attributed to al-Maʿarrī, 87–89; *hijāʾ* (invective poetry), 103; of Ibn al-Rūmī, 114; between Jarīr and al-Farazdaq, 29–30; of Labīd, on the oryx cow, 114; in *Leg over leg*, 132–33, 141; of al-Maʿarrī, Ibn al-ʿAdīm and al-Badīʿī's study of, 92–96; al-Mutanabbī, 70, 166; plagiarism (*sariqa*), 107; Plato's attack on, 55–56; poet as savior figure, 130; on social influence through adab, 26–27; study of, for the *adīb*, 4–6; *sukhf* genre, 160; virtual experience, 53–54, 152; wine poetry (*khamriyyāt*), 159
political leaders, 128
Political Regime (*al-Siyāsa al-madaniyya*) (al-Fārābī), 69
polyetymology, 125
polynomasia, 125
polysemy, 125, 132
Pope, Alexander, 83–84
power: and adab, 19, 26–29, 120; and knowledge, 120
prefaces, significance of, 44–46, 140–41
prejudice (*Vorurteil*), 80
premodern texts: *āthār*, usage of the word, 163; conception of past, compared with modern conceptions, 165; emotional nuance in, 159; lexicons, 127; relationship between language and truth, 143; Rushdi's devaluation of, 135–36; al-Shidyāq's references to, 125; understanding, as an effect of history, 150. See also *turāth*
preparedness, role of, in murūʾa, 22
prescriptiveness, in adab manuals, 8
princes: "mirrors for princes" genre, 39, 53; study of Arab culture, 4
Principia (Newton), 82
private and public morals, 31–32
professional class, and development of adab, 4
professionalism (*al-takhaṣṣuṣ*), 33
progress: dismissal of premodern texts, 156–57; education, role of, in al-Ṭahṭāwī's thought, 31–33; European idea of, 82, 165–66; marginalization of the Arabic language, 15, 147, 161; Najm and Rushdi's Western-centric literary benchmarks, 135–36; race for first Arabic novel, 146; Taha Hussein's ideas on, 158–59, 166–67. *See also* cosmopolitanism; modernity
pronunciation, mockery of, 138
prophecy and philosophy, 69
Prophet Muḥammad: anti-literary critics of, 58–59; horse of (*al-baḥr*), 118; on murūʾa, 23, 26, 28, 98; semantic expansion of adab, 3; *sunna* of, 116
public and private morals, 31–32
public sphere, 42–43, 54, 168
pulpit, dream of (in *Leg over Leg*), 129

punishment systems in society, 31–32
purity and virtue (*al-'iffa*), 24, 35

Qabḍ al-rīḥ (al-Māzinī), 155
qalb (*inversion*), 139
al-Qāmghār, Muḥammad b. 'Alī, 96
al-Qarṭājannī, Ḥāzim, 101, 109
Qaṭām bt. Shinja, 114–15
Qays b. al-Mulawwaḥ, 112
al-Qazwīnī, 95
al-Qifṭī, 88
qiyās, 115–16, 118
Qizughlī (Sibṭ Ibn al-Jawzī), 88
al-Qunūjī, Ṣiddīq, 7
Qur'an: allegorical language (*mutashābihāt*) of, 58–61; analogy of beasts, 74; attempt at *'āmmiyya* rendering, 139; as banquet of knowledge and virtuousness, 3; Cain and Abel, 66; on doing good (*iḥsān*), 23; on failure of self-critique, 49–50; false allegations against al-Ma'arrī regarding, 91–92; illusory nature of the world, 75–76; on justice, as prevailing over blood ties, 97–98; light, verse of, 59–60; misinterpretations of falsifiers, 94; Moses and Pharoah, 77; origin of humankind, 66; story of Abraham (Ibrāhīm), 67; story of the infant Moses, 65–66; "word as a tree" imagery, 55, 63. See also *tafsīr*

Rabelais, François, 122
Rajm al-'ifrīt (al-Khawāfī), 89–90
Rasā'il al-iṣlāḥ (Ḥussein), 34
Rawḍat al-'uqalā' wa-nuzhat al-fuḍalā' (Ibn Ḥibbān), 26
ra'y (deliberative thinking), 53–54, 64
al-Rāzī, Fakhr al-Dīn, 55, 67, 112
reader-author relationship, 43, 52, 57
readers: adabized, as critical and independent thinkers, 62; conditions of reading, 40, 41, 78; dissonance and failed readers, 140–45, 152, 157; in eighteenth-century Britain, 133; epistemological immunization in Orientalism, 80; hospitality to, 43, 46–48; Ibn al-Muqaffa''s hospitality to, 43–44, 46–48; imagined human as, 153; intellectual *inṣāf*, 82–83; interrogative mood, Absāl as example of, 77; laziness, antidote to, 48; nihilism in, 156–57; participatory reading, 62–63; predatory reading, 41, 94, 102; prefaces, significance of to, 44–46; *ṭa'n* (deliberate misinterpretation), 94; tradition of reading, 58–63; typology of, 46–48; universal common denominator, 48–49; virtual experience and social implications, 54. *See also* books
reading hospitality, 43
reality and truth (*al-ḥaqīqa*), 143
reason (*'aql*): adab, murū'a, and *'aql* triptych, 27; Ḥayy, as representing, 65; as humanized by murū'a, 32; intellective reasoning, 71; lack of, 29–30; on murū'a, as based on, 26; Pococke's view on limits of, 78; as prerequisite for a good life, 49; role of, in moral perfection, 25; as threat to naivete, 154; truth, reaching through, 72; virtue of, 21
refined litterateur (*al-adīb al-ẓarīf*), 23
reflection, 49; as requirement for seeking virtue, 49
reformist studies on murū'a, 31–36
religious leaders, 128
Remarks and Admonitions (Ibn Sīnā), 65
reproachment (*'itāb*), 22
Republic (Plato), 56
resolve and will, as requirements for seeking virtue, 49
reward systems in society, 31–32
Richardson, Samuel, 133
Ricoeur, Paul, 39
Risāla (al-Shāfi'ī), 115
al-Risāla al-kāmiliyya (Ibn al-Nafīs), 68
Risālat al-Ṣaḥāba (Ibn al-Muqaffa'), 40, 67
Risālat Ḥayy b. Yaqẓān (Ibn Sīnā), 65, 67
Romanticism, 24, 81–82, 161
Rosenthal, Franz, 92, 120
Rowson, Everett K., 104
Royal Asiatic Society, 139
al-Rūmī, Jalāl al-Dīn, 32
Rushdi, Rashad, 135–36, 139, 148

Sacks, Jeffrey, 126, 139
Sadan, Joseph, 23
al-Ṣafadī, Khalīl b. Aybak, 89, 105
safety, people of (*ahl al-salāma*), 70
al-Ṣaghānī, al-Ḥasan b. Muḥammad, 49, 111, 113, 115
al-Ṣāḥib b. 'Abbād, 106
Said, Edward, 43, 134
saj' prose, 135
al-Sakkākī, 143
Salafism, 57, 167
Salāmān, 14, 64, 74
Salih, Tayeb, 136
Saluki hounds, 113

Salūqī, 113
al-Sam'ānī, 'Abd al-Karīm b. Muḥammad, 106
Samarkand, 58
Sand, George, 24
sariqa (plagiarism), 107
al-Sarūjī, Abū Zayd (in *maqāmāt* of al-Ḥarīrī), 107
Sassanid court, 41
Satan, 32
satire in *Leg over leg*, 127, 137–38
school of murū'a blueprint, 33–34
scientific methodology, 66
Season of Migration to the North (Salih), 136
seclusion, 35
secretarial class, and development of adab, 4
self, purity of, 61–62
self-critique, 49–50
self-cultivation, 62
self-formation of ethical qualities, 33
self-respect, 22
Self-Taught Theologian, The, 68
semantic memories, 154
Seneca, 83
senselessness (*ḥumq*), 21, 25
Shaaban, Bouthaina, 146
al-Shāfi'ī, Muḥammad b. Idrīs, 115–16, 163
Shams al-'ulūm (al-Ḥimyarī), 112
sharḥ (commentary), genre of, 117–19
shar'iyya (legal) truths, 143
Sharma, Vishnu, 42
al-Shidyāq, Aḥmad Fāris: background of *Leg over Leg*, 122–24; as bridge between premodern adab and modernity, 161; emotional nuance in premodern texts, 159; failed reader, 140–45; genre-breaking form, 147–50; *al-Jāsūs 'alā al-qāmūs*, 126–27; leaders, criticism of, 128; lexicon-parodying novels by, 12; on loss of language, 15–16; *maqāmāt*, inclusion of, 134–35, 137–40; on the novel genre, 133–36; phenomenology of language, 125; readiness of, to defend *Leg over Leg*, 125; as representative of Lebanese *nahḍa*, 9; semantic memory, 154; unconventional literary form of *Leg over leg*, 132–37; views on Ottomans, 134; on waning of understanding of literary language, 124. See also *Leg over Leg*
al-Shifā' (Ibn Sīnā), 66
short stories, 135–36
shu'ūb al-ḥadīth (discourse) of Ibn al-Muqaffa', 44, 46, 52–55
shu'ūbiyya (Arab-Persian cultural wars), 29, 38
al-Sijistānī, Abū Dāwūd, 97–98
Silvestre de Sacy, 139
Sind, 34
al-Ṣīrāfī, Abū Sa'īd, 14, 105
al-Siyāsa (journal), 154
al-Siyāsa al-madaniyya (al-Fārābī), 69
skepticism: in al-Fārābī's writing, 69; in al-Ghazālī's pedagogical framework, 70, 161; and "learned ignorance," 77; of Taha Hussein, 154–55
social capital, 26–29
social *poiēsis*, 4, 13, 62, 132, 160
social standing, 22, 26–27
Socrates, 56–57, 122
solecism (*lathgha*), theorization of, 137–38
sophists (*ahl al-jadal*), 70
specialization (*al-takhaṣṣuṣ*), 4, 6, 33
speculum principis. *See* mirrors for princes genre
Spitzer, Leo, 125
St. Augustine, 164
status, social, 22, 26–27
Steiner, George, 38, 43
Stephen, Leslie, 82
Stetkevych, Suzanne, 102, 109
Stoicism, 83
strife, as essential for realizing murū'a, 35
al-Subḥ al-munbī (al-Badī'ī), 95
al-Subkī, Tāj al-Dīn, 143
Subrahmanyam, Sanjay, 84
su'dud (power/influence), 27–29, 32–33, 54, 120
Sufism, 57, 68, 70
al-Suhrawardī, Shihāb al-Dīn Yaḥyā, 67–68
sukhf genre, 160
Sulaymān b. 'Abd al-Malik, 140
al-Ṣūlī, 114
Sunan Abī Dāwūd (al-Sijistānī), 97
al-Suyūṭī, Jalāl al-Dīn: exoneration of al-Ma'arrī, 109–15; Ibn al-Khaymī's response to al-Ma'arrī, 96; impossibility of absolute mastery of Arabic, 115–16; *qiyās*, use of, in the *urjūza*, 116; *sharḥ* (commentary), *urjūza* as, 117–19; sources and textual relations, 105–6; *al-Tabarrī min ma'arrat al-Ma'arrī*, 9, 15, 104–5, 171–74; on the verse of light, 60
swords and war (*al-'ajūz*), 111–12
Sykes-Picot agreement, 7
synonyms, 106, 125
Syria, 9, 89

al-Ṭabarī, Muḥammad b. Jarīr, 59, 163
al-Tabarrī min ma'arrat al-Ma'arrī (al-Suyūṭī), 9, 15, 104–5, 109–15, 171–74
al-Tabrīzī, Abū Zakariyyā, 87–88

tafrīṭ (lack), 33
tafsīr (Qur'anic exegesis): light, verse of, 59–60; *mutashābihāt* (allegorical verses), al-Jurjānī's handling of, 59–60; story of Abraham (Ibrāhīm), 67; al-Zamakhsharī's explanation of *amthāl*, 58–59. *See also* Qur'an
al-Tahānawī, Muḥammad b. ʿAlī, 93
Tahdhīb al-akhlāq (Miskawayh), 30–31
Tahdhīb al-āthār (al-Ṭabarī), 163
al-Ṭahṭāwī, Rifāʿa, 31–35, 134, 168
al-takhaṣṣuṣ (professionalism), 33
Taliban, 167
ṭaʿn (deliberate misinterpretation), 94
taqlīd (servile imitation): as antonym to *baṣar*, 50; al-Badīʿī's critique of, 96; al-Bīrūnī on necessary reliance on books of the past, 164; in defaming al-Maʿarrī, 89, 91; in theoretical Sufism, 70
Ṭarafa b. al-ʿAbd, 3
Tārīkh ādāb al-lugha al-ʿarabiyya (Zaydān), 6
Tārīkh al-adab al-ʿarabī (Farrūkh), 41–42
Taşkopruzade, Ahmet, 7
al-Tawḥīdī, Abū Ḥayyān, 87, 119, 160
Telemachus (in the *Odyssey*), 11
testament (*waṣiyya*), 40
textual empathy, 10, 16, 153
Thaʿlab, 24
al-Thaʿlabī, Aḥmad b. Muḥammad, 59
al-Thawrī, 163
Theologus autodidactus, 68
theoretical Sufism (*ahl al-naẓar*), 70
thinking, deliberative (*raʾy*), 53–54, 64
Thousand and One Nights, 80, 135
"thrownness" (Gadamer), 155
al-Ṭībī, Sharaf al-Dīn, 46
time, experiencing as threefold flow, 164–65
Toto (in *The Wizard of Oz*), 103
tradition: continuity of conflict, 126; as discursive, 58; of reading, 58–63; Talal Asad's definition, 162
translation: ethos of, 39; of *Ḥayy b. Yaqẓān* into English, 78; as intellectual hospitality, 39–40
travel, as means of truly knowing someone, 22
travelogue, 15
tree, allegory of, in the Qur'an, 55
Trojan War, 164
truth: Kantian influences on Western philosophy, 166; and reality (*al-ḥaqīqa*), 143; in translation of foreign works, 40, 166
Tunisia, 34
turāth (tradition): attitude of modernist approaches to, 162–66; literary heritage as, 149; as resistance to erasure, 135
"Turk," use of, in expressions, 133
typology of readers, 47–48

al-ʿUklī, Abū Ḥizām, 106
ʿUmar b. al-Khaṭṭāb, 28, 75, 168
al-ʿUmarī, Ibn Faḍlallāh, 93–94
Umayyad period, 4, 34, 37, 120
understanding: defined, 93; as an "effect" of history, 150; as a perpetual crisis, 64
urbanity, 31, 35. *See also* modernity; progress
ʿurfiyya (customary) truths, 143
urjūzas, 104–5, 110–15
utterance (*lafẓ*), 54
ʿUyūn al-akhbār (Ibn Qutayba), 28, 131

Valeurs (magazine), 166
Vatican, the, 135
vendettas, 25
Venture of Islam, The (Hodgson), 162
vertical reader typologies, 48
virtual experience, poetics of, 53–54, 152
virtue-ethics, 4, 17; *inṣāf* as, 97; pedagogic processes as part of adab, 18
virtues, cultivation of, 33
Vishnu Sharma, 42
Voltaire, 81
Vorurteil (prejudice), 80
Vorverständnis (fore-understanding), 80

warfare, murūʾa as courage and perseverance in, 34
al-Washshāʾ, Abū al-Ṭayyib Muḥammad b. Isḥāq, 23–25, 32, 35
Wayy, idhan lastu bi-ifranjī (Khūrī), 146
wealth, seeking social influence through, weakness of, 26–28. See also *suʿdud*
Weber, Max, 57
"well-tempered," meaning of term, 10
Well-Tempered Clavier, The (Bach), 10
Weltliteratur (world literature), 43. *See also* world literature
Western culture, 158
Western philosophy, 55–58
will and resolve, as requirement for seeking virtue, 49–51
Willcocks, Sir William, 139
Williams, Raymond, 2
wine poetry (*khamriyyāt*), 159
wisdom (*ḥikma*), 39
wit, compared with judgment, 80–81
Wizard of Oz, The, 103
wolf intervals, as metaphor for dissonant reading, 10, 41, 94

women: ascendance of, in knowledge, 123; bad behavior toward, 30; unhistorical treatment of under Taliban rule, 167–68
world literature: Aravamudan's advocacy for multiple historical cosmopolitanisms, 82; recovering obscured histories through, 84; *Weltliteratur*, 43

al-Yamanī, Abū ʿAbd Allāh Muḥammad, 44, 62
al-Yamānī, Ibn al-Wazīr, 96
Yemen, 112, 115, 168
young readers, 47–48

al-Zabīdī, Murtaḍā, 50, 111–15, 138
Zajr al-nābiḥ (al-Maʿarrī), 9, 14–15, 85–87, 91–92, 101–2
al-Zamakhsharī, Maḥmūd b. ʿUmar, 20, 49, 58–59
ẓarf (character refinement), 24–25
Zargar, Cyrus Ali, 56
ẓarīf, 20–21; vs. *sakhīf* trope, 141
Zaydān, Jurjī, 6–7
Zaynab bt. Abī Aḥmad ʿAbd al-Wāḥid, 20
Zaynab (Heikal), 146
zuhd (asceticism), 35
ẓulm (injustice): misreading works as, 14, 86–87. *See also* readers

Founded in 1893,
UNIVERSITY OF CALIFORNIA PRESS
publishes bold, progressive books and journals on topics in the arts, humanities, social sciences, and natural sciences—with a focus on social justice issues—that inspire thought and action among readers worldwide.

The UC PRESS FOUNDATION
raises funds to uphold the press's vital role as an independent, nonprofit publisher, and receives philanthropic support from a wide range of individuals and institutions—and from committed readers like you. To learn more, visit ucpress.edu/supportus.

Founded in 1893,
UNIVERSITY OF CALIFORNIA PRESS
publishes bold, progressive books and journals on topics in the arts, humanities, social sciences, and natural sciences—with a focus on social justice issues—that inspire thought and action among readers worldwide.

The UC PRESS FOUNDATION
raises funds to uphold the press's vital role as an independent, nonprofit publisher, and receives philanthropic support from a wide range of individuals and institutions—and from committed readers like you. To learn more, visit ucpress.edu/supportus.